Blessing
journey!
Manal M/c

Earth School

A Fresh Perspective
on the Human Condition

Moriah Marston
and the Tibetan

ISBN 0-7414-3276-5

Published by:

INFINITY
PUBLISHING.COM

1094 New DeHaven Street, Suite 100
West Conshohocken, PA 19428-2713
Info@buybooksontheweb.com
www.buybooksontheweb.com
Toll-free (877) BUY BOOK
Local Phone (610) 941-9999
Fax (610) 941-9959

Printed in the United States of America

Printed on Recycled Paper

Published August 2006

WORDS OF PRAISE FOR
EARTH SCHOOL

"In *Earth School*, Moriah and the Tibetan take you on a guided tour of the subterranean levels of consciousness, shining a bright healing light onto all aspects of the human condition. Deeply psychological, informative and transformative, this powerful work is destined to be the standard text for all students of the earth plane."

—Mary Arsenault, Publisher, Wisdom Magazine

"I've been a student of Moriah Marston and the Tibetan since about 1995, and the lessons have altered my perception of the world, intensified my awareness of how I spend my energy...completely changed my life. It's as if the essence of different 'religions' has been distilled into a powerful elixir, infusing my days with a simpler, more direct sense of spiritual connection—to the cosmos and to my fellow creatures. I've come to see that each of us has a part to fulfill in the Divine Plan that is unfolding and by sharing our unique gifts, inborn and learned, we can experience the infinite mysteries, wonders and pleasures of Earth School. For that I will always be grateful...and always ready for the next lesson."

—Ellen Lovinger Eller, Shelburne Falls, MA

"I just wanted to let you know your article in *Wisdom* magazine spoke to me first hand. As I continued reading, I was struck and amazed at how insightful and real the words became to me personally. Years of searching, reading, counseling could not have uncovered such an empowering truth as your article did to me, in minutes, and at such a place and time in my life that required just that knowledge, just then to clear a path along my journey. A true soul connection. Thank you!"

—a grateful reader, TC –MA (Cape Cod)

"I read your article last evening that was in the *Wisdom* magazine. I was scanning the pages looking for something that I desperately needed to hear about what I was going through presently in my life. You put everything into perspective for me in a page in a half. My soul & spirit heard it. I'm not jumping for joy today but, I have a better idea that I'm not the only one who is feeling such confusion and disorientation.

Thank you for your insight on the forces of energy taking place within and without."

—**George T Jr.**

"I wanted to express my appreciation for your article that appeared in *Wisdom*, June, 2005 entitled 'Selfish vs. Selfless'— your insights were profoundly helpful to me and spoke so directly to issues I have been wrestling with for some time. It was also extremely helpful in talking with my daughter about these themes in her life. We have read the article many times—each time getting yet another insight from it. Again, thank you for a wonderful article."

—**Karen G, Boston, MA**

"Thank you so much for your monthly column in *Wisdom Magazine*. My partner and I read your and The Tibetan's articles with great anticipation of the knowledge they contain and share and we find them of great assistance as we grow in awareness, daily it seems at times. We're both very excited to learn and practice Universal principles of life and want to, in time, share and promote them as well in our own life. We very much appreciate your work!"

—**Amy H, Northampton, MA**

"Your article 'Gratitude vs. Entitlement' really spoke to me. I had picked up a copy of *Wisdom* in a health food store in Princeton NJ and started to go through the publication Friday evening. Earlier, I had been taking an evening walk thinking a lot and admittedly, working my sense of entitlement.

"It is remarkable to me, but not surprising that I picked up the magazine just when I needed it most. Your insights are so helpful and your message about envy addressed an issue I have been dealing with for years. Thank you for an enlightening me!"

—**Susan L, New Jersey**

"I have been reading your articles and channeling of 'The Tibetan' in the *Wisdom* magazine for some time now. I have always enjoyed reading them and come away with new insights or affirmations each time. Your last article on 'Worthiness' particularly hit home... Thank you again for your offerings and your wonderful articles of inspiration and wisdom."

—Yvonne, NYC

"First of all, I want to say I look forward to reading your *Wisdom* articles each month. They truly hit a chord with me. I'm a 'holistic health counselor,' and so many of your topics are spot-on for my clients, as well as for me. Thank you for your 'guidance' each month!"

—Jennifer M, NYC

"I just reread your article in *Wisdom* magazine, and the article touched me. It gave me a hope that I might release myself from the grip of isolation that you described so well. Thank you!"

—Betsy, New Hope, PA

"I just want to thank you sooooooo much for this article on narcissism that you wrote. I have been a sounding board victim for most of my life too and for the longest time - I thought the problem was ME! That I was not interesting enough, not valuable enough, not worthy of having people want to hear about my life....How ironic that you wrote such a valuable article that proves what my Higher Self knew all along. We do live in a VERY self-absorbed society and I HOPE and PRAY that we can all just get over our selves and get on the higher matters at hand.

"Bravo to you for such a wonderful article. And thank you for making me feel not so alone. I am quickly losing interest in my narcissistic friends...but then I suppose the word 'friends' does not really apply anymore. Thank you!"

—Tracey B, Rhode Island

"I just read your February article 'React or Detach?' in the *Wisdom* publication...Your message is what I needed to hear, right here, right now..."

—Annette S, Vermont

"Thank you for that wonderful article. Only one who has been there can know what it means to 'go kicking and screaming over the abyss!'"

—**Kay B, Pennsylvania**

"I just got through reading your article in the *Wisdom Magazine* and it is brilliant!"

—**Laura S, New York**

"Have been reading your column in *Wisdom Magazine* for months and absolutely look forward to the gems of wisdom...Blessings to you for your great work!"

—**Sue C, NYC**

"I would just like to tell you your monthly articles in *Wisdom* are always right on target with what seems to be happening around me—and I look forward to them. Thank you and the Tibetan for your inspiration."

—**Laura Z, New Jersey**

"I just wanted to thank you for the article, 'React or Detach.' Your words have helped me to face and deal with my anger from a completely different and exciting vantage point...You will never know the impact you have had on my life, and I thank you for it!"

—**Linda L, Brunswick, ME**

READ *WISDOM MAGAZINE!*

The journey continues! Be sure to read on with Moriah and the Tibetan as they explore *new* slices of the human condition and our shared journey of transformation in her ongoing monthly column, "Soul Connection." Watch for Wisdom Magazine throughout the northeast and Puget Sound, or visit www.wisdom-magazine.com or call 1-888-828-6670.

✧ DEDICATION ✧

This book is dedicated to the Ascended Masters—the "Head Masters" of Earth School—who oversee and guide our journey through many lifetimes on the planet. Their loving presence, 24 hours a day, gives us the courage to move through all our soul assignments knowing that we are never unattended by our Grand Tutors whose steady, ever-present support, encouragement, healing and teaching make it possible for us to joyfully evolve forward on the path to total transformation.

✧ ACKNOWLEDGMENTS ✧

My profound thanks to the following:

Mary Arsenault for creating *Wisdom Magazine*, a powerful vehicle for bringing new teachings to the public, and for including me from the very beginning. This continues to be a wonderful opportunity to explore these relevant issues with the readership as Mary's inspiration and creativity extends *Wisdom* out into the world—a much needed and appreciated shining light for expanding consciousness.

Ellen Lovinger Eller for her amazing expertise and razor sharp editorial skills coupled with her sensitive attunement to these teachings and her supportive and creative involvement with the School of the Golden Discs.

My courageous clients and students of the School of the Golden Discs for their willingness to explore the depths of their souls and to open to transformation. They have taught me about the mysteries of the human psyche. I am deeply honored by their trust and commitment to go through the alchemical fire with me and the Tibetan. Without them this book would not be possible.

The readers of my column who have inspired me, through their words of appreciation, to continue to language the terrain of the soul.

The Tibetan for his infinite gifts of wisdom, patience, support, humor and unconditional love. He is ALWAYS there when I need him, ready to serve, heal, encourage and enlighten.

And, from the depth of my heart I want to thank my husband and soul mate, Zayne. This book would not be sitting in your hands right now without his incredible dedication, hard work, perseverance and creative inspiration. He diligently compiled this project and brilliantly wove it together—through his artful eye—into a wonder-filled tapestry.

✧ CONTENTS ✧

Part Three: *HUMAN RELATIONSHIPS*

Part Four: *TRANSFORMING THE SHADOW AND MASTERING THE DESCENT PROCESS*

Part Five: *SOUL LESSONS*

Part Six: *THE TRANSITION PROCESS*

Part Seven: *THE NEW CONSCIOUSNESS*

✦ INTRODUCTION ✦

This book is a treasure chest of articles from my column "Soul Connection," published in *Wisdom Magazine* (widely distributed throughout the Northeast and Puget Sound) from August 2000 through April 2006. They are an exploration of topics relevant to people from all walks of life, and also reflect the transformational process that everyone is undergoing in response to the heightened vibrations currently impacting the earth plane. The topics were generated by issues brought to therapy sessions by my clients as well as by my own insights, studies and soul searching.

Please join me in viewing our human experience from the paradigm that we are all students attending Earth School. Our lives are essentially a grand learning process, and there are many human teachers available for guidance. But in addition, the Earth School faculty includes a group of teachers on the spiritual plane called the Ascended Masters. These Masters work internally with humanity 24 hours a day, often while we are sleeping, to instruct, encourage, heal us and guide our evolution.

Djwhal Khul, also called "The Tibetan," is one of the Ascended Masters. He is known as the Great Psychologist because of his extensive wisdom regarding the human psyche, based in part on his own soul's development through lifetimes on planet earth. His last incarnation was in Tibet during the 20th Century. From 1919 to 1949, he telepathically transmitted metaphysical knowledge from his monastery in Tibet to Alice Bailey, who lived in England. She recorded these teachings in a series of books that became the foundation of the Arcane School.

The Tibetan's teachings describe the paradigm of an emerging new level of advanced collective consciousness—"the birth of a new Cosmic Day." Ushering in this new paradigm are groups of world servers dedicated to restoring the Divine Plan on earth. After his ascension in 1950, the Tibetan has continued to work from the spiritual plane with thousands of students to accelerate their awakening so that they may assist in the Great Work of invoking this momentous evolutionary leap for humanity.

Introduction

Since 1986, I have been a channel for Djwhal Khul. Channeling is the art of making contact and receiving information through expanded awareness with another vibration or energy field, like being a human radio. We all have energetic sensors that can pick up "stations" of higher vibrational frequencies and often receive these frequencies through our heart (heart chakra) and/or through the top of our head (crown chakra). This "gift" of channeling is our natural birthright—available to all—enabling us to tap into highly creative realms, wisdom and invention, as well as guidance from beings who dwell on the spiritual plane.

Since 1983, my exploration of the human psyche in private therapy practice has demonstrated to me that our lives are constellated around specific lessons—requirements for the evolution of the individual soul. Karmic assignments are not punishments for misdeeds in past lives but rather vehicles to delve into the rich texture of the human condition. These articles are written to help people develop a positive, productive attitude toward the divinely mandated circumstances engineered for transformation. They provide an expansive perspective, in collaboration with the Tibetan, to help readers accept their attendance at Earth School as a wonderful opportunity.

There is a Divine Plan that orchestrates our human process, galvanizing to the soul with its multitude of challenges and duality. We are free to collaborate with the Divine Plan to invoke the Grace that lubricates our journey through these soul assignments. Heightened awareness of the spiritual implications of these lessons inspires us to work with our life course rather than resist it with fear. We are then empowered to master the human condition.

These articles uplift our vision to the celestial realm while simultaneously plumbing the psychological depths within each puzzle piece. We learn how to sustain the greater spiritual perspective on the journey, which nourishes our search for meaning in daily life and allows us to release self-judgment.

I approach each topic through our shared human vulnerability and candidly describe my own confusion about the subject. Drawing on my professional skills, I psychologically work the issue through a bold inquiry—a journey down the Rabbit Hole of the psyche—that opens a fresh perspective on each slice of earthly life. Then the Tibetan takes the issue and elevates it to an expansive metaphysical perspective, which illuminates and clarifies the true essence of the riddle within the lesson.

Before reading each article, please let go of your preconceived notions about the theme. Allow yourself to be touched, inspired and opened through the therapeutic impact of these essays. They are designed to stimulate and invoke our deepest issues. I include questions to the reader as tools for reflection, journaling, soul searching, self-examination and illumination to help each student with their stupendous "scholarship" to Earth School—the human condition.

Turn to this book as a first-aid kit. Open to any relevant article when you are lost in the quagmire of your false beliefs, karmic debris and unconscious patterns. Then relax into the healing experience of self-compassion, comfort, insight, self-forgiveness, clarity and understanding that uplifts the soul, opens the heart, and settles the turbulence of this wild transformational ride we all share.

✧ <u>PREFACE</u> ✧

How It All Began

✧ Becoming a Channel ✧

August 2000

It was January, 1986. Totally focused on establishing a psychotherapy practice in Newton, MA, becoming a channel was the furthest thing from my mind. A friend called a few days after my 37th birthday to inform me of a woman, Kathlyn Kingdon, temporarily in town from Colorado who channeled an ascended Tibetan Master, Djwhal Khul. She'd just had a cancellation—would I like to fill it? My client, scheduled for the same time slot had just canceled leaving me no reason to say no. This synchronicity was more than I could ignore.

New to the world of channeling and blissfully unaware of what I was getting myself into, I arrived at the reading filled with curiosity. When the Tibetan "came through" Kathyln, his first words were, *When are you going to let me in?* Stunned and amazed in witnessing a being from the spirit plane talking to me directly, I was speechless. Laughing, he reassured me that it was OK to speak to him. Somehow I found my voice as something deep inside of me say "Now" to his request. As if presenting me with the benefits package of a job offer, Djwhal Khul encouraged me to open my channel in collaboration with him, highlighting the enhanced awareness it would provide for counseling my clients on a soul level. Tantalized by the idea of receiving expanded insight, wisdom and attunement to my clients' issues, I made the commitment to open my channel and work with this mysterious and powerful otherworldly being.

Pleased with my promise, Djwhal Khul then listed 100 false beliefs carried over from previous lifetimes needing to be removed in order for me to open fully. These beliefs centered on fears of possession and loss of control. *The channeling will come easily, but the real challenge will be to trust it*, he cautioned. Driving home, head spinning from this strange encounter, I wondered exactly what I had just committed to. Little did I realize from that moment on my life would never be the same.

During the next six months I spent most evenings alone in my office, diligently applying the Tibetan's instructions for opening the channel. His technique for removing false beliefs was to have me speak each one out loud while envisioning a stone in the body correlating to that belief—imagining a light-filled hand reaching into the top of my head (the crown chakra), removing the stone, throwing it against a concrete wall and watching it explode. My logic shot holes in this "foolish waste of time," seeing it as nothing more than imagination gone berserk. In spite of my critical rational mind's attempt to abort this process, I persisted, unable to shake the deep sense of duty permeating my commitment to this teacher.

Djwhal Khul told me to receive him through the back of my heart (chakra). He said:

There is deep scar tissue there from past life betrayals, physically and emotionally being stabbed in the back by those you trusted. Envision a small flashlight beaming light, dissolving the scar tissue and opening the heart fully.

After three months of letting my imagination describe the slow process of removing this "scar tissue," suddenly the passageway from the back of my heart to the front became unobstructed. It felt like a cork popping. The intake of energy was so strong I had to catch my breath. Much to my amazement, these exercises had really worked.

False beliefs removed, scar tissue dissolved, all that remained was the control issue. I envisioned meeting Djwhal Khul in the center of my heart. He came to me in his light body. Although I couldn't "see" a physical form, I recognized his energy as the same that spoke to me through Kathlyn. Past life fears of possession prompted me to test the safety of allowing in this teacher. As soon as I made contact with his energy in my heart, I demanded that he leave. Immediately the energy receded. I invited him in again, only to insist he leave moments later. Back and forth this went several times until I was satisfied, "in control," reassured that this patient Tibetan Master was infinitely respectful of my boundaries.

After eight months of experimentation and practice, I began to give channeled readings professionally. Anxious that my channeling was the result of an over active imagination, I decided it would be valid after giving 100 successful readings. Hundreds of readings given, psychotherapy clients pleased with my new level of insight and perspective on their process, several channeling classes taught and still I was uncertain about the "reality" of this phenomenon called channeling.

The validation process for channeling is challenging. There is no such thing as a completely *pure* channel. We all have an individual filter through which channeled material flows. This filter is shaped by our language, culture, preconceived perceptions, emotions, and unconscious material. Our filter blends with the higher vibratory rates we are receiving to create our unique experience of channeling. The more we practice channeling, the more the debris clouding our filter is eliminated. Channeling is a natural cleansing process. Interfacing with heightened energies burns away the dross that obscures our clarity. Eventually, in spite of a large ratio of unconscious material to higher truth, we transform our consciousness just as a muddy pond is slowly cleansed by a steady intake of clear water, however small the trickle.

I know that I am truly in channel when I experience the heightened current of energy known as Djwhal Khul moving through and heating up my body. Channeling to a group leaves me in an elevated state of consciousness—clear, joyful, expansive, positive and very loving. Negative thoughts and judgments melt away in the blend with this spiritual being. A few hours later my energy level drops, leaving me fatigued in response to the impact of embodying the Tibetan's frequency, a much stronger voltage than my own vibratory rate. After years of excessive channeled readings and classes resulting in physical burn-out, I realized that a good day's rest is mandatory in recouping the life force required to sustain Djwhal Khul's vibration coursing through my physical body. Monitoring his effect on my energy aids the validation process. Imagination can not "make up" the actual physical and emotional results of being in the channel.

The process of opening one's channel puts tremendous pressure on the ego's need to identify ourselves as separate from each other. To merge with a higher consciousness or receive another vibratory rate just as a radio "picks up" varied frequencies is to go beyond the domain of the ego. The ego often reacts with negative messages such as: "This isn't real. You are making up the entire experience. Who do you think you are to dare to tap into greater levels of wisdom, knowledge, creativity, and compassion?" Usually this is a good sign that one is indeed opening to greater levels of truth. It's best to be patient with the ego just as a parent lovingly quiets a child having a temper tantrum.

There are several techniques for opening the channel, including meditation, invocation, deep breathing, listening to music or using potent sounds such as the "Om." The natural law of resonance amplifies our intention to blend with a heightened vibrational flow. Imagining self as a column of light enables us to relax into a natural state of alignment that stimulates receptivity to our Higher Self, the Masters, guides and metaphysical knowledge available to all of us.

Djwhal Khul encourages this process:

To be in channel is everyone's <u>birthright</u>. It is the innate condition that links self to the Higher Self. It is as natural as breathing. Allow self to relax and trust that it is impossible not to be in channel. Release the illusion that self is disconnected from a greater reality than the limited world of the ego. As self trusts the channel, the gifts of deep wisdom, telepathic communication, Universal Love, and great outpourings of creativity are showered upon self. Opening the channel accelerates the awakening process, expands the vision and makes all things possible.

Ascended Master Djwhal Khul, The Tibetan

✧ <u>Part One</u> ✧

THE MYSTERY

✧ The Purpose of the Mystery ✧

March 2002

As soon as we land on the earth plane, amnesia sets in. All memory of previous lifetimes, our current birth, the spirit plane, our soul's purpose, our destiny around relationships, work, creativity, health and eventual death, slip into the recesses of our unconscious, impossible to retrieve. Why aren't we allowed to see the bigger picture? Wouldn't life be so much easier if we could see the future? Why can't we know what death brings? What is the process? Where do we end up? Why do we have to forget our truth, the essence of who we really are? Why do we have to rely on an amorphous sense of intuition to recreate the larger perspective on our journey?

If I just knew the future, or how I was going to die, or if I would be happy in old age, or where I went after death, I would feel so much better, more peaceful and accepting of my life. Why didn't Source simply reveal to us the Mysteries as tangibly as we experience our physical reality? That would at least have given us a running chance to succeed at this impossible assignment of being human. Why do we have to resort to intuition, sometimes nothing more than a vague hunch, to try to conjure up a sense of where we are going?

We all suffer from a sort of Alzheimer's, receiving momentary glimpses of the greater context in which we exist and then completely forgetting it all, isolating us from the big meaning. If Source provided a clear, substantive, irrevocable view of the larger picture, we would be so much more comfortable. I have always relied on a well-developed, intuitive muscle to guide me into the Mystery. With much bravado and "certainty," I have constructed descriptions of the Unknown based on imaginative reactions to intuitive hunches. My mental and spiritual egos clamp down on these non-scientific constructs as if they were absolute truth, so great is my need to define the Mystery in recognizable forms.

Sometimes, in moments of "weakness," my faith falters and I wonder, at a very deep level, if all of my intuitive impressions are illusion. In such moments, I come face to face with the Great Enigma. A cold chill seeps in as I move into existential bewilderment, fearful of the chaotic, unformed nature of the Unknown. This renders me humbled and vulnerable. If I can stand it, this encounter with the Mystery opens me to a place of awe, in spite of my ego's desperate attempt to manage the loss of control with yet another preconceived image.

The Unknown is always present, surrounding us with its dark veil, with no picture windows to show the landscape. The Universe dares us to walk blindly through life with no reference for the larger context. Yes, we can read countless metaphysical books, sit with spiritual teachers and devotedly follow various religions. But they have no precise maps of the Terrain of the Mysterious because it cannot be shown in the physical world. The Mystery, like a great ocean lapping at the beach, crashes in on us, sometimes ebbing during moments of "certainty," at least until the tide comes in, roaring away that intuitive certainty with the transpersonal smirk of the great Force that is the Unknowable.

The child within cries out to God, "Please tell me what's happening!" The familiar phrase, "I'm just dying to know," expresses the ego-death that occurs when we stand face-to-face with the Mystery. People spend lots of money to consult with psychics, hoping to gain a momentary vision of the Unknowable. If the psychic is skilled, the reading offers respite from the constant undermining quality and uneasy feeling that result from charging headlong into the Unknown. The client is temporarily reassured that there *is* a larger picture.

But would we really want to know how long we are going to live and the circumstances of our deaths? Do we really want to see the future, with all of its traumas and challenges? If we could see our soul's magnitude, could we stand the intensity of it? Do we have the courage to trust our intuition?

The Mystery obliterates any attachment to the future. Although the imagination may create lovely scenarios of the unfolding self, ultimately we don't know who we are becoming and the form it will take. It is useful to project intentions and images into the future to create our destiny, as much as Lady Fate will allow. However, as we toss these intentions into the cosmos, eager to manifest fulfillment, a moment will surface when we see those intentions drift into the ethers, like flimsy milkweed floating around, caught on the great currents of the Mystery to be directed wherever the Unknowable awaits, regardless of our mighty efforts to pin down a known tomorrow. This forces us to transcend the

3

logical, analytical mind seeking to structure our visions. The Mystery deposits us right into the present, sparing us any illusion of the future.

The greatest Mystery that we face is death, the moment when everything stops. Knowing that some day we will literally evaporate out of form, forced to relinquish our current place on earth, floods us with an eerie, unsettled feeling. Our ego begs to see the Bridge of Death so that it can project itself forward in a fearful attempt to postpone its inevitable annihilation. If only we could see our metamorphosis—know for sure that the caterpillar turns into the butterfly—we could rest easy and gracefully, surrendering to our transformation. But that would be like jumping ahead to the last chapter of a book without reading all the way through it.

There is power in the suspense, in the uncertainty. We hold our breath, hoping it will all turn out okay. In our fragile openness, we are deeply softened, highly accessible to the spiritualizing energies of the Mystery.

The Mystery is deeply feminine. She is the Void, the dark, blank space, holding all potential and revealing none. In this cocoon of the Unknown, the Mystery nourishes us with receptivity. We can only take in, not project out, for there is no screen on which to project. We can only let go, surrender and wait. In that moment of emptiness we are liberated from our attachments, helplessly freed to allow the forces to impact us.

The Mystery is the doorway to higher knowing. Frustrated with the limitations of the lower mind's nearsightedness, we struggle for a larger vantage point on the Unknown. In this struggle, we push through the veil into the higher mind, our intuitive function muscling its way up the mountain to get a better view. We have to develop our intuition because it is the only bridge to the realm of higher knowledge, where the Great Libraries on the Causal plane teach the metaphysical laws orchestrating our existence. The Mystery taunts us with unanswerable riddles designed to short-circuit our lower minds, so that we can be released from the small worlds designed by our egos and expand into spectacular vistas of the soul's terrain. The joy is in the remembering.

The Tibetan, delighting in this exploration, adds:

Through intuition, the student stretches into the formlessness to contact a place of knowing not limited by the human condition. If life were all spelled out in form, the student would not have to exercise the intuitive muscle that allows humankind to eventually go beyond the illusion that earthly life is separate from the rest of Creation. Like a scavenger hunt that delights the child with its challenge to play detective, the student must follow clues to uncover the truth. To make it too easy is to invite complacency. The dynamic tension between physical, provable reality and the Mystery is highly creative. The child is disappointed if the desired prize is provided without effort. To hunt for it, reaching out into the unknown, is to excite the mind, invoke inventiveness, determination, curiosity, frustration, alertness, creative uncertainty and, finally, a "foolish" faith that lets everything go, resulting in absolute trust.

Complete trust can <u>only</u> be cultivated in reaction to the Unknown. Just as the infant totally surrenders to the impact of the mother, with no cognitive awareness of his/her process, so too do the students surrender to the impact of the Mystery, which catalyzes the innate gift of primal trust. The Mystery dares the students to move forward in spite of the veils placed before their eyes. Ironically, it is only this complete surrender to blindness that can evoke the latent trust required to let go of the rational mind and be infused with a guidance that ultimately sheds light on all the Great Mysteries.

To burn away the veils that obscure the clarity of the inner "third" eye develops and blends extended vision with hard-earned wisdom. It is wisdom crystallized from the process of letting go over and over again, each time wearing away at the dominion of the ego. To develop intuition is to accept that there is a greater picture available to all. To trust one's intuition is to know that all Mysteries were designed to be explained and described as the intuitive channel eventually captures pieces of the puzzle and reconfigures the great horizon, revealing the Extraordinary World.

As the student surrenders to the Unknown, cellular memory is activated to a time when the Mystery was experienced as the Voice of Great Guidance. To bathe within the Mystery is to cleanse the soul of the burden of expectations. To know nothing is to experience everything.

To Know Nothing is to experience Everything

Part One: The Mystery

The Veils of Mystery were dropped on humankind to strengthen their conviction, develop courage, turn up the volume and raise the stakes of their quest...to make them hungry for more. The hunger drives them to remember that, indeed, there is something more. The process does not stop at death.

Beyond the veils lies a realm of magnificent beauty, a process of exquisite Love, a wellspring of wisdom sparking the inherent genius within all. When the student develops a foundation of trust and faith within the confines of the windowless room of the physical world, they internally draw powerful spiritual resources that catapult them into their magnitude. When the veils are lifted, the curtains opened, the light pours forth with such intensity and profound magnificence, the soul is swept into a world of recognition, seeing in all directions at once, and validating the innate knowing that guided it all along.

So bless the Mysterious Wonder that forces students to grope in the dark and to call for help, allowing them to finally receive the guidance magnetized by the call. Upon contact with this guidance, students open, realizing they "knew" all along. Faith is substantiated.

As the collective awakening unfolds on planet earth, all veils will drop away. Humankind will burn through the dross of forgetfulness. The presence of the Great Mystery lies sweetly on the horizon, beckoning the soul to pioneer farther into the Great outreaches of the Universe with the confidence that one can indeed see in the dark, if one simply opens the inner eyes, trusts, lets go and leaps. There is no end to the adventure, to the Unknown, to the quest— to the Mysterious enchantment of the Divine.

✧ Why We Incarnate ✧

May 2002

The glorious season of spring reminds us to celebrate being alive. Nature sings her awakening song as we watch the miracle of earthly birth unfold through rainbow colored flowers, emerald grasses and budding trees. Spring's beauty reminds us of the great opportunity to be physical on the earth plane with all of her glory. So why do so many of us resist our bodies and resent being physical?

The Tibetan tells me that souls are lined up around the cosmic block waiting for the opportunity to incarnate onto the earth plane. Most of us find this baffling. Why would any being choose to dive into this heavy, gravity-filled, dense world, impossibly orchestrated by paradox and limiting duality, when they could be singing with the angels in the light-filled, free flowing realm of spirit?

Many of us have trouble staying in our bodies, reflecting a basic resistance to being on the earth plane, to being incarnate. Most of our addictions are unconscious impulses to flee the physical plane into the spiritual dimension, where we feel lighter, more carefree. Addictions to drugs, alcohol, overworking, excessive TV, consumerism, etc., numb the body. Too much of anything creates a block to being fully present on the earth. Add poor diet and lack of exercise, and eventually we convince ourselves that we don't even have a body—it's just this thing that moves us around and gets in the way. The more we are "disembodied," the more we neglect our physical well-being. A neglected body develops all kinds of aches and pains that validate the collective belief that being physical means suffering and limitation.

Djwhal Khul, the Tibetan, encourages us to bring the soul into the body. He accentuates that, contrary to the usual spiritual teachings emphasizing the function of transcendence (which is to "rise above" our human condition, our flesh, in order to move to a more purified realm), it is time to anchor the soul in the body and onto the earth plane. We are to move from transcendence to infusion. Quite a switch!

Perhaps most of us spend more of our lives in non-physical dimensions than we realize. We may not notice that in times of stress, fear, and pain, we psychically lift up and out of our bodies. As children, when shock, trauma and/or chronic situations of physical and/or emotional neglect/abuse occur, we "escape" by leaving our physical bodies. In this experience of disassociation, we may feel as if we are tethered to our bodies, but there is an essential part of ourselves that has disconnected and traveled to another realm. We are usually not conscious of this splitting off until a later time, when we are healed enough to return the split-off part of our psyche into the body. Then we realize how vividly present we can be when our consciousness is fully embodied.

Carl Jung taught that the body speaks the language of the unconscious. Better yet, the body *is* the unconscious. In the unconscious we carry all of our karmic material—records of past and present wounds to be healed. Our current physical body is connected to all our past-life bodies. To be fully in the body is to make contact with not only the impact of our childhood, but also the wallop of every previous incarnation.

I can testify to the challenge of staying fully present in my physical body. In grade school, teachers criticized me for not living up to my potential. How could I? I wasn't even in the classroom. Yes, my body sat there, but my consciousness was off in distant regions of imagination, resisting the apparent confinement of the physical plane that seemed so cruel to my visionary, rebellious spirit.

This other-worldly reality pervaded throughout my 20s. While I functioned on the physical plane, most of my being was off somewhere. Hours passed and I would have no cognitive experience of the physical impact of my activities, even trivial ones such as tying my shoelaces. I wanted to be "anywhere but here."

While I dutifully went through the motions of carrying on physical responsibilities, making a living, eating, exercising, I couldn't settle comfortably into my body. It represented prison. To be fully embodied was to feel the hardship of my childhood, to feel disconnected from the spiritual plane, to be heavy, dense and frustrated with the incessant roadblocks of being human. I just wanted to merge with the hawks and fly off somewhere spiritually exotic. I tried my best to "leave" whenever possible, not daring to truly touch the earth. As I rounded into my late 30s, I realized that there was no escaping the phenomena of being physical. I needed a larger perspective on the purpose of incarnation to counteract my belief that life on the earth plane is too difficult, discouraging and relentlessly laborious.

Years of listening to the Tibetan have provided a broader vantage point on the "opportunity" of being on the earth. He ceaselessly reminds me that to be human is not a punishment but rather a gift—the spiritual plane augmented in form. The density of the earth plane provides an accelerated learning curve as it vivifies and crystallizes our soul's essence. The human condition is specifically designed to shape the soul with its richness of human emotions and passions.

Once I finally surrendered to my non-negotiable destiny of being here, I began to notice the richness of the senses, physical contact, and the tangibility of my spirit in form.

To be in a physical framework vividly expresses the soul's essence in an undeniable way. As I learn to reference pleasure as much as pain, I release the false belief that we have to leave the body in order to feel light and enlightened. I begin to glimpse the Taoist teaching that heaven on earth is the natural way of things, and that the physical body is the vehicle for this heightened consciousness as much as the mind is, if not more so. I now meet each day with gratitude for being incarnate, with deep love and respect for my physical body, and acceptance/ enjoyment of the human condition, so unique in this universe. I want to be here more than ever.

Pleased at my progress, the Tibetan smiles in agreement with my latest conclusions about earth-life. He adds:

Many spiritual traditions have denied the physical body. This reflects the false belief that the earth plane is less divine than the spiritual plane. Ironically, the earthly plane, based in duality, gives the soul the greatest opportunity for enlightenment. There is tremendous creative potential for the soul to evolve as it interfaces with the human condition. The spiritual dimension is forged in form with a density that enhances the Higher Self's essence in a vibrant, dramatic focus that allows the student to evolve rapidly. The human condition is a crash course in Self-exploration.

The soul is filled with false beliefs generated from core confusions about the nature of Source (God) and Its essential love for all of Its creation. Examples of false beliefs are, "Source does not love me," or "Source has abandoned me." These false beliefs did not originate from earthly experiences, but stemmed forth from the original level, called the Monad, of separating or differentiating the individual out from Source. The monadic level extends down to the Higher Self, or Oversoul, which extends to the soul, which then extends to the earth plane in an effort to gather enough experiences and wisdom to resolve these original distortions.

As the soul incarnates, the original or monadic level of confusion is played out in the rich drama of the human condition. The student has an opportunity, often after several lifetimes of repeating the same patterns, to break through the illusion of false beliefs. This breakthrough is then energetically transmitted to the soul, from the soul to the Oversoul, and ultimately back to the monadic level.

The student has a specific set of assignments with each lifetime. These requirements are to explore, through his/her human sensitivities, new possibilities of understanding and attunement to Source's true Being. The earth plane is a powerful theater where the substantive dramatization of the soul's essence drives home the awareness of monadic illusion. It is an intense learning curve. The student's humanity mirrors the soul back to itself in a tangible format in order to burn through its illusions, transmuting the false beliefs blocking the soul's return arc homeward to Source.

In the new millennium, humankind needs to be more physical than ever. The more embodied the students are, the more they can resonate with mother earth and serve as conductors of light to augment her healing. As the students clear their bodies, their enlightened physicality highlights and enhances the earth's enlightenment process. Heaven on earth is inevitable.

The physical body is the last frontier of unresolved karma. Many students have burned through karmic debris in their mental bodies as they clarify thought patterns and open to new paradigms of perception. They are also working diligently to cleanse their emotional bodies by integrating powerful feelings of rage and fear with higher levels of love and joy.

The remaining residues of undigested karmic material render down into the physical body. These are the most stubborn levels of illusion to release. The student's physical body has agreed to carry this debris in order to cleanse it for once and for all.

The physical body was designed by Source to be an exquisite channel for heightened energy. The meridians that form an energetic grid work in the body carry tremendous electrical currents. Although the body appears solid and dense, it is far more space than form. It is essentially held together by Light and Love. As the students evolve, the body is experienced more as pure energy than as dense substance.

The kundalini is the life force that lies curled up like a snake at the base of the spine while dormant. When activated, it rises up the spine and sparks the electrical system of the body, which catalyzes awakening. The body offers the most tangible experience of the electrical nature of enlightenment. The kundalini awakens the light centers in the head, which activate large, unused sections of the brain by amplifying the sparking of synapses. Like inserting a plug into a socket, the connection is made. The juice flows and all illusions of separation, even at the monadic level, dissolve.

Trust that the physical body can handle and ground the strong energy of enlightenment. That's what it was designed for! Students can expect enlightenment through the physical body first as the last remnants of karma are materialized and transmuted through the endless loving service of this corporeal temple of the soul. The body is the electrical conduit for heightened Love and Light. Therefore, the sheer experience of being physical is an enlightening experience.

Allow self to touch the Divine as you touch your body, the earth and each other. Trust the body's memory to recall not only past traumas, but also ancient memories of Lightness of Being. Rejoice in the body's prismatic mirroring of all aspects of the soul. Celebrate the human condition—earth school—knowing that as it sculpts the soul, it liberates the spirit.

✧ Why We Die ✧

June 2002

Sitting with my father at the moment of his death from bone cancer, I watched his face transform. Just after he took his last breath, the lines of bitterness and cynicism melted as a sweet smile of peace softened his expression. For the past 32 years since his transition I have cherished that memory of his face, kinder and more yielding in death than in life. I have wondered what happened to him at the point of departure to invoke such beauty. Isn't death something to be feared, dreaded?

The ego tightens up in terror at the prospect of its own demise. Yet there is a bigger picture beyond our ego's domain that exalts the mystery of death to the same miraculous level as birth. There are cultures that celebrate when people die and grieve when they are born. What do those people know that we don't? How would our attitude toward death be different if we celebrated it? Would it ease our transition? Animals model full surrender to death, allowing their instinct to inform them of the grace within the passage. Why must we resist it so?

Since childhood I have "known" that I was destined to live to be very old. Is this wishful thinking? Perhaps. But I believe we can remember our karmic contract describing the appropriate time/ place/ mode of death for this incarnation. There is some room for negotiation in this contract if it is in keeping with our soul's evolution. Death, the ultimate ambassador for Lady Fate, is the supreme teacher of the precious gift of life. It sits on our left shoulder whispering in our ear of its inevitable presence, teaching us to live life as intensely as possible.

We often feel helpless in the face of death. But are we? How much control or choice do we have? Some go merrily along in life, oblivious to death, which is viewed as a vague point on a distant horizon that never arrives, as if it only happens to other people. Others, seduced by its mystery, flirt with death, tempting its hand whenever possible. Some people exist in constant fear of death, disempowered by it to the point of living only a near-life experience. Most of us agree that it's better not to know when and how we will die. The ego can't bear the awareness.

Death teaches the polarity of will vs. surrender. We hear miraculous stories of people who have willed themselves to live through insurmountable odds. Others fight death, extending their suffering, postponing the inevitable lesson of surrender that eases the pain and liberates the spirit. There are advanced spiritual teachers like Yogananda, who have demonstrated conscious exit of the body. Their knowledge, to transition at will, is the mastery we all need to acquire at some point in our evolution.

Our ability to surrender is greatly affected by our beliefs. If we are convinced that this life is all there is, with no eternal nature of the soul/spirit, we may be more reluctant to leave, hanging on for "dear life" to this one bit of opportunity to be on the earth plane—viewing death as utter darkness, the void, nothingness, the end of all there is. Those who believe there is "something" after death—the eternal essence of Self, the opportunity for reincarnation, the heavenly realms—perhaps let go a little easier.

A believer in reincarnation, I laugh at the notion that the death process is unknown. We have exercised the experience of dying hundreds of times in previous lives. Processing past-life death experiences through light trance work with clients over the past 11 years, I have observed uniform patterns. Initially, clients observe themselves floating above the body looking down at the final scene of death, then into the death tunnel—dark, sometimes elongated, sometimes short—then out into the light. Is their unconscious simply parroting information read from books or heard from other people's near-death experiences?

Their bodies shake, shiver, writhe around with an accelerated breathing pattern in the final stages of the past-life death they are reliving, and then finally deeply relax as they exit that lifetime. This cannot only be imagination. The current body has a cellular memory of past-life dying experiences, complete with all the traumas, pain and inevitable liberation from the physical body. Clients describe this release as a sudden flow of expansion, relaxation, lightness of being, like shedding a suit of clothes that is too tight.

Reliving my own past-life deaths, no matter how horrific the process, always leaves me with a profound feeling of lightness, buoyancy and speed...a sense of lifting up and out—accelerating through the death tunnel into a brilliant light indescribable to earthly eyes. The experience has consistently repeated itself, regardless of the content of the past life. Perhaps we only experience a prolonged death-tunnel transition when we believe that this life is all there is. Attachment to death being "the eternal dark" can conjure feelings of being stuck in the death tunnel.

Still relatively young in my evolution, I marvel at the Masters of the Far East who inhabit their physical bodies for hundreds of years, defying the illusion of earthly limitations. With wide-eyed anticipation, I eagerly await the Tibetan's assistance in learning how to consciously exit the body at will. I know that this is graduate-level material, overwhelming to my "elementary school" consciousness. But the day will come, sooner than we think, when we will all be collaboratively dancing with death from a place of joy and creativity.

The Tibetan, delighting in my appetite for challenges, teaches:

The impact of dying is one of the soul's most potent earthly experiences. Death is a process to be mastered, as much a course requirement as the mastery of life. Prior to each incarnation, the soul "signs" a contract to leave at a precise time, place and manner. There are firm guidelines for one's stay on earth, but they are not set in stone.

As the student burns through karma, new energies are released that reorganize the requirements for one's earthly stay. More "free will" is available to the student who completes his/her work ahead of schedule, creating space for an improvisational response to the original karmic contract. Some students may be ready to leave earlier, the souls eager to pursue studies on the etheric planes. Others may choose to stay longer to explore higher levels of consciousness within the human condition and serve in new ways. It is not a punishment to stay longer or leave earlier. During the sleep state, the student often meets with the karmic board to review progress, revisiting the original contract to discern its current effectiveness in the soul's evolution. EVERYTHING is open to change.

Each incarnation is designed according to an estimated time for the student to fulfill karmic obligations to others, develop new qualities/ gifts/ insights, and "do time" for purification in situations designed to burn through illusions that created pain or suffering in self and others in the past. This alchemical process breaks down the hardened emotional pockets of karmic rage/fear. Each lifetime requires a specific amount of time to "cook" the soul for transformation to occur and to provide room for the random creation of new destinies of a higher order. The estimated time includes space for chaos to impact the student in new and surprising ways.

Lives that appear prematurely cut off through accident/ natural disaster/ war are 90% preplanned to provide a pinnacle experience through the shock of sudden, unexpected death. This "trauma" has a profound transformative effect on the soul, even though humankind perceives the "tragedy" as cruel and unloving. It shatters crystallized patterns that the student was unable to transmute while living.

The impact of one's mode of death is designed to have a powerful effect on everyone connected to the person. How one exits is not only relevant to his or her own soul, but also the result of karma owed to others. The shock of sudden or "premature" death can serve as a wake-up call to those connected, teaching them flexibility and increased engagement in life.

Souls who choose a prolonged death through illness "cross over" and return several times to integrate the awareness that the very thin veil between dimensions is, indeed, only illusion. This tenderly acclimates the ego as the soul anchors its essence onto the spirit plane, making the final act of untethering from physical form a gentle one. People connected to a dying person have the opportunity to express unspoken truths, repair disputes, practice devotional care/sacrifice, and witness the illusion of separation as they watch their beloved return each time with comments about the "other side," often experienced as dreams by the terminally ill.

The mode of death is precisely designed to release unresolved karmic material. It may be either a continuation of previous deaths on an overt or subtle level, or it may be entirely different, to expand the soul's awareness. The student can change the circumstance of his/her death according to the present life's evolutionary progress. The need for a violent death might be transmuted through release of internal rage, fear, or disempowerment before the actual set date of death. Also, resolution with others might dissolve the need to be the "victim" of another's violence.

How one dies shapes the soul very specifically and reflects its orientation to the greater picture. Students who have agreed to work at the mastery level consciously design their deaths, holding a focused attention on that image which creates that very death. This teaches that ultimately death is not a punishment, a fixed fate that is irrevocable, but rather a process that is open to change and increased alignment of the personal will with the Divine Will.

It is useful for all students to plan for the future by envisioning their deaths in exactly the ways they wish them to occur. Someone's fear of a terrible death can come true possibly because he/she is sensing the karmic contract for that kind of death. However, more often, one's creative energy is actualizing the fear. This is not to scare the students into thinking that their worst fears will come true, but rather to alert them to the potency of the union of fear and imagination. Imagine self transitioning in a most exalted experience of celebration and liberation that generates a profoundly loving impact on one's beloveds.

Usually students are notified of their impending departure. Often this occurs unconsciously, although some are able to register the information consciously. Since death is not designed to hurt but rather to strengthen and deepen the soul, the knowledge of its imminent arrival is available to all. This knowing is often distorted in students who are so apprehensive about death that they fear it at the door throughout their lives. Separate out the fear from the intuitive knowing that indeed the time has come to journey forth to greater dimensions.

Once through the death tunnel, the soul enters a realm of profound light where all aspects of the life just lived are displayed for evaluation. The karmic board is present to advise the next step. From there, the soul either reincarnates or travels forth into learning situations in other spectrums. The soul looks back on the previous incarnation from a profoundly expanded view, vividly observing the full impact of that lifetime's actions, thoughts, feelings and spiritual attunement—a moment of crystalline clarity that sets the stage for future incarnations.

The death process is essentially an ecstatic experience. Physical cells release the soul orgasmically into the Oneness of the spiritual plane. This is the moment of profound truth, when all doors open to enlighten the soul to the full nature and advancement of its recent incarnation. Those who have diligently applied themselves receive a glorious round of applause from the karmic board. Those who were entrenched in illusion or negativity are sobered by the awareness of the extended course work required to untangle their distortions—not punishment, but rather a profound clarification.

Rejoice in the death process and the enhanced wisdom it provides. View it as the ultimate reminder that earthly life is but a small part of a larger universal context in which the soul journeys forth into expanded levels of awakening. Death opens the door to a vast realm of possibilities. Accepting the gift of death prepares the student for the experience of passing through the veil of illusion, the death tunnel, into a light so profound that it burns through all the dross of earthly attachment. Death is the catalyst, the mighty transformer, and the conduit to a greater continent of the Divine.

✧ From Loss Into Infinity ✧

January 2004

Supposedly nothing is ever really lost in the Universe. All of creation, every being, is infinite in nature and therefore ultimately impervious to annihilation. However, when we lose loved ones, animal friends, long-term employment, health, parts of ourselves and/or outmoded dreams, the loss (so painfully "real") threatens to devastate our faith and spirit. Lately, heightened energetic frequencies are impacting the earth plane propelling us forward at lightning speed as if we were on an express train with no local stops at which to get off and look around, take a break, regroup. This express train speeds up our clearing process. Losses are compounding on themselves as we are being forced to radically let go of aspects of our life experience too profoundly near and dear to imagine relinquishing.

Last week my beloved eight-year old Belgian sheepdog, "Zulu," died after two weeks of battling a fast-moving bone cancer. Because I work at home, Zulu and I were almost constantly together since we first adopted him at ten weeks old. His astounding physical beauty, advanced intelligence, unconditional love, relentless joy, childlike playfulness and utter devotion were nutritional mainstays for my soul. These gifts provided me with the courage, stamina, support and faith to continue to move forward through the intense rigors of the accelerated soul alchemy process of transformation that heats up and discharges all dark pockets in the unconscious. I savored every minute of Zulu's presence in my life, never taking the gift of his love for granted. His unexpected, premature death exploded like a shotgun in my heart. As the shock slowly wears off, a profound grief spreads its tendrils into my soul, unearthing all previous grief not yet touched, accepted, worked, integrated from this lifetime and previous lives. It just takes one grave loss to uncork the ocean of tears waiting in the psychic wings to carry off dear attachments to cherished life experiences.

Human beings are hard-wired for attachment. We must bind to others and fasten to life in order to deeply immerse ourselves in our earthly lessons. Yet, ultimately we are expected to release all attachments if we are to be enlightened. My pessimism views this as a cruel cosmic joke. Many of us would like to skim the surface of life to protect ourselves from getting too involved. Supposedly this would ward off the painful devastation of loss. But maybe that's not true. Perhaps the deepest loss is to push away the profound bond that comes from being fully hitched to all that we cherish.

Lately, as our attachments are being ripped from us at an alarming rate, it appears that grief levels are high for many of us. We are being called to expel everything that stands in the way of our ultimate liberation. Normally we are given lifetimes to achieve this disengagement, but with the accelerated energies powering the express train locomotive, daily new challenges surface in the area of accepting loss, letting go and trusting that loss ultimately transmutes into gain. The sheer volume of release currently required by the Divine Plan plummets us into layers of shock followed by the agony of breaking attachments deeply rooted in the soul. It is not only death that brings this acute pain, but any area of physical, emotional, mental or spiritual cords that are suddenly or slowly ripped from their bedrock. Like being flung from a slingshot, this loss sends us reeling into chaotic disorientation. These days, any areas that we hold onto for dear life (with excessive attachment) are precisely the ones on the front burner for dismantling.

While my spiritually-based mind accepts this rigorous soul-unshackling as an opportunity to lighten my load, release illusion and free my spirit, my human heart aches from the demands of letting go. Often it makes no sense to us when we lose someone or something important. At the time, screaming grief blocks our ability to imagine anything good resulting from the many levels of loss that we endure. Why would our Higher Self require that we lose "the good stuff" in our lives? The need to release bad marriages, miserable jobs, unsupportive friends, unhealthy lifestyles, self-destructive patterns, etc. is obvious. (Ironically, our attachment to the "bad stuff" can be equally painful to surrender because it can be such a source of distorted comfort/familiarity.) But the grief that comes from having to let go of the irreplaceable joys, dreams fulfilled, loving relationships, fruitful careers, satisfying lifestyles, secure belief systems and jubilant health that have enriched us beyond measure seems insurmountable and senseless. Sometimes we can't perceive the subtle levels of stagnation creeping into our areas of fulfillment that begin to undermine our evolution. Or our soul may simply need the experience of letting go, starting a new chapter, or learning to deal with loss. On the surface however, most of these losses seem downright wrong—a mistake on the part of the Divine Plan.

One of our greatest challenges is to be able to give an elevated meaning to our losses. How do we uncover the benefits within the loss? When the caterpillar becomes mush in the cocoon it cannot possibly know what a creature of beauty it is destined to become. Perhaps in the cocoon, when missing previous caterpillar definition, identity, mobility, it seems that all is lost. There is no way to foresee the great flight that awaits those mighty butterfly wings metamorphasized from caterpillar legs. So we are asked to "have faith" that somehow, in some way, this wrenching away of our attachments is bringing us to a better place. The Masters encourage us to count on the Divine Plan and to assume that Source wants only what is best for us. But the mystery inherent in transformation requires blind obedience to trust as we find ourselves subjected to new vibrational frequencies stripping away our invaluable tethers with lightning speed. To reduce unnecessary levels of suffering, we must create a healthy, soothing, healing and higher perspective on loss.

Some of us try to stay out of the attachment loop to avoid the torment of letting go. However, this protection prevents us from realizing the rich happiness inherent in the human impulse to attach. Self-exiled from the exquisite bonds of human passions/ engagement/ exchange, our detachment forces us to live in the in-between worlds—our life a "black-and-white" movie getting grayer by the moment. To be vitally alive is to open ourselves to the total impact of our earthly life as we submit to our soul's passions and allow our compelling human engagement to fix us deeply into our experience. Then, exhaustively saturated by the potency of this full immersion (attachment), we must inevitably release our precious "holdings" to open to greater advancement and possibility. Loss is not a limiting process. It cleanses away parts of the old no longer relevant to self's evolutionary cutting edge. Loss is the gateway into expansion.

The Tibetan strides toward me with Zulu prancing along by his side. Together they broadcast the loving reminder that truly nothing is ever lost. He teaches:

All students must walk the razor's edge of deep immersion in their human journey. This inevitably requires attachment to self's experience. Evolution demands that all attachments be broken.

Therefore, the students must express their innate human impulse to "glue themselves" to life events that provide them with rich earthly learning, while remembering that ultimately all "sticky energy" that carries the fear of loss must be released.

Yes, the students are being wrung out at a cellular level. No stone is left unturned. The Masters can safely predict that as the ensuing dawning paradigm merges with and metamorphasizes the old, purging obsolete levels of human experience, students will have to learn the art of "graceful dismount" fueled by the faith that allows them to positively embrace the required sacrifice of the old in order to birth the new. Many students are learning the art of moving through gut-wrenching grief while simultaneously touching an expanded consciousness beyond all that they have ever known. To hold both loss and gain at the same time is to embody the paradox of earthly life and to evolve beyond duality. At the apex of grief and expansion, the students can comprehend that loss is an illusion.

All aspects of the third dimensional reality will ultimately be "lost" to the fifth dimensional energetic issuance into the Age of Aquarius. Students will have an opportunity to live through the illusion of loss and revisit all unresolved losses from previous lifetimes. While transmuting this illusion, students feel the convincing clench of finality that loss conveys with all the emotional turmoil, collapsing of faith, confused thought patterns and aberration of separation. As the students move through these heaps of losses, they begin to realize at a cellular level that all losses are nothing but a metamorphosis of the soul and its expression in earthly life. Currently, because most students are still caught in the vivid illusion that loss is real, their awareness that loss is simply a metamorphosis of form is experienced only at a subliminal level. However, as the losses compound upon themselves due to humankind's transition through multi-leveled gateways of initiation, students will very rapidly realize that all defunct pieces of themselves are still there—glorified in authenticity and essence revealed. Ultimately the only real loss is the loss of illusion.

It is useful to track where the losses are in one's life. Begin to follow the threads of those losses. Open to the challenge of perceiving the reconfiguration of these threads into new forms, experiences, opportunities, loves, etc. As the students repeatedly examine the possibilities in these losses, they will eagerly move through the grief process that facilitates true release, knowing full well that great possibility awaits them from deep within the "hole" that is left from the discharge of the old. The students then realize that form is temporary as a static point and yet eternal in evolving essence.

As students attune to the eternal essence that infuses their reality, the pain of loss dims, replaced with profound joy. Consciousness is then transformed. The blizzard of losses tenderizes humankind's rigid orientation toward separation and allows their perception to expand and penetrate the veil that obscures the undying energetic root within departed relationships/loved ones, bygone parts of self, outworn dreams and idolized illusions. This enables self to see all "losses" in their recycled core as this center energetic nucleus breaks down its expressed form and reorganizes into a higher, more effective version of itself.

When humankind finally expels the illusion of loss, the earthly plane will resound in celebration of what has always been—the Eternal. All fear of loss will fall away into a distant sea of tears, no longer necessary to cleanse the soul through grief. Through this emancipation from the tyranny of loss, the collective consciousness will transform into gold. This is the gold that possesses the wisdom of true inter-dimensional connection, where humankind can feel, hear and see the etheric presence of all beings, including all past, present, and future aspects of Self. This evolution brings the students' consciousness to dwell in the heart of the Universal Holographic Matrix, where all existential points connect to the Center to create the infinity 8—the ultimate Universal Truth.

So allow self's grief, the final release conduit, to flow and shed all attachments. Accept this process without an agenda for how long the grief should last. Trust the psyche's genius that produces just enough tears and heartache to honor what has been, to breathe in its treasured essence and to let go of the old shell that truly has lived out its earthly purpose. Then the grief naturally abates as the acute pain modifies into a dull ache which converts into sweet nostalgia which transforms into a rich presence of life deeply lived—the transfiguration into the Eternal. Then this monumental acceleration of awakening becomes a joyous process, free from the fear of loss, which ecstatically ushers in a Universal View of Permanence that opens the heart to full embrace of All That IS.

✧ The Divine Plan ✧

December 2000

The Tibetan continually encourages us to collaborate with the Divine Plan. What does that mean? Is there really a Divine Plan? If so, how do we recognize it in our lives?

Once in a while, we experience the sense that "after all is said and done, it all comes together in the end." Life seems like a Charles Dickens novel—filled with characters and events revealed at the end to be intricately interconnected. At such times I "know" that the Divine Plan is at work in my life. The knowing brings clarity, allowing me to recognize life as an unfolding story written by a Force greater than myself. While it is my job to put the puzzle pieces together, a larger Plan originated the overall picture before it was chopped up into little pieces to be deciphered and reassembled.

A useful map, a smaller portion of that overall picture, is the astrological chart. Like the blow-up section of a larger state map reflecting an intricate system of street names in a particular city, the chart shows the intricate system of planetary energies propelling our individual karma in this lifetime. While the larger map reflects the Divine Plan for the universal evolution of creation, this section is enlarged for our personal work. We are equally a part of the larger map and the smaller, more individual one.

Often I feel at the mercy of the inherent, seemingly random nature of life. Experiences and events blow past me like a blizzard, relentlessly tossing me here and there without any overall purpose or direction I can discern. In those moments, in spite of my intuitive knowing that we are *not* indiscriminately flung out from the universe onto planet earth to blindly blunder around in an essentially chaotic world, I wonder what life is really all about.

Our soul's purpose is deeply etched into the karmic contract carried into each incarnation. This contract is a direct expression of the Divine Plan. Although we cannot glimpse the supreme landscape of the Divine Plan due to the limited vantage point of our human condition, we can sense "rightness" when things "fall into place" in our lives. That sense of "place" is our energetic response to the Divine Plan.

Synchronicity offers us "proof" of a larger order. If we heighten our awareness of the amount of "coincidences" in our lives, people and experiences hooking up just at the right moment, we have to admit that the principle of synchronicity is an expression of the Divine Plan. While we may not be able to clearly put all the puzzle pieces together until the end of the story, we can recognize that this great scavenger hunt we are all on has very definite instructions, clues, and endpoints.

Often we say, "What are the odds of that happening?" When observing the likelihood of certain events in our lives, we realize that most of what we experience is not based on mathematically sustainable statistics. This is useful to keep in mind when we are discouraged about what appears to be the low probability for the fulfillment of our wishes.

If a woman is looking for a mate in a town that is factually low on available men, then she might get discouraged about the possibility of meeting someone appropriate. However, if she views it as collaborating with the Divine Plan, which is geared to fulfill her soul's needs, then she can throw the statistics out the window and follow the synchronicities which lead her directly to her soul mate, provided finding a soul mate is in keeping with the Divine Plan. The same is true for finding the right home, employment, friends—everything!

The first step in collaborating with the Divine Plan is to surrender to it. Difficult karmic situations or relationships are thrust upon us as direct mandates from this cosmic blueprint. If we can positively surrender to them for learning, releasing the notion of random bad luck, we've won half the battle.

Djwhal Khul adds:

When humankind truly recognizes the presence of the Divine Plan in their lives, they enter a state of relaxation, and release the personal will or laborious effort imagined as a requirement for a satisfying life. The power of the Divine Plan to bring forth the fulfillment of one's life destiny cannot be impacted by the ego/ personality. However, this does not exclude the necessity to bring one's creative focus into collaboration with the Sacred Agenda.

Collaborating with the Divine Plan, I heighten my attunement to receiving guidance/ instructions, and then act on that directive with my own unique inventive response. Djwhal Khul teases that we have to be willing to do the "assignment" because it is "due" whether we like it or not! The extent to which we consciously, positively collaborate with our awareness of the Divine Plan impacts our ease factor. Resisting the Divine Plan makes the assignments more difficult, causing undue suffering from the illusion that we could possibly fulfill our life's inner and outer work without completing all the "course requirements."

How do we attune to the Divine Plan? The Tibetan responds:

The biggest factor in attuning to the Divine Plan is to encourage the conscious mind to fully embrace the premise that indeed there is a Divine Plan. Then the lower mind automatically opens to the higher mind, which is capable of extended vision. Increased comprehension of the grand scheme of things, the larger map, heightens one's faith in the Plan, enhancing a joyful response to this collaboration. The student begins to truly trust this "map" describing the terrain of the soul, and the most efficient and satisfying routes to get to their destination. Eventually the student recognizes the Divine Plan in action, every moment of their lives, no longer needing dramatic experiences of synchronicity to prove it exists.

Be alert to the ego's need to discount a reality larger than itself. The ego prefers that the student stay in the realm of coincidences and not venture into the dimension of synchronicity. When needed, the Higher Self and Masters provide a striking experience of the Divine Plan at play. This provides the student with concrete proof of a larger cosmic design to catalyze the awakening from a narrow ego-based reality into a higher mind-based universal context in which to recognize one's soul.

I am reminded of the wake-up call I received from Djwhal Khul, the Tibetan, three years after opening my channel. I was still struggling with my persistent ego in the form of monster doubt, despite having given hundreds of readings. Nagging disbelief tried to convince me that there was no Divine Plan...that my channeling of the Tibetan was nothing more than delusion.

One busy day at my office, I received a call from a man named Harry. He introduced himself to me as a 60-year-old physicist living in Nashua, NH, with his wife. Awkwardly apologizing, he conveyed that, not knowing who I was, he had no idea why he was making this strange call. Harry explained that he and his son, playing with the Ouija board one evening, had received a phone number—mine! At the time I was living in Newton, part of the greater Boston area, filled with thousands of phone numbers. Since my services were not advertised, he could not have seen my name in a local publication.

Harry asked if I would be willing to tell him who I was and what I did for a living. Describing myself as a therapist and channel for Ascended Master Djwhal Khul, Harry caught his breath, stumbling over his words. He had been a student for 20 years in the Arcane school (based on the teachings of Djwhal Khul transmitted to Alice Bailey in the early 1900s), and was rewriting these esoteric teachings to make them more reader-friendly for the mainstream. Feeling blocked in his connection with the material, he had been uncertain that his efforts were accurately reflecting the Tibetan's teachings.

Awestruck by this "coincidence," I urged Harry to come immediately for a reading, which eventually led to him taking my four-month channeling course. At the end of the course Harry felt sufficiently "opened" to fulfill his "assignment" to work with the material and offer it to others. Together we delighted in this opportunity to experience the Divine Plan at work so concretely that neither his scientific skepticism nor my suspicious cynicism could discredit the lesson! Never again did I question the existence of a Divine Plan!

The Tibetan concludes:

To attune to the Divine Plan is to go beyond the logical mind into the illogical terrain of the soul. Accepting that life doesn't always make immediate rational sense allows one to open to a broader perspective on the journey. The path of the soul's evolution springs from the Divine Plan.

The responsibility of the student is to bring curiosity and alertness to the reflections of the Divine Plan at work in everyday life. Assign the mind the task of noticing when things fall into place. Pay extra attention to the gifts inherent in the Divine Plan and delight in this recognition. The willingness to observe synchronicities and expressions of Grace bringing forth self's true destiny heightens the collaboration with the higher self. The creative flow is increased, enlivening the Divine Plan and invoking its full potential. Release all notions of being lost in a random universe. Relax into this glorious Plan that carries self on a magic carpet into full transformation, self-knowledge, and ecstatic possibility.

✧ Serendipity ✧

December 2004

Just when I'm at the end of my rope—fed up with the frustrations and dead ends of life—serendipity strikes! Suddenly I'm rescued from my suffocating linear, rational, well-planned existence. Serendipitous events shake loose my moorings and catapult me into a new reality. What a breath of fresh air! Serendipity ushers in the unexpected, the impossible, the unfathomable, revealing the incredible joining of all beings through a Divine Plan that coordinates our encounters through events so exquisitely timed that our sense of destiny is renewed.

Lady Fate's precision orchestrates serendipitous events within a time frame of seconds—a moment too early or too late would forfeit these "chance" encounters. To recognize all received gifts of serendipity would humble our egos with gratitude for this rich display of the Divine Plan in action through its brilliant manifestation of improbable circumstance. Serendipity demonstrates ordinary miracles—the divine synthesis that holds our kismet to its course.

When willful agendas crash and there is nothing MORE that I can possibly do with my life, I throw up my hands in surrender (usually after much struggle) and plead with the Universe for a serendipitous event to eject me from the quicksand...the stuckness. But serendipity, by definition won't be forced in spite of our beseeching. When there are painfully long stretches between Divine Coincidences, we must remember that serendipity is *inevitable*. It is the underpinning of the scavenger hunt that unveils clues when least expected and desperately needed to the next riddle/ answer which will unfold our pathway. If we don't give proper credence to the divine mandate within our serendipitous moments, we lose our ability to decipher these pointers. It becomes insurmountable to decode our soul's earthly trek. Denial of serendipity wicks the magic out of life and stunts the wonder required to claim the magical child within—the gateway to liberation.

We can't attach to serendipity. It bursts in like a rainbow butterfly that we encounter, wish upon, and release within moments. Serendipitous events are visitations from the angelic realm. They shock people into the heart of the unexpected and bedazzle us with electrifying moments—reminders that we haven't been forgotten by the Universe.

Serendipity may come in the form of startling encounters with strange people who materialize to deliver a pungent message and then quickly disappear, or old friends you never expected to see again, or a wrong turn on the road that leads you to discover a beautiful new world filled with possibility. Serendipity is the arm of the Divine that reaches in to catch us off guard and unglue our everyday paradigm. Serendipity has PURPOSE. There are no coincidences—just the GRACE of serendipitous events that bathe us in opportunity.

Serendipity is the karmic whimsy that toys with all of us. How often, when a book practically falls off the shelf to call to us when browsing in a bookstore, do we randomly open it to discover just the message we need. Our only obligation to this synchronistic magic is to notice it!

But if we are oblivious to the serendipity in our lives because our egos discredit the greater intelligence that orchestrates our timing, its enchantment fades. Most of our extraordinary experiences appear through serendipitous channels. Serendipity is the trickster that sideswipes our rationality. We ask ourselves, "What are the odds of that happening?" But serendipity, the Cosmic Jester, mocks and defies the odds. So we are taught that *anything* is possible.

Life would be so humdrum without Divine Coincidence. There would be no evidence of the magic that facilitates transformation. Without the confluence of events designed to open gateways to our destiny, we would live a miserable rote existence of predictable statistical reality with no wizardly curveballs to redirect our attention to where it needs to be and to remind us that there are larger Forces at play.

If we recorded all our serendipitous experiences, they would paint a picture of the impact of Divine intervention and how synchronistic promptings, like road signs, not only moved us in the right direction at the perfect time but also demonstrated the specificity and purpose within our destiny. Synchronicity, like the phenomenal language of dolphins and whales, expresses a supernatural sonar resonance beamed out to connect us with each other in particular circumstances as if we were responding to an electrical charge—the Divine Call. Serendipity is the Universe's response to our calls for help—perhaps issued even years earlier and just now activating the energy we need—with perfect timing.

We may unwittingly block the instruments of magic that fuel serendipity if we are too skeptical, rational or circumspect to trust its mystery. Doubtfulness arrests our ability to register the Wand of the Divine as it plays us in the theater of the human condition. Despite our distrust, serendipity still happens; it just isn't recognized. Those precious mystical events then fade behind the veils, and we wonder why nothing special ever happens to us.

But regardless of our blindness, serendipity is a focal point for our Universe's all-pervading Grace and Goodness. Serendipitous events expose the connection points in the Divine Grid that cradles our souls safely in good hands.

Recently, my husband and I made a last-minute decision to keep a promise we made to visit an old friend in Ithaca, NY. The only two days we were free to travel coincided with Cornell University's parents' weekend. All lodgings were filled. Why would we pick the one weekend of the year when everyplace was booked? Finally we tracked down three B&Bs (Bed & Breakfast inns) 20 minutes away from town. Only one of them, just opened two months prior, had a vacancy. Upon arrival we discovered that the B&B's host was an avid student of the Masters and metaphysics.

For years we've enjoyed talking with innkeepers throughout the country but never met one with whom we could discuss these interests. We joyfully recognized our soul connection with the innkeeper, and she immediately initiated plans for us to hold seminars in her area. The odds are slim that we would have met this person under "normal" conditions. The Tibetan certainly had his serendipitous play with us as we found ourselves unexpectedly in just the right place at the right moment.

Because serendipity is a force field that surrounds us, we can enhance its influence in our lives by staying playfully tuned in and open to the impossible. This is especially important during these times of global challenge, when our pathways for evolution seem blocked by negative energies. Once we agree to wholeheartedly serve the Divine Plan, we discover that we are serendipitous instruments for others, and increasingly we find ourselves in situations with people who need us to spark their consciousness in that moment.

Soon, as the emerging Aquarian Age establishes itself, we will experience greater and greater levels of serendipity. To dance on streams of synchronicity will be a way of life that reflects the holographic essence that units us together in a tapestry of genius.

Lost in my thoughts, I'm startled to notice that suddenly the Tibetan has appeared "out of the blue." He recounts all the times he sent me messages through loved ones, strangers, animals, books—anything to catch my attention. He teases that serendipity is one of the few ways that humankind will allow in the spiritual plane. The Masters work through the principle of serendipity as they align their energy with us in exquisite precision timing that clicks in just when we are ripe. Djwhal Khul teaches:

The Masters love to employ the dynamics of serendipity to catch the attention of the student. When life beats the odds and unlikely events occur, the student spontaneously opens to a sense of mystery and connection with the higher planes. Serendipity momentarily baffles the ego/ personality and suspends its rigid perceptual control. In that instant the student is available for contact with his/her Higher Self.

The teachings of the Masters appear in unexpected ways and through "chance coincidences." Students who have "fallen asleep" wake up to their spiritual essence when reminded that their sojourn on the earthly plane is nothing more than an ongoing series of synchronistic events specifically designed to promote liberation.

Ask the spiritual plane to shower self with gifts of Divine Coincidence to inspire the exploration of the magical juncture where the personal will ends and the Divine Will takes over. As humankind opens to its spiritual essence and remembers that it is energetic in nature and therefore electrically connected to all beings, it will notice increasing sparks of resonance that create all serendipitous moments.

Ultimately the issuance into the New Age is one of synchronicity—when the prison door flies open against all odds through an astonishing chance encounter with a mysterious unfoldment of events. Then self is free—open, available to the miraculous...the extraordinary—and fills with gratitude for breakthroughs to full soul manifestation. These synchronistic Cosmic Interventions pave a way that short circuits proven statistics and goes to the heart of things—where Love promotes a dance of opportunity that carries the fulfillment of all of the soul's needs.

Pay attention to synchronicity. Don't let the clues pass by unclaimed. Bear witness to the eternal spring of messages carried forth. Follow these Cosmic Communiqués to their Source—where the Mystery meets the Known and serendipity giggles in delight at the spark of recognition that teaches students they are not victims of statistics, sober consequence, or the probable, but rather apprentices of magic in the Realm of Chance Encounters with the Divine.

✧ The Path ✧

August 2001

"Do you think I'm on the right path?" Wrestling with that question myself, this is a frequent inquiry from clients hoping for some kind of confirmation of wise choices pursuing their life direction. Life itself is a sacred journey. Most of us agree we are "going someplace" in spite of often having no idea where. There is no road map, mileage chart or recognizable destination. Yet to reference our experience as a pathway gives us a sense of movement and growth, a way to bear witness to our evolution.

We use external journeys as vehicles to express the internal sojourn of the soul. These journeys reflect the longing for a pilgrimage culminating in clear vision of the most expedient pathway to awakening, revealing all blockages that stand in the way of true freedom. Deep in our hearts we know that there really is no endpoint to our journey. Only the mystery smiles back at us when we reach the top of the mountain, laughing at our desire to map out the path from an all-knowing perspective. Ironically, we often conclude our journey with more questions to live through. At the summit, we view other, taller mountains magnetizing our curiosity—our longing to go "all the way."

The journey unfolds, winding around the landscape of our soul, dipping into unforeseen adventures, reaching plateaus with delicious vistas that lull us into fleeting moments of grasping the unfathomable nature of our path. We breathe a sigh of relief, "Ah ha, we've finally arrived," only to be catapulted off again into the riddle held within our life's adventure. In that riddle there is a central point of confluence where all the different tributaries to our path converge into a clear reflection of our soul's essence.

This Divine Matrix orchestrates the many voices of the soul calling to us to "go in this or that direction." Knowing that all pathways ultimately wind up the mountain allows us to indulge these voices—to wander off on "side roads" that offer the enchantment of falling in love with different parts of ourselves. Discovering these parts of self is like having an affair with a special lover, sharing precious moments in mutual delight yet knowing we must return to the central pathway while weaving in these newly claimed pieces of the soul.

Ultimately we learn that the path is a PROCESS not an endpoint, woven as we journey along like a spider creating its own unique web mandala. In hindsight, we review our path, perceiving how it all fits together to create the "yellow brick road" leading us into our truth. Because what we do is essentially soul driven, all choices, even those that seem to take us far a field of our life's purpose, eventually rejoin us with the pathway. "Everything comes full circle" as we wind through the woods, meadows, storms, jungles, deserts and mountain peaks in our soul only to return home to ourselves, right where we started, with a PhD in Wisdom to show for it!

Many of us suffer from guilt and regret for having taken the "wrong" road in life. We believe we have wasted time moving in an erroneous direction. Ironically, the only "wrongness" about the road is the overlay of regret we place upon it. We are not expected to always know exactly where we are going and how to get there. Like cosmic pioneers, we must forge our pathway into enlightenment. Accepting this not-knowing (releasing the perfection standard of being absolutely sure of who we are) allows us to experiment with the path we choose, accepting its apparent failure without remorse. Every "wrong road" is a counterpoint, honing our ability to attune to our truest pathway.

Disillusionment in the path we previously believed in so fervently is inevitable. The path presents itself to us in layers. As each layer outlives its usefulness it falls away like a snake shedding its skin. When shedding, we feel like an aimless wanderer free-floating in the universe tossed about by circumstances. As if we were driving through dense fog with no sense of the four directions, our compass is useless when our road disappears into illusion. Then we learn to walk like a blind person—trusting that all is unfolding as it should until the clarity and "certainty" return, reassuring us that we have not lost our way but rather have grown to a deeper attunement to our soul's path.

Doubting our path is an exercise in clarification. To not occasionally doubt and scrutinize our course would be a step-up for a big fall from the naive assumption that we know exactly where we are going. Raising the question, "What really is the best pathway to explore my soul in this lifetime," helps to remind us that the road is ever renewing and rearranging its unfoldment to reflect the emerging self.

Attunement to our path involves coupling the vision of our emerging self with what actually presents itself in our daily life. We strike out in a direction that appears to hold the promise of fulfilling our vision. However, eventually we bump into the impact of the Divine Will revealed in the path we actually find ourselves walking. We question—are we walking this "other path" from our original vision because we are resisting our soul desire or are blocked in opening to who we really are, OR is the Divine Will expressing itself through Lady Fate, unfolding a truer pathway for our soul's evolution, indicating that perhaps our original vision may have misrepresented our true destiny?

Developing our vision is essential. By opening our inner eye (third eye chakra) we begin to trust the images offering movies of our future self. Exercising vision increases clairvoyance and insight into our soul's direction.

We then need the Willingness to act on what we see! Many spiritual seekers receive incredible insight/ images of their potentiality, but they experience it only on the mental plane rather than acting on it in external life. If we don't fuel the vehicle, it doesn't go anywhere no matter how great its potential for movement. That means trusting our vision enough to commit. Waking our vision includes remembering that this foresight is merely a small glimpse of the full picture of our soul's artery to enlightenment. To move blindly, dedicatedly and joyfully into the mystery with the certainty that sustains commitment is to live the freedom of the Fool. Like the Fool card in the tarot, with our cosmic knapsack over our shoulder and dog at our side, we allow our innocence to inspire our path trusting the Divine Order that orchestrates our soul's matrix of evolution.

Crossroads on the path are particularly challenging. Most of us stand shell-shocked at these intersections, suspended in ambivalence and indecisiveness. Frozen, we can spend our entire life spellbound by these junctures. Midlife often brings these crossroads, teasing us with the possibility of going in a completely new direction. Intuition, prayer and a foolhardy willingness to "go for it" help us leap through this gateway hoping for the best! Better to move than to stall.

The Tibetan jumps in:

Part One: The Mystery

It is impossible not to be on your path! The path, a trajectory of the soul's evolution, is a collaborative effort coupling the soul's karmic mandate with self's improvisational response to the chaos within the Divine Order. The student is the artist that receives the image/knowing of the Higher Self's path and puts it into form.

Use the third eye, the inner beacon of light, as the headlights of a car revealing the immediate road as self approaches it, although unable to light up the entire highway. The pathway is enshrouded in mystery but can be clearly revealed when the student learns how to access the "high beams." Trusting this inner beacon of light allows the student to enthusiastically journey forth recognizing the pathway step by step.

The Masters remind the students that indeed they <u>are on a path</u>—a true journey that ultimately circles them homeward. Knowing that everyone has his/her unique pathway allows self to release the illusion of being lost in life. The route is a precise arc (current of energy) literally conducting each student into full union with the divine. Conscious participation with this movement allows self to be in the driver's seat knowing that, paradoxically, the car is automated by the Divine Order. To courageously drive into the night, fueled by a trust in the illuminating beam of spirit gleaming forth, hones the soul.

As co-creator of the unfoldment process, be willing to describe the path trusting that the route has already been established yet is always brand new. Road blocks, construction, potholes, no safe shoulders on which to pull over are all stimulates to the soul's growth. These apparent counterpoints to "progress" or "getting there" are vital resistances that provide the dynamic tension inherent within all earthly life. Do not struggle with them like outraged motorists caught in Friday afternoon traffic crawling along at 5 miles an hour. Rather, view these delays /obstacles as an opportunity to relax, let go and develop patience, knowing that eventually <u>all reach their destination point.</u>

Be the spiritual initiate embracing life as a voyage. The great Highway to the Divine lies within. Allow the path to take you for a ride you will never forget—one that expands your paradigm, stretches the mind, fills the heart, enlivens the spirit, exhilarates your being, brings you to the edge of your seat, and feels like the wind blowing through your hair stimulated by the Great Forces propelling the path onward into eternity.

The path is evolution—emerging truth—the soul's ultimate joy. The path is within every breath. The path is ensouled in the bottom of the feet encoded to march the student in the right direction. To be on the path is to be up for adventure—in the moment—open to serendipity—to be free, to explore, to be curious, to wander into the Divine, to trust the process. Journey forth, riding the Cosmic Railway to dimensions of experience accessing unknown territory. The path will go the distance and more, making all things possible for self's awakening.

Don't hesitate to step on board. Take the express train. Don't even think about getting off. As the inner vision clears, there are fewer stops along the way. Before you know it, you have arrived. Stepping off the train, you catch your breath, remembering this train station from eons ago when humankind beheld the magnificent grid work of pathways intermingling together in the Cosmic Design of Homecoming. From this place of unification, all pathways become One—and self is liberated.

✧ The Eye of the Hurricane ✧

January 2005

I loved the mighty hurricanes that sporadically blasted my New York childhood home in Bay Shore, Long Island. Riveted to the window as I watched trees mercilessly blown around, I couldn't wait until the eye of the storm arrived, when I had permission to run outside and taste the eerie calm of the tempest's void. As my front yard filled with a spooky light, my heart raced in response to this strange, compelling magnetism of quiet. Mystified, I marveled at the bizarre juxtaposition of the hurricane's drumfire and its abrupt halt into soundlessness. Even my little-girl innocence sensed that larger forces of the Universe were making their presence felt in those moments of unearthly hush as I bathed in the awesome wonderment of the Great Mystery.

Lately, an unnerving supernatural stillness is coloring our existential climate. Like the Hanged Man card in the tarot, we seem to be suspended upside down in the void. Although we're still exposed to today's cacophony of disturbance, chaos, travail and upheaval, the Eye of the Hurricane has captured us as we hover in the vacuum, filled with an urgent anticipation to see what's going to happen next. It's hard to get a purchase on this disorienting energy, especially for folks like myself who fuel on activity, focus, goals, action and relatedness. This Eye feels surreal, impersonal, detached. It is the center of the vortex of enormous CHANGE that is upon us. In the hiatus, our melodramas are neutralized by reflections of absolute placidity.

But how can we relax in the Eye when we know a larger storm system is still building? Do we fearfully crouch in the corner as we await our fate? Do we boldly explore and therefore expose ourselves to this twilight zone vortex—daring it to have its way with us? Can we trust this bizarre lull? Where is the energy taking us? Is it a gateway to enhanced consciousness? Or is it simply a menacing intermission, geared to intensify anxiety about the storm's ensuing ferocity that will surely flatten us all?

The Eye of the Hurricane is a great in-breath. Accustomed to projecting ourselves onto external reality, we must curb our tendency to fill this inhalation with projections of fears based on false beliefs that interpret this Cessation Juncture as a sign of failure, abandonment, lostness. Overwhelmed with excitation or agitation, we often forget to breathe. Shallow breathing blocks the ability to experience a real in-breath, one so deep that our process is momentarily suspended. What an opportunity to break attachment to willfulness and simply receive the Universe into our being. This prodigious Eye teaches us to yield to the in-breath of the Divine Plan.

Much of the extraneous levels of self have been decimated by the storms swirling through our collective consciousness. Stripped down, we stand naked in the Eye, laid open to its magnetic Gateway. Uncovered, we're available to resonate with its huge concentric circles of heightened vibrations that reshape us on a cellular level. The Gateway, a medium of the resplendent Divine Feminine, emanates a force of non-doing in which we simply exist in the Divine Pause that refreshes the soul and allows eternity to sneak a peek at our process. Eternity, enveloped within the Feminine and accessed through the Void, reminds us to let go. So we might as well cooperate with the impact of the current Eye and employ its calm for introspection.

How can we reap the benefits the Eye when life is roiling around us, violently ripping open our wounds, relentlessly burning karmic material, squeezing the hope right out of us, perpetually unveiling walls and blockades, as our heavy hearts fill with discouragement? The little girl inside of me who marveled at the Universe's wonders knows that the source of magic is in the Eye of the Hurricanes that thrilled her so. It is the place of confluence where intentions arrive at their destination, multiplicities become one, hopes are consummated, goals accomplished, pathways end and begin, and we are truly liberated from our chronic attachment to life's storms. Centered within our core, may we weather these storms with grace and acceptance as we become the magicians who playfully engage the transformational Forces within these colossal Cosmic Commotions.

The potent blizzard of karmic material currently being released requires a balancing counterpoint. Overflowing with unassimilated chaotic energy, we've reached the boiling point. The more that we can sustain the composure of our inner center, the Eye, the less we will aggravate this collective storm. Taoists teach that stillness is at the heart of all movement, the yin within the yang. To be utterly still is to encounter all possibilities. Creation springs forth from the Feminine's rich quiescence and allows us to go the distance in our transformation. Resources within the Wellspring of Quietude that lives beyond earthly drama feed us the energy to endure today's gigantic energy storms.

In surrender, I attempt to bow to the wisdom of the Divine Plan when it abruptly halts relentless tempests of bombarding chaos to usher in the Great Suspension. In the Respite of the Intermission, I learn to wait...listen...breathe...and believe. From the hushed Wilderness of Pausation, I remember to release the melodrama of my existence, no matter how compelling. I remember why I'm on the planet at this momentous time—my soul's mandate to experience a life of metamorphosis. I remember who I am. As I breathe deeply, my cells are recharged with spiritual fortitude—the electrical charge of the Divine Feminine, who feeds us the essential nutrients to propel our soul through the alchemical process. The Eye teaches me to step off the wheel of compulsions and delicately await my fate with the trust of a newborn babe.

The Eye demonstrates that our collective clearing process ebbs and flows rhythmically in waves, regardless of its relentlessness. Increased sensitivity to the impact of the Eye augments its "deep nothing" benefits of ultimate recharge. No matter how arduous our collective climb up the spiritual mountain, the Eye holds us in a mystical dimension that surpasses all accomplishment/ activity/ movement and opens our extrasensory gifts to the awareness of the innate pulse of our being. From this realm of rarefied stillness, we truly KNOW that all is well.

Calm and collected, the Tibetan emerges from a tornado-like vortex, deeply at peace within the Eye of the storm. He teaches:

Monumental storm systems currently energizing the collective consciousness of humankind are orchestrated to uproot the known. The receptive energy of the Divine Feminine contains the central vortex that formulates the precise cycles of these erupting alchemical flares. In the labor process of birthing the New Cosmic Day on planet earth, the collective consciousness is being "dilated"—opened, expanded. But this is not the time to push out the "baby"—the new consciousness. Although humankind is used to striving and thrusting itself forward, this is a period of waiting, allowing and being impacted upon. Breathe with this emergence of the Feminine to enhance a spacious response to the transformative impact of these labor pains.

Daunted by the vacuum of the Eye, students fear a failed labor—a stillbirth—because they cannot imagine that the spark of Creation can exist and endure through the deep stillness of the Feminine. Please trust the precious emptiness of this hushful sequence. Resist the impulse to push until the time is ready.

The Eye is the heart of the mystery, a true panorama of not-knowing. In this yin phase, students develop patience, acceptance and even joyful anticipation of their momentous participation in the tremendous birth of the emerging paradigm. All external storms are mere extensions of internal upheaval. Cultivate the super-ordinary calm gifted by the Eye to quiet the soul into sweet surrender. Appreciate its respite from the topsy-turvy of the Divine Disorder currently disintegrating the old world order. The Eye is the mystical portal through which the soul beholds its truth. When all the wailing voices of conflict, confusion, frustration and grief are suspended, self sits within the Eye and is nursed by the Divine Feminine into full satiety of spirit. Then all subsequent violent storms are weathered from the sweet inner garden of the Great Mother, who reminds self that the towering Forces of Crisis that usher in the transformed Soul are balanced by a place of deep motionlessness—Being-ness. This awareness fortifies humankind to enter the climatic changes in the collective consciousness well prepared and fit for the rigors of metamorphosis.

The Eye is the entry point into the new paradigm—the Aquarian Age. Cycles of karma encoded in the collective mind of humankind that hold humanity's expectations of earthly existence in a predictable format are now reversed in the Gateway. The circuitry of the brain is scrambled to allow something NEW to occur. The Eye's Gateway is a vortex that inverts customary energetic dynamics, and issues an original, fresh magnetic influence on humankind's collective brain patterns. This catalyzes the opening of light centers in the head, which register the new dimensional frequencies on one's radar screen. From this broadened view shed, humankind is reassured that the process of immersion in the alchemical cauldron is a finite one. The loving shock of the electrical charge in the Eye that makes possible all reversals of expectation/ understanding the status quo frees up the imagination to register the new. It demonstrates that the old paradigm is outmoded, changeable, releasable, and sets humankind upon a newly sprung, broad stage of wonder that defies expectations, reveals miracles and demonstrates that all suffering is nothing more than a bad dream from which humankind has agreed to awaken at this momentous time on the planet, as everyone moves forward through the Gateway into the Universal Orbit of Spiritual Renaissance and Mastery.

✧ Trusting the Wisdom of the Forces ✧

March 2003

Many powerful forces are at play in our lives. Do we trust enough to surrender to these potent cosmic battalions? Do we recognize the deep wisdom within these force fields buffeting our lives about like milkweed dancing on wind currents? When I remember that the Universe is beyond-genius brilliant, I can appropriately honor the superior Intelligence within the Forces that shape my life. Then I relax into sweet surrender and allow the cosmic laser beams of power to judiciously impact my life, designing all experiences to evoke my soul's essence. The more I open spiritually, the more I acquiesce to the Forces as I begin to put the puzzle pieces of my life together to reveal the grand scheme within my destiny.

When my ego is in charge and my unconscious is brewing up a toxic stream of undigested past-life debris, I lose sight of the inherent Wisdom within the Forces. I assume that this Universe is full of dead ends, engineered by a not-so-smart Source who could care less about me! At these times there is no ultimate convergence of experience reflecting the brilliant architecture of our Creator. Without this Divine synthesis, I assume that all forces are randomly, chaotically, cruelly having a joke at my expense. It's easy to think that the Universe is out to get us when life throws us a curve ball with no apparent rhyme or reason. We assume we are just getting clobbered by dense energetics ignorant of our needs.

The Tibetan continually reminds me how the frequencies of the force field containing the earth plane are speeding up—upping their ampage, bombarding us with heightened vibrations foreign to our lower voltages. Unfamiliar frequencies demand that we open our senses/ innate knowing to trust that these emerging Forces are issued from a wisdom bank, a "trust fund," designed precisely for this time of collective awakening—cosmic birth. These forces accelerate our processes, wrenching up gobs of karmic debris for transmutation NOW.

The forces are exquisitely designed to extract long-forgotten karmic blockages from their hiding places within the soul to provide access and healing. Many of us are feeling internal pressure, to talk to certain people, to take certain actions that we wouldn't normally take. Although we are being propelled into a blizzard of never-ending work, the cosmic wind is truly at our back. Trusting the tempests of the forces has been a challenge at any time in human history. However, the challenge is greatest now as we collectively brace ourselves within these tsunami wave-like force fields sweeping us off our earthly feet into greater cosmic communion. My clients report: "I'm really blown away lately, blasted, disoriented, pushed, propelled"—all signs of our individual energetic response to these heightened Forces.

When we see a tsunami wave approaching, do we trust it to be the very best thing that could happen to us in that moment? I'm the first one to run! Resisting these heightened force fields only creates a feeling of disempowerment. This feeds fear. Fear contracts the chakras, the very centers within our energy bodies that the forces are auguring their way into to clear blockages to full soul alignment. We fear that a tsunami wave will crush every bone in our bodies. It's true. These forces are designated to pulverize age-old crusty defense structures walling off access to the much-needed cosmic energy contained within our individual chakra systems.

In hindsight, we recognize the synchronicity of our lives. Serendipity places us exactly where we need to be to meet the right people or experience a confluence of energies that catalyze our awakening. In retrospect, we see the Genius within the Forces that urge/ push/ compel us forward. Yet our egos, fearful of innate helplessness in the face of the forces, feel puppeted around like dummies. Egos, unwilling to perceive, acknowledge, accept the innate superior intelligence within these forces, assume they can do it better—rationalizing that the forces are nothing more than random energetic spurts.

What would our lives be like if we truly trusted the Wisdom of the Forces? Imagine unfurling a huge sail as we lean into the wind, open to the Divine embrace of our destiny. Resistance lowered, the sail fills up with cosmic energies fueling an express trip to full awakening.

Who's to say what is good or bad? My limited vision obscures the big picture unfolding through pre-designed forces. Suspending conclusions, even in the face of tough times, I can glimpse the larger opportunity within the force field delivering these hardships. We're taught not to read the end of a book before we plow through the entire story. But it's mighty tempting to want to know how things are resolved.

Currently we are in a drama that keeps us on the edge of our seats. Oh, how we wish to jump to the end of the story, to find out what happened so we can prepare for what is going on! This is the point of trust—to accept our experience without premature judgment, suspending notions of good/ bad to allow the Forces to deliver their ultimate teaching. With so much karmic debris being dredged up, our vision feels "whitened out" by this internal blizzard of past-life wreckage littering the clarity of our third eye, thereby requiring blind trust in the cosmic design that orchestrates these jumbo currents inundating our world.

Women have to yield to birth contractions overwhelming their bodies, rendering them as vessels for other souls to incarnate. Collectively, we have to submit to the Great Labor, pulsing energies expanding/ contracting us through the cosmic birth canal—the porthole into the next dimension of consciousness. Women wonder if they can survive an arduous labor. But something larger possesses their bodies requiring full surrender to the natural order of the mystery. Can we endure the rigors of the birth of the New Cosmic Day? All we can do is trust this great Labor of Love as it dilates our consciousness, catalyzing attunement to the forces bearing down on us for final liberation.

I'm the queen of control, the last one to abandon myself to the forces! My ego still tries to convince me that I know more about what's going on than any amorphous electric currents sweeping through me. I try to second guess the Forces—yes, jumping to the end of the story to see where all of this is taking me so I can gain some measure of control over my flimsy life! However, my snap conclusions invariably prove premature, wrong, and distorted, because the meat of the process is missing. The process is the Mystery inherent within the Forces precisely aimed at every cell in the body. Instead of opening to Grace, I clutch onto flat concepts of reality, blocking the spontaneous impact of these mighty currents. Mind sealed shut; I lose the opportunity to consciously collaborate with these frequencies, stubbornly fighting them through my insistence that I have it figured out. This leads me down dead ends. Then the curve balls of reality shock me back to my divine senses as I remember that I am only a fool on a foolhardy quest for meaning. In that moment of supreme vulnerability, my eyes soften. The mind melts. I begin to trust the Wisdom of the Forces.

Despite my attempts at "control," the Forces orchestrate infinite opportunities for my transformation. I simply have to accept the process, let go, pay attention, relax, and yield to the eddies of the celestial whirlpools that always deposit me exactly where I need to be on the beach of earthly life. As my ego fails in its effort to be the supreme, all-knowing center of my universe, I begin to trust the brilliant serendipity of the forces. Sometimes, I can actually relax into them with the trust of a new-born babe, gleefully suckling their eternal spring of celestial milk. Then I notice the road signs, subtle clues revealing my soul's architectural design, cosmic plans laid out well before my ego set up shop. Sporadic intuitive flashes then have fertile ground to reproduce as I blend my mind with a willingness to resonate with the mystery— to be "used" by the Universe for a higher purpose—to know that within the random stage of experience is an exquisite Wisdom holding the chaos together. Where will my life take me when I completely get out of my own way, fully embracing the Forces at play in my life?

The Tibetan, twinkling in amusement at my control issues, teaches:

Taking control away from humankind is like prying a toy away from a toddler whose little hand is tightly gripped around his/her plaything. So the Masters tease the students into letting go— reminding them, as a parent reminds a child, that they have "lived" longer and perhaps know more than the child. Asking humankind to perceive/ trust the ancient wisdom of the forces as it is directed through the auspices of the Masters is like trying to convince a teenager that he/she may not know everything.

During this time of heightened chaos, humankind attempts to batten down the hatches, board off the tornadoes of transmutation, and take refuge in the cellar (the seemingly fixed terrain of the lower mind). Ironically, it is far more dangerous to huddle within old belief systems while waiting for the storm to end, because that is precisely the area that the Cosmic Wisdom directs the forces to pummel! Better to fling open the fallout shelter door, expose self to the divine hurricane currently blowing apart entrenched defense structures, and cast one's fate to the Universal Wind. It is safer to take flight on the air currents of divine wisdom than to be cemented into the underbelly of self's blind spots disguised as knowing.

The dawning of the Aquarian Age ushers in a revolution in consciousness through heightening the voltage of the collective electrical body. Humankind is experiencing changes in its energetic flow. Students feel electrocuted, suffering from a deep sense of shock to the old self. Yet the ampage must be pronounced if it is to crack apart the entrenched past-life blockages in the soul. If self yields to these extreme energetics, then the resultant transition through anarchy becomes a playground for original thought, alignment with the ultimate genius of Source. Otherwise, the student refutes the Wisdom of the Forces through his/her insistence that the old world order be obeyed at all costs— continuing to allow self to be "taxed" by the monarchs of a fading paradigm.

It is easy to forget, during times of extreme chaos, that there is an Intelligence within these fields of disturbance. How do revolutionaries remember that they are fighting for a higher cause when their instinct to emerge victorious from repression is almost extinguished by the adversities/ traumas of upheaval? Exhausted, disoriented, crazed, many students are beginning to question the wisdom of the forces over-turning all security and comfort.

How does a woman yield to the rigors of birthing? She remembers that she is the instrument of a great process, the miracle of creation. So, too, must students remember that humankind is birthing itself to a new level of freedom. Humankind is now the instrument that physically enhances/ grounds the intergalactic voltage pulsing around and through the earthly plane to push out the baby—the New World Order. Trust this divine instinct to stretch the collective body to issue itself forth into glorious spiritual emergence. Pulse the contractions sweeping through self's daily life, breathing in and out as these relentless Forces bear down upon the soul, inducing its full alignment into form. Now is the time to push. Dare to bring forth self's magnitude.

Fully abandon self to this great collective mission knowing that the magnificent Intelligence of the Forces sets fire to the light centers in the cerebrum providing access to the brain's full capacity. As the higher mind fires up, humankind cannot help but truly understand the genius of the forces, rejoicing in this blessed honor to be incarnate in a time of unprecedented human potential.

Through trusting the Wisdom of the Forces, one's process of enlightenment accelerates beyond all expectation as self rides the cosmic rapids through the vaginal sleuth way ushering in the New Cosmic Day.

Play detective. Look for clues from these Forces that would gladly expose their direction when listened to and trusted. Feel the joy of effervescent champagne as all that has been hidden/ denied bubbles up. Without these great benign forces of Source's Being, the earthly plane would calcify in its outgrown density, leaving humankind dry/ unillumined/ trapped. At long last, the forces have blown open the prison door. Don't huddle in the back of the cell looking for some long forgotten illusion of security. Go forth in bold expectation of all that is possible and more, while self rides the Wisdom of the Forces into effortless ecstasy!

✧ <u>Part Two</u> ✧

LIFE ON PLANET EARTH

✧ The Ego: Who Do You Think You Are? ✧

February 2001

Banish the Ego! Transcend it! Chop it up into little pieces! Get it as far behind you as possible or it will absolutely crush your chances for enlightenment.

We all know the ego will corrupt us. Haven't we been told by all spiritual teachers that the monster ego must be conquered if we are to save our souls?

When I first started my spiritual quest for "true freedom" in 1981, I was amazed at the amount of potent warnings about not falling prey to the ego. In my early 20s, naive about the spiritual pathways, I conjured up images of the ego as an insidiously controlling beast, a reflection of the lowest level of the human condition. While I read countless spiritual books and meditated and prayed with groups from various religious orientations, collectively they all shared the same fear—the fear of being blinded by ego-hunger and dominion. I was confused that this force from the psyche called the ego could be so daunting to so many "advanced" students on "The Path." My own ego reacted with statements of self-negation—advising me to give up on this enlightenment stuff because surely I would never accomplish self-transcendence if they couldn't.

At the time I was struggling to find myself, and hated the thought of having to give up my identity to find God. I felt I hadn't yet reveled in the joys of having a self, and was reluctant to sacrifice the notion of who I thought I was in order to merge into an amorphous blob of consciousness called "The One." Was this resistance the voice of ego undermining my spiritual progress? Or was it an inner knowing that perhaps there was a more compassionate approach to nurturing the ego that might leave more room for a unique self?

Still experiencing this elongated identity crisis decades years later, I laugh at the notion of trying to pin down a personal description of self. The ego is a function that reflects the temporary nature of earthly life. Whenever I have decided, "Now I finally know who I am," my consciousness shifts and new dimensions within my being emerge, needing to be integrated into an already antiquated image of self-identification.

And yet, the ego allows our ever-evolving sense of self to have form—an identity that distinguishes and differentiates us from each other. This identity does not have to block our empathic communion with each other. Ironically, it can enhance our sense of collective unity because it offers us a reference point, revealing how our unique spark of consciousness adds more spice to the collective soup.

To let go of the judgment around having an ego is to let go of the notion of original sin. The ego is not something that humanity "made up" on the sly, hoping that Source wouldn't notice. Source built it into our psychic structure for a purpose—a divine purpose.

Ironically, when we try so hard to rise above ourselves—transcend the ego—we often push our egos down into the unconscious, hoping to bury them somewhere no one spiritual can see it. We then feel strangely split off from ourselves—perhaps ungrounded—as a subtle but unmistakable, spiritual ego takes over, convincing us that we have conquered the lower levels of our being. Jumping up and over our natural need for self-identity, self-importance and self-expression leaves the ego hungrier than ever to be fed. The hunger gnaws at us, unmercilessly demanding satisfaction, and this appetite drives an ego function, largely unconscious, that takes over our expression and actions. The need to inflate self through grandiosity is the sign of an unloved, unfed, judged and exiled ego.

A consciously fed ego is a happy ego. From this satiated state, the ego relaxes, moving into a complacency that allows the Higher Self to work *with it* without having to fight its way past the stronghold of the personality. The non judged ego becomes more passive when it receives acceptance. This passivity heightens the ego's ability to receive and yield to instruction from higher levels of consciousness without having to resist this instruction out of fear of ego death. When the ego feels as if it is part of the Great Collaboration, its need for "being important and special" is fulfilled. To embrace the ego is to identify our need to have a unique self and to offer ourselves whatever is needed to develop and establish that self in the context of unconditional love. When the ego feels really loved and cherished, it can relax into the highest level of its divine function, which is to give full human expression to the Soul.

This does not negate the need for us to be continually vigilant about the ego's need to control our reality. However, this vigilance is not meant to launch a crusade to "hang" the ego. Rather, it is the necessity to work at bringing the ego's domain into full consciousness—to be aware of when self needs to feed the ego attention, applause and importance, emphasizing one's uniqueness. When done consciously, we can avoid the illusion that the ego is all there is. Just like taking a child to the candy store, we can "treat" it to an indulgent narcissism that satisfies its immature cravings. Once indulged, the ego purrs like a contented kitten, more easily surrendered to the requirements of the Higher Self.

The Tibetan teaches:

The task is to refine and evolve the ego, not destroy it. To destroy the ego is to destroy an aspect of Source's creation. Humankind judges the ego as the culprit in the crime of separation. However, it is not the ego that fosters the experience of separation. The sense of separation is generated by the collective false belief that the divine exists only within certain levels of one's being, instead of permeating all aspects of the self, including the ego that generates separation.

To fight the ego is to perpetuate the illusion of separation. This illusion suggests that the ego is not part of self's divinity, but rather something separate, as if from some distant realm beyond Source's creation. From this perspective, humankind hopes to move beyond the experience of isolation by destroying the ego. Ironically, it only enhances the disunion by separating off a part of self that it judges as unspiritual and unworthy of Source's love. This prolongs the illusion that heaven and earth can never be one. While purification and refinement of self is crucial to the mastery of the human condition, the ego is not a blotch on the soul that must be eliminated. Rather, it too must be purified and refined to heighten its potential to serve the Divine Plan.

Imagine the ego as the pencil point, the pencil being the soul. The ego interfaces with the human condition, giving form to the soul's essence within the limitations of the earthly realm. Without this focalizer for framing, shaping and structuring the soul's matrix through human personification, the soul would remain in the realm of the formless, losing the opportunity to interface with the human realm in full earthly individuation of its unique spark.

When observing a pencil, one notices that the pencil point is just the tip of the potential of the pencil. There is so much more to the pencil than that surface spot. As humankind remembers that its ego function is simply a <u>tool</u> in service to the Higher Self, then it will stop dissipating its precious energy in the struggle to annihilate an aspect of its divinity that is integral to the process of evolution. It can then assign the ego its proper place, working with it to enhance full expression of the Higher Self. Then the pencil point is sharpened, ready to draw true and clear descriptive lines reflecting the Higher Self in form.

Many people believe the ego to be all that they are. Then the pencil point becomes the large messy black smudge of a magic marker. The individuated self is overdone, overstated and exaggerated, blocking out the true flow of the Higher Self, constricting its impact and richness of portrayal. Then it seems as if the ego is the cause of this "disconnect" from the Higher Self. However, it is the student's perspective and perception of the ego that give the sense of true disconnection.

Identification only with the ego creates an inner emptiness— as if the pencil point was floating out in space with nothing to spring from or connect to. Then the student tries harder to make the ego fill the spiritual void usually through inflation and grandiosity. However, trying to inflate the ego to match the size of the Higher Self is like trying to blow up a balloon to the size of a star. Desperate and fearful, self keeps inflating the balloon until it pops, and then vainly struggles to blow up another balloon.

Precious life force is wasted in this attempt to make the ego into God. The Higher Self appears to recede as the student focuses completely on the ego's constant hunger to be acknowledged as something more than it is or can ever be. This heightened attachment to the pencil point crystallizes and solidifies the ego. Then it seems truly set in stone, unable to be cracked open to receive the full onset of the soul. At that point, the ego is judged as harmful, when in reality it has simply been employed for something it is not designed to do. It can never touch the vast domain of the eternal Self, the soul. It can only represent, like an ambassador, the continent of the soul to the human dimension in a particular lifetime.

As the student breaks through the illusion that ego is all there is, he/she releases the illusion that life on the earth plane is all there is. Opening to the greater reality of the heavenly realms, flowing through countless dimensions within this particular universe, self realizes the microscopic nature of the ego. Then the student can work with this minuscule level of being, refining it into the optimum manifestation of itself, completely honed to receive with exquisite accuracy and precision the requirements of the soul in its journey on the earth plane.

The ego changes from lifetime to lifetime, but the soul is the same soul throughout all incarnations. Just as wearing one's favorite outfit encourages self to shine and sparkle, embrace the ego, creatively refining it to fully magnetize the essence of soul pouring through its countenance. So, celebrate self's unique representation of divinity in form. Love the ego as the servant to this great opportunity to delight in self's distinctive expression of singular brilliance within a cosmos of multiplicity in oneness.

✧ Personality ✧

July 2002

What happens to our personality when we die? Does it dissolve into an amorphous sea of retired personas, discarded and collecting cosmic dust like outgrown stage costumes, disembodied beings, stashed in the back room of a theater after the final curtain call? It's such a shame to put so much energy into creating just the right personality to express self, only to have it fall away, apparently underutilized by lives that pass too quickly within the overall cosmic scheme of things. Though I don't mind wiping hard to remove stage make up with Noxzema when I choose to end the performance, I'm partial to my well-crafted persona and have no desire to lay it to rest.

With lifetimes piling up, we can't possibly hold onto all of our past-life personalities, nostalgically held in our soul's heart chakra. It's too cumbersome. Loving them all, I have no desire to let any go. I want to collect them, like karmic trophies of my hard-earned human wisdom. After all, they put themselves on the line in each of my previous lifetimes, going to the "front" to interact with other souls dressed up in persona costumes. They took the flack of my confusion, aggression, fear, rage, bewilderment, distrust. They used the discipline to develop my soul's gifts, wisdom, knowledge, talents, etc. They should be honored in the Personality Hall of Fame for actions above and beyond the call of cosmic duty!

My personality delights in the attention as I study my face in the mirror. How do I look? What is the social image I convey? Is my deeper soul-self coming through my eyes? Do my clothes, hair and body reflect my essence? Is my face revealing the emotional tumultuousness of this lifetime? Does my intensity show, or have I crafted a persona that safely masks it away from the judgment of others? Is my personality working to make sure that it's doing the job of true self-representation? Is my attachment to my external reflection simply superficial ego gratification, separating me from my soul-self? Or am I keenly aware of its importance in spearheading my soul's evolution in this lifetime?

The ego is the pencil point of the soul, extended onto the earth plane to represent the Higher Self. The personality, an expression of the ego specifically designed for the lessons of this incarnation embodies the fabric of the soul. If the soul carries unresolved anger from ancient lifetimes, the personality reveals this in flushes of "random rage" projected onto self and others. Personality traits carry uncompromising threads of soul looking for refinement, maturation and healing. There is no point in struggling with who we are. Acceptance of our personalities yields to self-love within soul-embrace.

The personality appears to disintegrate when we die. But does it? Psychics like John Edwards, substantiating rapport with the spirit plane, communicate with the *personalities* of our dearly departed. We might have trouble recognizing them without their familiar costumes on, but clearly these personalities do not dissolve in death. My parents, deceased for over 35 years, have "communicated" with me through various psychics. Their personalities, difficult and troubled, were undeniably present in the connection, enabling to recognize our on-going soul relationship.

The holographic perspective, beyond time and space, indicates that everything happens simultaneously. Paradoxically, as the personality disintegrates at death it also maintains its differentiation. All past-life personalities, concurrently operant, are accessible through recognition of the costume of that lifetime—vibrant, expressive, fully alive within the soul's matrix. Therefore, the personality *does* exist outside of time and space.

Do the theater costumes dissolve in the backstage trunk, or are they simply waiting there, ready for the actor, filled with passion, to bring that particular role back to life? Identities are not ephemeral illusions. They are extensions of the soul and therefore include an eternal essence impervious to the shifting sands of time. Every personality is interwoven into the essence of the soul, perhaps taking a back seat to emerging personas pioneering the soul's current evolution, but never really losing its moment on center stage.

In past-life regressions, the personality of the lifetime being explored vibrantly surfaces as if hundreds or even thousands of years had not passed since it was the leading actor in the soul's theater. The terrain of the soul holds a magnificent banquet hall—hundreds of faces seated around the great table and eating from the same source, the soul. Like any extended family event, this gathering is filled with interpersonal dynamics. Often our childhood family dynamics reflect on-going soul-personality relationships.

When we are born, the planets are in specific mathematical relationship to each other. In astrology these relationships are called aspects. Benign aspects, trines or sextiles, reflect harmony and resolution among previous past- life personalities. Challenging aspects, squares or oppositions, carry points of tension/conflict within the personality-filled soul family. When we feel at war with ourselves, perhaps our soul's personalities have shown up to have it out with each other for once and for all. When we are at peace with ourselves, perhaps the wisdom-filled mature personalities have stepped in to remind us that "we" are all one soul!

Personalities shift according to our ego's maturity. The maturation level of the soul is expressed through the emotional and physical body, profoundly coloring the personality. As we refine our energies and fear transmutes into love, the personality shifts—more cleanly reflecting the fully-realized soul.

In my therapy work with clients, many sub-personalities surface—expressions of the soul that may be largely unconscious until one dives deep into the psyche. These sub-personalities ultimately integrate through a central organizing personality that mirrors the essential Self- the conductor that directs all sub-personalities into a harmonic symphony of soul expression. If the soul's growth is ensnared by a particularly dominant personality from a past-life, that personality can overpower all the other past life selves, resisting collective harmony. When we meet someone with a very imbalanced personality, they are usually "hung up" at the karmic juncture of a past- life personality still sparking its energetic charge, like a fallen electrical wire, prohibiting full conversion of its vibration into the smooth conduction of soul's overall multiplicity. Warring parts of one's personality indicate where the soul needs work, and we can track these irritants to past-lives that need healing.

What makes a "good" or "bad" personality? When we try to negate our personality and adopt one that doesn't match our internal truth, it feels like we are wearing a plastic face. Our essence suffocates behind the mask, chafes against the soul. Our essential Self is straight-jacketed by our attachment to societal notions of appropriateness, can't flourish—restricted by a personality that limits its coloration rather than enhances it.

If we don't cultivate our self-expression the soul is blocked. Developing our personalities is not the shallow endeavor some may judge it to be, but rather spiritually enriching, possibly bringing resolution between discordant karmic selves. The personality interfaces our soul with other's souls for heightened communion. The quest is to consider how to best represent the soul in our interactions with each other.

The Tibetan's dynamic personality sparks with mine to respond:

The personality is a construct, the countenance of the externalized ego. Expression of the ego is not to be judged, for it brings the artist's touch, awash with colors, to the planet. Without the personality, the ego (the paintbrush of the soul) would have no paints for Self-illustration.

Certain aspects of the soul need to be expressed in a particular incarnation. Therefore, one's personality is somewhat predestined. Some fruits are tart and others sweet. So too are the personalities karmically fashioned to provide just the right flavor to the collective soup.

The Masters assume a distinct persona that organizes their energy into a precise tool for optimum impact on the student. Some students require strict, cool and detached teachers to stimulate their disciplined determination and help release them from self-indulgence. Other students blossom with a teacher who is soft, warm, easygoing, humorous, because such traits foster trust and the release of the illusion that Source is harshly judging them. This illustrates the importance of accepting one's basic persona without judgment. To assume a false personality creates an experience of disconnect from the Higher Self. The personality sings the specific music of the soul. Who can say whether the passionate dramatic music of Beethoven is better than the dreamy softness of Debussy? All contribute to the Universal orchestral symphony.

Personality traits must be refined into greater balance with the soul's essence. Students may be caught in negative past-life personality characteristics. These negative characteristics impede the flow of one's energy and produce a deep sense of stagnation. The soul retreats into the karmic prison created through redundant long-term limiting characterizations of Self. The student must break the karmic lineage, even though ancient personalities do have lives of their own.

Students often have the same personality traits as their parents reflecting the propagation of generational soul family archetypes. The student has the responsibility to these clan members from countless lifetimes to purify those personality characteristics that imprison the entire soul group. They can transmute the karmic family legacy into one of joy-filled expression where all family members experience their birthright of competition-free spaciousness to display the rich coloration of the soul.

Try on a costume in this lifetime that facilitates expansion, fulfillment, and empowerment. Disregard spiritual notions of what the personality should be like when self is spiritually advanced. God wears many faces and so does the soul. Yes, all of these historical faces still continue to exist in the time frame from which they emerged. However, previous personalities lose their centrality in the game of evolution, fading into the background. At the highest level, they are merged as one into the matrix of the soul. At the coarse level of the lower planes, they reflect multiplicity—the many strands of the rainbow that arcs over the soul's terrain. These personas have "their place"—karmically anchored to the temporal space of their incarnation. Outlived personalities are not discarded to randomly float around the Universe. After death, they weave back into the soul through the Akashic records, holding all karmic imprints.

Personalities are products of a particular time/ place, and yet paradoxically hold within their core all of the soul's capacity for expression and can be interchangeable with other personas at a fundamental level. The personality needs to be well formed yet elastic. Flexibility enables the personality to flow with the increasing demands of the soul as self approaches the gateway of enlightenment.

There is no such thing as a "good" personality but rather a persona that is a perfect "fit" for the soul's essence. Please accept without judgment the spicy temperament, "having an edge," of one's persona, knowing that without the spice the soup would be bland. Accepting Self's inherent disposition releases judgment about the temperament of others so that all can enjoy the rich drama of the interplay between passion/ sweetness, ruggedness/ softness, firmness/ fluidity.

The Causal plane, which stores the karmic register, has a room in the Great Hall of Records where all of the soul's personalities dwell. Each is loyal to the color of its incarnation and waits patiently for the final soul representation to join them, concluding their last incarnation on earth. When this final personality unites with the other personas a great alchemical process assimilates all the personas into a brilliant mandala catalyzing the soul to an amplified vibratory rate. This mandala floods the soul with the vibrancy of each personality's contribution. Hundreds of faces of the soul are still distinct in their ephemeral application. It appears that the room is filled with individuals. However, from another angle the room is pulsing with the arch of a rainbow, all countenances merged and yet distinct.

From this place of "take-off," the soul treasures its personas, so devotedly offered to enable the soul to take the center stage in each incarnation as the resplendent being that it is. With the fulfillment of this profound creative accomplishment the soul journeys forth to other dimensions where new expressions of its divinity emerge buoyed and enhanced by the rich foundation of earthly human personality deeply imprinted in its fabric. Through these personalities the soul has known itself in form, explored the human condition, recorded its karmic history and delighted in broadcasting itself to the earthly world and beyond.

✧ How Spiritual Do We Have to Be? ✧

November 2001

With life's frenetic pace pushing us all to the brink, even those of us who are dedicated to spiritual growth are "falling behind" in our daily commitment to working our spiritual life. Others are just plain losing interest. Collectively, anxious voices abound with self-recriminating thoughts like, "Gee, I've really been bad—haven't meditated in two weeks." "I don't go to church or temple anymore—don't know why." "My spiritual practices are falling by the wayside—life's too busy." "I'm probably not making any progress." "I haven't prayed in months—am losing my grip on my soul." "I used to do yoga all the time—don't seem to care anymore." "My daily life is too damn busy—there's no time for God or all that other spiritual mumbo jumbo." "How can I possibly raise a family, have a career, pay the bills, deal with my marriage, and still have a spiritual life?" "It's all too much." My mind is filled with worries, routine details, negativity—I'm a million miles away from my Higher Self." "Everyone is going to reach enlightenment before me, leaving me in the dust like a retarded child."

Is it possible for our earthly life to "take us away" from our divinity—from Source (God)? How can we infuse our daily life with a sense of Divine Connection if we are not making the time, or we have no interest in spiritual practices? How spiritual do we have to be in order to be okay? Do we have to feed our spiritual life like we water the garden? Does our Higher Self wilt and wither away if we neglect our spiritual practices? Is it possible to be "disconnected" from our soul? Do we stop growing when we don't take time to focus on Source?

Clients often ask how frequently I meditate, assuming that since I am a channel for an Ascended Master, I must meditate a lot. Sheepishly, I answer that I never meditate! It wasn't meditation that opened my channel. Rather, I used imagery work to release false beliefs and open blocked areas in my heart chakra. Being a wired, high-strung Aquarian, with a devilishly over-active mind, I can't possibly sit still long enough to quietly go inside and focus on my breath, a mantra, or the "Great Nothing." Does this mean that I am not energizing my spiritual life? I hope not!

In my early 20s I realized that my "Mexican jumping bean" type of temperament would not easily lend itself to quiet introspection. Diligently trying to meditate for two years resulted in being swallowed up in feelings of failure for not being able to sustain the inner journey. I ultimately gave up, deciding that I would have to "get" a spiritual life another way. Jumping up from any attempt at meditation, frustrated and critical, I often ran out the door, bee-lining it to the woods. There I would roam around with my German Shepherd dog for a few hours just to blow off steam. Little did I realize that I was charging into my true "church"—nature. Nature's solace and teaching delivered more spiritual nourishment, uplifting my spirit more effectively than the "shoulds" of an official spiritual practice.

Unable to recognize that these soulful sojourns into the woods were sacred rituals, I continued to judge myself as irresponsibly unspiritual for several years, until I eventually released the old notion that to be spiritual is to sit in meditation or deep prayer for several hours daily. I finally recognized that my soul was prayerfully breathing in spirit through the trees, grasses, winds and waters. In addition, I soon began a path of service, still continuing 24 years later, that has "grown" my soul more than I ever could have imagined.

It's difficult to hold ourselves accountable to a rigid paradigm describing the "right" way of spiritual cultivation. Life tosses us about in its usual chaotic fashion, challenging us to experience our spirituality whether we are doing the dishes, arguing with our lover, driving in rush hour traffic, fretting over the bills, or watching some idiotic TV show while munching popcorn.

Some folks, having meditated a lot in previous lifetimes, don't need to keep working that particular spiritual muscle. Rather, their spiritual task in this lifetime may be to develop and relish an earthly life—sensual, mundane, pragmatic—discovering the joys of being in a physical body with all of its pleasures and possibilities. Just because their lives are filled with errands, details and the mental buzz of householders and business people, doesn't mean that they are not evolving. Ironically, if they were to force themselves to withdraw from their worldly lives to become more spiritual, they might be counteracting the very benefits their souls requested them to develop this time around.

This does not negate the essential need some people have to meditate, pray and attend religious functions. For them, perhaps in past lives too little focus was brought to the world of spirituality and its interfaces with the physical plane. They may need to absorb, through meditation/ prayer, abundant spiritual energy to feed a soul starved for spiritual nourishment due to possible past-life excessive family/ work responsibilities, attachments to earthly seductions, or worldly ambitions, leaving little time for spiritual replenishment.

We all need to experience the feeling of being in contact with a spiritual source. Everyone benefits from prayer, meditation, and/or religious communion. However, what invokes the aura of the Sacred can be expanded to include all aspects of our daily lives. It all boils down to our state of consciousness while we are doing our lives.

Internal hunger directs us to the best "food group" for our spiritual nourishment. We just have to suspend our notions as to what that is supposed to be. Some people may experience more of a spiritual high from hanging out with folks at the local coffee shop learning the art of making small talk with folks about the weather, perhaps balancing out too many past lives immersed in solitary esoteric research and contemplation.

Evolution requires that we refine our energy. This refinement usually necessitates some kind of spiritual practice. But who's to say what a spiritual practice is?

Traditional spiritual practices involve techniques for quieting the mind, turning awareness inward, purifying negative emotions, cleansing the physical body, opening up central channels, releasing negative/ limiting thought patterns, bringing attention to higher levels of being/ spirit, and opening the heart's capacity for unconditional love. With consistent practice, these techniques accelerate our spiritual evolution. However, not having the time, inclination or discipline to perform these practices does not mean that we stop growing spiritually or have dashed our opportunity for awakening.

We may lose interest in our practices not because we are lazy or irresponsible, but because our current cycle of growth demands that our attention and creative energy change its focus. Our spiritual growth cycles inward for a while and then balances through an equalized and external projection. During inward cycles, undistracted by the "noise" of outer life, there is more of a natural inclination to meditate, pray, open up chakras, explore our inner landscape, and easily remember our divinity at all times. During the outward cycles, we are often required to externalize our growth through heightened activity/ social engagement and worldly enterprise/ service. These cycles may last days, months, years or even entire lifetimes. To fight these rhythms through judgment ironically impedes our growth, wasting precious energy by resisting our Cosmic Study Plan in this lifetime.

Nodding in agreement, the Tibetan responds:

The vibrational rate of the earth plane is accelerating, creating a shift in the cosmic "time table." No longer is it necessary to clock- in months and years doing yogic practices, renouncing the world, fasting, spending hours of meditation and prayer. The student must seize the moment, every moment, to experience the divine spark within. Living as an enlightened being, seeing no division between worldly life and. spiritual life, is the greatest service one can provide humankind today. Wearing spiritual glasses/ filters through which to perceive all of life dissolves the 'separation' between heaven and earth.

Humankind is evolving to a state of consciousness where spiritual practices become outmoded. All of life becomes a meditation—a prayerful YES to Source—a natural alignment with the Higher Self. The student simply breathes in universal love and breathes out devotion to the earthly world so treasured by its Creator.

Yes, this process is enhanced by practices, rituals and sacred events reminding humankind that everyone is a student on a spiritual pathway. However, how one holds these practices is the key to their success. To view them as heavy obligations is to negate their impact, creating unnecessary resistance to a natural process. Likewise, to be blind to the spiritually inspirational effect of earthly daily life is to be caught in the illusion that one has to separate from the world in order to cultivate the soul.

Many students have spent countless lifetimes immersed in strict routines of spiritual practices. These lifetimes leave cellular memories describing the "right and wrong" of how to grow the spiritual body. However, the earth plane was vibrating at a lower rate—creating a denser field of energy through which to access one's spiritual essence. Humanity, still immature, required fundamental guidelines for evolution, just as a kindergartner needs firm behavioral guidelines to channel childish impulses in a productive direction.

In the new millennium, humankind is rapidly accelerating to new heights of maturation. This increases the responsibility for each individual to explore their own unique optimum combination of activities/ practices, coupled with the proper balance of inner and outer life. The earthly vibrational field is lightening, making it easier to access the spiritual plane. This challenges humankind to ground the spiritual dimension within one's earthly format—a healthy physical vehicle, proper livelihood, fulfilling soul-level relationships, self-love, flowing creativity, a higher sense of purpose, and the willingness to release all false beliefs carrying the illusion that self must wait lifetimes before being worthy of enlightenment. These are the trustworthy baseline spiritual practices required for the evolution of the human condition.

With this energetic acceleration, many students simply don't have the time to clock in hours of spiritual practices. Fortunately, the karmic dispensation available now is the impact of accelerated energies cleansing karmic debris pushed up to the surface by the increased vibratory rate. This allows the student to release the limitations of the past and open to the current collective spiritual mandate, which is to infuse the earth with as much light as possible to accelerate her awakening.

All "bad" habits (i.e. poor diet, negative thoughts, stagnant negative emotions) will be alchemized by the energies streaming through the earth plane in the new millennium. Enjoy any "spiritual practices" that self wishes. Joyfully embrace all opportunities to bear witness to Source, opening the heart to the spiritual wonder of the miracle of collective awakening on a planet that is awakening as well. The ultimate spiritual practice is to allow self to be swept into full communion with all beings, evolving beyond all elementary notions of what a spiritual life should be. From this place of sublime celebration, self plays out the heart of earthly human life, reveling in the freedom to simply BE—connected at all levels through the brilliant imagination that is Source.

✧ Power ✧

January 2001

"Watch out for power—it's dangerous, especially if you are on a spiritual path. Better to sidestep the entire issue. It's safer to keep self small, diminished, invisible, even victimized than to face the responsibility of empowerment." Sound familiar?

How can we contemplate our enlightenment if we can't handle power? Aren't all the great spiritual teachers beings of tremendous power? How do they escape the seduction of power while still allowing the force and magnetism of their charisma to shine forth?

A common issue in my work with clients is the fear of power. Most of us have been hurt by people who have abused power. As children, we are all too vulnerable to the adults in our lives. These "grown-ups" vary in their true maturity. When undeveloped themselves, they unconsciously readily abuse the power they have over the children in their lives. Tyrannical, abusive adults make a deep imprint on a child's psyche. Often, children inwardly make a solemn promise to never, *ever*, be like the mean, unfair, unloving, insensitive adults who held power over them.

So we grow up determined to do it "right," never to be like "them." Unconsciously, our psyches imprint this intention on our creative filter. This imprint alters creative energy, tweaking it in such a way that whenever we get close to power, we undermine it. Undoing power relieves us of the fear of abusing it.

Although consciously we tell ourselves we are ready to be fully empowered, there is a vulnerable child within, tenaciously holding on to the memories of being a victim of abusive power. The potency of that inner child's resolve is formidable. In spite of the adult understanding of childhood events and circumstances that maturation brings, convincing the inner child that it is safe to loosen his/her grip is like trying to convince a rock climber to unlock the safety line as he hangs over a precipice. Not an option!

And if this isn't enough to stop us, cellular past-life memories release further foreboding alarms stopping us dead in our tracks as we near the Terrain of Power! Undoubtedly we all have many past lives filled with trauma from the abuse of power. This abuse may have been the result of political repression, corrupt "justice" systems, chronically punishing parents, slavery, restrictively rigid educational systems, spiritual communities fraught with ego corruption and competition, employment under bosses of steel, arranged marriages resulting in bondage and cruelty, etc. The list goes on and on we when contemplate all the ways humanity has distorted the natural flow of power available to everyone. No wonder we are timid when it comes to the prospect of assuming power. There are so few role models for empowerment and so many overwhelming memories of how power can be distorted and exploited.

Past life imprints go as deep as a cherry stain on fresh wood. Trying to "sand" it out is impossible. How can we ever return to the original state of innocence where power flows freely, fresh and neutral, carrying the potency of a great waterfall, without hurting others or ourselves?

The ultimate irony in all of this is that if we don't assume our rightful power, it ends up leaking out of us unconsciously. The unconscious leakage of power usually expresses itself in the same patterns and dynamics established by authority figures in our childhood (reflecting past life imprints). Our efforts to avoid hurting others with our power backfires if we don't claim our birthright of intense strength. Unconscious power flows through the shadow lands of the psyche, inevitably distorting its true, potentially loving nature because of our attempt to deny it. Ironically the monster we struggle to avoid becoming possesses us when least expected. And so we hand down the legacy of abuse of power to our children, and they to their children.

Collectively we huddle in the corner, fearful of our potency while distortions of power flow through us, dominating our lives through unconscious force. Consciously we may feel more protected when we identify with false humility, disempowerment or even victimhood rather than approach the red hot issue of personal power. However, unconsciously we are the very tyrannical powerhouses we have struggled to resist.

We become "disempowered" by our very fear of power. Unable to approach it, we attempt to bury it like nuclear waste, hoping it will disintegrate. We all know nuclear waste just doesn't go away. And so with power the issue remains, lifetime after lifetime, until we are bold and courageous enough to seize it, praying for the wisdom and true humility to ride the potency of the force with the compassion of the Buddha.

My own process around power has been tumultuous, having an inner child who fervently believed it was far safer to swallow power than to own and express it. This repression of power inverts the energy, causing it to turn in on itself. The illusion, that I could actually *hide* my power, resulted in a lot of "swallowing" as I matured into an adult uncertain of the worthiness of having power.

In my mid-30's, I finally felt strong enough to tackle this issue. To contemplate becoming a healer and channel required addressing power. The solar plexus (the chakra just below the rib cage) is our power center. My physical body reacted violently with each step I took toward assuming more power. Our past life material, stored in our cells, is often carried into full consciousness through the body. Nausea and vomiting were the results of my conscious effort to accept the responsibility of power. Deeply blocked by fear of moving into power, my body's reaction was to literally discharge anything in the way.

Persistent internal work cleared the way for greater currents of power to flow. These currents encountered a determined little girl within who fiercely stood her ground, holding her commitment to prevent the gates of power from outwardly opening. Not only was she plagued by parents who unwittingly abused their power, but also by vague past-life memories of power misused, of being both the victim and the victimizer. As children, we are strongly susceptible to past-life imprints, still fresh and open to the causal plane with its records of our karmic history. Eventually I was able to transmute the intense fear associated with power so that initiations into greater power would not have such a violent physical impact.

Power is available to everyone. In order to grow and evolve, we must confront the issue of our magnitude. It is integral to the freeing up of our energetic truth. Those who use it positively have worked through their issues around power. The potent energy streaming through them is light and clear. People who exercise a threatening quality of life force are the least empowered, needing to establish dominance as compensation for a weak fear-based inner foundation. The majority of us vacillate, letting our power flow in spurts. Often, after making a powerful statement or action, we are unnerved and intimidated. The tendency is to immediately retract our potency, hoping no one noticed our force! After all, we don't want to get in trouble for being "too much."

What does it feel like to hold back our power? There is a price to pay for inhibiting life force. At the very least, the physical body bears the brunt of this contraction, attempting to contain energies which, by their very nature, need to be emanated, expressed and directed.

The mighty bugaboo we collectively tackle is the conflict of power versus spirituality. Most of us, elevating images of holy beings like St. Francis of Assisi, prefer to spiritually identify with expressions of gentleness, kindness and compassion. These qualities, not usually associated with power, are most powerful. Attempting to be appropriately spiritually humble, we deny the potency of our force, fearful that its formidability would corrupt our "Christ-consciousness." This leaves us with a watered-down spiritual charge devoid of the red-hot juice that powers true spiritual passion.

The Tibetan charges in, smiling in amusement over my exploration:

The true responsibility of power is to allow self to accept the imperfection of the human condition, thereby releasing all shame connected to past-life or current-life "mistakes." True power does not belong to the ego but rather to the Higher Self and beyond. Self humbly accepts the opportunity to channel this divine force through the creative intention to express self's highest possible essence. Accepting the limitations inherent in the evolving human condition, self can bravely move forward into power, holding the intention to funnel this magnitude for the good of all.

Potent energies, predestined to be available to all who open to their Higher Self, must be embraced with trust and a true desire to serve the Divine Plan. Release all false beliefs describing self as unworthy of power. These false beliefs undermine linkage to the universal forces required for evolution and manifestation. In the connection with greater currents of power, self offers this force up to the highest possible consciousness, allowing the emphatically vivid divine flow to be administered with wisdom and compassion for all beings. Allow self to fill with gratitude for the opportunity to be a conduit of power, knowing that these immense currents of Force carry the blessings that await all who embrace the quest to transform, heal and liberate the world.

✧ Money ✧

June 2003

Why is money such a charged issue? After all, it's only money—supposedly a neutral vehicle for exchange of goods and services. Throughout the globe most cultures use money as a central organizing vehicle for giving and receiving energy. Yet many of us cringe when we think about money. We don't talk about how much money we make, how much we have, spend, owe because of some strange mystique that money carries. Money is as mysterious and taboo as sex—the hot sphere that we all desire and experience but are cautious about revealing to each other.

"Money is the root of all evil." Why? If money is neutral, how can it be an ambassador of the wicked? Many "spiritual" people judge money as a" lower" level need. They are embarrassed to want money. Can we have/want money and still be spiritual? These people disdain money only to struggle with rent payments, bills, and the limitations of poverty. But they often feel righteous in their "indifference" to the finer things that money can buy—clothes, houses, vacations, dining out, workshops—pleased that they are not enslaved to the material concerns and lusts of this world. This sense of righteousness often generates judgments against the wealthy, as if they are lost souls.

Honoring St. Francis' example, must we renounce the material pleasures that only money can buy in order to preserve our spiritual integrity and purity? Does poverty bring us closer to God? Is renouncement still an appropriate vehicle for transformation?

Many spiritual students are embarrassed about their desire for money, fearful of exposing shadows of greed. People become irate if they feel that spiritual teachers ask for too much money. Yes, exploitation of anything leaves a sour taste in our mouths. But a reasonable income supporting spiritual service alienates many who believe that ultimately one's life, fully spiritually based, should magically support itself—like levitating above one's earthly path—neither touching, nor soiling self with base material concerns. This reflects old notions that the earth plane, with all of its density, is a "lesser" realm that diminishes rather than enhances elevated consciousness.

Money is neutral energy, to be manifested and used in whatever way we want. So, how do we arrive at a dispassionate relationship with money—liberated from the usual projections of power, disempowerment, fear, frustration, obsession that load our financial perspective with dread and control issues? Where did these projections come from? What process do we need to go through in order to purge the collective conditioning around money?

Raised by a self-serving, affluent family, I had the luxury of disdaining money in my twenties. My hippie values rebelled against materialism as I quested for "higher" virtues—love, harmony, peace. Pure in my intentions, no mortgages/ loans, I was immune from the sticky earthly net of money ensnaring and enslaving others. Orphaned and penniless at 21, I had no relatives to fall back on for financial support. This simplified my life, leaving me with only immediate material concerns—groceries, cheap rent, clothes from rummage sales and gas for my used 1966 Mustang.

In my mid-thirties I moved from Ithaca, N.Y, to Boston to become a therapist. The hippie transmuted into a yuppie. Suddenly, all the repressed money hunger surfaced. I wanted everything that money could buy! At 42 I finally broke down and acquired a credit card - soon to be unleashed in the world of acquisitions. Now at 54, deeply immersed in the material world—mortgages, loans, credit cards, and unending desires to do things that require funds, I realize the compelling nature of money. I have moved through denial, judgment, frustration, desire and overwhelm, all in the name of this supposedly neutral energy. What strange power money holds in our collective unconscious.

It took years to admit that I wanted money. Fearful of carrying my parents callous materialism, I was ashamed of my greed. Secretly, I wondered how people made money. What trick did they know? While I spent my twenties and early thirties trying to get away from money, some of my peers spent that time making gobs of money. Were they less spiritual than me? Perhaps this was my way of hiding power. If I were poor, others wouldn't be threatened, and I wouldn't have to assume responsibility for my magnitude.

It's foolish to measure our inner wealth by externals and equally ludicrous to deny the expression of inner wealth in form due to fear of exposure, false humility and self-denial. This crimps our divine creativity that naturally brings all energy full circle. Inner creates outer. To block outer expression suffocates inner expansion. To blindly obsess over our earthly manifestations veils our wisdom about the true Source of Wealth.

I now understand that money is only what we make it. Issues of disempowerment, inferiority, lovelessness are lodged in our financial flow—contracting or expanding this cosmic hose according to the evolution of our values and self-worth. Coming full circle, I still want all that money can buy but am deeply content with the great bounty filling my life. My spiritual life is supported by physical comfort and prosperity while I work to simplify the complex nature of money that carries the desire for MORE.

That desire for more is not the fault of money. Money is only the messenger broadcasting our longing for fulfillment at the deepest level. We get sidetracked thinking that we won't be fulfilled until we own a house, vacation in Hawaii, drive a Mercedes, pay off all our bills, revamp our wardrobe, accumulate art and sacred objects, send the kids to college and on and on. Endless money pits with snakes of yearning feed on the illusion within our negotiations with the Divine. How often during the day do we say to ourselves: "I can't follow my heart's desires, live my true lifestyle, be creative, follow my soul's calling, because I don't have the money. Until then I can't let go, be at peace, experience gratitude, or see the glass half full." So we allow money to be our big excuse for resisting growth, not taking risks, and denying Grace.

Perhaps our enslavement to money (desire for or rejection of) is a huge balancing out from lifetimes of self-denial—yes, the St. Francis complex of tossing away all earthly goods in the name of pure devotion to God. If so, we can now learn that all earthly creations are direct offspring of divine inspiration. It is impossible to be contaminated by too much form. However, some of us may need to divest ourselves of our greed, softening our grasp on the material plane to open to the finer, more subtle nature of the etheric realm and the intangible values that it holds. Perhaps too many lifetimes were spent entrenched in material plane stuff, assuming that physical satisfactions were the ultimate treasures of life. Eventually we realize that this isn't an either/or situation. Money simply carries our belief systems about ourselves and our place in the universe.

The Tibetan strides forth, teasingly scattering weighty golden coins, like flower petals, on the grounds—a carpet of glittering riches, teaching:

Yes, from where the Masters sit, money is irrelevant. But we understand the potent energetics inherent in money. The great Master Kuthumi, in one of his incarnations, was responsible for creating the Taj Mahal. Master St. Germain lived the rich lifestyle of a European count. These Masters demonstrated the inherent abundance of Source. Humankind need not fear the material plane's expression of divine wealth. Play with it like candy, knowing that eventually all students have to master the physical plane and come to terms with the metamorphosis of divine value into earthly manifestation.

This is a uniquely individualized karmic assignment designed to reflect the soul's quest for pure expression of the spirit in form. If the soul is saturated from lifetimes of acquisition blocking the golden sparkle of the Divine, then self must renounce attachment to money. If the soul is weakened, disheartened by an earthly plane laden with too much hardship and impoverishment, then the soul becomes sick from the illusion of limitation and disconnection from the Royal Source of Bounty. Mastery of the earthly plane involves balance, the true interface between form and spirit.

Western culture is fat with materialism. Rather than judge the glut of manifestation, allow it to fill the physical desires to the point of saturation, discharging the hunger for more-in-form so that the true yearning for soul-alignment is finally revealed. Then allow that longing to be fully supported through earthly resources, manifesting the neutral energy of money required to carry self forth into enlightenment. To deny money is to attach to it. Explore the deeper reasons that charge money with such misery.

Historically, renouncement was an appropriate learning device for humankind in its infancy to modify its excessive attachment to the physical plane. Students expressed their willingness to divest themselves of all physical attachments in pursuit of their divine essence. However, St. Francis' teachings have been distorted in their interpretation that material riches are evil or anti-spirit. This false belief has caused as much suffering as excessive attachment to money. Either way, humankind has been enslaved to the illusion of giving material wealth too much power.

Many students are afraid to step on their spiritual path because they believe they must give up all physical pleasures and comforts. Ironically, spirituality breeds prosperity because enhanced self-love lubricates the flow of all creation. Self-negation never brought the students closer to Source, only further from themselves and their soul.

Those who obsess over money may be afraid to look beyond the physical, assuming that nothing lies there. Then money has to be their God, which leaves them frightened and grasping for more to ward off the illusion of existential vacuousness. Western culture is compulsively driven toward financial accumulation. This reflects a deeper spiritual starvation resulting from a lifestyle devoid of spiritual meaning as the storm of frenetic amassment clogs the third eye's vision of what is possible, burdens the heart's joy with financial concerns and churns up the solar plexus with disempowering hungers that can never be satiated by money. Bringing spirituality into daily life lightens the earthly load, lubricates wealth on all levels and breaks attachments to the limitations of monetary restrictions.

Unworthiness is an illusion that crimps physical manifestation. There is no being that does not merit prosperity. All of humankind DESERVES abundance. All souls are rich in value. Once this is understood, the student is liberated to employ the vehicle of money to manifest a lifestyle rich in ease, soul alignment, precise expression of the Higher Self's harvest and gifts, with not too much or too little emphasis placed on the fuel (money) that carries this manifestation forth.

Once the student relaxes into the fullness of his/her physical life, just as it is right in this moment, a door opens—a porthole to the Banquet of Wealth from the spiritual plane. Then money takes its proper place—simply a pipeline for Source to shower Its creations with gifts. Poverty consciousness is released at long last. The truly empowered student, in complete alignment with the mandate of his/her Higher Self, extends forth into human existence with a cosmic pocket full of resources richly supporting Self's evolutionary journey through a delightful walk on the earthly plane. Pure mastery involves no attachment to money, with the complete freedom to have as much of it, spend as much of it and delight in it as a playground for creativity, perpetually demonstrating Source's magnificent GENEROSITY showered on all.

✧ Energy ✧

November 2000

How many of us are truly comfortable with our energy level? Do we have enough of it? Too much? Our human experience reflects limited energy, but when we run out of it we die.

The Tibetan talks about limitless energy, the infinite expression of Source (God). He reminds us that we are extensions of Source with the potential to embody the infinite. That means infinite energy. Collectively, can we really believe it is possible to encompass unlimited energy?

The Tibetan teaches the same thing over and over again:

Don't forget, you are energetic beings. See yourself as pure energy with limitless potential. Understanding one's essential energetic nature brings freedom from the restrictions associated with the density of form.

Recognizing their true energetic nature, the students experience the spaciousness of their physical being. There is more space in the physical body than density. What fills that space? Energy—the energy of Source.

Energy is a precise reflection of belief systems. When students reference their being as purely energetic, the following false beliefs can be released: "The earth plane is too heavy and dense". "I am stuck in my limitations which prevent me from transforming." "It is impossible to clear out blockages—due to their sheer 'weight.'" "I simply don't have the energy to do what I really want to do with my life."

Energy is movement. Energy is change. Energy can speed up and change vibratory rates. When energy accelerates, old forms resonant only with lower vibratory rates naturally fall away. Energy is indestructible. Energy powers transformation.

It is one thing to theorize about energetic attunement. It is another to actually experience ourselves as fundamentally energetic in nature. What does energy feel like as it moves through our supposedly "spacious" bodies?

Twenty years ago, as a new student of T'ai Chi, my instructor taught the microcosmic orbit, an energetic route naturally flowing up from the base of the spine and down the front of the body. After extensive T'ai Chi movement and subsequent meditation, he instructed us to "feel" the energy in the orbit. I felt absolutely nothing! I couldn't even imagine what he was talking about. Lying on the floor, trying so hard to feel this illusive thing called energy, I felt like a lump of flesh and bones. Maybe there was energy there somewhere, but I couldn't figure out how to get to it. I tried to convince myself I was moving energy with all this T'ai Chi and meditation. But it was only my theoretical mind trying to offer reassurance that I was making progress in the energy department.

A slow learner, it took me several years to recognize the sensation of energy moving through the pathways in my body. The warmth in my hands and tingling sensations in arms and feet alerted me to the awareness that just maybe energy was finally moving.

Five years of practicing T'ai Chi later, I started to channel the Tibetan. Ironically, this led to a fear of too much energy. Would I be able to match the potency of Djwhal Khul's energy? Twenty years of Tai Chi coupled with 14 years of channeling have taught me to relax into the wonderful experience of being deeply open to the great outpouring of energy available to all. In channel I experience Djwhal Khul's energy as a powerful waterfall cascading in and around my being, a wonderful demonstration of the abundant nature of energy.

Determination and focus are required to cut through the collective belief that the physical plane is solid and dense. If it is indeed only solid and dense, then we face the issue of limited or bound-up energy. If it is spacious and essentially energetic, then we are limitless in form. If we believe we are low on energy, then we lose our connection to the vast abundance of universal energy. If we believe energy can hurt us, then we experience kundalini (life force) eruptions resulting in a vast array of physical, emotional and mental suffering. If we believe we don't deserve our energy, then others steal it. If we believe energy is scare and limited, then we steal energy from others and our beloved planet. We compete for energy.

Releasing these limited beliefs frees us to take responsibility for the cultivation of energy, which is to swim with the flow, not against it. This energetic cultivation taps us into our birthright, an inherent connection to the universal life force. Following the natural laws of health stimulates greater energetic movement.

The more we imagine ourselves as purely energetic, the more energy flows. This increased energy enhances aliveness, heightens the five senses, clears the mind and amplifies the positive charge. Energy cultivation and recognition is a spiritual pathway.

Primarily our soul dwells on the etheric plane (higher level dimension), not the earth plane. Our earthly orientation has no reference point for the recognition of the soul due to its lack of substance. Therefore, in contemplating alignment with our Higher Self (soul), we can only imagine the soul in energetic terms, not physical. The Tibetan adds:

When the student perceives life from an energetic perspective, "barriers" to one's divinity break down. The Higher Self exists beyond the physical realm. Energy springs from and flows beyond time and space, allowing instant connection to one's Higher Self. The bridge between personality and soul can only be an energetic one.

This bridge is enlivened by the student's awareness that his/her being is far greater than the immediate physical realm reflecting self's existence. This greater realm is only recognizable in energetic terms. Opening up awareness of energy, the student begins to perceive the energetic field that surrounds the physical body, called the aura. The aura varies in size and color depending on one's state of mind, physical and emotional health, and level of spiritual maturation.

When fantasizing about all the wonderful things to accomplish in my lifetime, I inevitably run into the bottom line stumbling block—my false beliefs about energy. Waffling between fears of having too much energy versus running out of energy has impacted my ability to take the initiative to fully manifest my potential. Encouraging me to toss away these foolish false beliefs the, Tibetan refutes each of them:

False belief: "I could probably fulfill my dreams if I only had enough energy."

Djwhal Khul: *Only fear prevents humankind from fulfilling their dreams. Energy flows freely and unimpeded when fear is released. Fear constricts the energetic channels. It kinks the "cosmic hose" of infinite energy, reducing the great outpouring of life force to a mere trickle.*

False belief: "I have to conserve energy to get through the day."

Djwhal Khul: *There is more than enough energy to get through the day, even with only one hour of sleep each night. Respecting one's energy is important, viewing it as a divine gift. However, hoarding energy, rationing it out in bits and pieces, is not necessary. This thinking reflects the scarcity illusion so deeply embedded in the collective consciousness resulting in diminished energy.*

False Belief: "It is dangerous to have too much energy, I might overwhelm others. I can't handle other people's energy; it's too much for me."

Djwhal Khul: *Once self is comfortable with the potency of his/her own energy, others will be as well. Vibrant heightened energy serves as a catalyst for awakening in others. It is a source of inspiration and a demonstration that the fire of life burns brightly within all beings. If others judge self as being too energetic, they are envious, so hungry is humankind to know the full extent of its aliveness. The fear of being overwhelmed by others' energy is the flip side of the same coin. In this case, self is repressing his/her natural radiant flow due to fear of being "too much." Discomfort with expressing one's full energetic nature can unconsciously invite others to usurp one's energy. It is impossible to be too much.*

False Belief: "If I have too much energy moving through my body, my circuits will be fried."

Djwhal Khul: *"The physical body is energetic in nature. Energy is neutral and therefore harmless to the body. The challenge is to address blockages pushed to the surface by the energetic flow in the body. The more that the student clears out these blockages, the greater the capacity for heightened energy. Ultimately the physical body, as well as the emotional and mental body, is designed to be an empty vessel able to receive* outpourings of universal energy to be channeled into the human experience. *The more relaxed humankind becomes with its own nature, the more open it will be to the energetic waterfall of life. The challenge is to ground this life force in form through the release of all energy-related fears.*

False Belief: "Energy is too mysterious to cultivate. I don't know how to access much less direct it."

Djwhal Khul: *Yes, energy is mysterious, as are all aspects of Source. However, mysterious or not, it is possible to master one's attunement to the true essence of life, energy. Experiment with it. Pretend it has substance. Play with it. There is no right or wrong approach to energetic attunement. Imagine seeing it streaming from your fingertips. Shape it. Visualize filling favorite visions and dreams with energy. It is cosmic fuel. Energy is friendly. Energy is light. Allow self to envision energy in the body as a current of love whose sole function is to give self life. Gratitude for this infinite gift enhances its flow.*

As usual, the Tibetan counters my concerns with loving insight. His teaching inspires me to explore the full extent of my energetic nature, knowing that this attunement will heighten resonance with my Higher Self. Joyfully we all play in the garden of life, allowing the infinitude of energy to dissolve fears of change, loss, and death. Life force unites us all into eternity reflecting our oneness with Source in this wondrous swirling universe of boundless ageless energy.

✧ React or Detach? ✧

February 2005

If I were really spiritually advanced, I'd let everything slide off my back. I'd be a transcendent being, impervious to whatever life presents. Isn't that the cosmic goal—pure non-attachment? To arrive spiritually, must we embody the Buddha's serenity? Is it more desirable to be in a state of pure emptiness than to ride the passions of the human condition, in vivid Technicolor? What is the spiritual price for our heated reaction indulgences vs. the human price for sustaining detachment in situations that beg for the responsive emotional flow of the human heart?

We often berate ourselves for our strong reactions to others. If only we were more nonattached, our interpersonal messes would end. We could float through life unscathed by the slings and arrows of our shared human melodrama. To be hooked by unfair/hurtful dynamics just sets us up to be raked over the coals by the tangled fur ball of projections bouncing back and forth in our relationships. However, to hide behind elevated levels of detachment may wick out the human blood, sweat and tears that transform the soul. Then our spiritual cool is nothing more than a prison of transcendence, too sterile to honor the bitter juices that accelerate our alchemical process in their pungent dismantling of the ego. Although our disdainful spiritual egos would judge them as setbacks, all reactions, however ugly, serve our transformation.

The right to react to violations in our relationships is integral to our evolution. When striving to be an empty vessel, we may be repressing gut-level reactions that inform us about our needs. Survival depends on our freedom to react. Mastery of the human condition requires healthy boundaries. Reactions are fabulous mirrors that display hidden parts of our psyche, provide clues to our authentic self and describe our soul's learning curve. Is it really necessary to transcend our basic instinct to engage each other through the ping-pong ball of reactions that web us together in the impossibly gummy mess called human relationships?

If responsibility means "the ability to respond," then isn't true responsibility to our soul based on our uncensored reaction to earthly life? What a vantage point! Reactions provide information about each other that might otherwise be masked by too much spiritual nonchalance. The dynamic tension in our relationships is the grit that creates the pearl. Our spiritual egos may seduce us into believing that we are "beyond" certain reactions. Certainly, the more we work through our illusions, the less our wounds are kicked up in reaction to others.

However, if we haven't completed the arduous task of healing all our soul's wounds, there is bound to be some sticky stuff inside that is dying to react when poked or prodded by interpersonal dynamics. If we talk ourselves out of our reaction in order to be spiritually correct, then we risk depression. Depression, often symptomatic of self-repression, fuels self-denial, self-judgment and inauthenticity. Besides, repressed reactions take so much energy to keep buried within the unconscious—ultimately exhausting and disempowering.

Is the range of raw human reactions truly non-spiritual? In spite of the bumpy road, I would rather be an authentically wild, reactive banshee than an inauthentically unflappable, spiritually self-composed being. Nothing that is repressed ever disappears. Like nuclear waste, all repressed reactions smolder within the unconscious, waiting for the day to release their fire. I'd rather take my chances with explosive daily reactions, and the mess they create, than be insulated in a spiritual lofty tower that denies the roiling within my guts, and eventually erupts an unconscious volcano to cause widespread destruction throughout my relationships. Then, dropped into the sludge of corrosive negativity (covered and suspended for years in the spiritual glamour of false serenity), I would be covered with the putrid stagnation of censored frozen reactions that would indeed lower my lofty vibrations.

How do we know when it's okay to react or not? Spiritual teachers encourage us to not sweat the small stuff. But isn't it the small stuff, the microcosm, that reflects the greater, macrocosm, climate in the soul? Don't we learn from the trial and error of varying reactions in order to locate our authentic self? Paradoxically, if we're all unconsciously bouncing off of each other like bumper cars, we pile up in a heap of disaster as our reactions serve as needless destructo-machines that pulverize fragile trust in ourselves and others. Often, after we've been *so* convinced that someone did us wrong, a few days will pass and we'll begin to see reality through their eyes. Suddenly our potent reaction seems extreme, unnecessarily hurtful, and regretfully we wish we had the spiritual wisdom to initially step back from the process, breathe, expand our consciousness and allow an acceptance of what has occurred to temper our fire into understanding.

Perhaps the key is consciousness. If we're driven by unconscious reactions, we squander precious life energy in needless overreactions and loss of self-containment. It helps to buy some time—practice detachment without denying the gut-level genius that gives us the "gooch" to fully show up on our behalf in relationships. Then we have the choice to bring full awareness to the deeper levels within our reactions and what they are calling for, rather than be enslaved to blind reactions that leave trails of disaster in their wake. We can employ our spiritual savvy to decide when and how to react to others, if at all. The ultimate mastery is to react in ways that enlighten us and others. When allowed the full range of reactions, eventually we lose fascination for our favorite interpersonal melodramas, like boring, rerun movies. If we're stuck in predictable chronic reactions, maybe we're not gleaning what we need to learn. In this case, practicing some non-attachment might bring the breath of fresh air required to experience new, more informative reactions.

For many years I reacted to a friend's dramatic tendencies to throw curve balls in our plans. I felt trapped by my inability to control my reactions to his craziness. Finally, something snapped. I understood the deeper reasons for my attachment to those dynamics, and was free at last to be blissfully neutral in reaction to his patterns. Without the hook, our dysfunctional dance came to an immediate stop—no need to fight about it. I simply withdrew the energy that had previously fed our dynamics. However, I had to earn this level of liberating non-attachment by working on all the sticky areas within that magnetized those painful dynamics. Healing awareness of my wounds released the need for me to "hire" him to reenact my hurts and gifted me with the spaciousness of projection less loving indifference. What a relief! What freedom!

The Tibetan "reacts" to my exploration with the deeply engaged love of a teacher for his student. No need for non-attachment here as he shares my awakening. He teaches:

Most spiritual students hold impossible standards of non-attachment. They assume that any human reaction other than love, acceptance and kindness is a sign of devolvement. Some souls spend lifetimes transcending the human condition, which may strengthen the spiritual body, but retards their exploration of duality through physicality, emotions and thought. The soul requires deep emersion in rich, interpersonal dynamics colorfully expressed through reaction to others, to learn acceptance of perceptual differences, an understanding of give and take, about the rights of self and others, and to sort through priorities. The courage to be honest and forthcoming in self's reactions builds backbone. Souls who hide behind non-attachment postpone their earthly assignment of swimming naked in the human condition. Unprotected exposure to the tapestry of human relationships fills the soul's wisdom bank. Please don't judge self's flow of reaction or attempt to lift above the raw material within that begs for purification through the human predicament. Rather, harvest the awareness gifted through this process.

Humankind is designed to react to its environment, like a baby whose sensitive response to the mother completes the loving bond of survival. Metaphysical law never issued arbitrary spiritual handcuffs of non-attachment to tame the human spirit's reaction to its existence. True detachment results from a series of reactions that involve the soul's need to establish mutuality in relationships. All interactions that don't express this divine harmony require a corrective reaction. Usually it takes more than one incident to inform the student that long-standing reactive patterns are no longer necessary. Then surrender is as easy as a ripe fruit falling from the tree as self finally perceives and releases the entire melodrama. Non-attachment's neutrality can't be forced because it is the result of the process of reacting, learning and then surrendering.

However, to be like a top spinning out of control through unceasing blind reactions, depletes self and reenergizes false beliefs. The conscious student must react responsibly, with a self-containment that strengthens the energy body and concentrates the force field within significant reactions to enhance their designated impact on the soul. Ultimately, the student must embrace the negativity within their reactions, not in denial or judgment, but as important energy that wards off violation/ imbalance. To contain this energy enhances connection to self without giving over precious life force to others' unconscious dynamics. The wise sage reacts while containing energy, issues chi without self-depletion. That is the art of Conscious Response. So allow the theater to unfold in the dazzling display of reactions and counter-reactions. All forms of divine creativity bounce off each other in an exquisite dance of interrelatedness and shared evolution. From that great Arch of Response all beings are enlightened.

✧ Psychic Protection ✧

People often ask how I protect myself when I'm channeling. To be in channel, I must be very OPEN to be wholly available to the greater vibrational field of the Tibetan. Does this leave me vulnerable to dark energies "getting in" at the same time?

Many of us are spiritually opening up quite rapidly as we shed ancient karmic defense structures. Challenged to evolve beyond our childhood conditioning which is based on our entire karmic matrix, we are stripping away psychic protections developed by our unconscious that help us to survive physical, emotional and spiritual wounds sustained during infancy, childhood and teenage years. As we cast off this psychological armor, we feel naked/exposed.

To progress beyond old paradigms of abuse, we must break down the defenses that straight-jacket us. Although protection makes us feel safe, we pay a price. While hurtful energy is blocked out, good energy is equally as obstructed. Novocain thankfully blocks the pain of getting our teeth drilled, but it also prevents us from fully tasting our food for a while. That numbness is worth a few hours of trade off, but most of us are carrying protections that entrap us in the Numb Zone for most of our lives. Because it suffocates the spirit, the Numb Zone eventually becomes more unbearable than the pain we're trying to avoid. We came to the earth plane to FEEL. When this suffocation becomes unbearable, we dive into therapy, meditation and other modalities to break free of our imprisoning shields. Eager to feel again, we decide to brave the rigors of exposure to ourselves, others, the world, the universe. But does that make us sitting ducks?

How can we possibly open up and expand if our growth leaves us vulnerable to negative energies? In addition to dealing with the hazards of fully feeling all of our unhealed wounds, does this disarmoring leave us defenseless to the perils of psychic assault, or at the very least, indirect attack by others who unconsciously allow their imbalanced states to be conduits of negative energy? Why should we discard our heavy rubber slickers if we are standing in the middle of a hurricane? This storm is the result of the current spiritual mandate to clear bundles of past-life debris, and the release work inadvertently spews out gobs of negative energy. Blizzards of karmic toxins are being propelled and sprayed everywhere.

Teachers of spirituality often urge students to employ protective mechanisms to shield their sensitive, freshly-awakening chakras from dark-force violations—or simply to prevent them from "picking up" negative energy from others. Those of us who believe in recycling try to transmute our individual karmic fall-out through spiritual/ healing practices. However, many are oblivious to this monumental collective clearing process and are unconsciously littering the astral field and the collective emotional body with tons of dark garbage. Do we need to protect ourselves from being contaminated by this mess?

When people are unconsciously ensnared in wounds filled with fear and anger, they unwittingly become easy vessels for negative forces. Unable to take responsibility for their denied injuries/ negativity, they project them out and violate others. The potential for psychic attack increases—terrorism on the emotional/spiritual level—as the heightened frequencies currently impacting our planet heat up the alchemical stew that is cooking us all.

In alchemy, the first step of turning lead into gold is the blackening stage, which breaks down old configurations in order to usher in full metamorphosis. In terms of spiritual advancement, the blackening stage can be shadowy, ugly, bleak, and dark. Many of us are in the blackening stage as we break down the old paradigm in consciousness in order to reach the "gold" of collective awakening. It's quite the challenge to strip away all defenses blocking our expansion while being psychically exposed to a blizzard of blackening energy.

My issue with psychic attack is that it's invisible! If someone points a gun at me, I know I better run. But if someone is forcing a sugary smile while cloaking a heart hardened by negativity, I might not realize that I'm in danger. If my heart opens to that person's false smile, does that make me a target for their displaced shadow? Psychic attack *is* invisible, immeasurable—like noxious gas. It can't be seen but sure can kill you. Or can it? What happens when people plant "mean seeds" in someone? We all know what it's like to have another person's "poison words" lodge in our soul and fester, ulcerating our wholeness with pockets of venom. How do we protect ourselves from that if we're totally naked in our openness?

In channel, I imagine myself in a protective violet bubble that allows positive energy to be issued forth while preventing negative energy from being absorbed. This technique enables me to relax enough to fully open to the powerful thrust of the Tibetan's force. Perhaps it's just a placebo, but it works! However, I am always aware that the next step awaits me—full surrender to the Divine embrace, unencumbered by any cultivated psychic devices designed to buffer the Great Flow.

There is nothing that can be done to us that we're not already doing to ourselves. Psychic attack, like a dart, only sticks if we are carrying an internal matrix of self-aggression/ self-abuse easily activated by external negativities. Sensors wired into our own self-destructive impulses "pick up" negative frequencies and magnetize them into ourselves. The healing impact of self-love, compassion, kindness, patience, insight and inner work releases the magnetic charge that draws nasty energy to us. However, the period of transition between opening up our deepest self in order to expose our wounds and to having those wounds fully healed is challenging. During that process—spanning days, weeks, even years—we feel exceedingly vulnerable to any harsh energies that would duplicate our original wounds. Do we need protection en route to our wholeness?

We swaddle our newborn babies in layers of comforters to protect their sensitive systems from the elements. We, too, need to be cocooned as we rebirth ourselves to protect the freshly revealed authentic self from the demolishing forces of darkness that are only too happy to undo all our hard labor. Do we need the Divine Mother, the Source of Ultimate Protective Nurturance, to remind us to "put a coat on" as we venture out into the maelstrom of negative energy being released during this time? If we've been burned in the past, and we release our protection, it is unbearable to let anything near the burns. Acute pain makes us recoil in self-protection as we try to gauge how much exposure we can tolerate in order to allow the wounds to heal in the light of our consciousness. So we must wear our temporary protection lightly, without attachment, and be willing to discard it when necessary, like the patient who acquiesces to the doctor's need to pull off the bandages and explore how the wound is healing.

Fearful of attack, people assume that if they open, there are legions of "bad guys" out there on the astral plane waiting to nail them. If we accidentally leave a wallet in a public place, we automatically assume it will be stolen. It always comes as a pleasant surprise when we go back to retrieve it and it's actually still sitting there—untouched—right where we left it. Perhaps it's time to assume that we can be safe as we open—time to believe that a benign force is permeating our reality, gracing our path and nullifying negative magnetics.

The Tibetan OPENLY embraces me on the inner planes—allowing our energy to intermingle freely. He teaches:

If one's need for protection is fear-based, then it only serves to contract self's innate channel. Ultimately, one's desire for protection is connected to the deeper need for immunity from self. Psychic attacks are heat-seeking missiles triggered by the holes in self's auric field—unhealed wounds highly receptive to negative energy. Rather than focus on putting up protection from the dark force "out there," self is safest when focusing on healing self's wounds with Divine Love.

Many students have spent lifetimes fighting the malevolent forces. As warriors, they have been fully armored against the malignant poison spewing from dark vortexes. In this lifetime, as one's awareness of dark/ light energies increases, self's cellular instinct is to build blockades to ward off attack. This requires much energy/ attention placed on psychic defense. One's energetic "defense budget" robs other areas of self's life—creativity, relationships, service. Ironically, garnering excessive energy for psychic defense calls out to the dark force to do battle. Self is throwing down the gauntlet. While this may not be a conscious decision, at a cellular level, self is broadcasting this impulse for combat.

Most students assume they are inferior to the dark force—that they are helpless targets in the cosmic arena of dark vs. light. They feebly put up protection, hoping somehow that the knives of negativity won't penetrate. A common collective false belief is that to be vulnerable and open is to be in a weakened, disadvantaged state. However, unobstructed vulnerability is truly the only place of empowerment available to humankind. Wholehearted openness allows students to tap into the rich indomitable spirit of the human condition that expresses their Divine core. This profound human essence is impervious to any dark attacks because it IS the earthly manifestation of Source's Ultimate Potency.

There is nothing "out there" that can undo the Divine Matrix As students anchor deeply into their divinity; they're automatically aligned with Source's magnificent muscle of Light and Love. This teaches that inner peace is self's ultimate shield of "protection"— the full-blown relaxation that surrenders all notions of struggle, warfare and attack. Students sweetly yield to a force field so LARGE that nothing in this Universe can hurt them. Instead of creating protection with psychic shields/ swords /armor, focus on generating self's force field, strengthening self's vibratory rate, and stabilizing self's inner center by doing meditation, prayer, deep soul searching and energetic practices that heighten one's positive charge.

All difficult people, energies and events that block one's pathway are descriptions of self's false beliefs from past lives. Explore and release these illusions. Vulnerability is the arena of superior strength, because in this place of soft receptivity, nothing blocks self's contact with the Great Celestial Flow. This Colossal Spiritual Issuance magnetizes such Light and Love that it literally neutralizes any discordant energy that resist full communal resonance. Self then is truly HELD within a Force Field so Loving that any protective layers seem as foolish and unnecessary as wearing a rubber diving suit under full-length fur coat on a hot, sunny day.

Don't waste precious creative energy constructing gigantic blockades, shoring up medieval moat-like barriers because of fearful anticipation of retaliation for self's willingness to unfold/ open. If students put that same amount of energy into charging their field with love, light, the sound current and compassion, the war against the dark force would immediately end. To sit in the Garden of Peace with the Buddha reveals the absurd foolishness emanating from any negative energy that assumes it could destroy the Eternal.

Yes, the unfoldment process heightens exposure to the collective release of karmic debris—decaying, malignant energy. It's important to cleanse self during this opening. Imagine taking showers of light through toning, meditation, prayer and simply sitting in the sun as the warm rays burn away any sludge stuck to self's aura.

Most people wouldn't consider going a week without bathing. Yet many students are oblivious to the astral psychic garbage they're exposed to in this great collective clearing process. Ask Mother Earth to transmute this muck, the Angelic force to scour self's energy body, and the Masters to launder self's aura in the cosmic Maytag that employs Light/ Love as the maximum detergent.

There is no excuse to abate the opening process. Appreciate the exquisitely tender nature of the emerging Self. Place that delicacy/ fragility in the hands of the Divine Mother. Allow the spirit plane to midwife this process.

"Mean seeds" and "poison words" directed from others may lodge themselves in self's field. But ironically they inevitably serve the healing purpose of revealing self's unconscious areas of fear, impotence, illusion, and victim hood. Supported by Divine Assistants, lovingly remove these malignant bullets. Then self's full consciousness of these hidden pockets makes it IMPOSSIBLE to be attacked in those areas again. There is simply no magnetic affinity to draw this artillery.

Release old conditioning that self need be a victim of psychic attack. Don't look back at ancients wars against the forces of undoing. Look forward to the emerging Garden of Peace encoded in the DNA of all of humankind as it releases the need to struggle, fear, fail, "prove worthiness," or be undermine in any way. TO BE OPEN IS TO BE ULTIMATELY SAFE! Model the courage to trust that allows full exposure of self's divinity. Demonstrate that no harm can come to those in full alignment with the Source of their existence. To protect is to close. To align is to open. To stand in a cosmic shower more powerful than Niagara Falls, the roar of Love is so great that one cannot even hear the feeble efforts of unilluminated energies trying to nip at self's heels. This alignment brings everyone together in a Circle of Safety, the Strongbox of the Divine, the Universal Vault of Exemption from all lower-level aggression. Then all are drawn through the Porthole of Sanctuary, the threshold of the Golden Age.

✧ Aging ✧

October 2002

All of us, even children, are aging—subject to the inevitable passage of time and its impact on our bodies, minds and souls. In our youth we feel impervious to aging while we ironically count the years, maturing us until we are old enough to be on our own. We lie about our age to convince others that we are older than we appear. Later on in life, we lie about our age to convince others we are younger than we appear. Aging is relative.

At 38 years old I felt ancient. I had done it all. This was the way life would be forever, or so I thought. Usually that sense of feeling aged sets in just before major breakthroughs, when repressed parts of Self explode up to the surface to take center stage, ushering in the youthfulness of new beginnings and possibilities. Struck by the immediacy of uncharted territory, when midlife changes hit at 40, I felt like a wide-eyed baby taking in life with no preconceived expectations. Aging has a lot to do with the known and unknown. Too much known makes us feel stagnant—old. Too little known makes us feel confused, bewildered, uncertain—young. Age is a subjective experience often unrelated to physical reality.

Why is it that some people seem so young while others are old before their time? The physical body carries our emotional reality, expressing the voice of the unconscious. The body ages rapidly when emotionally we are old, worn-out, used up. When we are filled with vital life force, our bodies age more slowly and beautifully, with a grace that goes beyond time. Yes, genetics have their impact. But we also have free choice to either imbue our DNA structure with vital energy or roll over and play dead long before our spirits leave the body.

I am 53 years old—and sometimes I look it! Other times I look in the mirror and see a vibrant 21 year old or an ancient 100 year old. I can watch my face age and "youthe" within minutes, depending on the angle of my perception and energetic flow in that moment. The physical form is malleable, highly impacted by the impressions of our thoughts and beliefs.

Collectively, we expect to age. It's a pre-described formula. No one is immune to the age conveyor belt moving us steadily along to our destiny of corporeal deterioration. Physically, we mirror back to each other our shared beliefs about aging. Where might we find ourselves if we collectively made the leap into a new paradigm impervious to long-held cultural notions of aging?

Our beliefs about the onset of old age have evolved as life expectancy has lengthened. 300 years ago we expected to be old at 40. Now, it's 70. Why not shift our expectations to 150 as the onset of old age? Is this not simply a matter of opening to new beliefs? Isn't the quest for the Fountain of Youth fulfilled by exploring the mind's ability to establish new thought forms to usher in our ancient legacy of longevity? The Masters of the Far East demonstrate longevity by inhabiting youthful vehicles for hundreds of years. If *they* can, why can't we?

Studies have shown that the body is designed to live well over a century. Yet so few of us accept that it is natural to go beyond widely held, crushing age limitations. Real aging starts in our minds and beliefs and works its way into our bodies. We feel lucky to get to 70 and hope that the last chunk of life won't be too brutal. We dread the diseases and deterioration of old age expected to show up by 65 and increase mercilessly from there. We are victims of time. Yet the golden years are truly that—golden, if we simply think outside the box and claim our birthright of venerable vitality.

Our high- stress, toxin-filled environment and diet prematurely age us. However, perhaps our process of aging carries a greater element of choice than we assume. There are many powerful ways to slow down the aging process: enzyme-rich food, exercise, clean water/air, meditation, stress management, loving relationships, sleep, creativity. These are the foundations of longevity. "Internal" martial artists practicing chi gong/ tai chi reach their full stride in the 80's as compared to Olympic athletes who hit prime in their 20's.

Movement is the antidote to age. If we keep our minds, hearts, bodies and souls active we renew our personal bank account of vital life force. When we start to shut down and stagnate within familiar limiting patterns we atrophy, slowly curling up and preparing for death, sometimes decades before our "time." So much of aging depends on our attitudes and expectations. If we expect to live to 150, hitting our prime at 80, and we take full responsibility for our health, then nothing need stop us! We need to leave the collective thought matrix that teaches us to retire at 65 and prepare to get sick, weak and old by 70.

Worry is the great thief of longevity. If we face aging with dread, we get old fast. If we think outside the box and move into extended levels of maturation with excitement and creative anticipation we can remain forever young. How does the human process of aging enhance our soul's evolution?

Maturation brings enhanced wisdom if we are willing to claim it. I now have permission to step forward into my authority and speak my mind. Aging provides the seasoned vantage point that we are all "fools" on a foolhardy quest for awakening, allowing me to play this human game with a large grain of salty humor. Age has taught me to step back from my own melodrama, release judgments and broaden compassion. Age has revealed a road map of life patterns that display my soul's purpose. Age has taught me to appreciate and conserve energy—to cultivate a powerful life force in order to fulfill my destiny.

Age teaches me the power of NOW. I can't waste time postponing my soul's curriculum, waiting until I am ready. Age, teaching that we are never ready, pushes us to go forward, ready or not. Age is the Universe's way of saying, "Final exams are coming up—have you studied?" Age banishes stagnancy in the face of soul hunger for we are no longer willing to passively wait to be fed.

Aging reveals frailties through signs of emotional/ physical dis-ease that threaten to overturn my life if I don't honor these vulnerabilities. My arrogant youth, impervious to limitations, burned through brain cells, life force, my nervous system, with the unconsciousness of someone who leaves all the lights on, water faucets running and heat turned up with no regard to energy conservation. Age teaches me to slow down, be gentle, bask in my physical limitations—forcing me to take long hot baths and melt into the Universe. I am more active at 53 than at 23. I now can value the well-being of my physical body and want to love it into longevity. Ironically, the quality of my daily life is more vibrant than the couch potato, pizza-eating days of my 20's. Age relieves me of the need to be "drop-dead beautiful." It's no longer expected. Age breaks my attachment to surface images. I am opened to a deeper exploration of beauty.

Age challenges me to contemplate eternal youth, daring to break the mold of deterioration. Age turns up the volume on my clarity. Age reflects my progress and demonstrates staying power. Age mellows my competitive nature into greater acceptance of everyone's place on the planet. Age allows me to be a funky, unstoppable post-menopausal woman. Age offers a history of victories to reference when wondering if I will make it up the mountain I am currently climbing. Aging bequeaths beautiful wrinkles around my eyes, revealing how many hours I have spent laughing at the absurdity of life. Age teaches me to treasure those I love and to reach out more. Age gives me permission to do EXACTLY what I want NOW. Age dilutes the power of fear through decades of testing and retesting the trustworthiness of the Divine Plan. There is no better teacher than aging to evoke the soul into its full glory. If I am this enhanced by my aging process at 53, I can only imagine how profound my life force will be at 95!

The Tibetan's beautiful, ageless face appears to me on the inner planes, ancient eyes sparkling in delightful response to my outburst of age appreciation. He adds:

When humankind revels in the JOY of aging, it will be free to move beyond the illusion of time. The soul wears the aging body as playfully as it wears the young body. One's essence shines through an aged body, like wearing a magnificent antique gown, reflecting the creative collaboration between the physical body and the soul over decades.

Aging is a teaching tool for the soul to experience physical metamorphosis. Aging allows the physical body to record one's life process and prepares the ego to detach from the physical vehicle at death. Aging is an outlet for the tension of spirit in form within the gravitational field. Aging teaches humility, inspires humankind to look beyond the ego trappings of the physical plane and demonstrates the ephemeral nature of the physical vehicle.

By experiencing the discrepancy between feeling young internally while seeing an old face in the mirror, humankind realizes they are only spiritual beings observing themselves in form. This challenges the student to emphasize the soul's needs, which ironically leads to a heightened awareness of the unconditional eternal youth of the soul regardless of the age of the body. Therefore, aging facilitates non-attachment to the ego so that self can truly become an instrument of the Divine.

Age allows the students to observe their "ancient selves" in form—the materialized wisdom selves. Then the students can try on their mastery. The costume is already there which gives each student permission to "arrive." Age records time yet reveals that it is an illusion of time because the wrinkled body does not reflect the vibrant consciousness of the spirit. The body ages, thinning out formidable physical walls, to allow the spark of the soul greater prominence and radiance. As the student welcomes age, the soul is given the green light to take center stage within the body.

However, aging is only a temporary vehicle for learning. Once humankind realizes its innate elasticity, it can play around on the time continuum like a child plays on monkey bars—hoping on and off at will, donning young or old bodies according to the soul's latest creative requirements. All concepts of youth-oriented beauty break down as humankind reorients itself to the vast Universal Beauty that unites all. Humankind will be free to realize the Fountain of Youth existing in the inner Shambala of the heart, where the soul dips into its waters, forever refreshing and renewing, to further its journey homeward. Human beings become magicians who through non-attachment, work the forces of life to allow longevity of 1,000 years or more while keeping the bodies of 30- year olds, laughingly remembering the elementary lessons of aging early on in their evolution.

As humankind fulfills its mastery of the earthly plane, it can at long last discard the function of physical aging to explore the eternal nature of the soul in form—choosing just the right "age" to represent the soul's glory in that moment, fully open to and aware of the elasticity of the gravitational field. The body's divinity extends beyond the gravitational field, forever renewing the essence of soul/ spirit through form. Allow that essence to shine through the physical body. All who expand their minds into the larger Universe of Limitlessness will rejoice in the body's ability to perpetually renew itself as it claims its birthright of eternal youth. Birthdays will be celebrated into the 1,000's—so many candles on the cake—a brilliant reflection of the eternal Light of Source sparkling through Self's ageless wonder.

✧ The Process and the Goal ✧

November 2004

I'm tethered to my life goals like a leashed dog. Filled with inordinate amounts of determination/ striving, I can't imagine being content unless all ambitions are accomplished. But goals are cyclical, fulfilled one moment and then swallowed up in defeat/ futility the next. During times of frustrating fruitlessness, I curse the day I ever believed I could realize my dreams. What folly! What was I thinking? People say it's not the goal but the process that counts. But I'm not convinced.

Goals teach us how to focus intention. To meet our passionate objectives we must employ mind, heart, body and soul to fuel determination. Why not put all our eggs in one hot, potent, IMPORTANT basket—with full permission to unleash all of our zeal, longing, persistence. Then our lives would be on fire. We really care about where we're going. Everything would be at stake—nothing watered down.

But too much attachment to goals enslaves us to an idealized future that may never happen. Tethered, like the carrot before the donkey, we rotely strive toward the goal long after we've forgotten the passion that initiated our sense of possibility. Blindly we strain for years to get to a destination that may have lost its relevance. Ironically, goals are not endpoints. They are catalysts for the powerful process of aligning imagination with intention to fuel a vision of what we could achieve, and to finally arrive at our desires and feel nothing but hollow disappointment indicates that perhaps we haven't honored the process. If we don't bring consciousness to the process, we are blindsided when the goals manifest.

It's exhilarating to conjure up a goal—to suspend negativity long enough to see great possibilities. Excitedly we lunge into plans/action to realize our target—FAST. As we dare to stretch the envelope, inertia sets in. It's too hard…there's not enough time… all efforts doomed to failure… this goal isn't "realistic"… better pick a less ambitious goal—less important, less true, less compelling—to avoid profound DISAPPOINTMENT.

Maybe it's just not worth it to create goals. They only evoke suffering and self-judgment. To live goal-less would bring us into the preciousness of the present moment. But our creative imagination aches for a focal point for expressed advancement—to out-picture our evolution. Otherwise we blur into the vague quicksand of a pale, indistinct reality. To be goal-less is to be lost in space with a weakened, diffused focus not nearly meaty enough to manifest our earthly human intentions. So how do we set appropriate goals without being eaten alive or dumped into the trash heap of nullified possibility?

Non-attachment doesn't mean goalessness. We need to be in the game of life—ardently engaged in our enterprises. But goals shouldn't imprison us. We must strike the exquisite paradox of putting our ALL into the goal while simultaneously releasing it. Just because we choose the goal doesn't mean we have control over the process of its attainment. The moment we set our aim, the target develops a mind/will of its own and controls us! Impassioned goals take us down an unpredictable road fraught with obstacles, twists and turns. There are no direct routes to our dreams. The complexity within the process of goal attainment reveals the multilayered underpinnings of karmic material that express the soul's need to fulfill a particular purpose. Where we imagined we would end up is never where we actually arrive because of these deeper soul agendas. Goals require freedom from expectations to surprise us with the end product. Goals are fluid visions of becoming—not fixed points of accomplishment.

Our goals and process must dance together in a yin/ yang interplay of action and letting go. The goal is the known. The process is the unknown. The goal is the catalyst for listening to our soul. It initiates and contains the process. The process carries the goal. Both are mutually indispensable which creates a powerful alchemy. Goals fire up our soul's process of becoming by setting into motion deep desires that transport us through profound soul terrain. The ensuing process allows us to attain our goals and fulfill our soul's destiny. Goals seduce us into the mystery within the process as we put one foot in front of the other with no guarantees. The process strengthens our faith/ vision. Goals structure/ ground our focus and provide symbols for our passions. They reveal what gives us meaning.

The process carries all past-life issues with unrealized goals, fearful expectations of failure, and issues with the sacrifices required to attain goals. The process resolves our karma, cultivates wisdom, provides insight into our worst fears and wildest dreams and enhances self-esteem. Past-life cravings set the stage for current-life desires. Therefore we are responding to a powerful urge to resolve, balance, strengthen and heal the soul body through the fulfillment of specific goals. This is the challenge to break new ground in the process of goal fulfillment.

Goals need permeability to adapt to the process. The process continually informs the goal of its applicability to daily life. The process pierces the veils of illusion from moment to moment, which can be demoralizing, as we are hit with one disillusionment after the next in order to get to the core essence of our soul's goal. Our chosen destination point propels us into the void left in the wake of repeated disillusionments. This void appears to mock the ideals that convinced us to believe in our dreams—a perfect moment to trash our desires. From the Sea of Mystery, our goals seem to be sheer nonsense. But the vision that impresses itself on our hearts/ minds persists. The soul longs to achieve this incarnation's purpose, and will not accept a diluted version of its destination.

There is no backdoor escape from the soul's mandates. We have no choice but to be ferried forward toward our goals, as we gulp down disappointments, frustrations, disillusionments, and keep surfacing for air to see if the vision is clarified. Goals are ultimately the RESULT of the process' metamorphasizing impact. To attain a goal is to UNCOVER it—not to manifest it. Goals exist all along deep in our soul's heart, waiting for the day when the strength of our faith enables us to tolerate the heat and mystery within the process. Although the will is good for initiating goals (painting the vision on a blank canvas), it's helpless within the rigors of the process. There comes a point when we must surrender to the life inherent in our objective, as if the goal were an entity of its own, and let it take the lead in its dance with us. We can only be led to wherever its real destination lies. The goal, which structures our intent, ultimately unlocks the gateway to the great Sea of Becoming, where our soul's process of transformation is revealed in all of its divine glory.

The Tibetan applauds my exploration of this dance of attainment and teaches:

Humankind designs its goals through imagination, intuition, soul urges and past-life illusions. Choose goals wisely and then immediately release attachment. Embrace the ensuing process of riding the oceanic waves that zig zag self, topsy turvy, to the pot of gold at the end of the rainbow. Release all time agendas for manifest goals. Students have no idea what they are unleashing when they set their intention into motion because past-life issues surface the moment the commitment is made. All goals are karmically mandated and include a rigorous process of sloughing through childhood and past-life pain/ failure deep in the unconscious to clear the way for the soul's liberation.

Do not be enslaved to the ego's goals, which only serve the illusion of separateness, control, vanity, inflation. Rather, listen to the sweet promptings of the soul's persistent song which brings the genius inherent in the Divine Plan to route the journey into one's true magnitude. Grace lubricates movement toward the soul's goals while the personal will exhausts itself in the struggle to make the ego's goals important.

There is no goal that is out of alignment with the Divine Plan. Even "wrong" goals eventually lead self full circle, back to a truer starting plan coupled with a deeper vantage point gained from the dissolution of the initial goal. Then, released from the folly of karmically misdirected intentions, self eventually chooses the soul's razor's edge of accomplishment. Watch for obstinacy in sticking to goals that cause endless suffering. Observe the promptings from the soul to move in new and unexpected directions.

Many students go to their deathbed filled with remorse/ regret/ shame for unrealized goals, and expect the karmic board to judge their lack of achievement. But the karmic board evaluates the <u>process</u> unleashed by the goal, not the end result. It is the transmutation of the debris extracted by the goal that truly measures progress. To break undue levels of past-life striving, self may require a lifetime of forfeiting most ambitions. Other students may need to balance stifled/ aborted past-life initiatives with strong objectives requiring a lifetime of determination to fulfill.

It's not necessary to crack the whip with hardened willpower to fulfill intentions. Breathe with the goal. Pulse the process instead of relentlessly bearing down, the way one lays on the horn to override a traffic jam. Forward movement always yields to an ebbing back (magnetized by the soul's pull toward the familiar).

Goals are vehicles to practice manifestation, power of intention/ focus, persistence, discipline and letting go. The soul is honored and embodied by goal setting. True mastery is expressed through the sheer joy of creating arbitrary endpoints of delight that enliven self's essence into an exquisite process of unfoldment, in a mystery so profound that all goals bear fruit on the great Tree of Life.

✧ Time ✧

August 2002

Rushing to my computer today, already too late to meet the deadline for this month's column, I realize that I am once again right up against time. Just thinking about time makes me cranky. There is never enough of it. I am usually late, not early, with my life. Time slips through my fingers in spite of all attempts to hoard it. Racing through my day, I wonder what the rush is about. Sometimes I look at the clock and watch the hands go around and around. Time is melting my future into the present with a cold relentlessness akin to death. This feeds my frustrations with the limitations of earthly life. Ceaseless thoughts like, "I have no time anymore—I'm too busy," "I had no idea everything would take so much time," or "I can't get it all done in time," fuel my exasperation.

Yes, I am a true victim of time, struggling to stay ahead of it before it captures me in its tenacious grasp and rings the final bell we all dread: "Sorry, you are now out of time"—you've reached the end of the game, end of possibilities, end of options. It's over—just because of time?

Metaphysicians teach that time is an illusion. Yet to me it feels uncompromisingly real, "larger than life." Spiritual concepts fall short when I find myself getting less and less sleep because I don't have the time to fulfill all commitments in the day. Time closes in on me with a suffocating grasp that creates a feeling of compression and lack of space. Time and space are intricately linked together in a powerful illusion, enslaving us all.

I ineffectively try to outwit time, using my imagination to elongate it when I'm late for an appointment, hoping to do the impossible by making it there in half the time, or to shorten it when I'm sitting in the dentist chair, or counting the minutes until I leave on vacation. Surprisingly, when least expected, sometimes I do manage to make it to my destination in half the time. How?

My short-fused reaction to time comes from fighting it. In surrendering to time, we can relax, open and expand into infinity. Our belief that time is real creates suffering. When I don't watch the clock, time actually fades, opening a space to accomplish more. Is it my struggle with time that creates the compression? When I try to control time, I lose. To let go of the clock is to trust the natural unfoldment of things. The more deeply we are engaged in life, the more irrelevant time becomes. Flowers don't check their watches to see if they have bloomed on time.

"Time waits for no one"—except for the enlightened ones. If we place our imagination outside of time, we can open to the vast spectrum of possibilities, unbounded by the obstinate pulse of time. We need not be slaves to it. Time, relative to our experience, is more elastic than we might imagine. When in crisis, accident or trauma, time often "stops" as we are suspended between the worlds. Our egos are momentarily neutralized, allowing us a window on the true nature of reality—timelessness.

There is an old adage that describes the nature of earthly life: "Time is a way of preventing everything from happening at once." Our learning occurs within the time-space continuum. This dimension, carrying the illusion of limitation through time, obscures our holographic perceptual matrix and reorganizes it into a linear format manageable to our logical, lower minds. Time is like a Zen koan or a riddle from Merlin, teasing us to crack open its mystery. It is the delusional box we have to work our way out of in order to claim our wisdom.

Time heals. But does it? Time and space spring from the same dimension of the illusion of separation. When I am in pain, if I look at the clock, I often wonder if I can get through the pain. When I expand to a larger sense of timelessness, it eases the immediacy of the pain. I can then see that my wounds are part of a holographic simultaneous alchemical mix. I am not stuck in the "blackening" stage of alchemy, but have already become "gold."

When fully convinced of time, we experience limitation, boundaries, form, a container for our boundless Self. To persuade the boundless Self that it is containable is futile. Something appears sacrificed in the process. Is it time that washes away our pain, or the psychological distance resulting from increased wisdom and expanded perspective that allows us to detach from our wounds? Great healers like Master Jesus have demonstrated that all wounds, physical, emotional or spiritual, can be "miraculously" healed instantaneously outside of time.

Time is simply a measuring device for our process, which is perceived as a linear unfoldment, from one point to the next. We forget the multiplicity of the soul that recognizes all lifetimes in a simultaneous reality. Parallel lifetimes defy logic. Time, a cloak that descends when we land on earth, creates a sense of urgency to motivate us to cherish this precious opportunity to be in form.

Everyone talks about running out of time. Even children, usually accustomed to a rich sense of never-ending time, are feeling rushed. What's happening? Is time really speeding up, or are we all losing our minds?

The more I try to master time, the more it speeds up. Is this a sign of failure? Or am I truly "running out" of time—evolving faster and faster through the band of dimensional energy called time, out the other side into the realms beyond?

The Tibetan eagerly jumps in to catch the sphere of time and throw it outside the boundaries of the ballpark:

Yes, humankind is making a shift in its perception of time. As the collective evolves, it realizes the illusion of time. The dimension that holds the earthly plane has dramatically increased its vibratory rate a thousand-fold since 1990. Time is a permeable veil that is thinning as the accelerating energies speed up the vibratory rate of the earth plane. Heightened vibrations dissolve the density of time.

Humankind perceives time as speeding up because the logical mind registers these accelerated energies through a spatial context. With energy stepped up, life appears to be moving faster. This perception is not only the result of advanced technology increasing the pace of life. It is humankind's energetic response to heightened vibrations.

Technological progress is the <u>outcome</u> of these increased energies. Advanced technology provides heightened connection among all peoples around the globe. This diminishes the illusion of space and shatters the spell of time. Increased vibrations allow the old paradigm to dissolve. The entire contextual framework for humankind expands, opens, and lightens. Time is revealed for the illusion that it is. For example, when a cassette tape is rewound, it quickens as it approaches the end. Then it stops! Similarly, in this perceptual shift, humankind can no longer attach to the density of time as the veils thin. Current potent vibratory rates pulse rapidly, driving students into the "timelessness" of the present moment.

Humankind is still desperately clinging to its old paradigm by trying to reference this heightened energy through the familiar context of time. This creates a friction between the emerging consciousness and old collective false beliefs. The friction generates the frenzy about time. Humankind is literally being spun off the wheel of time and space. Let go.

From where the Masters sit, everything has already happened. Existence in the heavenly realms is not subject to the boundaries of time and space. Our consciousness extends in a circular, non-linear fashion. There is no beginning or end to one's being and therefore to one's experience. This eternal flow of life is the core matrix for all beings in Source's Creation. We perceive the students' earthly incarnations as mere blinks of an eye expressing a simultaneous reality that is the unifying principle of All.

The central purpose of time is to slow down the vibratory rate of the soul so that it can interface with the dense gravitational field of the earthly plane. The soul extends itself into a format that appears to be a progression of events, measured through a global incremental perception of the pulsation of energy—time. There, it cultivates awareness of its essential divinity through form. Form heightens the experience of energy, light, love, and evolution.

Time was created to remind the student of the temporal nature of earthly life. The harnessed world of time provides a counterpart to the immortal nature of the soul. Time is a reminder that the earth plane is but one aspect of the soul's experience. Impermanence heightens the dramatic experience of being human. In this amplified drama, the soul fills with color, wisdom, power and love.

When humankind was young in its evolution, like a toddler it required greater boundaries. Time served as a "playpen." Humankind was teased into believing that time was real, that there wasn't a larger yard outside the walls of the playpen. This appropriately contained humankind until it matured enough to assume increased levels of responsibility for itself and its impact on mother earth and the galaxy. Time corralled humankind's free will and creative power until it was experientially wise enough to handle it. Like a training ground or boot camp, time offered a strict program within which humankind could refine its collective consciousness beyond the illusion of separation.

The rigor of time's limitations has never sat well with humankind. Frustrated and cramped, students have challenged themselves to push through the veil of time. As one's awareness opens, uneasiness with time immediately surfaces. The disturbance signals the emergence of clarity, revealing one's eternal nature.

As humankind matures and awakens, they will collectively access the vast realm beyond time. Then they will no longer energize the "time" program that has been the central contextual framework for earth school. As the collective releases the false belief that "time is real," a profound level of light will pour forth into the minds, hearts and bodies of humankind, flooding the earth with love, and revealing the truth of eternity.

It is now "time" to open to infinity. Remember the grace of timelessness. Allow self to create life experiences outside of time. Imagine energizing one's intentions and desires beyond the context of time. Release all expectations about how much time is required to accomplish something. Trust that all karmic mandates for this incarnation will be fulfilled regardless of whether self references time or not!

The unfoldment of self's magnitude has already happened. Self can relax outside the illusory grid work of time, which has been nothing more than fake bars on a window designed to convince the students to stay in their rooms until they have internalized their divinity and rooted themselves in wisdom. Once this is accomplished, they are free to exercise their creative options in ways that will only enhance, not threaten, intergalactic life.

Take off the straightjacket of time. Trust that self will be more efficient than ever, uncompromised by the loss of energy from anxiety about not having enough time. It is impossible to not have enough time. Challenge self to trust the timelessness. Let go of the clock's illusion and attune to the already enlightened Self that "speedily" magnetizes and propels self into an embrace with all that has already happened.

And what a Celebration it is!

✧ The Interface Between Realism and Vision ✧

February 2006

Now is the time to envision a brand-new paradigm. We need vision to pull ourselves forward into our ultimate potential. But how can we open our view shed to what might be possible while we're holding on for dear life to the world we've always known?

Most of us live in "reality prisons" that confine us to the past. Our expectations fall in the box of our conditioning. The logical mind keeps us practical, predictable and careful. But rational thinking forces us to "ration" out our imagination. This prevents our imagination from sweeping us to the edge of the mystery that spawns all true visions. Too few are willing to slip into the unknown to ideate. We usually fish inside our reality box for visions—flat, passionless, predictable, small, stagnant images fostered in a bog of stifling rationality. There we assume that we are safe and sound in the known, but ironically are in danger of under-extension.

Paradoxically, without realism we dysfunctionally float off into pipe dreams. Pie-in-the-sky fantasies usually fall to earth with a thud that wounds the spirit and hardens the heart. We protect ourselves from this disillusionment with an ironclad realism that disparages flights of fancy as foolish meandering into never-never land. How can we use our realism to protect us from delusion without limiting fruitful panoramas of possibility?

We all want to manifest our visions. But are we stuck with overriding metaphysical laws—the underpinnings of our "realistic" parameters? If our vision strays too far from theses precepts, will we be bucking the "way of things" and fall into a chasm of distortion? If we create visions that counter our true requirements, such as, "I am floating in a sea of perfection and consequently have no work to do on my soul in this lifetime," then we're attempting to live beyond the gravitational field. Flights of fancy may fling us too far out onto the etheric fringe where manifestation is impossible. Yet we must travel to the brink of these parameters in order to seek the impressions cosmically designed to guide us through this Threshold of Change.

When we invest our energy into the manifestation of a vision that proves improbable, we become frustrated, swear off all envisioning, and attempt to lead a realistic life. We seesaw between an intense commitment to dreams and a hardened determination to keep our feet on the ground—no more visions for us!

We must create a belief system that holds the interface between vision and realism, for without vision we can't employ the imagination to stretch us to our cutting edge. All leaps of faith are fueled by vision. But if we're unwilling to accept today's earthly parameters, we'll never materialize our goals. We'll suffer chronic disappointments as the tide of realism relentlessly washes away the sand castles of our visions.

What is the source of our visions? Do they simply carry our desire to escape the restrictive laws that govern humanity? Or are they transmissions from our soul that remind us who we really are? We usually discard these implausible glimpses of our destiny with the self-admonishment to "get real." This narrow version of reality wet-blankets the inspired imagination and sense of possibility. Although we assume that vision and realism are like oil and water, they actually *do* mix. Mastery of the human condition requires us to find a way to believe in these unlikely visions with a white-hot passion that literally melts the confines of our fathomed reality to allow for expansion and leaps of faith.

We're required to bring the mystery into the known. As we take a stand in the flow that envisions our evolved self, we learn to trust that, ultimately, "reality" is malleable, receptive, in sync with our destiny and magnetically charged to manifest our evolution. The soul's growth insists that we find a way out of the reality box. Realism is based on what we've already encountered. So why would we give it the clout to block us from touching what we haven't yet experienced? It takes courage to follow these new soul visions while our outworn reality-alarms fill us with disbelief.

The emerging paradigm brings visions that seem diametrically opposed to our normal expectations. This is a 180-degree shift in the collective consciousness. Hunger for control compels us to rigidly adhere to conventional expectations in an attempt to deny the creative mandate to envision the new human being. It's much easier to stay in our comfort zone than to explore strange new frontiers. Visions catapult us forward. We don't have the option to designate the visionary work to others who seem more inspired, willing, or courageous. We ALL share the same karma to pry ourselves away from our "reality securities" long enough to touch the outskirts of our true human potential.

Is our version of reality grounding or imprisoning? What is it that allows some people to follow their vision and succeed in its implementation, however unfeasible, while others pursue visions that never manifest? An intense determination is required to anchor vision in form, coupled with a desire to collaborate with our soul's unfoldment process, no matter what the odds against us may seem to be.

Vision is an enhancement of reality, not an escape. We must employ realism to help us manifest our visions. True visions spring from the soul's relentless presence in our psyche. Given half a chance, a vision of our soul's agenda for this lifetime pops up on our internal computer screen, eager to be received, honored, and implemented. All we have to do is ask and trust these precious clues to our unfoldment despite images that are vague or incomplete.

The only conclusive reality we must honor is the karma that carries this lifetime's lessons. If we use visions to escape our karma, they fail. All the fanciful visions in the world won't release us from our soul's course work until we've learned our lessons. Once those lessons are fulfilled, our visions tell us to move on, and what direction to take.

We may fear our visions because they propel us into the mystery. Often we can't identify with these images of our evolving self. Fear of failure to manifest these visions compels us to take refuge in a "realism" that rationalizes an unwillingness to even try. Our actuality perspective is usually based on beliefs handed to us as children, which also include the collective "reality matrix" that prescribes who we are, what we do, what we can be. We have to integrate our history to ground our vision. Otherwise, our vision stays on the etheric plane, weakened because it loses the powerful pull of the gravitational field, and this feeds the acid of disappointment that erodes the conviction required to manifest vision.

I'm amazed how trees manage to grow on inhospitable hard ledge. The tree finds soil and a way to take root through cracks and breaks in the rock. It follows the path of least resistance. The force of the soul is equally resolute. Eventually it will establish all visions that reflect its truth. Our encrusted realism, the "hard ledge," ultimately yields to the soul's doggedness. Our visions unveil the openings in the rock, however miniscule. Then we can plunge our intention deep into these fissures to bring in new life that seems inconceivable. The key is to release our historic-societal-familial conditioning and reorient ourselves to the soul as the ultimate realizer.

The Tibetan appears in a crystal-clear vision and teaches:

Etheric-plane visions are the central organizing principle behind earthly life. Humankind cannot stay purely in the realm of vision because it is mandated to manifest divinity in form.

Some students who fondly remember their pre-incarnate environment of ephemeral unfolding visions aren't fully committed to the earthly plane and are reluctant to materialize these images. Others feel lost when these etheric impressions, so clearly delineated through the imaginal valve, appear incongruous with their attachment to established reality.

Currently, all etheric visions are out picturing the rising shift in consciousness. Humankind must trust these visions even though there's no lower-mind framework for such remarkable terrain. The lower mind's attachment to these visions only distorts and blocks their manifestation. Then the student, feeling betrayed by Source simply because of a misperception of vision, reverts to the "logical," the "rational." But that only imprisons his/her consciousness in the past. Because the emerging consciousness hasn't fully revealed itself; incoming visions appear hazy. The veil between the dimensions is not yet completely dissolved, but one can playfully peek around that veil to catch a glimpse of the new light factor that illuminates an extraordinary sense of potential

Vision is the wellspring of all great archetypes of creation, invention, artistry and human understanding. Full-scale commitment to these "gifts of sight" has allowed humanity to evolve, even though visions may mutate from moment to moment. The onset of metamorphosis in the human condition is too vast and rapid to hold tight to one vision. Therefore, students must commit to the process *of envisioning. Accept the bafflement that these flowing, changing visions catalyze. TRUST that they herald total transformation. As humankind softens its "realistic mind," it will catch a glimpse of the New World Order that awaits right around the next bend in the road. From this glorious vista, the new realism sets in. Then humanity truly comprehends that all visions are divine messengers that open the mind and imagination, guiding the soul's spirit to its Divine Destiny.*

✧ Animal Friends ✧

July 2001

What is that exquisite love showered upon us from our beloved animal friends? So often in times of deep pain, darkness and hopelessness, the sweet lick of a rough tongue and a warm, wet nuzzle on my cheek has literally saved me from plummeting into a vortex of bottomless despair. Looking into the eyes of my beloved "fur-babies" (three cats and two dogs), anger melts, fear subsides as love fills my heart, clearing my vision and uplifting my soul. Through their eyes, I am reminded of the universal love that unites us all. I remember that I am not alone in this world. I am unconditionally loved for all of who I am, regardless of what I see as my endless imperfections.

Our animal companions bring us into the realm of total acceptance. In their world, we are absolutely free to be ourselves as they teach us to take time to play, walk, marvel at nature, roll around on the floor, howl at the moon, sing silly songs, sit patiently while they curl up on our laps to receive their quota of daily petting, and step off the treadmill of unceasing responsibilities long enough to sink our hands and faces into the delicious pleasure of soft, rich, luscious, living fur.

Faithfulness, honor, reverence and compassion are their gifts to the human race. They teach us the art of DEVOTION. What would the world be like if we honored each other with even half the level of devotion our animal friends lavish upon us? They hold no grudges when we disappoint them; return sweet kisses and purrs when we off-load the frustration of a difficult day onto their sensitive ears; remain patient when our unexpected delays keep them waiting hours longer than their natural schedule for eating, walking, and playing; nurture our healing process by curling themselves around us when we are sick; adore us with their eyes, no matter what we look like; and are always ready to spontaneously connect with exuberant joy.

They often "take the hit" for us when negative energy is directed our way. We may not even see the negative energy, but it is palpable to our animal friends. They gladly sacrifice themselves to receive the brunt of any harmful energy rather than allow us to get hurt. Sometimes they get sick when we are sick, taking on some of our toxicity to work through their bodies so that we are not too burdened by our cleansing process. Their unique love is truly a balm to the soul—soothing all the hurt places, enhancing our instinctual response to life, reminding us to be in the present, and bringing a smile to our faces even in the darkest of times.

It is not uncommon for my clients, wondering if something is really wrong with them, to confess to me that they grieved more for the loss of their dog or cat than for the death of a parent. I explain that far from being "wrong," such grief is their psyche registering the loss of a *quality* of absolute love found nowhere else on the planet. This pure animal love, as opposed to the human emotion, seems to transcend our earth plane of duality. There are no price tags attached to it, just the infinite outpouring of a steady heart not susceptible to the ambivalence of our human condition.

Because our relationship with them infuses us with all-encompassing love, the death of an animal friend brings up every loss we have ever suffered. When I had to "put down" my eight-year old German shepherd, Star, due to inoperable cancer, I was devastated, and continued to actively grieve for over two years. Not even joy at the arrival of my wonderful Belgian sheepdog, Zulu, four months after Star's death, could mitigate the internal ache of longing to hold her one more time and melt into the mystery deep within her wolf eyes.

I know that Star is with me on the spirit plane, watching over things, reminding me to take good care of myself. Always my protector in life, in spirit she walks by my side, forever loyal. She is with all the animal companions I have had the honor to love in this lifetime, circling around me in eternal devotion.

At long last we humans are evolving our sensitivity to animal friends. It's impossible for me to say, "Zulu was *only* a dog," or "my cat Zsa Zsa is *only* a cat". They are so much more than our society's stereotypical perceptions. Collectively, we are finally beginning to appreciate their emotional life, their sense of mission and purpose, the complex dynamics they have with us and each other, as well as their own unique sets of karmic conditions that govern their present life. Animal communicators are becoming more widely recognized as viable, credible mediators to bridge the gap between our world with the sometimes unfathomable world of our pets. The more we heighten our communication with our animal friends, the more we realize the precious quality of connectedness inherent among all beings.

The Tibetan listens to my words of animal adoration with a knowing smile on his face, remembering his own joyful relationships with animals in previous earthly incarnations. He adds:

Domesticated animals make the soul choice to be of full service to humankind. The earthly counterpart to the angelic realm, they offer a great field of support to all who are willing to receive it. These earthly angelic emissaries cannot intervene with the destiny of their "owners'" individual karma. However, they can soften the impact by acting as filters for karmic debris. Through these filters, they absorb some of the difficulty by sharing their guardians' energetic field, helping to shoulder the karmic storms circling throughout.

Animal companions are particularly attuned to fear and grief—projecting a field of safety that restructures their guardians' anxious energy into a feeling of protection. In times of grief, they serve as bridges to the spiritual plane. Blending their energy with the field of the deceased loved ones, they heighten their guardians' ability to "touch" the etheric bodies of the loved ones.

Other experiences of grief have to do with loss of self, and they are assuaged by the animal's ability to mirror back, through their eyes, the full authentic self that is the guardian's ultimate truth. 100% responsible to their service at all times, domesticated animals' purpose is infused with dignity and determination.

The attuned animal takes on the psychological and spiritual complexes of his owner. If the owner carries great rage, the animal absorbs the rage, feeling compelled to take unnecessary aggressive stands. The animal understands the fear base from which the rage springs forth, but may not be able to crack out of the protective aggression until the owner makes a breakthrough of his own. Therefore it is critically important for the owner to take full responsibility for negative emotions, and to encourage beloved animal companions not to carry this negativity. The karmic contract mandating that animal friends must help shoulder the physical, emotional and mental climate of their owners can then shift. Then the pet demonstrates openings in the auric field that allow greater levels of light to penetrate the wounded areas within their owner, so that the owner may evolve to a heightened state of consciousness.

Animals extend forth to the earth plane from a collective soul group. Although they are individuated in form, they share a "Higher Self" with all the other members of their species. Within this group soul, their telepathic ability is heightened, allowing them to collectively respond to all loving or hurtful actions that touch any one of them, at any time, anywhere on the planet. Amplified telepathic communication enables them to tune in to the minds and hearts of humankind with great sensitivity of perception. This enhances their ability to lean into the soul of their guardian, thereby making their energetic presence felt no matter how clouded over their guardian's auric field may be. This magnified merge with their guardian's energy body allows the full impact of their angelic "love boost" to be received.

Many animals' lives are considerably shorter than humankind's life span so that people learn to cherish their presence. This profound love bond creates a pathway for the guardian to attune to the deceased pet's presence on the spirit plane. Animal friends are continually connected throughout their owners' lives, serving them from the spirit plane and demonstrating the linkage that is only a veil away. Students can use their loving bond with a deceased animal to break through the illusion of that veil, imaging the very real contact of the beloved pet sitting on their lap (root and second chakras) or chest (heart chakra), natural places for the animal spirit to settle into extending full devotion and communion.

The accelerated energies currently impacting the earth plane are not only speeding up humankind's evolution but the evolution of animals as well. The animal kingdom is releasing old instinctual responses of aggressive territoriality that led to indiscriminate warfare among species. The collective animal souls are also releasing illusions of scarcity, allowing them to share their bounty on all levels. The refinement of their energies transforms their instinctual need to eat flesh as they discover the abundant innate life force that sustains them far beyond meat and water. This allows them to serve Mother Earth in her awakening as evolving animal consciousness conducts amplified love through their channels into the center of her being.

As the collective souls of animal friends refine their energies, they incarnate on the earth as "special pets," seeming to read minds, to show up just when needed, to "train" themselves, lovingly embrace other animals—including those that might once have been seen as threats—and transmit just the right message to their human guardians at crucial moments. In this accelerated evolution, the "peaceable kingdom" returns to the plane—a clear reflection of the Garden of Eden, where all beings harmonize.

From the inner Center of Deep Gratitude, offer animals an open heart, lovingly caring for their needs as they offer their service to you. Expect their wisdom to override your knowing. Follow them to the interface where instinctual prowess and spiritual wisdom meet. Allow their loyalty to demonstrate what really is important—the Eternal Unbreakable Bond invulnerable to negativity or death. Let these blessed teachers pave the way for telepathic communion among all beings.

This dissolves the differential illusion of separation...the false hierarchy that places humankind on top and the rest of the animal kingdom below. Recognizing animals as Saintly Benefactors frees humankind to accept and embrace the gifts they offer, and follow as animal friends pioneer the road to collective awakening.

✧ <u>Part Three</u> ✧

HUMAN RELATIONSHIPS

✧ Overcoming Isolation ✧

December 2003

How are we going to move into the shared communion/ community required to catalyze our collective awakening if we still feel so isolated from each other? The Tibetan describes our essential interconnectedness like a string of lights on a Christmas tree. Automatically, as one of us lights up, awakens, we all light up. Yet many of us allow our illusion of separation to extend itself into a profound existential experience of penetrating isolation. Even in large groups we still feel isolated. Regardless of whether we live in large cities or rural communities, we might as well be alone in the Arctic wasteland given our widespread loneliness. What generates this sense of inner exile? Why are we perpetuating such disconnect from each other when essentially we all share the same quest for aliveness, fulfillment, joy, love, inner peace, success, spirituality?

Ultimately, we all walk the same pathway. Is our attachment to isolation the last frontier to be transmuted before we can pass through the gateway of liberation? Our shared enlightenment depends on letting go of this illusion of mutual alienation.

Throughout much of this lifetime (in past lives too), I have identified myself as a lone wolf. My visceral negative gut reaction to society convinced me that I would be alone baying at the moon for many more lifetimes. I have used my attachment to isolation as a shield against the inevitable disappointments experienced in human relationships. Not willing to have my heart broken, suffer betrayal, feel misunderstood and judged, I refused to join the human parade—preferring to wait life out watching silently from behind the wilderness in my soul. This has afforded me a great vantage point on humanity. But I forfeited the fulfillment of deep human contact rich in duality, mystery, love, support.

With the accelerated energies kicking up my core karmic debris, I still struggle with the existential crisis inherent in isolation, feeling distinctly separate, alienated and lonely. Yet this inner experience doesn't jibe with my outer life rich in human relationships, community, marriage, love. This core of isolation rises up in my psyche like the Baltic Sea with icy shafts of loneliness chilling my bones, contracting my heart and filling my mind with pessimism and negativity. Self-quarantined (when false beliefs urge me to keep my space from others), the vacuousness of isolation settles into my soul, dropping me onto the desolate inner landscape of emptiness.

I find that many of my clients also struggle with loneliness and this frigid world of withdrawal. How do we connect with others who seem caught up in their own lives, not interested, unavailable? Many of us try to join groups, find friends, develop community only to recoil when it seems that others don't really know who we are, can't perceive our reality, don't care about us. Self judgment sets in, scolding that we're not good enough to be a part of the community that appears "out there" with its doors locked, entrance unattainable. We conclude that it's easier to go it alone, with an unnatural attachment to self-sufficiency. God forbid we should be "co-dependent" on each other! After all, we insist that we have everything we need inside of ourselves. Yet paradoxically, we preach that "no man is an island."

Our communities lack rituals that bond and unite people. While we may participate in gatherings, how many of us actually share our souls with each other? Together on the surface, meeting for dinners, walks, sports events, family outings, festivities, we give the appearance of being connected. But we often go home feeling emptier than when we left. Why?

Our isolation supports our greatest illusion—that we are actually alone. How can we be truly alone if we are all one? This riddle still plagues my mind when I'm in situations that strike that deep frigid chord of isolation longstanding in my soul. I, as well as others, usually react to the aberration of isolation by separating out, withdrawing, disconnecting. This becomes the self-fulfilling fallacy that it is possible to separate from each other.

As I evolve, my relationships grow deeper, richer, more fulfilling. This catalyzes the inevitable healing crisis that flushes up deeper levels of my original isolation wound. As my outer life fills with community, my soul, reverberating with ancient echoes of self imposed isolation, endures the transmutation of poisons spewing from unceasing banishment. I stand at the crossroads of tasting, touching true interconnectedness, while being flooded with the memories of the lone wolf who insists that no one can really enter my soul and love who I am.

We all stand at this crossroads as we confront the spiritual call to greater community, interdependence, collective awakening, and shared transformation. We can't deny that we're all simmering in the collective alchemical cauldron together as our karma melts away and transmutes into expanded consciousness. We must take the leap of trust and dare to believe that lifetimes of isolation have been based on the delusion of estrangement. We're not destined to have our souls shrivel from the loneliness springing from the existential hinterlands of this wasting disease called isolation.

Many of us are feeling more isolated than ever as we're dramatically blown open up by the powerful energies bombarding our planet. We assume that others won't understand this strange, disorienting process we're undergoing. So we hide our process from the feared judgments of others at a time when we need to connect more than ever. Cemented behind the walls around our souls, we suffer unnecessarily. In order to make it possible to "go the distance" we must share this intense process. If we fall prey to the seduction of the call of isolation, this mighty collective spiritual endeavor will fail.

Often when we go through trauma, it seems that no one can hear our pain or recognize our wounds. This "proves" the false belief that fundamentally we function on discordant wavelengths undecipherable to each other. We feel invisible, de-valued, unimportant, retarded, alienated, frightened. This inevitably leads to isolation from ourselves, our truth, which is then mirrored back to us through a chasm of unrelated ness with others. When isolated from ourselves, our passion dies.

After lifetimes of isolation we get pretty good at it as we take pride in our self-sufficiency while hoping that ultimately we don't need anyone other than ourselves. We think that separatism makes life so much easier. But regardless of the trials of relationships, it is only through our human connectedness that we can begin to imagine the realm of Divine Union that unites us all and burns away notions of unrelated ness. When we venture past our fortress of exile we discover that essentially we are all the same and therefore not unreachable, unfathomable, and unlovable by others. To release the notion that we're outcasts from our communal essence dismantles the stronghold of disconnect.

The Tibetan walks toward me arm in arm with all the other Masters that guide our earthly world demonstrating the Cosmic Fellowship of All. He teaches:

Isolation wounds start with the monadic imprint. The monad is the original level of Self's being when Source split off from Itself. The monad extended forth to the Oversoul, then to the soul and finally to the earthly plane. This original level of splitting off created a monadic imprint—an illusion, misinterpretation, that Source could actually disconnect from Itself and therefore that human beings could actually be severed from their spiritual Source and Universe. Humankind's assignment is to see through the illusion of separation, betrayal and abandonment from Source at the monadic level. After releasing this distortion, students then understand that Source's extension of Itself did not reflect separation but rather <u>enhanced expression</u>.

Everyone needs to relish in their solitude, bask in individual space and self-exploration, for periods of time in order to release blinding attachments to others, to reclaim and define self, to heal and rejoice in singularity. However, this elected solitude is not the same as feeling trapped in a prison of isolation because self can't fit in, connect or relate to community. When students believe that they are forced to be alone because no one will love them, or because they refuse to love others, then the suffering of loneliness sets in like a dismal murky veil in the soul which instantly catalyzes the original monadic distortion that endorses the myth that Source has turned It's back on humankind. Humankind personalizes this by believing that others can't relate or are not available, and that somehow alone, unprepared, unloved, humankind is being asked to exist in a void with no support from others, the earth, the universe and Source. Existential pain carries this shock of apparent disconnect—the monadic imprint.

Usually the demoralizing chill of isolation makes its presence felt in childhood at that moment when the child first senses his/her difference from others in the tribe/ family/ community or through an experience of being let down by others in a crucial and intimate way. Then the child begins to identify self as separate from others which often leads to external self-exile in order to preserve the sense of unique self or internal self-exile while trying to conform externally. Either reaction touches the karmic bedrock of isolation carrying past life selves desperate to connect. Ironically, no one has ever been alone in this or in greater worlds.

When students begin to open up spiritually they expect to access an increased communion with all beings. However, their opening process automatically clears deeper and deeper levels of past life isolation which creates the experience that they are further than ever from their spiritual goal of enhanced oneness. This reinforces the common false belief that as one opens spiritually there will be increased difficulty relating to others (still spiritually asleep) which makes it harder to stay connected to one's community. Remember that this surfacing isolation is being purged and transmuted, as a critical component in the transition to the endpoint of rich, heartfelt togetherness.

To heal this isolation, imagine tapping into the Colossal Electrical Network of Cohesion—the nexus that displays and sparks awareness of interconnectedness among all beings and within all Universes. When students feel this grid, as an electrical fusion with the frequency of all others, attachment to isolation is broken. Then students taste the Divine Embrace that holds all beings together on the lap of the Great Celestial Mother. Her milk of acceptance, love, and nurturance eradicates the illusion of existential emptiness and fills humankind's soul with sweet alliance.

Do not take pride in isolation, as if it is a feather in one's cap to endure/ survive completely alone. This is a time on the earthly plane when all levels of distortion around disconnect must be released in order for students to catalyze each other's awakening. Now is the time to reference common ground, to breathe each other's dreams /visions, to recognize self in other, and to find the courage to reach out to each other in mutual recognition of divine linkage. To reach out is to challenge the illusion of isolation and truly remember that humankind springs from one root system based on the essential joining of all beings.

This outreach accelerates everyone's awakening process as they remember to share deeply of their souls with each other, to allow themselves to relate to all. This expressed fellowship ignites all the lights on the Christmas tree. Humankind is then dispatched through the gateway of collective enlightenment that melts away the pain of isolation and transports the earthly plane to a greater consciousness (the fifth dimension) which manifests the ultimate Divine Society. The dark force that would seduce humankind into believing that the monadic imprint was based on Source's exile of Its children is shattered through this camaraderie of shared liberation.

The beauty of the birth of the New Cosmic Day on earth is that it is <u>impossible</u> for students to enter the fifth dimensional portal *alone. It is mandatory that this spiritual emergence happens in groups to display the essential fabric, brotherhood/ sisterhood, of the human condition. Therefore all beings who would pass through the portal must release their fortress of isolation complete with its hollow loneliness in order to hold hands into and through this dimensional shift. Then all previous lifetimes of isolation carrying the monadic distortion are instantly healed, and collectively at long last humankind can experience itself at the monadic level as a differentiated, but profoundly related, expression of Source's essence.*

When that collective understanding gels in the shared heart of humankind, the entire Universe will resound in joyous celebration of Oneness and no one's voice, no one's heart, no one's soul will ever be left out in the cold of the existential wasteland of isolation. So COME TOGETHER WITH EACH OTHER and break the curse of disunion. Teach each other, love each other, heal each other, remind each other that all are on the pathway and all are popular, accepted, received in the Greater Community of the Macrocosm. To begin each day with the knowledge that self is deeply loved and joined with all others fills the unremitting sunken ache of loneliness with song, sweet nectar, and the exquisite lightness of being that marries all together in the exalted Blessing of Oneness.

✧ Soul Mates ✧

June 2001

We all want to meet our soul mate. We dream of that one person who would fulfill our soul's deepest desires, and imagine the heavens bringing us together in some wildly synchronistic event. The moment we look into each other's eyes, we will be captivated by our souls' lightning recognition of our pre-determined agreement to blend as one. In that instant, the world will stop turning, our hearts will pound in recognition. All darkness will fade and will be filled with sunshine and joy, certain that everything is possible at long last!

Are we just corny romantics caught in fantastic illusions of going off into the sunset to live together happily ever after? Or are we sensing a profound yearning within, reminding us of our Higher Self's agreement to join with another soul in mystical union?

Collectively, we are moving into greater alignment with our soul, which heightens the need for reunion with soul mates. Discontented with ego-based relationships, we ache for something deeper, grander, and more compelling in our connection with a beloved. This powerful bond with our soul's cherished counterpart has an eternal quality to it, as if it could continue beyond death, having survived many shared lifetimes.

There is nothing wrong with ego-based relationships. They can be quite fulfilling, delightfully enhancing, expanding and healing to our sense of self identity. Our immediate emotional, physical and mental needs can be met with great satisfaction, like a delicious dinner at a lovely romantic restaurant. We bask in each other's gaze through the candlelight, taking a moment to enjoy the sweet pleasure of loving and being loved. We feel good about ourselves as we soak in the companionship of our connection. We might get along "famously" and learn to function together as "quite a team." Other may view us as the "perfect couple," so convinced are we that we have the "best thing going."

Then the unspeakable happens—whether it is after two, ten or thirty years. We split up, leaving friends and family thoroughly stunned! We can't help wondering whether we simply got bored with each other. We decided that the romance played out after endless renditions of the same old romantic dinner, or that we outgrew each other. Or perhaps there was a deeper hunger within, despite our satiated egos.

"Why are there so many divorces"? We ask ourselves. Some people believe we just don't have the "staying power" we used to. If so, then why not? A deeper relational paradigm is emerging, irresistible beyond all that we have known, stirring our soul with restless anticipation of something "so much more" that could be possible. This is the need for a partner who would recognize and touch our soul at its core level, unimpeded by the demands and distractions of the ego

Personality-based relationships that do not evolve into soul union fall away, unable to be tethered through the fulfillment of ego-needs alone. Those of us who decide to continue to live on the ego level find another partner, content to simply feel good again. The rest of us "soul-hungry" people, continue to search for the true beloved, determined to go beyond all boundaries in our quest for divine union.

Sometimes, when meeting our soul mate, there appears to be limited common ground to justify our intense sense of connectedness. Values may differ, perceptions clash, personal preferences seem to be at war with each other, disharmony over religious practices, political views, ect. Yet a tenacious energy glues us together beyond all personal protests of impossibility, danger and fear. The soul's passion, once caught on fire, ignites the heart chakra with such force that the ego/ personality fades into the background, disoriented and overwhelmed by a strange, unspeakable sense of destiny with this other person—someone who "I never would have chosen."

In soul mate liaisons, our egos often go hungry, frustrated with the lack of "sugar" in the relationship's diet. The purpose of the soul mate partnership is not to fatten the ego, but to evolve the soul. This evolution requires total surrender. Self is challenged to mature into a higher state of consciousness through this union. The ego feels as if it is taking a beating when former soul-level dynamics surface in the relationship. These dynamics reflect the soul's karmic core pattern of false beliefs. Being caught in the alchemical cauldron of a very hot relationship certainly turns up the heat on defense structures, lifetimes old, needing to be broken down to allow for the two souls' magnitude to emerge.

We envision our soul mate on the etheric plane—filled with lighted perfection—elegant beyond words in his/her reflection of our greatest possibility. It's easy to believe we have met our soul mate while in the throes of freshly discovered passion, usually good for a joy-ride of about six bliss-filled months. Then the glamour wears off. We are "stuck" with this other person and all of his/her flaws. In the dense limitations of their human condition, we wonder, if this could really be our soul mate.

Yet the energetic chord binding soul mates is unbreakable, able to endure the greatest of human disillusionment. This staying power has the potency of nuclear energy, giving us the feeling that we just can't get away from this individual no matter how much our ego kicks and screams.

How do we recognize our soul mate? Often our meeting is serendipitous. We can't force it, but we can invoke it. We feel a strong energetic response to the person regardless of how casual our introduction. There is an energetic rush—a deep sense of familiarity and recognition, as if we have known each other before. A transpersonal force exists between us, far greater than our ego-based identities. As the relationship unfolds, our sense of connectedness to our individual soul is heightened, along with an expanded awareness of our karmic past. Gazing into each other's eyes, we can actually see or sense former lives together and the karmic contract we carried into this incarnation.

This soul contract includes reaping the rewards of positive karma as well as resolving negative karma. There are areas in the relationship filled with grace, as if supported by angels from the heavenly realms. These areas reflect previous lives together, when we mastered the art of loving at its highest level. Free to bask in wondrous love in this lifetime, we discover a source of eternal treasure reminding us of our infinite nature.

Inevitably, negative karma will rear its ugly head. How can we grow to trust, much less love each other, if we have possibly tormented or even killed one another in previous lives? What were those ancient struggles? How do they reflect our souls' false beliefs? Our current relationship enlivens those old dynamics with such precision that at times we wonder where all the rage, jealousy or fear is coming from. Navigating this tumultuous terrain requires an unshakable determination to unite in spite of age-old karmic storms circling through the causal (karmic) body for hundreds or even thousands of years. Through this union we learn how to truly love.

In 1991, planning to begin channeling again after a two-year break, I told the Tibetan that I needed a soul partner in order to fulfill my karmic agreement to offer his teachings and establish the School of the Golden Discs. Suddenly, I felt compelled to move to a carriage house in Montague, a small, quiet village in western Massachusetts. Not knowing anyone, unfamiliar with the area, I wondered what I was doing in this strange place. Then one month later I met Zayne while reading a flyer he had posted on the outdoor bulletin board at the local post office. (He was advertising nutritional supplements.)

Ten years together feels like ten lifetimes. We have worked through deep emotional issues, explored the heights of pleasure, supported our mutual clearing of gobs of karmic debris, co-created the School, served the Masters and encouraged each other to open to our magnitude. Our union daily reminds us that we are "on the right track" as together we forge ahead into the unknown, knowing that our love makes all things possible.

Smiling with a twinkle in his eye, Djwhal Khul adds:

Do not fear that self may not find a soul mate in this lifetime. That thinking reflects the illusion of scarcity when it comes to Source's great love for humankind. Relationships are the vehicle for attunement to the loving bounty that is available to all. It is not as if self has only one soul mate and is doomed to be unfulfilled in relationships if self doesn't meet that person. Self's willingness to unite with another at a soul level creates a magnetic draw, attracting precisely the right soul partner. Use the power of invocation to call forth this partner, asking that this person catalyze, enhance and accelerate self's journey into enlightenment as the relationship heals karmic wounds, burns away the veils that obscure self's vision, and demonstrates the power of love to remove all obstacles. This partnership teaches the unity of all beings through Love.

The Masters delight in the wondrous fireworks that ignite when two souls merge together in deep recognition of each other's essence. In this union, self is transported beyond the plane of duality into the great Oneness. Angels ring celestial bells heralding the true cosmic marriage of the unification of the spiritual plane with the human condition. Look into each other's eyes and see the magnitude of the soul. Allow this gateway to the soul to transport self into the universes that lie within connecting all worlds through the Cosmic Kiss, which is the miracle of life.

✧ Making Love ✧

February 2002

The mating instinct is alive and well within all of us. Some of us relish it. Others would prefer the sexual impulse to simply go away—to not be bothered with the complex, demanding nature of this potent terrain. In spite of efforts to bury our sexuality under layers of denial, redirect it into creative projects, parenting or excessive work demands, or transcend it through spiritual practices that encourage going beyond the flesh, it still makes its presence felt like a distinct undercurrent threatening to shake our reality if we unleash it. Ironically, it has a greater potential to undermine our fulfillment if we don't give it its proper due.

This doesn't mean that we have to be having sex with each other all the time. The quest is to honor the erotic charge that fills our universe, our bodies our souls and the earth. The erotic charge is most concentrated in the physical act of making love. When riding this electrical impulse we are transported into an ongoing state of mystical love-making with all beings. One can practice physical celibacy, like nuns or priests, while still filling with immeasurable pleasure through "making love" to God.

However, for most folks it is far more satisfying and tangibly transformative to physically make love with a beloved. The mating instinct is not simply for procreation. My hunch is that Source would have offered a simpler, more efficient, less threatening process for the one-pointed purpose of conceiving children.

The mating instinct propels us past the ego, fueling us to open not only our bodies but our souls to each other in a most irrational manner. When blinded by the love-light that excites our erotic flow, the faults of our lover dissolve into a sea of sweet pleasure and deep relaxation. When truly open at that level, we are icons of acceptance and compassion, allowing ourselves to be delivered into the oneness that emerges through our coupling. In that moment, we experience our divinity mirrored in our lover's eyes.

Through the microcosm of our physical embrace we touch the macrocosm of the Divine Embrace lovingly holding us through all incarnations. Making love expands our awareness. Sexual pleasure helps us to loosen our grip and dissolve fears. It heals the body, soothes emotions, grounds us, opens chakras and brings magic into ordinary life. Through erotic union we touch the angelic realm with our love sounds, tears of joy and release, and are transported through a pleasure vehicle into greater dimensions far beyond the ego. Tantric sexual practices from India, as well as Chinese Taoist sexual practices, invite us to ride the sexual current into full union with the Divine.

Reading this, most people would say: "How come I don't feel that way when I'm making love with my partner?" "Yeah right, only in the movies and romance novels." "After a short while in a relationship the sex fades and becomes boring, predictable, and unfulfilling and eventually disappears." "It's too complicated—makes my life crazy." "I get hurt when I open up on that level." "There are no good lovers." "Sex is just for people in their 20's." "I can't let go. It requires too much trust." "I don't have the time." "My partner doesn't even notice me anymore, much less desire me." "It only leads to trouble."

What is it that makes us push away a divine vehicle that brings us enormous joy, pleasure, spiritual awareness, love and healing? It requires quite a bit of energy to repress the relentlessness of the mating instinct. All the sublimation in the world won't take the edge off desire-bodies engineered for sexual union. What are we so afraid of? Everyone craves a healthy, flowing sexuality. Are we afraid to face intimate connection and exposure? Is it our ego's grip, not wanting to budge from its domain of control and predictability? Making love moves us into the mystery. Even long-term lovers, when truly open to the moment and free of expectations, can't predict what will sexually unfold between them. To accept the mating instinct is to embrace the mystery.

Perhaps we forget the true function of making love. It's not just for physical release or making babies. It is to provide the opportunity to open our souls to each other. Can we really trust at that deep level? What makes us shut off our sexuality? If we have been hurt by a lover, do we secretly decide never to be swept away again? How can we be fully immersed in the mating game if we don't allow ourselves to be physically possessed by the erotic currents charging our lives? Even if we are single, we still have to deal with our sexuality. Auto-erotic experiences allow us to explore the same instinct that unites us all.

Some religions teach that the mating instinct used other than for procreation, is "bad." This judgment caps a natural flow, filling us with guilt whenever our desire for making love manages to find its way to the surface among the repressive sea of religious distortions. Ironically, the more we open spiritually, the more erotically charged we become. Our sexuality grows in leaps and bounds as we move closer to Source. The sexual force, known as the kundalini, is the essence of all life energy. The more we remove blockages to our soul, the more we fill with life force. It is ironic that religions attempt to control, even annihilate, this instinctual life force that naturally increases the more we pray and meditate.

The mating instinct carries us deeper into ourselves and each other. If we are not experiencing this depth with our lover, there are probably blockages. Sexuality only gets rote, dry, predictable, empty and flat if we don't open up to the mystery. Attempting to simply take our pleasure, or physical release, on a surface level leaves us empty and unfulfilled. Over time it is tempting to fall into a routine with our lover numbing us with preconceived expectations. Instinctively we know that making love can move us into challenging emotions and memories (past-life or present). We defend ourselves from the surfacing of this deep material by either negating our sexuality or keeping it on the surface—just a "physical" act. This compromises the true function of making love. We feel out of sorts, blocked, unable to get turned on, and/or frustrated with our partner. We then decide to either get a new lover or give up sex. Both options miss the point, which is to bravely allow our sexuality to unconditionally transport us into our soul, with all of its hidden demons as well as gifts.

I have always been propelled by a relentless sexual drive. Promiscuity in my hippie days taught me a lot about "free love." While my Aquarian nature basked in this wild, idealistic freedom, my soul began to hunger for something deeper as I matured. I found myself remembering past-life days as a courtesan in France, exploring the power of the divine consort. This led me to earlier memories of ancient times as a sacred prostitute, revered in the Temple of Aphrodite.. The sacred prostitute healed men, nurturing them into heightened levels of awakening through pleasure.

Maturing into mid-life, my sexuality evolved to a deeper place as I integrated the sacred prostitute into a monogamous relationship. I was ready to honor the sacred container of marriage as a perfect cauldron to house my erotic flow. In this containment, my sexual life was enriched, potent in its impact on my body and soul. Marriage continues to provide the opportunity to deepen my ability to trust not only my lover but also the uncontrolled erotic flow blasting open deep doors in my psyche. After eleven years of making love with my husband, I know that sexual passion doesn't have to fade in a long-term relationship or be dampened by aging into our 50's. On the contrary, making love intensifies with increased trust, communication, appreciation, attention and acceptance of each other's process.

The Tibetan's eyes sparkle in response to my reflections. He adds:

If all of humankind were to make love in joyous recognition of the divine gift that it is the world would experience immense healing. There has been much confusion, fear and misinterpretation about sexual energy. The essential nature of making love is pleasure. Evolution through pleasure is the next frontier for humankind as it releases its attachment to pain and suffering. Making love is designed to teach humankind about the potency of pleasure and the true nature of Source, which are love, joy, bliss and ecstasy.

Through the ecstatic current, humankind breaks through old barriers of fear and illusion. The ego is threatened by orgasmic energy because it propels self into a realm far beyond the domain of the ego. Humankind attempts to repress or control the mating instinct in an effort to dominate the process of unfoldment. However, one can only enter the gates of enlightenment by letting go on all levels and being "swept away" into the larger dimensions of reality.

Ironically, while students complain about the amount of pain in the process of being human, they are far more fearful of pleasure. Erotic pleasure teaches the student about the Loving Force that weaves all aspects of the Universe together into a cohesive whole. It is not necessary to practice celibacy based on the illusion that transcending the mating instinct brings one closer to God. Yes, there have been many spiritual teachers who have renounced their sexuality. This is not to be interpreted that mating is unspiritual. Usually these teachers are directing their sexual energy into a mission requiring the containment and issuance of tremendous life force.

Practicing celibacy is appropriate when one wishes to incubate the erotic current to heighten the process of

132

transmutation. The erotic current, kundalini, is a very powerful transformative force that heats up the alchemical process. There are times when it is rightful to contain the sexual fire within to break attachment to an ego-driven lust blocking the student from traveling deeper through true tantric union. This containment is also suitable during times when the student needs to be single in order to heal and heighten their sense of identity and self-worth. This breaks the attachment to the notion that only through another can self be happy.

Judgment placed on sexual desires is very harmful to the soul because it attempts to sever a vital life force essential to awakening. This judgment carries the illusion that Source created a world contaminated by sexuality. Actually, the world is amplified and magnified by the great opportunity for physical union with a beloved. When lovers unite, the world lightens. Mastery of the human condition requires the release of all judgments, fears, control and negativity that repress and deny one's mating instinct. Incorporate the mating instinct into a spiritual paradigm that applauds, makes sacred, and reveres making love as the Divine Conduit that it is.

To welcome a healthy, flowing sexuality is to say YES to the ecstatic current, deeply trusting union on all levels. If left unaddressed in this incarnation, the work continues into future lifetimes until the student celebrates the art of making love with a beloved, with self, with Source. This brings the Divine Intoxication of making love within a universe where all beings are bonded through a force so powerful and transformative that the body, mind, heart and soul are joyfully merged within the pleasure dimension of the Ecstatic World.

✧ Jealousy ✧

September 2001

Don't trust anyone who *never* gets jealous! After all, it's a natural human reaction. If we were to be really honest, don't we all feel twinges of jealousy when our lover notices someone else's sexual allure, or when someone else makes more money, has more fun, has sweeter children, has a really exciting job, is tight with a special group of friends, has a gorgeous house, has opportunities just falling into their lap, is more powerful, is more spiritually advanced or, maybe, just plain *happier* than we are?

Ah, the list goes on an on when one contemplates all the things to be jealous about. Whatever is lacking in our life is fertile ground for the seeds of jealousy to take root. It won't take long to look around and find someone who seems to be flaunting what we don't have right in our face. They usually seem to have whatever it is in spades!

Jealousy falls in two categories: when our territory is being threatened, especially our sexual territory, and when others have what we crave.

As an idealistic Aquarian in my 20s, I decided that sexual jealousy was simply not an option. My expansive, freedom-loving nature demanded that I be "above" this lowly impulse. Suppressing homicidal twinges when someone flirted with my boyfriend, I convinced myself there was enough room in this universe for everyone to "do their thing" no matter how much it might violate my territory.

Years of betrayal and disloyalty from lovers finally broke me down, humbling my superior notions of advanced consciousness. I had to face the inner conflict of trying to unconditionally accept my lover's unbridled thoughts and actions versus wanting to tear the face of a gorgeous woman tantalizing him seductively if I'm not vigilant, forever tightening my claim on his body and soul. Finally I had to surrender to my instinct rising up like a viper ready to strike when my territory is threatened. Submitting to instinct was the door to liberation. I stopped struggling with the animal within, who cares nothing for a spiritual ego determined to transcend such unevolved feelings as jealousy. This enabled me to claim my totem animal—a very wild wolf!

Appreciating that wolves mate for life, I realized that we all need to "pee" on our boundaries, marking our territory with bodily fluids smelling like "stay away or you'll be sorry." Embracing the wolf allowed me to let go of my narrow judgmental paradigm, declaring jealousy as "wrong". Opening to instinct freed me to growl, pace and gnash my teeth when jealousy surfaced, bringing me more into my physical body and sexual fire.

From this deepened connection to myself I no longer struggled with instinctual boundaries. Twenty years later, at age 42, I happily and proudly announced when Zayne and I became lovers that I would probably tear him to shreds with my teeth if he ever betrayed me. Laughing inside when making this declaration, I felt liberated from old spiritual conditioning that demanded that I transcend the need to possess. There had to be equal room for the animal as well as the spiritual being. Heaven meets earth.

The issue is not to repress jealousy, but to use it as a barometer of the emotional climate in our sexual relationships. If we don't admit our jealousy, we may be more inclined to act upon it unconsciously. Approaching the boiling point in our possessiveness might be a signal of unmet needs in the relationship or inner conflicts around ideals vs. human/ animal requirements. We don't have to blindly act on jealousy by shooting our lover. Rather, we need to allow this gut-wrenching internal volcano to alchemize us into a keen blending with our animal instinct. This reflects our passion, vulnerability, possessiveness, needs, yearning, lust and domain. In the acceptance of our creature-drive, we can reference jealous surges as gut-level clues describing where our boundaries need to be set as well as teaching us about fears of loss and betrayal. Openly communicating these fears to our lover eases "unwarranted" amounts of jealousy, loosening its feverish grip on our heart.

Yes, jealousy is ugly. In the spacious and unconditionally loving heavenly realms, there is no need for jealousy. However, down here on the earth plane, jealousy is REAL. To repress it is to fight a visceral reaction that is as purely physical as salivating. To judge it is to deny a part of our divinely human instinct. It is integral to our passion. To fight it is to water down our blood. The challenge is to accept it, working with it as an information tool to teach us about the "unreasonable" parts of ourselves that make us the richly vulnerable human beings we are.

Jealousy of what others have is the second category. Not falling in the domain of instinct, this form of jealousy reflects fear, scarcity, inadequacy, unworthiness and self-negation. At some point in our lives, we all dip into painful, jealousy-breeding beliefs, asserting: "I'll never have what others have." Such illusion stimulates a profound resentment, usually of God, about the "unfairness" in the human condition. This resentment stimulates our desire to negate what others have through envious competition.

This form of jealousy represents an internal emptiness that we either haven't consciously explored or that we believe can never be filled. Jealousy reveals hungry parts of our soul waiting for attention and fulfillment. Rather than resent others for having what we wish we had, we can use jealous energy to catalyze our determination to do the following: reach out for what we need, examine false beliefs that imply our needs and desires can't be met, view jealous reactions as clues to what our soul may be hungering for at an unconscious level, and explore the world view that says if others have what we want, there won't be enough left for us.

Jealous energy is the heat of desire. Following this desire-fire describes the path we need to walk for ultimate fulfillment. Desires evolve and refine themselves so that, eventually, we grow from being jealous of someone's shiny new car to being jealous of someone's inner peace. Jealous energy needs to be acknowledged as a reflection of how we may be withholding what we really need from ourselves.

To focus jealousy in a competitive or demeaning way toward others is to dissipate our potential to fulfill our desire-body at its truest, deepest level. Superficial jealousies are easily released when we ask ourselves, "How important is it that we have our neighbor's gorgeous house?" However, after examining the fulfilled aspects of our life, if jealousies persist, then they are acting as guides to soul voices clamoring for attention.

The Tibetan, eyes twinkling with delight, adds:

Jealousy springs from humankind's most widespread collective false beliefs. These beliefs include: "My needs won't be met." "There isn't enough to go around." "Source favors others more than me." "Others are more worthy of Source's bounty than I am." Such sibling rivalry among humankind is everyone's attempt to get Source's attention before others do—to get the best piece of pie before the entire pie vanishes.

From where the Masters sit, the banquet is infinite, illustrating never-ending abundance on all levels. Source's love is immeasurable. There is no need to be jealous over what others have when self's plate can be full to overflowing.

To feed jealousy about others having more than self is to waste precious energy needed for manifestation of self's deepest desires. Ironically, frustrated resentment over other's good fortune steals the purpose of desire by sidetracking one's thinking into competition and fruitless comparison of self vs. other. Self is bogged down by referencing other people's reality as more valid than self's, missing the point. Referencing self's limitations through other's acquisitions, on whatever level, dissipates creative energy and obscures the true picture of self's potential and value. Respect jealousy as a signal that self is in a negation attitude, undermining what is possible for self. Use the blistering focus of jealousy to direct purposeful invocation of all that self desires and deserves.

Sexual jealousy reflects the complexity of mystical union with a beloved. In this union, two beings are merged as one. This oneness requires a sacred container that honors the exquisite delicacy of this merge. When the container for this merge is threatened or violated by intrusion and betrayal (even if it is only a mental betrayal), the visceral torment of being separated from one's beloved triggers the original memory of being split off from Source.

All of humankind is craving unification with the Higher Self, with Spirit, with Source. Unification is a sacred process requiring ultimate loyalty to one's commitment and connection with the Divine. The instinctual response of jealousy toward a threat to one's sexual union reflects the wisdom in the animal kingdom's appreciation of Divine Union, expressed among all who unite in soul merge, especially through physical coupling. Humankind has the opportunity to use this instinctual awareness of sacred boundary to deepen its spiritual consciousness through heightened understanding of true union. One does not have to act on jealous instincts, but rather use that emotional energy to enhance wisdom about the requirements of trust and honor when invoking sexual energy for spiritual (tantric) awakening.

Do not judge the jealous currents flowing through self. Allow these currents to inform self of the precious quality of connectedness resulting from opening the body and soul to another in mystical union. From this informed place, self can assume full responsibility for all actions and prerequisites for joyful sexual exchange.

Jealousy is one of the universal human emotions—a feeling/ passion shared by all of humankind. Release all judgment about this aspect of human nature. Challenge self to understand the divine function of jealousy. This function is to integrate the lower chakras, often judged as the "base" level of the human condition, with the heart's capacity for acceptance and unconditional love. This "base" level is the rich soil in which the human condition tempers, shapes, hones and fills the soul with earthly color and passion unrivaled anywhere else in this universe.

Jealousy then becomes a teacher for the soul as self embraces the full spectrum of the human condition including all emotional flows that propel self out of the rational mind into the great creative chaos of the second chakra and solar plexus. This creative chaos catapults self beyond the ego into a terrain of instinct, wonder, mystery, wisdom and depth. In this Domain of the Irrational, jealousy presides as a great teacher, making its impact on the soul in a way that self can never forget and need not deny. Once accepted, the red hot flow of jealousy transforms into a golden thread in the tapestry of the human heart as it interfaces with the soul. From this place of enrichment, self grows in wisdom, awareness and acceptance of the unfathomable nature of the human condition emerging from the wilderness of instinct held within the core of spirit.

✧ Selfish vs. Selfless ✧

June 2005

Sometimes I just want to say NO to everyone but myself! It would be so lovely to bask in my reality and block out the world of OTHERS. I'd follow my inclinations on my own timetable and give myself all the time I need for ME. I'd be immune to others' needs as I unleashed a passionate journey into self, for self, about self. BUT, we know that's too selfish. To be truly spiritual means that we have to go beyond ourselves and be dedicated to others. We must learn how to give selflessly and be happy about it! We must make everyone's reality more important than ours. Then we're really practicing Universal Love. We're taming—even transcending—our hungry egos. We're conquering self-serving, egomaniacal impulses and rechanneling them into thoughts, actions, arenas beyond narcissism. Ahh, to be truly selfless—pure agent of the Divine—to give like a saint with no concern for self. Surely that would make the karmic board proud of us!

Reactively I protest, "What about me?" "Don't I count?" Are these objections simply my egotistical demons obstructing the "no-self" required for these great spiritual endeavors? Or are they cries of a neglected soul-self overlooked for too many lifetimes under the Divine Directive of imposed selflessness? If so, the soul is starved for attention and constructive self-involvement. Otherwise exercises in selfless giving are hollow gestures based in self-denial and filled with grudging resentment and sadness. There are karmic developmental phases when deep self-absorption is mandatory to nurture/ heal/ enrich the soul. If we judge others for being too selfish, maybe we're green with envy.

I've struggled with the false belief that I'm allowed to exist only if I serve others. To live for myself exclusively would certainly be the end of me. My profession requires pure selflessness to hold a transformational container for others' processes. For years, piercing migraines were barometers that alerted me to karmic patterns of extreme self-sacrifice, and I discovered that extremes of selflessness must be balanced by rich self-involvement. Otherwise I'm drained by too much giving.

We need to have a self before we can give it away. How deeply do we take our selfishness? Can we set aside time/ activities/ energy only for ourselves without guilt? Are we truly free to merrily go our own way without thinking of others? How often do we make a self-serving choice that is immediately captured in the sticky web of guilt that scornfully reminds us that we're not alone on this planet—we must take others into account at all times. Guilt convinces us that our needs aren't as important as our obligations to others. Apparently, their "selfness" must have greater significance than our own.

Yes, the pure service of putting ourselves aside for others is truly rewarding as our divinity smiles in approval of this self-transcendent exercise. This brings deep satisfaction. But too much selflessness starves us. The rewards of fulfilling others provide limited nourishment for our neglected self. Direct self-interest, uncompromised by other-directedness, is like a vitamin B shot to our withered, neglected self.

What would the world be like if we were all truly comfortable with healthy selfish needs? How guilty do you feel when you take time just for yourself—when you don't pick up the phone knowing a friend in need is calling... when you duck out of the office and leave co-workers to complete deadlines... when you ignore your kids' hunger for attention because you're too tired... when you insist on doing what you want rather than caving in to your lover's agenda? To carry guilt into these selfish acts is an unconscious way of compensating for self-involvement. Guilt bridles our free dive into self. We can't possibly fall madly in love with ourselves while simultaneously self-inflicting the punishment of draconian guilt. How painful is it to say no to the needs of others? Surely guilt holds no place at the Gateway of Liberation.

Where do we draw the line between healthy self-involvement and narcissistic blindness? This line continually shifts according to outmoded patterns that require counterbalance. If we've spent a lifetime of giving, we might need to answer to no one for at least a year. Would that extent of self-involvement detract from our divinity? Ironically, if we're too other-directed in our lofty spiritual quest, there's not enough self-love to fill our ministry.

Perhaps we take refuge in self-renunciation so that we don't have to face ourselves and find out who we are. We avoid our inner life. We may smugly count up our cosmic brownie points from selfless offerings but the passion of self-discovery dulls as we take ourselves out of the game and sit by the sidelines assuming that this is the more virtuous path.

How can we not resent a God who awards weighty significance to everyone but ourselves? It's scary to really assess how much time/ space we might need as individuals. If these needs are unleashed, we may never care about anyone else again! But how will we ever uncover our authentic self if it lies buried under layers of self-abandonment?

So how do we discern how much and when to give versus when to sink deeply into self and turn an indifferent eye to others? We should trust our gut when it argues with our spiritual ego. If our acts of selflessness truly energize us, we're probably right in balance. But if we're easily drained by other-directedness, the well has run dry. We're suffering from self-neglect. Too much self-sacrifice rivals narcissism in its obstruction to liberation.

However, let us not condone a lifestyle of blind egoistic self-indulgence. We can't help but be repulsed at the destructive level of selfishness in today's world. The attitude of it's a dog-eat-dog world—"we better be out for number one"—is bringing the planet to its knees. Lack of caring about others cements all borders and seals us away from our unity. It's impossible to grow spiritually if we are absolutely selfish. Egocentric self-indulgence hardens the energy body. We get so wrapped up in ourselves that we block loving energetic exchange with others. We become the center of our universe. As our entitlement prevails, self-interest narrows our world view. We believe that people only exist for us—to meet our every need. Lifetimes of that attitude demand the counterbalance of incarnations of selfless service and self-sacrifice.

May we master the interface between self and other, and neglect neither, through the exploration of Love as it flows into us, through us and around us.

The Tibetan, full of his wonderful cosmic Self while unreservedly focused on his student, teaches:

The human heart, deeply held within the Field of Universal Love, can't help but respond to the needs of others. It instinctively corrects imbalances of selfishness. The heart anchors the Central Organizing Principle of Unity, opens the door to limitless Divine energy, which enhances availability to others. However, humankind's belief that selflessness is a denial of self restricts the heart vessel's flow to a trickle. To fully embrace one's self-ness provides a substantive vessel for the Divine flow. The greater the self-fulfillment, the greater the capacity for other-directedness. Self is always ennobled when Universal Love interfaces with the willingness to pour forth nourishment for others.

It all boils down to attitude. Grumpy selflessness negates the expansive principle of Love. Healthy selfishness invites satisfaction that overflows into gift-giving. Yes to others doesn't mean No to self, or vice versa. Yes to self simultaneously generates a Yes to others. Integrate the duality. Close the perceived gap between self and other. Then all acts of selfishness automatically link in largess to others. Healthy selflessness reinforces the self through offerings that circle back to feed self tenfold.

Too much selfishness breeds a fear of scarcity because self cuts off from the flow that unites all, singularly energizing only self, and therefore blocks the bounty received from acknowledging others. Fear of loss of self feeds the scarcity illusion that giving to others empties one's vessel rather than simultaneously filling it. Then healthy boundaries become walls that offer protection against being drained by others, but ironically only diminish self's expansive nature.

Excessive selflessness perpetuates the illusion that self is not significant/ essential to this world and the greater Universe. Self-diminishment only fosters the illusion of unworthiness. All beings on the planet are equal in distinction. To neglect self is to starve the soul. What is the quality of service from a neglected vessel? How much bounty can possibly pour forth from a wasteland of self-nourishment?

Celebrate Self! Unconditionally embrace self-interest as a statement of Source's Love for self and the need to nourish the manifestation of self's divinity into full flower. The Garden of the Divine bears fruit from this commitment to self-discovery and the soul is carried forth in its appropriate splendor. The joy that results from this unconditional self-journey emanates forth to heighten sensitive awareness of others with a pure impulse to honor them in all ways. This joy is a natural abandon that forgets the separation between self and others and unites all in mutual illumination.

✧ Narcissism ✧

July 2004

Have you ever been at a party where you found yourself doing all the listening to others with little or no inquiry returning to you? Have you ever tried talking to someone who goes on and on about themselves, perhaps for hours, without pausing to see how you are doing? Or if they do inquire about your life, they quickly interrupt your sharing, unable to tolerate any lack of attention for even a moment? Do you ever find yourself shutting down, becoming mute and/or numb in a conversation with someone who expects you to be nothing more than one big ear for their never-ending rantings about themselves? Do you ever leave a social gathering feeling empty, invisible, resentful, frustrated, mute or shabby? Perhaps you were spending time with narcissists!

Narcissism is the preoccupation with one's own self-reflection. We are all narcissistic to varying degrees. Healthy narcissism is nothing more than constructive self-interest, self-expression, and self-exploration. However, many people cross this healthy line into the realm of blind narcissism—a hard-core bottom-line type of self-involvement that literally blocks out the reality of others. Narcissism prevents the possibility of true exchange. It creates a wall behind which only lives the narcissist.

Narcissists internally suffer from a deep lack of self. So they work excessively to make sure that everyone around them mirrors the sense of themselves that they want to see (and believe). We are all on a learning curve to discover our truest, deepest self, and indeed we all use others to mirror back the authentic self that we wish to claim. However, in the midst of this process we must also hold an awareness of other people—not just as our "hired" mirrors, but as distinct individuals worthy of our attention, interest, curiosity. When we connect with someone who has found the balance between self and other, we experience a true give-and-take in the conversation. We bounce the "interest ball" back and forth like a ping pong game instead of hogging the ball for ourselves, blindly assuming that the other person will be forever fascinated by us.

Narcissists are energetic vampires. They take too much by creating a high gravity field, a black hole of demand that sucks others in as victims of narcissists. In our relationships with narcissistic people, we begin to disappear as their reality commands all the space. This shrinking, invisible feeling eats away at our self-esteem. All beings require ATTENTION! Like planting a garden, we must put full loving attention on each flower for it to bloom. When overshadowed by "attention mongers," we simply don't flower. That is painful.

I grew up in a family of narcissists. My stepmother talked for hours about herself without any inquisitiveness into my reality. My father and brother were silent narcissists, lost in themselves and once again, oblivious to my reality. I grew up assuming that I didn't have a right to take up space in the conversation. Others might find me boring. My job was to ask questions, listen and then slink away to be alone where I could finally focus on myself. Fearful of being narcissistic like my family, I was afraid to receive attention from others. As a young adult, I chose mostly narcissistic friends. It felt familiar and safe to listen to others. If I listened to them, they would love me. After exploring this issue in therapy, I courageously challenged their narcissistic wall with statements like, "I have some things I would like to share about *my* "life." This isn't easy with a narcissist. Twenty years later, I have *no* tolerance for narcissists. Time is too precious to waste being someone's sounding board. I simply walk away from them—fast! To be with someone who never manages to get around to focusing on my life reinforces old wounds of narcissistic neglect. Why bother!

Are you a narcissist or a sounding board? Either polarity generates isolation. It's useful to ask ourselves, after spending time with someone, what did we just discover about them? Did we interrupt their statements with our own hurried need to represent ourselves? Were we able to hold our loving attention on their process for more than a few minutes? Did we go away feeling puffed up, self-satisfied, bloated with stolen attention? If so, we might want to courageously look into the mirror to confront the narcissist within. Why not heal ourselves with a self-penetrating love-driven focus rather than hold others hostage while forcibly extracting the last vestiges of their wilted, exhausted attention. We need to transform the inner narcissist into an adult (most narcissists are literally stuck in early childhood demanding "parental" attention), and remember that others are just as important as self.

Those of us who are victims of narcissists must break the "listening spell" and resign from our job of being someone's mirror. The entrainment that holds our attention captive while convincing us that our reality comes second must be shattered. It is essential to notice when we are becoming drained by the interaction and immediately stop it! Narcissists' relentless broadcasting of themselves puts others into trance. With silent narcissists, so deep in their world and unwilling to make the effort to relate to others, we end up doing all the inquiry/ reaching out. If we end up feeling drained, unseen, alienated, we've been taken hostage again. We've caught their contagious disease of insignificance and we've disconnected from Self. To be used this way doesn't help the narcissist to grow; it reinforces self-negation and wounds self-esteem while creating false images of relatedness, connection, friendship. True relationships encourage both parties to take center stage and shine in the spotlight of loving attention and interest.

It's shocking to witness how too few people are truly interested in others. Collective narcissism produces a very lonely society. It's hard enough to attempt to have meaningful relationships with supremely self-absorbed people. But an entire society entrenched in narcissism can have devastating global effects. If we can't pull ourselves out of our narrow insular reality long enough to bring our full awareness to others, how will we ever acknowledge/ honor the larger worlds of diverse cultures? If we can't grow up and get outside of ourselves, how will we ever become a unified global village? Narcissists, preoccupied with their drama, are oblivious to the challenges others face and narcissistic societies have little compassion/ concern for the hardships experienced in other nations. This collective blindness intensifies separation, isolation, judgment, selfishness, negativity, competition and cruelty. We must mature before it's too late. As spiritual beings we are called to "get over ourselves" in order to recognize the rich, complex existence of all "others," regardless of how foreign and non-mirroring of Self they may appear.

The Tibetan strides forward holding a hand mirror. Detached from his own reflection, he turns the mirror outward toward others. He teaches:

All beings are natural mirrors for each other. Students must find the courage to look into that mirror expressed through others and see the real Self. It is futile to try to determine, control, manipulate others into mirroring back what self's narcissism wishes to see. That only creates distortion and feeds fear. The dense self-absorption that eclipses others also imprisons self in the Void of Oblivion—an "isolette" of deep, internal emptiness. In this isolation, there is no "reality check" for self's distortions/ delusions. Inability to perceive the impact of one's illusions on others fortifies one's prison of false beliefs.

Globally, national narcissism reinforces the illusion that one's country has the ultimate truth. Other cultures barely exist through the narcissistic eyes of the homeland. This is a root cause of world suffering. It requires great maturity to suspend self's reality long enough to fully acknowledge the experience of others. World evolution demands this maturity during this delicate historical time. Humankind must expand their awareness of <u>all</u> "others"— other cultures, other dimensions of being, others from the spirit plane and extraterrestrial realms. The immature "me, me, me" attitude of humankind reinforces its belief that the world/ universe revolves around itself. This self-aggrandizement prevents many students from connecting with and receiving gifts from dissimilar, otherworldly, "unrelated" forces. To block these resources retards evolution.

What is the real root of narcissism? Humankind looks into its own mirror to ultimately discover its divinity. However, the ego's need to be special or important distorts the mirror's reflection by exaggerating the importance of self ABOVE all others. In order to uphold this perception illusion, the ego has to work overtime to continue to feed its fattened aberration. Victims of narcissists allow their rights to be gobbled up, their own significance to be overshadowed. This is the inversion of the narcissistic inflated ego.

The need to prove one's significance stems from a deep emptiness. This emptiness, a dark cavern in the soul, develops through lifetimes of narcissistic wounds. This gloomy cavity is filled with the desperation to be absolutely visible and significant to Source. Humankind shoves its significance onto others with demands that <u>they</u> fill this emptiness. No one can satiate someone's narcissism. Rather, narcissists must step back from their ego's viewpoint and risk facing them as nothing, deflating

146

the balloon of ego grandiosity. *Only then can they comprehend that they are EVERYTHING—they are Source.*

Humankind must drop to its narcissistic knees and pray for the humility to release its self-fixation and extend its awareness to other outstanding realities. Break free of the prison of self-absorption and enjoy the SUPERLATIVE VISTAS that await. Only then can the spell of Narcissus be broken and humankind set free to look around, enjoy the bigger picture and behold Self's true place in a vast realm of others. Open to the Divine Flow that allows the student to fill with the eternal SELF that can ONLY complete itself through the domain of Other—Oneness—its SOURCE.

✧ The Divine Function of Anger ✧

April 2006

Most of us try to hide our anger. After all, it's embarrassing to show this rather unspiritual part of our psyches. We struggle to talk ourselves out of it. But it just keeps festering in our guts, summoning us to heed its aggravated churning. No matter how we try to elevate our consciousness and rationalize the conditions that invoke anger, its burning indignation pierces our thoughts and interrupts our harmonious transcendence, dragging us down to the bowels of the unconscious where we must confront all denied hurts, assaults, insults, betrayals.

Why are we so afraid of revealing our temper? Society, parents and spiritual teachers admonish us for our ire because anger equals destructiveness, hurtfulness, judgment, selfishness, lack of compassion. Children who feel safe and free enough to express fury are often punished for tantrums. Taught that we're not lovable when we're mad, we associate anger with rejection. So we tuck it away where nobody sees it, assuming it will simply dissolve on its own as we tell ourselves, "I got over that violation. It's okay—not that important. I can let it go." But anger, akin to nuclear waste, can't be buried or destroyed. When repressed, it makes us toxic. Like Mother Earth's repulsion to nuclear poisons, our precious body pays the price. Years of unresolved anger collects in the liver and joints, while the gall bladder is choked with all that "galls" us.

Anger won't dissipate until it has fulfilled its Divine function—to stop transgressions against our birthrights and negations of our very existence. When we block anger, we cut ourselves off at the knees and inescapably become victims. Loss of anger equals loss of power. Angerless sanctity won't steel us for our journey through the rugged terrain of the human jungle, where beings constantly collide. How can we keep pace with the evolutionary challenge of survival of the fittest if we're not allowed to protect ourselves with anger's natural instinct to STOP all negation of self?

Human emotions, brimming with Source's genius, are teachers. Anger, a formidable Divine Force propelling the natural instinct of self-preservation, must be honored rather than shunned. It clarifies boundaries and conveys information about ourselves and others. Bristling arguments expose our hurts, disappointments, rights, needs previously unnoticed or ignored by the other person. Expressed annoyance clears the air like a striking thunderstorm on a hot, sticky summer afternoon—the atmosphere so dense you can "cut it with a knife." When we hide our resentments, we're really hiding ourselves—fearful that we won't be loved if we admit our true boundaries/needs. Finally, when this inauthentic self-representation becomes intolerable, wrathful furies erupt to re-establish balance and foster the self-advocacy that undoubtedly ensures we are loved for who we truly are.

The question is not whether we should be angry, but rather how to master and responsibly channel this Divine Instinct. There's no point in fighting it when our anger declares that something just isn't sitting right. Instead, we must skillfully direct our outrage, rather than secretly stew, and experiment with focusing just enough of anger's clarifying energy, not too much or too little.

We all know the devastation caused by people who express their anger over minor infringements with hurricane force. This overkill usually reflects a conflict about their right to take care of themselves. Destructive, excessive anger expresses the belief that we must destroy the whole situation rather than the violating piece. We don't need an entire forest fire to eliminate a few diseased trees. Like surgeons, we must precisely focus our anger to the particular area of imbalance.

Patterns of self-negation, self-denial or self-repression are the source of extreme rage stemming from an uncertainty about one's rights. Fearful of being violated, defensive anger is often used to unconsciously drive others away to protect ourselves. Anger is the radar that alerts us to behaviors of self-betrayal. When repressed, its siren's shrill goes unheeded in the unconscious for years and leaks out in inappropriate ways. People who scream at the top of their lungs to make their point are probably feeling impotent in their fury. They're not able to go the distance with their anger's purpose/message and inevitably become enraged at their self-imprisonment. Long-term repressed anger turns into rage, then fury—culminating in crystallized hatred. When we are unable to fully claim ourselves, the acid of disempowered anger creates disease.

Once we revamp our relationship to our needs/rights, we won't have to overkill to stop a violation—we simply draw a clear line. Directed, self-responsible anger flows like a cool, clear laser beam that commands respect and establishes self-dominion. Anger, a natural issuance from the psyche, dissipates immediately when fulfilled. If anger festers and eats away at us, we're still withholding permission to have our existential rights.

Fearful of being too much, we often half-step in expressing whatever riles us, ironically prolonging infuriation because anger can't dissolve until we've completely corrected all trespasses. Because anger's alarms describe our natural, innate boundaries—the shape of our being—it's nonnegotiable; we cannot be okay with what really isn't okay. Restrained reactions to whatever offends us, buried in practiced compassion, are futile. Sympathy for others doesn't negate our needs.

Life without anger—that hot flare from the gut that alerts us to our boundaries—is frightening. It creates defenseless victims who feel they must submit to all insults without recourse. When we express too little anger, we dilute our passion and hide our true colors. The displaced ire that leaves us quietly muttering and fuming under our breath, kicking the cat or yelling at other drivers on the road, totally misses the direction in which our exasperation must be fired. If parents scoffed at "silly, childish" anger and we learned to chide ourselves for our furies, or if we're afraid that our anger won't be taken seriously for some reason, we cannot give ample clout to self-advocacy. The result is that we're left even more agitated.

All conflicts between who we are/what we need vs. whom and what we *think* we should be/have are filled with anger. When we try to be "good," our anger leaks out unconsciously and puts others on the defensive. Disowned anger can be dangerous. It fosters random, pointless battles/attacks and leads to depression, chronic resentment, martyrdom, bitterness and disconnection from self.

The need to cloak my anger became the source of agonizing migraines. Efforts to override my deservedness in order to be caring and accommodating resulted in one big headache time after time. Fearful of confrontations and of being perceived as demanding, ungrateful, unloving, I analyzed every angry impulse to decide whether it was justified, rather than simply trusting its message and following its clues to the area within that needed self-advocacy skillfully directed, without guilt.

Potent use of the laser-like nuclear energy of anger doesn't require tyranny, abuse, criticism, judgment or battering. When we are vividly clear in our undeniable representation of self, we can express our anger with authority and sensitivity. Anger used to obtain power only leads to disempowerment. Honored anger that alerts us to violation allows us to establish and sustain our human rights—a state of true power.

The Tibetan elaborates:

Anger, the interface between yes and no, represents the Cosmic NO that counteracts any distortion of the Divine Plan. If one's Divine Rights, as encoded in the Divine Plan, are blocked, then anger is a reactive instinct that says YES. It is part of everyone's divinely mandated gift of existence. Anger's YES to the Divine Plan stops all negation of spiritual essence in form. Complete self-love is the outcome.

Don't judge anger as an aberration of one's Divinity. Misgivings of one's furies reflect trepidation around power and the instinct to live. Fear of anger retards the students' ability to consciously take charge of their wrath and evolve it from raw instinct to skillful application. Nonattached, adroitly channeled anger terminates all hurtful situations.

Mastery of anger involves acceptance of needs through clear self-assessment, the willingness to express awareness of violations and to stop, with a minimum of energy or dramatics, any negation of self and of all earthly beings. Ire dissipates when there's ample spaciousness for self's being on all levels. Anger brings the opportunity to work out inner conflicts regarding the relationship between one's spirituality and human instincts/necessities. To impose a spiritual idealism that describes the enlightened self as angerless blocks the integration of the crown chakra (spiritual center at top of the head) and third chakra (solar plexus), leaving self disempowered and ungrounded.

Anger is not meant to be spiteful, vengeful or vicious, but rather to right all wrongs. Although the notion of wrong is subjective, anger's instinct is pure—emanating from an inborn source of knowing that disallows lovelessness. Bring curiosity to your anger. Follow its clues, like a detective, to the bottom of the issues it unveils—illusions about scarcity, separation, abandonment and betrayal projected onto Source's relationship to self and the planet.

Source wants self and all of Its beloved humankind to exist in fulfillment, joy, empowerment, clarity and full Spaciousness of Being. These are everyone's birthright. Constructive anger, the insurance that ultimately all will arrive at this level of dominion, relentlessly works to prevent self from settling for less than the gifts of existence. There is no selling short of the soul's earthly needs—only full commitment to the Divine Right to dwell in this wondrous Universe of Love.

✧ Dare to Drop Your Defenses! ✧

September 2005

What would the world be like if we stopped all "defense spending," especially in our personal relationships? In spite of proclamations of openness, our reality filters are shaped by subtle, ingrained, unconscious defense structures that distort our perceptions. Automatically triggered munitions make us oblivious to our defensive reactions. Are we ever completely open and available to each other?

The battle of self-preservation triggers the impulse to reinforce armor and shore up lines of defense. After all, we must preserve our self-righteous, judgmental points of view at all costs. The solar plexus retaliates with heavy artillery if anyone dares to shake up our reality. At the Impasse of Incongruence between our assumptions and others' reflections, we must PROVE WE'RE RIGHT! Where did we ever get the notion that right and wrong were absolutes? Human nature exists in shades of gray fueled by polarities that bounce us back and forth.

Our spiritual growth craves deeper, soul-based contact within all relationships. When our defenses are up, we can't possibly hear the souls of others. Our strongholds of justification exaggerate their "crimes" or "faults." We become so obsessed with feeling attacked or offended that we completely lose sight of the real issues. Our defense system instantly engages, often before we've even let someone else finish their sentence. Like clockwork, chronic unconscious injuries repeatedly fire up defensive patterns based on narrow, distorted conclusions. Defenses maintain the illusion that we have to come out fighting and protect our turf, because essentially we're adversaries—not beloveds.

Our armament creates the illusion that we are safe from injury. Does defenselessness invite attack or make us appear weak, incapable of self-representation? A strong defense system doesn't ensure immunity to hurt. Our shields can't heal the festering wounds they guard. Although it gives the illusion of invulnerability, no stronghold is impenetrable. Our essential unity prevents us from blocking mutual impact. We may scurry to buttress our psyches, but inevitably there are loopholes that magnetize impact from others. We must lay down our guns to experience the genuine healing fostered by trust-based loving contact. Empowerment ultimately emanates from defenselessness.

When I decide that someone is attacking/ judging/ criticizing me, I vehemently rush to my defense, drill my point home. I "explain" myself so they know the "truth" of the situation, and they don't make that mistake again. How dare they reveal an aspect of myself that I don't want to see! God forbid I should really let them in. I may not be ready to hear their insights. It might hurt too much. Armored steel doors slam shut and block out any opportunity for resolution.

Defensiveness is contagious. The more we employ heavy artillery, the more vicious the other person's retort. Then it's simply a matter of who wears out who first. If we "stick to our guns," supposedly we win. Our opponents capitulate out of sheer exhaustion, but there is no heartfelt reconciliation. The opportunity to learn from each other is lost. Our "victory" only delays our growth. Now that they've seen the error of their ways, we're top dog, smug in our fortress. Sadly, this "triumph" only indicates that we are better buttressed, less yielding and/or compassionate, more frightened and smaller than the other person, regardless of our puffed-up weighty imperiousness. How can we abort self-protective impulses and open our hearts to receive others as teachers, in spite of their poison words/ actions?

It takes remarkable courage to be the first to drop defenses. If we're "big" enough, we'll resist the impulse to ram our truth home and retaliate by undercutting the other person's reality. Then we have a chance to touch the common ground we share with our worst enemies. America's gigantic defense budget is paltry compared to the loss of precious creative life energy we use individually to sustain our stances of self-protection.

Defenses are ultimately isolating. They block the very messengers we "hired" to broadcast the good or bad news about ourselves. Others' hurtful projections provide the opportunity to see through those accusations and reinforce self-love. However, if there is truth in the attack, then we can learn more about our shadow—those aspects of self we would rather deny. Either way, undefended, we win!

True defenselessness indicates a level of trust in self, not necessarily in the other person. All interactions are important vehicles for self-discovery rather than threats to personal existence. In couple's counseling, I've sadly witnessed too many wrecked partnerships undermined by defensiveness. We're so hasty to make our beloveds the enemy. Love withers behind oppositional fortresses.

The need to defend ourselves comes from the belief that we are wrong, bad, unlovable, and not enough. As we invalidate these illusions and experience wholeness, we are fully available to the perceptions of others, regardless of their transference. Wounded by critical parents, I vigilantly blockade anyone's hurtful presumptions or angry attacks by making sure nobody catches me off guard. Ironically, the need to defend myself gives others the power to hurt me.

I'm learning to hold steady when being "fired upon" by loved ones or strangers, to embrace everyone's reality simultaneously and surrender all righteous interpretations. Struggling to keep a cool head as my guts knot up into a hot fist, I try to be magnanimous, spacious, spiritual, compassionate and non-attached enough to make room for the antagonist. But it takes so much maturity, discipline, focus and self-love to not reach for our guns in the onslaught of someone's illusion-based projections. I have to bite my lip, remember to breathe (as if facing a firing squad), soften the constriction in my heart and validate myself as a worthy human being.

I continue to practice a fearless trust of self-exposure. After all, what could anyone possibly say or do to us that we haven't said or done to ourselves? They only reveal internal pockets of self-negation that need love. From this perspective, we can willingly meet all confrontations undefended and discover more about the nuances of our being.

The Tibetan enthusiastically teaches:

There is no divine armament. Why would Source protect Itself from Itself? To truly emulate its Creator, humankind must advance by transcending its hair-trigger instinct to guard against mutual impact by squaring off against itself. Only when all defenses are dismantled can humankind begin to experience One Love. If humankind cannot lower its interpersonal walls, how will it open its heart to beings from other planets and dimensions? The emergence of the New World Order mandates full exposure to All That Is.

Steel-walled collective defenses have girdled the human soul since the beginning of time. Humanity even believes it must defend itself against its Source! Archaic notions of a God who is a judgmental, vengeful, punishing parent motivated humanity to stockpile endless variations of weaponry in the collective unconscious to protect itself from the wrath of this divine prosecutor. In its early stages of incarnation, humankind's immaturity—the lack of self-discipline and self-responsibility—was the filter through which it perceived its Source to be a displeased parent who mercilessly unleashed Its fury in order to manage Its unruly child (humanity). Unable to look into its own heart and inner terrain, humankind projected that Source would superficially judge its behaviors from a compassionless, righteous disdain of the human condition. Because humanity believed it was impossible to achieve the lofty standard of Source, admonishing attacks from the spiritual plane seemed inevitable.

Like children, desperate for pardon who try to defend themselves for being late for school, breaking a dish, getting into tussles with peers, not doing their chores, humankind forever defends itself to God. But humanity perceived God, or Source, to be eternally dissatisfied, always outraged by Its improbable creation—the human condition! Children become frustrated with parents who don't offer understanding and compassionate guidance. They vent on their friends through bullying or defensiveness.

And so the wars began. The daily interpersonal skirmishes that compel humankind to shore up defenses compound exponentially, until personal combat escalates into global warfare. What a mournfully convoluted attempt to receive love and acceptance.

Please release the illusion of this parental deity and trust the true Source Who only knows Love for Its Creation. Source beholds the gem within humankind's essence and compassionately understands the rigors of earth school. Students are unfailingly guided, never abandoned, in an aura of such gratitude that the young soul feels safe to stumble, fall, and confront its limitations/darkness without the need for self-defense.

Humankind, secure with its Source, can expose itself to the tremendous spiritual Forces of Divine Love. The final stronghold of self-defense is based on the soul's struggle with the illusion of separation from Source. Once this ultimate veil is pierced, then all defenses—weaponry, justifications, excuses, self-pride, stony denial, brutal attacks, retaliation—become like discarded toys, broken and useless, from a bygone day when such things mattered. The Universe smiles as the magical child finally recognizes the compassionate heart of the Divine Father and Divine Mother within his/ her Source—and runs to leap into the arms of the Cosmos, free at last from the shields that have blocked Essence, Light, and Joy.

✧ <u>Part Four</u> ✧

TRANSFORMING THE SHADOW AND MASTERING THE DESCENT PROCESS

"The deeper you go, the higher you fly."
John Lennon, the White Album

✧ Existential Blues ✧

February 2003

It's easy to catch the existential blues in the dark, cold, dead of winter. Without the sunshine and song birds to warm our optimism, we might ask ourselves what life is all about anyway? When we fall into the disorientating wasteland of existential angst, life seems meaningless. We feel like a speck of sand in an indifferent, heartless, random universe. All our spiritual woes surface, causing us to wonder if indeed there is a Divine Plan within this sea of emptiness. Lately, regardless of the season, more and more of us are succumbing to attacks of the existential blues. Why?

My existential pain (despair, hopelessness, isolation, disconnection) surfaces when I experience the discrepancy between my sense of potential and my current, limited self. There is a gap between my vision of all that I was meant become in this incarnation and who I actually turned out to be. If we hold our ideals too high, is that fodder for an existential descent? When we fall short of our idealized, self-actualized being, is there nothing left to hang on to? Is that gap simply the juncture between fantasy and harsh reality? Or is it the interface between the dimension of the soul (fully-actualized Self) and the ego/personality (small self)?

Our first contact with our soul may be accompanied by weird, ghostly pains unrelated to our current life. Many of us are venturing toward the threshold of enlightenment. In this threshold, deep soul aches surface. All past lives of the soul emerge to bring profound qualities of feeling, saturating our current emotional body.

Collectively we are moving to a new level of consciousness. The route to this frontier brings a loss of meaning as we leave the old paradigm. In this new dimension, uncharted and foreign with no maps of meaning, we miss the nostalgia of the old paradigm. As we cross the chasm to the new world order, all of the old ways are stripped down, depositing us into an existential cauldron designed to bring up all past life meaninglessness. Because we haven't touched the new frontier, we rely on faith alone to believe that it does indeed exist. Like Columbus, we are way out on the water, hoping for dear life that the new land will eventually reveal itself. Otherwise, we may fall off the "edge of the world" into nothing. This nothing is the seductive existential realm.

As we leave the old dimension our values shift. Priorities of the ego give way to the values of the soul. The ego no longer generates the meaning through which we direct our lives. There is a gap between all that we have known (in our small reality) and the new dimension of our highest truth. In that gap we can plummet into a meaningless abyss with no handholds to grab on to. Is this a test? How do we cross that abyss?

I can be sailing along through life filled with a great sense of progress. The existential blues suddenly descend like a dark cloud. Waking up with them in the morning is like waking up with the flu. Existential sickness plagues my heart as my mind scrambles for some understanding of this internal weather system that is robbing my joy and inner peace. The more I try to put aside this heavy weight of bleakness the more it tenaciously settles in, determined not to let me off the cosmic hook. All of my tricks for battling the emptiness, like communing with nature, practicing my favorite chi gung forms or playing the piano, feebly fall by the wayside of my "blues." Engulfing despair flattens reality into a one-dimensional cartoon that is not funny. I lose all clarity as reality blurs into this magnetic flood of illusions, usurping my "knowing." The tsunami wave of futility and meaninglessness has me in its grasp, devouring my enlightened, inspired self, convincing me that there is no place to go from here. The walls close in, shrinking my reality into a gray cement box, a coffin that buries all motivation while it annihilates vision and understanding. I try to connect with higher frequencies like the Tibetan or the angelic realm, to provide a portal to the larger picture that would explain this quicksand of misery I've fallen into. Inevitably, all I can "pick up" during these storms is static, like a computer that crashes. These existential blizzards last a few minutes or several weeks.

To avoid the narcissistic pull of these energies that generate complete self-absorption which further blocks out the big picture, I have learned to talk about this pain with loved ones. Sometimes I wait, hoping to hear the encouraging subtle voice of higher consciousness. Service helps. When I focus on others, my angst recedes. But there are times when nothing works. There I sit, holding on for dear life as my internal fabric of wellbeing recedes like a shrinking island. I must dare to stretch beyond the known. Existential crises challenge me to puncture my bubble of wisdom into a larger order of knowing while swimming through the gulf of the abyss where all the dead bodies of my outgrown self float. Yes, the existential blues carry death of the old meaning. If only I could avoid this torment—somehow get it right next time and be spared this awful human experience of spiritual dismemberment.

The Tibetan reaches out his arms, exuding compassion, reminding me that the spiritual plane is always available for comfort. He says:

Once soul development through the paradigm of duality is fully harvested, students release the belief structures of the third dimension and find themselves vulnerable in a wasteland where old skins are shed. Obsolete meanings lose potency while self struggles to make contact with the emerging, still undecipherable significance of the next level. All that self has worked for—cleansing, purification, healing, opening—has been to leave the small room of the ego to venture into the vast terrain of the Magnificent Self.

Once out of the nest, students may be surprised by what they encounter. Expecting a celebration, soberly they find themselves in a dimensional hinterland that must be resolved in order to merge into a greater field of being. At that moment self says: "I want to go back into that warm small house where I knew who I was." Yet the door is shut. The house fades. The universe won't allow retreat. Knocking on the door to get back in only perpetuates the existential blues. Ambivalence about going back prevents self from accelerating through this dimensional field into higher ground. Evoke the courage to move through the existential blues by remembering that self is braving terrain that has never been closer to enlightenment.

Disillusioned with the old paradigm, deep grief emerges from self's inability to believe in what used to be important. This feels isolating because many are not yet emancipated from their small self. In this gap between the unrealized and the potential Self surfaces a soul ache that carries the profound longing/ desire/ heartache for the Higher Self. From lifetimes of experiencing enlightenment as an unattainable consciousness beyond the student's reach, deep levels of disappointment/ sadness create an existential climate of starvation and hopelessness. Today's accelerated energies generate an intense spiritual hunger that cannot be fed in the old ways. The student falls into a pocket of emptiness, a strange nostalgia, where all the earthly rewards fall short of deep fulfillment. In past lives, when there was a gap between the Higher Self not yet in form and the current self struggling to break through illusion, like children with noses pressed up against a locked candy store, there developed a searing, inconsolable feeling of disappointment.

Invoke the Light of Acceptance to heal the gap between the magnificent and unawakened self. In this gap is the illusion, fostering humanity's greatest suffering, that self is not yet awakened. When existential pain emerges through the emotional/ mental body, self is closer than ever to the deepest terrain of the soul. Ironically, the existential blues reflect the crash and burn of illusion. Despite the discomfort of traversing the "gap," self has attained a state of spaciousness never touched before. It may not feel like spaciousness because the heart contracts in this hinterland while it reorients itself, through a breakdown process, from personal to impersonal love. Self is exploring a terrain with no support from the mainstream because third dimensional reality cannot perceive it. It truly is another spectrum.

Accept the existential blues with gratitude. Bring curiosity to them. Trust that a greater reality, in profound communion with all beings, is ushering in a light factor whose brilliance will quickly overshadow the diminished light of the small house. Fill that small room that used to hold the old world with a large love. This eases existential bewilderment and reminds self that haunting pangs are aches of recognition of the Higher Self's true domain. The ache of longing still carries the illusion that self is not yet within that Magnitudinal Self, while a greater ache of resonance indicates that self is finally dislodged from the small room to touch this larger domain.

The ache is the memory of all lifetimes when self could not respond to the Call now ushering forth. When self froze in the gap, paralyzed, a deep sense of failure and impossibility, experienced like an ice storm, crystallized. Surrender allows the existential blues to shift in their color, creating a profoundly peaceful acceptance of this requirement to leave the nest of the small self. Embrace the wondrous climates and weather systems that shape and hone the soul, evoking wisdom and transmutation. Then self is established on the new land, no longer traveling back and forth.

Meditate on the ache. Ask for guidance from the heart chakra. A blocked heart, holding the illusion that heaven and earth are not together, feeds the existential blues. The ache surfaces for clearing as the student evolves closer than ever to the union of heaven and earth within. As this ache informs self of the immediacy of this greater domain, the student responds by creatively giving it expression, form and LOVE. Creativity pulls up and transmutes all unconscious memories of past lives at this threshold. Through creativity, the wisdom within the ache emerges into a form—a pathway ferrying self through this liminal state. Trust that there is a magnetic field in this existential wilderness that literally transports the student through this inter-dimensional band of emptiness.

If the student is desperately trying to get back to the small room for comfort or standing within the existential realm reaching negative conclusions such as: "I am abandoned. I will never feel connected. My life has no meaning," then the creative energy will pour through these false constructs to manifest another small room, joyless because it is no longer the room of the small self required to germinate and grow through warmth and love. It becomes a room of resistance, capturing the existential pain as a permanent place rather than as a part of the great labor and birth of the Magnificent Self.

This gap is pure mystery, uncharted by most of humankind, with no reference points from the small room. Many students have stubbornly clung to their fear of moving through it. Yet even the most tenacious have eventually been ousted from this dismal shroud because it is ultimately illusion. Remind self that it is <u>impossible</u> to stop one's unfoldment. Self cannot fail to awaken. Embrace the pure not-knowing of existential crisis. Those who have crossed great bodies of water in stormy seas and dark nights, not knowing what awaited them, have had to face similar issues of faith. When the sun peeks through these gray clouds, it sends forth great shafts of light upon which rainbows dance which are the ladders into the Greater Domain of Being through which all students harvest their liberation. From this elevated kingdom, the existential blues fade like gossamer veils to reveal the New World Order—a place of great Purpose, profound Meaning and utter Joy lavished upon humankind like the pot of gold so richly deserved at the end of a long, arduous journey of Faith.

✧ Self Sabotage ✧

January 2006

I hate shooting myself in the foot. Don't you? It's humiliating to be a victim of self-undoing. Sure, we strive to conquer the unconscious impulse to yank the rug out from under ourselves. But no one is immune to the all-mighty inner saboteur's cruel destruction. We all dread its devilishly orchestrated wreckage of our best intentions and efforts. As we enter a new year, filled with positive resolutions for self-improvement, we wonder who will win the battle this year—our good will, aligned with the Divine Will's highest vision for our soul, or that dark creature from the basement of our unconscious, who gleefully pulls the plug on our reservoirs of fortitude, determination, self-love, self-esteem, self-discipline, healing and transformation.

Is this monster of subversion really necessary for our evolution? Does its undermining impact foster our eventual mastery of the human condition through its chafing insistence that we can't win? Like irritating sand that creates the pearl, does the process of self-sabotage eventually produce a powerhouse of determination and spiritual strength? Or is it just an aberration essentially out of synch with the Divine Plan? Can we hope for a life of such profound alignment, balance and integration that the habit of self-sabotage eventually disappears, because there are no illusions remaining to ignite its Vortex of Downfall?

We give our power over to the saboteur because we don't understand its function. Baffled by a deep impulse for self-ruin and feeling impotent to intervene, we helplessly witness our self-created demise. The saboteur—slippery, sneaky, enigmatic—wields a tremendous influence on our decisions as it oversees our "falls from grace." It scatters landmines along our path that detonate right in the face of our best efforts. Always on duty, the saboteur salivates in blithesome anticipation of our arrogant assumption that we can win the race this time, without unconsciously holding an invisible wire across the track that sends us flying down the mud hole of ruin.

I am dropped to my knees by my inner saboteur whenever I set intentions for self-improvement. No matter how extensively I scan for self-created pitfalls, somehow the saboteur inevitably infiltrates my endeavors with its undermining ways. It victoriously gloats when apathy blankets my resolve to continue new disciplines, when I recklessly scatter precious creative energy or manufacture excuses for not ennobling my visions with action and persistence, and/or when I start to believe all the internal voices that perpetrate lies of impossibility, ineffectiveness and self-diminishment.

The saboteur leaves no stone unturned in its search for our unconscious weak spots. It latches onto these vulnerabilities with the tenacity of a pit bull, tearing away the flesh of our convictions. Usually these "attacks" of self-sabotage seem to come out of the blue with a force so powerful that we feel catapulted backward.

Self-sabotage can be dramatically obvious: when we defiantly head for the bakery on our third week of a healing diet, or for the bar when our doctor has warned us to cut back on alcohol; when we turn off the alarm clock and return to sleep, pretending not to care about our boss's admonitions regarding lateness; when we don't return the call of a blind date referred by trusted friend because it's safer to retreat into ourselves than take a chance on love; when we give away valuable time for writing that book, painting that picture, practicing that instrument, because "more important" things take precedence; when we silently swallow our words, carefully rehearsed for a much-needed confrontation with our parents, children, friends, lovers and employers, because it won't make a difference anyway; when we say something stupid/ cruel/ insensitive to a new lover before the trust has solidified; when we're on the verge of achieving our goals—completing that Ph.D., paying off that final credit card, losing that last 10 pounds, finalizing that project—and then, for no apparent reason, stop short. We certainly don't want to disappoint the saboteur who counts on our flimsy spirits to buckle just before the finish line.

Self-sabotage also operates insidiously, subtly entering and contaminating our mind stream with narrow parameters that starve our positivity, imagination and sense of potential. When we really care about something, the saboteur tosses an unavoidable monkey wrench into the mix. We can try not to care too much—to trick the saboteur with our detachment. But when there is a lot at stake, self-sabotage arises from the very guts that fuel our passions. Are our positive convictions strong enough to hold back the tide of wreckage masterminded by the part of ourselves bloated with hindrances, damage, and blockage? Most of us want to go the distance in our lives. So what "possesses" us to fall astray?

We unknowingly feed our saboteur by making impossible leaps forward—headstrong and certain that we're unstoppable. We unrealistically vault to higher places without acknowledging the power of opposing agendas in our unconscious. We must respect this deep inner world's richly potent unrefined energy, where our monsters of undoing are housed. Self-sabotage tells a different story about who we are—equally valid in spite of the huge discrepancy between that evaluation and who we think we should be. If we don't honor these contradictory impulses, when denied, they accumulate enough force to demolish all our best intentions.

We must discern whether self-sabotage is an indication that we aren't paying attention to contradictory parts of our psyche, or an ingrained self-destructive pattern triggered when too much "good stuff" is happening. If we believe that when life is too joyful, something bad has to happen, we will gladly live within chronic episodes of self-sabotage in order to ward off the "brink of happiness." We agree to be pushovers and to reinforce the belief that the saboteur always rules.

If we struggle with the saboteur, it just gains energy. We need to observe where and why we self-abort. What is the story within the pattern of our sabotage? What is our favorite form of self-undoing? Does it out-picture an unmet need in the soul? Or is it simply a frozen pocket filled with fear of advancement?

Self-sabotage is addictive: a quick fix that produces a strange self-destructive high on a rickety roller coaster, seducing us with cheap thrills that seem more tantalizing than the "monotony" of the steady, even-keeled advancement and persistence required to fulfill our mandate to become master builders of the soul.

What would it be like to exist without self-sabotage? Can we tolerate smooth sailing as we steadily apply ourselves to our evolution without the melodrama of self-devastation? As we bring loving inquiry and acceptance to our saboteur, we claim yet another chunk of our soul. We must negotiate with the saboteur and hear its perspective. Then we can patiently adjust our expectations by integrating this vortex of subversion into our paradigm as an invaluable kink in the flow that paradoxically fosters self-trust. Eventually the saboteur comes around in full cooperation once its riddle has been solved and we have embraced its needs. Then the saboteur lends its incredible force field to our endeavors and we're in full alignment with the Divine Will.

The Tibetan, approaching me at light speed, unimpeded, teaches:

Everyone has a saboteur who embodies his or her ultimate resistance to liberation. This resistance contains memories of self-betrayal in previous incarnations. Humankind fears its absolute attainment because spiritual prosperity is such a foreign paradigm compared to their usual dispirited and downcast earthly journey. With too few cornerstones to anchor the awareness that humankind's birthright is a grace-filled triumph, unconscious false beliefs dominate the student's choices, actions and thoughts with stories of undoing.

The saboteur, one of the inner terrorists that reside in the collective unconscious, randomly makes a botchery of the pathway, reinforcing the common false belief, "I can't trust myself." Fundamentally, humankind is terrified of its own self-destruction. However ironically, it's more afraid of discovering its ultimate magnificence. So it sabotages itself just before entry to higher levels of consciousness, awareness, self-responsibility and advancement.

Students arrive at the Gateways of Initiation and falter in belittlement and unworthiness. The saboteur has a field day at these inaugural junctures. However, the thresholds are invincibly magnetic and inevitably draw the students forth, regardless of the saboteur's defiance. The saboteur is only as strong as the illusion that it represents. Because illusion is empty of validity, it is devoid of any real potency and easily crumbled, regardless of one's addiction to undermining self-obstruction. Humankind must recognize that the saboteur is only an empty shell—a minor bump in the road. From this vantage point, this monstrous dynamic in the collective unconscious is neutralized.

Self-distrust is the primary, underlying matrix of self-sabotage. There is no need to cripple self in order to catalyze growthful descents into the unconscious. A deliberate and unhasty pace of unfoldment allows the student to lovingly honor all discordant parts of the soul and nullifies the need for the saboteur's speed bumps in the road. As humankind truly practices and experiences self-love, it need not damage itself in fear of its ultimate spiritual disentanglement and exposure. Release all self-hatred fostered by the saboteur and instead rejoice in the opportunity to pierce the veil of resistance with the soul's resiliency and determination to unveil its consummate glory.

✧ Negativity ✧

May 2003

Many of us latch onto negative thoughts and perceptions as if they were God, our ultimate truth. When viewing whether the glass is half full or empty, most of us have to strain to see the fullness, while the lack readily imprints itself on our attitude. If we give equal import to the positive experiences in our lives, the world would change. I'm not suggesting we have to block out the negativity, but rather that we put it in its rightful place. We live on a plane of duality where learning through negativity is inevitable. But why must we exaggerate the negative currents moving through our lives, as if that were all there is?

Clients tell me that they attach to the negative because it gives them a sense of control. We believe it is safer to perceive/ expect the negative than to anchor ourselves in the positive and risk losing it. Perhaps we fear the joy that allows us to relax, trust, smile, open our hearts and embrace the mystery of our becoming. Happiness feels too vulnerable. So we armor ourselves into a shield of negativity designed to protect us against all the possible horrors of life. Ironically, our creative flow pours through this negative filter, bringing us exactly what we expect—a miserable lifetime. Then we sit justified in our anticipations as we count all the rotten things that have gone down in the day, almost satisfied that our expectations were right.

How can we possibly make the leap into greater consciousness if we shrink our world through negativity? Don't leaps of faith require openness to the probability of a positive outcome? Otherwise, we leap and fall to the bottom, our negativity as heavy as cement, dragging down expectations, blocking flight, constricting vision and crippling enthusiasm. This compounds on itself as we pick up our shattered body, firmly resolving never to be so idiotic as to believe that anything good could possibly happen to us, or even if it does happen, that it can't be sustained. So our world withers as our negativity imprisons us in a glass perpetually half empty.

Negativity robs us of the present moment. Instead of breathing in the bounty, our critical eye searches for flaws. Perhaps we are afraid of gaining too much altitude, so we search for anything that can bring us down. Eventually we lose the elasticity/ resilience of positivity and simply stay down like a lead weight, locking in the following "proven" false beliefs: "It's impossible to be happy. My needs will never be met. Life is too hard. I never get any breaks, opportunities, love. Everyone else has it better than me."

Negativity is a nasty habit. Resistance to my birthright of joy hits me first thing in the morning before I even get out of bed. My mind jolts me awake, already at work on the List of Discontent, scanning how hard the day is going to be, looking for what I might do wrong, and tenaciously reminding me of yesterday's frustrations carried over onto today's agenda. I forget to notice the gifts of health, safety, intelligence, love, creativity as my mind is kidnapped by the negativity police who begin their endless interrogation before I'm even fully awake. I have to force myself to remember what a bonus it is to be alive, to be grateful for the day's prospects and all the spiritual endowments nourishing me. So I practice chi gong and hike up hills with my dog, Zulu, attempting to burn off this negativity and open some small space in my consciousness where I can perceive the glass half full.

Negativity is most destructive through attacks of self-annihilation. We often enter or end our day with a litany of self-scolding, reminding ourselves, lest we forget, how badly we have failed at relationships, career, finances, parenting, spirituality. Most of us wouldn't tolerate this disparaging input from others, but don't hesitate to shred ourselves with it. Our negativity creates such a groove in our perceptions that our consciousness automatically flows toward it, like a magnet for woe, emerges victorious, in control as it colors our sense of possibility.

To what extent does our negativity stop us from committing to our dreams? Negativity, subtly deadly like noxious gas, poisons our thinking, aborting original responses to life's challenges, setting up never-ending red stop-lights that say: "Don't you dare." "You can't possibility do that;" "You're not good enough;" "It's too hard;" "This won't make you happy anyhow;" "It's impossible to be happy."

Negativity feeds resignation, failure of imagination, depression, physical disease. It blocks energy, convincing us that we don't have the internal resources to go the distance into our transformation. Must we wait until we are on our deathbed to recognize the quintessential thief that negativity really is, as we lament wasted energy, time, missed opportunities, unrealized dreams all because we believed its insistent pessimistic lies?

Negativity is contagious. We all know what it feels like to be with a negative person. After a few minutes we become depressed—then hopeless—then numb. Radioactive negativity projects out, broadcasted by gloomy people, creating a black cloud infiltrating our right to exist under blue skies. Their cynical field of impossibility wraps itself around us and takes us down, like quicksand, into the realm of dulling contraction. Like oil spills in the ocean, it contaminates everyone.

This serves the dark force which, feeding on the death of our creativity, smothers catalytic sparks of light designed to open vistas of achievable potential. Voices of Undoing seduce us into thinking that somehow we are safer trusting the limitations, frustrations, losses, let-downs of our life than the joy, love, expansion, possibilities, visions, gifts. Wherever we focus our attention is where our energy flows. If we are steeped in negativity, our energy inevitably charges that pessimism, yielding a life of supreme dissatisfaction. Nothing happens. Nothing works. Nothing succeeds. Nothing matters. Why bother?

When I register the glass half full, keenly appreciating my life's treasures and horizons of potential, I get scared! This is too much! Like a hot potato, I can hardly touch my positivity, much less hold it. It's too expansive. How will I stay grounded if I'm not tethered by negativity? Perhaps I'd be bored, no compelling pathetic melodrama to spice up my day. I would have to be more responsible, creative, present, appreciative and giving in return for all the abundance in my life.

Maybe I just want to be lazy and hang out in my suffering and regret, swimming in its oily, sticky, stultifying oxygen-depriving sludge that mucks up my chakras and contracts the channel. That keeps me in the collective stew of the familiar. After all, isn't that what we expect—a negative outcome? If I try to drop the negativity even for a moment, I get anxious. Now what? It's dangerous to trust the positive. There is no control. I might fall on my face, embarrassed and ashamed, that I would be so unsophisticated as to believe life is essentially a favorable experience.

Edison believed that 1,000 failed experiments brought him closer to a successful discovery. His positivity channeled him into the land of invention as his buoyant imagination burned through the web of negativity that could have buried his genius forever, leaving all of us so much the poorer. I reference him when I struggle with giving up on my dreams, and resolve to strengthen my affirmative flow, viewing the negative as tonifying challenges to my spiritual muscles and soul's determination.

To see the glass half full provides a sneak preview of my magnitude. Taking daily stock of all the good things paints a beautiful soul-based self-portrait. With that as my platform, negative voices lose their dominance as I am positively fueled into great expectations!

The Tibetan, all smiles in applause of this discussion, gives me a sunny embrace and teaches:

Humankind is fascinated, entrained, by the negative aspect (a required counterpart to the positive flow) of the earth plane's learning format of duality. Subliminally, humankind remembers the singularity of its Divinity, the Oneness that abounds beyond the polarities, and is disturbed by what feels like a distortion of the Divine. The apparent confines of the negative learning curve run counter to one's limitless spiritual essence. Compelled by an inability to accept and assimilate this negative counterpoint, humankind expects the worst.

Negativity is a counterpoint, not an endpoint, to strengthen the soul and develop wisdom. When saturated in its negativity, humankind loses sight of its true nature and cannot assume responsibility for co-creation with the Divine Plan. Then students feel weak, restricted, disempowered—becoming helpless children who believe there is never enough, self is unloved, and it's too hard to try. Release all beliefs indicating that earthly life is meant to be woeful and mediocre. Students cannot be spiritual athletes if they succumb so easily to the negative polarity. Everyone is responsible to each other to emanate positive energy, so that all can lift the veils of negation from their eyes.

Humankind clings to negativity because it fears its expanded nature. The ego can identify itself only through the confines of limitation. When one's consciousness becomes too large to be contained within the realm of duality, the ego fears annihilation. So it attaches to "what isn't or can't be" in order to reassure itself that it won't be eclipsed by the Higher Self's spiritual magnitude. The ego convinces self that it is dangerous to become too happy. Self might fall from grace. This is impossible, because grace is built into the matrix of the human condition. Without grace, one's life would abound with disasters. The only fall from grace is the fear-filled paralyzing imprisonment of the ego's negativity. To attach to negativity is to glut the ego, fattening it with limitation and denied light, which smothers the soul in impossibility. The learning curve of duality, distorted by the exaggerated negative, is then unable to teach the true multiplicity that yields wisdom.

Negativity aborts birth. To say YES is to magnetize a great opening. To say no is to block the collective emergence. Dare to live in the YES, even as the negative challenges of duality lap at one's consciousness. From this platform of YES, students embrace the duality while simultaneously rising above it into infinitude. From this heightened consciousness, self touches the archetypal realm where the roots of all imagination reside, representing the Great Inspiration that is Source. From this altitude, one's vision opens. Vistas of truth are revealed. Self is energized by a boundless life force.

Accept negativity as a strengthening tool, like bar bells used to develop muscles. But remember to put the bar bells down after one's workout and relish the exquisite lightness of being that comes from being in good cosmic shape! Then one is ready to spring into action, spiritual muscles well-developed, to implement visions from the third eye into form and service. If students keep pumping the bar bells ceaselessly, their entire being exhausts itself into depression and generates the illusion of inherent impotence, ineffectiveness, inferiority, fueling the shrinkage of possibilities within their world view. Then there is less joy to fire the spirit, which by default drops the energy into the negative pool in which most of humankind swims, enslaving itself to the false belief that it is trapped, punished, unworthy, feeble. Denying the momentous bounty of positivity and gifts available to all, many people reference themselves as paupers, hopelessly throwing their hands up in the air, eager to embrace defeat before even trying.

With the onset of the Aquarian Age, collective awakening on the horizon, humankind cannot AFFORD to indulge its negative stagnation. The heightened vibrations impacting the earth plane will not tolerate it. Karma is mightily magnified by these accelerated energies. Therefore, the potency of one's negativity intensifies its profound undermining of the soul's advancement as well as karmic contracts owed to others.

When someone has a cold, they are careful not to be around others who might catch it. But few recognize how contagious their negativity is; sickening all those they come in contact with. Rise to the challenge! Face the negative elements in self's life. Greet them as opportunities for profound transformation. This unblocks self's gratitude and possibility. Embrace the bar bells with gusto, eager to prove to self one's ultimate capacity for creation.

Then the student is finally AVAILABLE to the Masters and angelic force to step to the front in humankind's transformation, impervious to the seduction of the collective sea of negative expectations, embodying the YES for others. Self then serves as teacher and leader, positively charging the collective electrical grid with possibility while neutralizing the poison of negativity. Gateways of perception then open. Self perceives and anchors the birthright of bliss.

Practice positivity. Dare to behold the glass half full. Watch it ultimately fill to the brim and overflow with good fortune. Get used to the altitude. Learn to breathe in the brilliant atmosphere of the positive force. Don't be ashamed to tell others of the natural order of things. They will quicken at a cellular level to this truth, realizing that so much more is possible. Accessible and immediate, humankind's treasures of grace, abundance and spiritual wealth forever compound upon themselves. It is written in the YES that is Creation.

✧ The Divine Function of Depression ✧

April 2004

Why is everyone so down? Our use of anti-depressants is sky-rocketing. We think nothing of taking all kinds of "medication" for our chronic blues. We give it to our children like candy. Is this collective depression so contagious that even our children have lost their innocent joy? When depressed, we automatically assume that we need to get a prescription, as if anti-depressants were vitamin pills that provide essential nutrition for the soul. What did we do before medication became the "solution" to our problems?

Theoretically, anti-depressants put us back in balance. But they also exact a price for this chemical adjustment to the soul. They flat line our passions, and sexuality into a "manageable" reality. Supposedly, this "balancing" provides us a stable platform on which to do our inner work. However, many of us simply go from one anti-depressant to another without responding to the need of the unconscious for deep exploration. It's easier for many professionals to simply prescribe medication rather than accompany their clients through the underworld of depression and out the other side.

Admittedly, some people who have crippling chemical imbalances really benefit from medication. But too many of us are throwing our hands up in the air in resignation that we are victims of depression and must submit to the side effects of the all-mighty drugs. Advertising and the media constantly reminds us that we can't handle our psychic pain on our own—we need pharmaceuticals. Just take a pill and all your problems will vanish.

Only now are we beginning to see some of the harmful effects from these drugs. In the long run, what price will we have to pay for taking the edge off a process that is designed specifically to call attention to the soul? At best, anti-depressants are useful as temporary scaffolding, allowing the psyche to stabilize itself in order to begin the labor of deep inner healing, not for long-term dependency.

Regardless, we are becoming a society steeped in deep depression. What is the Divine function of this plague of blues that has swept throughout our land? Depression is not a disease, although it may be viewed as pathology. It is really a powerful energetic in the psyche designed to create a downward vortex that pulls us into ourselves, freeing up imprisoned aspects of the soul, releasing buried emotions, discovering hidden resources and embracing our inner child. Most of us experience depression at some point in our lives with symptoms of despair, lethargy, immobilization, numbness, hopelessness. Depression also expresses itself through pent-up restlessness; we pace our inner prisons like caged animals.

Yet depression contains a spiritual message—information encoded in our unconscious. What is our psyche trying to tell us? We must be detectives to follow the clues within the depression that lead us to the buried treasure at the nadir of this downward vortex.

I'm certainly not immune to depression. It has persisted since childhood. When I find myself repeatedly sighing out loud, I can feel depression pushing itself up against my efforts to deny it. When I wake up with a leaden heart, depression has infiltrated my dream world. If my body feels heavy, I know that my cells are releasing hidden pockets of depression. When I can't remember my life's purpose or meaning, when my inner vision seems blocked, depression has caught me by the coat-tails, broadcasting thoughts of "why bother."

When I feel nothing but self-contempt, my depression is in full swing. When I find myself aimlessly contemplating how much I "want off" this plane, my depression is in full command.

My mother's depression led to her suicide when I was three years old. Depression can be genetic—passed down through our karmic lineage as we reincarnate with the same souls over and over again. My mother's death inspired my psychological work with people—a desire to open the Window of Light and Possibility to all who sit languishing in dark rooms of gloom.

Wrestling with depression, I've discovered that it "cooks" me for a precise amount of time and then spits me out from its bottomless darkness into a sun-drenched room in my psyche that has been just waiting for me to emerge into the light. Even as the depression walls close in, a small inner spark reminds me that there is a profound purpose to this process, as I am put in touch with pockets of pain, trauma and emptiness that my soul has carried for centuries. As I find the courage to touch these deep places with self-love and patience, the depression ceases its dark howling and the winds of despair dissipate.

I've learned to trust my depression. A vehicle for penetrating travel into self, it opens inner doors that appear to go nowhere but actually lead to great soul riches. I experience a profound lucidity when emerging from a depression cycle. This hard-earned insight and clarity come from the willingness to excavate the soul from its hidden dungeon of anguish. Simply my loving presence (along with the help of the Tibetan and other Divine resources) melts the veils that substantiate my despair. Depression is nothing more than denied imprisoned aspects of self that carry "life sentences"—with no hope for parole.

Depression is our way of saying NO to ourselves at the deepest level. This NO is the ultimate form of self-negation. When we believe that we are living in a loveless universe, we assume that the NO is a cosmic mandate. This generates great shame that our own Source would disown us. Contrite, we modify and debase ourselves by crawling into the depression pit to wait out our cosmic adjudication in divine disgrace.

We can't run from our depression. It chases us everywhere. Depression is a spiritual crisis. The Depression Wall blockades our connection to the Great Flow that contains our essential birthright of possibility. The soul may sit behind that wall for lifetimes as the illusion of being cut off from divine support entrenches itself. We assume that there is nothing that awaits us that could possibly make any difference in our lives. The soul, determined to be liberated, waits for the inner landscape of bleak despair to break apart. Eventually, the Depression Wall crumbles. Until then, we can't bypass this lifetime's soul issues. No matter how painful, we have to surrender to depression's alchemical effect on our psyches, trusting that we won't have to endure its crushing strangulation of the soul forever. When locked in the depression box, energy heats up, spiking this level of darkness to a pitch that drives us to rediscover our Source.

The Tibetan, apparently impervious to depression, walks toward me singing songs of delight. He teaches:

Humankind feels out of control as the disintegration of the old paradigm yields to the New Cosmic Day. This breakdown process stimulates feelings of helplessness and hopelessness. Humankind believes it can't make a difference in the face of this onslaught of negative energy, which stimulates karmic memories of all past-life traumas endured with apparently no help from the higher planes. The perceived abandonment caused humankind to contract into a consciousness of icy separation, which lowered its "ceiling" (blocked crown chakra). Continuing to bump their heads against that lowered ceiling, humankind dared not stand up straight and reach for the stars.

Over lifetimes, the bent-over gesture in the soul breaks down one's innate alignment with the Divine and produces a profound sense of self-diminishment, because the Higher Self feels inaccessible. This generates a powerful matrix of despair that blinds the soul to the Joystream that sustains all beings. Depression roots its tendrils in the blindness. One's current depression is the result of a long-standing depression for lifetimes. It's time to stop this karmic legacy. Journey through the barren terrain like torch-bearing pioneers who know, deep in their hearts, that a lush, colorful world awaits them just beyond the veil.

After much work, many students may be depression-free for months or years, only to have it return. Fearing failure, they may succumb to its obstinate message of woe—certain that there is no place to go, nothing to be done, no opportunity to pursue. Ironically, this subsequent layer of depression indicates that finally the student is accessing/ releasing even deeper soul blockages. Lifetimes of depression are surfacing to full consciousness for transmutation.

How does one walk through the corridors of despair and not be seduced by this spiritual crisis? Depression ultimately convinces one that life is not worth living—an inversion of the spiritual force field that mandates earthly life, feeds the spirit, and applauds the boundless potential of human existence. The formidability of this inverted force field is daunting to the ego/ personality, especially as it activates all previous soul memories of disconnecting emptiness.

When depression clamps the soul, self is right up against the portal of entry to a greater consciousness—as the vortex drives self deep inside to touch the most impenetrable inner stockades. The lowered ceiling keeps dropping to push the student to the subterranean level, where unworthiness and self-blame are housed. Depression is a useful tool for surrender. The ego's attempt to battle it ultimately fails.

The students MUST ask for HELP from the spiritual plane when confronting the magnetic vortex of their depression. They need enhanced light to tether themselves to the corrected force field that says YES to their being at ALL times. Please ask the Higher Self, Masters, Angelic Force, and Source Itself to be energetically LIFTED up above these darkened waters of pessimism without blocking off self's much-needed healing interaction with these karmic wounds. It truly is "darkest before dawn." Widespread depression is the final vortex of the separation illusion—the prelude to the dawning of the New Age. It is the last membrane of isolation or lovelessness before the soul bursts forth in full recognition of its rightful place in the Universe.

Depression leads the students to the collective core wound of separation. Like an express train into the dark, depression relentlessly clutches self until it has reached is miserable destination—a wasteland in the collective consciousness, where all beings feel exiled from their Creator. This presents the opportunity and challenge to realize the illusion of this imprisoning exile. As more students see beyond the veil, the collective Depression Wall crumbles. At this momentous time in human history, the Divine Mandate of collective awakening requires all of humankind to pierce the shroud of separation/ lovelessness and touch its true Essence.

As students openly share their experience of depression, they commune with each other, not in misery, but in mutual realization that depression is nothing more than an agreed-upon decision to lock self up in a deep, dark inner vault, and throw away the key. Ironically, it is impossible to throw away the key because self's conscious awareness IS the key. Simply the intent to find that vault and BELIEVE that it can be opened, freeing all exiled parts of self with the help of the spiritual plane, immediately softens depression's steely climate. Then the journey inward through this darkened corridor, while formidable, is not torturous punishment but rather a mysterious search for the cosmic clues that uncover the gems banked within the banned parts of the soul. Once reclaimed, the soul rejoices and depression is truly a thing of the past.

Chronic depression is an intense attachment to non-movement. Many students in previous lives responded to their illusion of disconnect by deciding to sit tight and wait it out— spending centuries awaiting Source's permission to emerge. But depression's persistence is the affirming genius within. It knows that if students continue to bump up against this bleak vortex, they will eventually dare to touch its acute pain with loving inquiry. Then the giant bugaboo of soul sickness will recede through the healing touch of cherished connectedness with self, others and the Universe.

Don't wait behind the Depression Wall. Accept the insistency of self's depression as a cosmic mandate to push forward into one's inner recesses to retrieve the soul's full essence. Though it may appear to be counter-intuitive, the willingness to move toward self's depression with open-heartedness melts despair. Don't push past depression. Rather, release undue attachment to external life to allow deep inward travel. This intention alone alleviates some of the depression. To avoid facing one's depression prolongs the ride on the karmic wheel of suffering. The inescapable dominion of the soul's glory insists that all blocks to its shining brilliance be dismantled.

Inevitably, humankind will be liberated from depression as it remembers its spiritual essence. As more students create shared rituals for the soul's passages/ initiations, depression's greatest weapon—isolation—is rendered impotent.

Shine the light for each other! Encourage this process of welcoming back exiled parts of self to the Whole, just as Source welcomes Its children back with joyous embrace. As more students heal their depression, others will boldly defy the collective false beliefs of futility and despair. Accompany others into their dark pits of separation to remind them that disconnect is impossible. Then the collective negativity will break apart like the great arctic ice, allowing the waters of Cosmic Consciousness to flow freely, washing away all vestiges of depression into a titanic waterfall of Boundless Possibility and Joy!

✧ Crimes of the Soul ✧

October 2001

Since Tuesday, Sept 11, 2001, I have awakened each morning to our immediate collective nightmare; feeling like the ground is giving way. How can our reality shift so radically in a matter of hours? With stomach churning, sinking, queasy, the mind jumps in to gain control over my repulsion. But there is no rationalization, no psychological or spiritual explanation, to release me from the sheer pain of trying to assimilate and digest the horror and devastation that has occurred. My heart, weeping over this needless disaster and desperate to stay open within its natural flow of compassion and forgiveness, struggles to resist the impulse to contract in self-protection and "hard-hearted" defeat at the futility of the human condition.

Angrily, I confront the Tibetan with: "I thought you said the human race was making progress? How can we ever consider ourselves 'spiritual beings' when we generate this kind of agony? We might as well be back in the dark ages, barbarically slaughtering each other over pointless land feuds. How can we possibly make a collective leap in consciousness when we are capable of mass murder? The light doesn't seem to be pervading on this planet. Maybe it never will. Are we all doomed to self-destruction, caught in the net of the 'dark forces?'

"No wonder our beloved mother earth is so contaminated by our irresponsibility. How can we possibly honor her if we can't honor each other? Why didn't the Masters and Angelic Force stop this horrendous crime? Is there no such thing as Divine Intervention? Are you, our supposedly dedicated helpers, going to stand by and let us annihilate each other? Is it really possible for you to protect us from ourselves? And what about this "New Age" that is supposedly carrying so much light, love and transformation? It must be all stupid delusion—a hollow fairy tale we tell ourselves to buffer the "reality" of our dense, dark, retarded little world. Don't lead us on anymore by seducing us to believe that world peace and collective awakening is within our reach. My trust is shattered."

Within moments after unleashing this rage on my beloved teacher, I sit down and weep, realizing that I'm looking for someone to blame, to be held accountable, perhaps to ease this unbearable feeling of helplessness. Like an angry child, I lash out at the one who loves me the most—my teacher and friend who has been devoted to me in spite of all my limitations, standing by me for countless incarnations as an anchor for my evolution. Admitting temporary blindness fueled by rage that filled me with zealous fire, I see the gut reaction: I not only want to destroy the "cause" of this crime, but also to nullify the part of me that would dare believe we could collectively evolve beyond this anguish-filled realm in which we live. It is too painful and disappointing to let myself really trust that we could mature forward to a time of true world peace.

If I, having worked so hard to make myself conscious, can be instantly consumed by blinding rage, so too can any of us strike out in venomous reaction to life's apparent injustices and betrayals. Dare we judge our enemy when we are cut from the same cloth? All the spiritual progress in the world doesn't exempt us from our collective shadow, a shadow we all feed from the dark undercurrents in our soul.

This becomes the real spiritual test. How do we hang on to our "highfalutin" ideals of universal love and oneness when so many of our loved ones are heartlessly destroyed by another's madness? Do we sink to their level, caught in the throes of revenge and retaliation? Do we immerse ourselves in compassion, leaving ourselves wide open and vulnerable to future attacks because we have not shown "them" that we mean business? They "need" punishment. How do we decide the punishment? Are we still at the primitive level of "an eye for an eye"?

Unable to answer any of these burning questions, I just want to bury myself in denial, pretending that there is nothing I can do about it anyway, abdicating my responsibility to the collective consciousness. My true responsibility includes holding the full impact of this trauma in my heart, without "Novocain"—no distractions, rationalizations, indifference or non-reality created by geographical distance. We all somehow contributed to this horrible event through our daily-indulged illusions of separation, competition, judgment, scarcity, greed, power struggles and lovelessness. No one is exempt from these crimes of the soul. We must all come to terms with the undeniable impact of our own darkness.

We all "died" on Tuesday, September 11, 2001. Something has irrevocably changed. I can only pray that this change will somehow alchemize us to a new level where collective crimes are not only intolerable, but inconceivable to all beings on this planet.

The Tibetan strides forward, long maroon robes flowing as he descends the steps in front of the "Hall of Records," our usual meeting place on the causal plane where the karmic records are stored. Arms stretched out, he envelopes me in an embrace that melts my heart in tender surrender to the inevitability of our current human condition. Remorsefully, I ask for forgiveness for my impatient rage and frustration. Lovingly waving aside my plea for forgiveness the Tibetan says:

The shock of this tragedy stimulates all trauma from past lives. How many times has self witnessed the pointless destruction of Source's creation? How many wars must the planet endure before humankind breaks through the veil of separation? Until humankind truly knows the consciousness of ONENESS, it will continue to burn itself up in the fires of negativity.

These negative forces cultivate the terrain of hopelessness, defeat, futility, emptiness, powerlessness and despair that drives the soul to strike out against anyone or anything that mirrors back its own prison. This is the prison of darkened consciousness—a consciousness sealed off from the experience of Source's Love. Within this unilluminated vortex, the soul withers away, starved by the lack of spiritual nourishment, barely able to receive a trickle of Source's bounty.

The darkness crystallizes into a potent force orchestrated to destroy anything or anyone that threatens its cocooned energetic corruption. There is tremendous energy in this crystallized dark force that leaks into the collective unconscious of humankind, feeding on the human inclination to believe that it is somehow separate from Source. Alone on the earth plane, apparently having to fend for itself, humankind sinks to the bestial level of rageful survival, angry at Source for creating such an unholy place as this planet earth.

The Masters continually implore the students to remember who they are—truly beings of Light. However, the Masters cannot shake all of humankind awake. We can prod, poke, tease, challenge, teach and inspire, but cannot force the consciousness open like a clam shell defiantly sealed shut. We can only wait patiently, determinedly present at all times as conduits for Divine intervention.

Divine intervention is not aggressive, not a forced expansion, but rather the warming breath of wisdom whispered over and over again until the student suddenly "comes to" in full awareness of the truth of their being. Until the soul warms to its truth, the Masters and Angelic Force can only hold the Great Invocation that reminds all of humankind about the inevitability of the Divine Plan. The Plan, established long ago, reveals the earth in her enlightened state.

The New Age is just beginning, with humankind emerging from thousands of years of darkness. This has created a long-standing inertia—a force that pulls the collective consciousness back into the confining paradigm of darkness and futility. All who have incarnated at this time have agreed to work at the Olympian task of withstanding the true weapon of the dark force, which is the cultivation of hatred and judgment.

Allow self to have the courage to believe in the new emerging paradigm, knowing that to change form is not an easy task. This process is filled with chaos and unpredictability. The collective leap in consciousness demands great determination to weather the storms of transformation and the "blackening" stage of alchemization.

Let these events unfolding upon the earth at this time crack open the collective defense structure reflecting the false belief that one must only concentrate on self. Encourage a heightened awareness of group consciousness to flow forth, knowing that all are brothers and sisters, responsible for each other—and all have souls longing for liberation. From that platform, imagine the resolution of this great tragedy, a resolution that honors the tremendous service of those dearly departed beings who were "victims" of this catalytic event. Let this resolution carry enough passion, heart, and grief to bring human beings closer to each other.

This great destructive force, a profound discharge of negative collective karma, can potentiate a transformation so profound as to blast all of humankind into a new realm, where all life is honored and revered. Pray from the depths of the soul to offer this tragic sacrifice as the final shock that breaks the spell of this dark force that would imprison humankind for eternity if left alone and unaddressed within each being. The Masters weep with humankind and hold them, encircled in love and great compassion for the courage to be incarnate in the year 2001.

In this time, the oppositional Forces confront each other for final resolution of all duality and the ultimate release of all karmic memories of Divine betrayal. This leads to the opportunity to KNOW safety, the true Net of the Divine that brings all souls through the eternal focus and substantiation of Source's outpouring of compassion and acceptance. Do not fall prey to the hungry ghosts of past lives telling self that the dark has won.

Remember that all is possible. Allow the trust to endure. Know that the Masters share the burden of fear, lightening the load, so that the true gold within the human heart can emerge, shining victorious at long last.

✧ The Question of War ✧

January 2002

It was 1968. I was a sophomore in college demanding PEACE, end the Vietnam War NOW, fully convinced of the absurdity of killing people to fuel political corruption. I *knew* I was right. How could anyone at any time condone war? My compassionate mind- set was repulsed by the military, considering them heartless bloodthirsty barbarians. From my youthful, idealistic, hippie perspective our only choice was to make love, not war; to "WAGE PEACE" no matter what.

Yet during those times of "absolute certainty" I was haunted by what I knew about WWll, won by the "good guys" a mere four years before my birth. I grimly imagined how my life would have been if Hitler had been the victor. That war against "evil," horrific criminals who could murder and incinerate their brothers and sisters seemed righteously mandatory.

My confusion about war surfaces repeatedly. How do we decide when and if war is justified? What happens to spiritual idealism when our beloved homeland is attacked, creating thousands of innocent victims?

Spiritual tradition teaches that war is wrong. The Taoists say to yield to one's opponent, flowing with the Way of the Tao. Gandhi inspired thousands to keep the peace by resisting the instinctual urge to fight back. Master Jesus taught us to turn the other cheek. Do the heavens ever use force to stop what seems to be a violation to the Divine Flow?

War is a volatile topic with no clear-cut resolution. It is tempting to simply retreat from this red hot issue, not wanting to touch subject with a ten-foot pole. But we have no choice. The war against terrorism is actively impacting us, whether consciously or subliminally, highlighting the bitter reality that there has always been war among humankind. Historically we were constantly fighting and killing each other.

We attempt to justify war among humankind by citing principles. However, our enemies are just as passionate about *their* principles. Where do we draw the line? What absolute principle surpasses all divisive concerns, permitting us to pull out all the stops to support it? We often agree that it's right to go to war if we are fighting for our freedom or survival. The need to protect oneself is pure animal instinct.

Spiritual teachings describe the body as a sacred vessel. Do we allow others to torture and destroy that sacred vessel without attempting to stop them? But how far do we extend self defense? Dropping the bomb on Japan to end the Pacific theater of WWII murdered thousands of innocent people. Was it justified? Do we destroy other "sacred vessels" in order to preserve ours? The impossibility of these questions leaves me overwhelmed with confusion, muddled in a bog of contradictions and uncertainty.

When I moved into my previous home in Montague, MA, I noticed one or two hornets flying around the bedroom. I tried to ignore them, hoping they would just go away. A week passed and more hornets arrived, bringing the number up to five or six. Each morning I awoke witnessing hornets flying around the ceiling, terrorizing me with their high-pitched buzz.

Idealistically practicing a passive, yielding approach, I tried to wait it out, hoping the October chill would send them on their way. Then I got stung. A large, inflamed, red hot welt, sent aching pain down my leg for two weeks. How could I ignore this? Maybe it was just a fluke. I resolved to let it go. Then Zayne got stung, and I got stung again, and he got stung again. Soon there were at least 50 hornets taking over our bedroom ceiling. They were forcing us to deal with them, like it or not.

After feeble attempts to humanely corral and usher them out the window, I called the exterminator. "Kill them all" I declared, determined to be done with those destructive monsters. I was at war. Nothing was going to stop me. My instinct for safety far overrode my spiritual desire to preserve all life. These were only insects I was killing, yet we knew the principle still applied.

When do we give ourselves permission to wipe out a plague that torments us, whether animal or human, and how do we justify the means by which we do that?

This instinctual dynamic is reflected in our medical approach to cancer. A cancerous condition is comprised of "enemy" cells basically eating us alive. Too often we feel defenseless in our attempts to stop the cellular war machine that is annihilating us systematically. How do we treat this terrorism? Sometimes the precision of surgery *can* remove only the cancer cells, leaving the rest of the healthy cells unharmed. And so we attempt to kill only the terrorists with precision bombing, sparing the life of the innocent and good.

However, sometimes the cancer cannot be surgically removed and the decision is made to bring out the heavy artillery of chemotherapy. Yes, they "cure" cancer by flooding the body with poison, but at the price of indiscriminately ravaging healthy cells right alongside the nasty cancer cells as it floods the body with poison. The entire body is weakened, almost destroyed by the "cure" itself. Is it worth it? Those who recover from cancer think so. Are the innocent lives inadvertently destroyed through unavoidably generalized attacks worth the sacrifice? Not only does this weaken the besieged country but collectively we are all shaken by this desperate shotgun approach to healing the apparent "incurables" of the world.

Confused to the point of a mental stalemate, I can only raise the questions. The great poet teacher, Rilke, teaches that we need to live the questions. The answers lie in a distant horizon, unfathomable to our limited human perspective. But the questions have their way with us, working on our obstinate belief systems, undermining our knowing, perhaps paving the way to true wisdom.

The Tibetan lovingly observes me struggling with this conflict in ideology and responds:

War has been a central component of the human process. External wars only reflect the internal war active within most people. To be at war with self is to attempt to obliterate conflicting parts of the soul needing to be integrated into a harmonious whole. The ego is often at war with the Higher Self, struggling to destroy the overriding principle that guides this incarnation in an effort to reign supreme, in control and dominant over karmic mandates. Let the student "cease fire" on self, expanding the ability to embrace every aspect of self with compassion and understanding. This matures the collective consciousness into self-responsibility, lessening the potential for external war.

War has an alchemical effect on the collective consciousness. Every war, in its irrevocable impact, has taught a particular lesson and evolved the awakening process in humankind. The towering impact of death and destruction, while crippling the heart and tormenting the soul, breaks down the false sense of security reflecting stagnant energy within global relationships.

War is ultimately an effort to break down barriers. Just as when friends or couples have angry arguments, hurtful statements to each other ironically are efforts to be heard in a new way, evoke new information, fracture rigid, suffocating boundaries, and aggressively demolish outgrown agreements that stifle the soul.

Within the current arena of duality an act of power is sometimes required to establish a higher order, evolving the earth plane closer to Universal Peace. This is reflected in nature when a forest fire destroys a beautiful old-growth forest, a natural act of power designated to break through an outmoded order, to usher in new expressions of the Divine in form. One weeps over the loss of the majestic ancient trees, but when the dust has settled, the fresh beauty of new grasses and wildflowers rebirthing the forest floor brings renewed faith. The death required for rebirth demonstrates the eternal within the temporal.

And so, in personal and global relationships, one may anguish over the loss of a harmonious connection, beautiful and serene. But this is replaced by an alert awareness of new energies emerging, a disturbance ultimately providing new possibilities in connection, understanding, relatedness and unification. Within the uncertainty created by warlike destruction of old forms, the global family loses its sense of place, position, hierarchy, structure. In this collective uncertainty, the smug confidence of believing that one is in control falls away. Then humankind is "reduced" to a level of open uncertainty, defenselessness and vulnerability that ultimately results in a softened state. The experience of soft exposure offers humankind the potential to experience greater love for each other, valuing the precious connection that links all within a universe that cannot be controlled or orchestrated by the ego. This heightened state of vulnerability and love nurtures a new level of global peace. Stalemates mirrored within attachments to positions of concretized power dismantle in the experience of a Universal Love that demonstrates the sameness among all peoples.

Humankind's oppositional relationship with the Divine provides abundant feeding ground for the dark force, is an anti-life dynamic that is programmed to undermine the Divine Plan. Until humankind moves its alchemical practice to the art of the enlightened magician, required acts of power to stop this anti-life force have to be expressed through an equally destructive response exemplified by war. Until humankind understands the potency of the Force of Love and its ability to neutralize all aggression, it will resort to the "necessary evil" of war in an effort to rout out the dark undercurrents in the human soul. Eventually, humankind will understand the responsibility of the magician, which is to work the Force from the sophisticated level of mind, alchemizing the barren terrain that houses the dark force—collective thought patterns steeped in lovelessness

Ultimately there will be world peace. Then evolution will not require a destructive breakdown for movement to higher levels of order. Rather, the principles of transformation and transmutation will be the central organizing dynamics in the collective mindset of humanity. This is reflected in the caterpillar who metamorphosizes into a heightened level of existence, the butterfly, through the complete destruction of its old form. Even the forest fire will be replaced by this model of transfiguration, allowing nature to be spared the "ravages" of its historic warlike conditions.

Enlightened Masters live on the plane of Universal Peace and Compassion. These teachers, both human and in spirit, model to the students an expanded perception of Divine Love. Humanity's instinct to war will melt away like a dark cloud on the horizon, leading to a Paradigm of Eternal Peace that reflects the birth of a new Cosmic Day within all Creation.

✧ Finding Meaning in 9/11 ✧

September 2002

We've somehow managed to go on with our lives since September 11, 2001. Are we changed, permanently wounded, transformed, defeated, inspired, weakened, and sobered? We have all suffered from post-traumatic stress. In the first year after that awful day, my dream work with clients revealed nightmarish images of toppling buildings, crashing airplanes, and flaming bodies—the psyche's way of trying to digest a terrifying event that still continues in our unconscious, as fresh as if it were happening today. Consciously we try to go forward, put it behind us, get over it. But collectively we were all hit, and collectively we have been trying to heal, questioning, fearing, and wondering. Did this terrible tragedy wound or strengthen our faith?

Disasters like this force people to strive for elevated understanding in order to heal. Higher meaning broadens our perspective, creating some spaciousness around the horror—the horror that doesn't break down no matter how many months pass. The human psyche can only assimilate so much. The remaining debris concretizes into a hard ball of trauma that sits in our collective belly like a rock. How much have we digested in the years since? How will we tolerate the indigestible core of horror? Can a higher meaning soften that unalterable pain? Will we ever get enough distance from it to be able to look back and imbue this upheaval with understanding?

How many of us are sidestepping that ball of terror, hungry to recapture the carefree spirit of the child once again? Yes, our collective innocence was shattered. Now we toggle between the impulse to return to the old consciousness as if nothing happened and the determination to soberly pick up the reins of responsible adulthood. What was the lesson? Did we learn it? What healing meaning could we possibly give such a shocking catastrophe? Is this kind of horror mandatory to shatter our innocence—a relentlessly present, indigestible fear that alchemizes us to a place of power through its constant irritation?

Some of us are reluctant to believe that such an event could have a positive transformative purpose. That thinking feels too sacrilegious. We believe we must continue to suffer that day over and over again in our hearts, imaginations, and souls in order to do penance for our collective crime. It would be too easy to give a higher benevolent meaning—like sliding out of doing hard time—too cavalier for the cries of the victims crashing to their deaths in that blistering nightmare. Some of us hope the philosophers, spiritual teachers, authorities will hand feed us enough mental resolve to sedate us into acceptance of the unacceptable.

We need to imbue 9/11 with a higher significance that bridges and integrates this event into our souls. If we don't give it meaning, we fall into despair, all "victims" of humanity's blindness. We must evolve our perception of this event based on what it has awakened in us collectively. Otherwise we are forever stunned by the moment, frozen in time, unable to synthesize the impact to fill our hearts with fresh determination, courage, forgiveness and faith.

I am just as guilty, only too happy to slide past the ghosts of that day, trying to block out their cries. I went to New York City in December to buy a piano and somehow allowed only enough time to get to the piano studio on 20th street and back home—no time to take the subway all the way downtown to the site of the crime. It didn't even cross my mind to go there, to pay homage, until I was "safely" back in western Mass, so deeply buried was my fear of facing the trauma. Then the guilt and the shame set in. What a coward I was not to bear witness, as if this crime happened to someone else, not me.

9/11 changed me. I don't take my freedom for granted. I know more fear, registered as vague anxiety relentlessly nipping at my happiness. I am more determined than ever to work on myself and others to consciously embrace/ transmute our internal demons. Ironically, this amplified commitment brings me greater joy. 9/11 removed "vacation time" from my internal work by demonstrating the urgency of these times. The collective reckoning of the poles has begun—dark clashing with light within our souls.

The rug was pulled out from under us. I have a greater empathy for others who live with terrorism. I lost the illusion of external security but gained the sanctuary of internal security, a spiritual harbor. Still haunted by that day, I can no longer be in denial about the fragility of our American life, or of our human existence. This lack of denial ironically evokes a deeper level of faith—one based on the raw awareness of collective unilluminated terrain. This yields a previously unreachable wisdom and newfound strength/ determination to go beyond the insanity of destruction.

Our faith is most fragile when we are in illusion and strongest when our eyes are open. This awakening brought greater clarity, tangibility, aliveness. It's become too painful to attempt to disassociate from our crimes of darkness. The heightened awareness stimulated by 9/11 burned a hole in our illusion of coherence, reminding us that we live in times of intense fragmentation, chaos, overwhelm. We shake our heads, painfully admitting that this is just the beginning—the loss of innocence and the gain of wisdom. No one is invulnerable to this event. Through the shared tragedy we know an unprecedented collective communion.

My clients have brought more transpersonal issues to our work this year. Burning personal issues are less compelling in light of the larger tragedy. Financial stress forced us to reexamine our values. Economic crunch pushed us toward simple pleasures, almost with a sigh of relief. Perhaps we are all tired of striving for the next acquisition, outputting gobs of money into soulless empty endeavors. 9/11 compelled us to drop our phony sophistication and reach out for what's really important. It forced us to ask: How do we feed our souls to eliminate all the spiritual starvation that sustains global monsters of aggression and hatred?

Initially, 9/11 shattered my assumption that humanity was making progress, sparking my rage at the Masters for their promise that collective enlightenment is on the horizon. In the face of this horror, the New Age suddenly seemed to be a bunch of hogwash. Now I understand that 9/11 blew a hole in our collective soul, leaving it bleeding but opened to new energies. We were frightened enough to finally take notice—to be alert—no longer numb to the heightened energies and the potential for transformation. Like lancing a collective boil, this kundalini shock blasted apart our attachment to isolation/ separation and merged our divergent perceptions. It fired up my sense of mission as I faced the immediacy of this time of awakening.

The accelerated vibratory rate currently impacting the collective consciousness has unearthed deep karmic debris for cleansing. This relentless energy pummels all blockages to full awakening. Catastrophes like 9/11 shake up the collective defense structure to augment access to these snowballing energies. Forced to wake up from our collective isolation myth, awareness of our interconnectedness deepened. This amplified our cognizance of the revolution in consciousness currently unfolding at the grassroots level.

9/11 demonstrated the illusion and pitfalls of worldly power, leaving us hungry for the presence of a greater power in our lives—the power of our divinity. The frustrations of our "enemies" mirrored our own, causing us to suspend judgment and cultivate compassion for everyone's pain. In our shared fragility we experienced true humility—the kind that opens our hearts to something greater than our small selves. Can something as abhorrent as 9/11 actually enhance our humanity—our spirituality? Yes!

The Tibetan sits patiently as I sort through my thoughts, deeply supportive of the need to integrate such a cataclysm. He teaches:

When the principle of shattering is applied, its sole function is to break apart stagnancy, density, illusion. This shattering of the old order makes way for a new higher order based on the Oneness that joins all beings. When one is stripped to the bone, the true Divine Skeleton is revealed, exposing the essential spiritual structure of the soul based on the unification of all beings through Love. Over the years since 9/11, countless students have transmuted their initial rage, fear, hatred, bewilderment into a new level of wisdom, dissolving many boundaries. The poison of their horror has transmuted into fertile soil for new growth. Most students have allowed themselves to stay open, resisting the seduction of cynicism and jaded self-protective perspectives on collective corruption. This upheaval dismantled walls of self-righteousness, allowing all peoples to stand in each other's shoes—to come together in mutual acknowledgement of loss, pain, wonderment. Sharing this mutually vulnerable place softens humankind to experience the inevitable link that unites us all.

Humankind matured from this crisis and strengthened its resolve to assume responsibility for the daily small but significant acts of violence, aggression, and lovelessness. Humankind, witnessing the extreme of its collective shadow, pulled back in repulsion. This loathing still leaks out its toxins in projected judgment of other cultures, nations, religions. However, a much greater percentage of students have assimilated this revulsion into their world view as a signal designed to turn the stomach, energetically alerting them to any violation of the Divine boundaries nourishing all of Source's creation.

Yes, this devastation haunts humankind—as well it should. In that haunting, humankind cannot rest so easily in it sleepy repose of indifference and narcissism. 9/11 produced victims throughout the globe, forcing humankind to explore the illusion of collective disempowerment. The existence of victims/ victimizers reflects an infantile humanity that still believes Source (God) is responsible for all of its miseries. 9/11 demonstrated the stark consequence of irresponsibility, immaturity and carelessness. This wake-up call helped humankind to comprehend that there are no victimizers— only people as vulnerable as their neighbors who appear to have so much more than they.

What are the mandates of this heightened maturation? In their commitment to never let this happen again, many students have taken greater responsibility for the seduction of rage, jealousy, hatred, aggression, judgment and scarcity. 9/11 expanded the students out of their small egoic worlds into the knowing that ultimately there can be no peace or joy until ALL beings are liberated. Many students are working on integrating their shadow—accepting it as the black coal that transforms into a diamond. Students are teaching each other to use the heightened awareness caused by this shock to see what is possible in the human condition—to look more deeply into each other's eyes...to open their hearts to each other's souls...to embrace the preciousness of life...to refuse to energize intolerance...to focus on higher qualities of love, joy, support, nourishment, peace, creativity.

The intolerable nature of 9/11 prevents humankind from going back to sleep. Startled awake, humankind is now available to invoke its birthright of collective magnitude. Many students have begun rolling up their sleeves, deeply aware of how much work there is to be done <u>and</u> of their ability to accomplish it. They are making the leap into a new world order based in love and communion, magnetizing others who are less conscious to join in this accelerated learning curve. The agonies of 9/11 tempered the collective soul and opened the collective third eye. Many students met in groups, exercising their imaginations to envision humankind's potential for rebirth/ regeneration.

As more groups met, students began to experience first hand the impact of the collective endeavor that invokes group awakening. When humanity rushes to each other's aid in support/ comfort, it finds itself in groups that build momentum in consciousness. Since September 11, that momentum burned through the dross of greed/ selfishness and burst open the collective heart chakra to reveal the power of Love in its highest sense. This is the Love that heals the unhealable, renews faith at a deeper level and dissolves all pain. Know that the beloved "victims" of 9/11 gave of their bodies in a soul agreement to add fuel to the alchemical fires in the human condition—so that all may know the heat that transforms and the magnificent opportunity for liberation that comes when humankind lets go of separation and holds the entire world within the collective heart.

✧ Leaving the Dread Zone: Overcoming Fear ✧

July 2003

How many of us walk around with a pit of anxiety in our stomachs so chronic that we can't even register its impact? What dread-filled expectations do we unconsciously carry to sustain that pit? When someone tells us to relax, we quickly insist that we ARE relaxed! Yet, our belly continues to tightly wrap itself into a frozen ball of negative expectation and our breathing stays shallow while our mind frantically searches for outside things to justify the persistence of this anxiety and dread. Yes, fear is our constant companion, day and night. Nightmare dreams wake us up in a sweat convinced that we are doomed to some horrible destiny. Frantically we search for ways to calm our nerves and quiet down the internal voices of catastrophe while forgetting to fully breathe, take in our surroundings, drop our shoulders, relax our stomach muscles, soften our eyes, release our furrowed brows and TRUST. Habits of fear-based motivation block our ability to imagine other incentive-fuels for growth. This compounds upon itself as the Dread Zone closes in on us, blocking possibility, exaggerating past traumas, difficulties, and dramatizing our collective doom.

Fear is contagious like a wicked plague that annihilates the spirit. We feel defenseless in the face of fear's relentless seduction. It NEVER leaves us alone. It thrives on the wee hours of the night when we wake up, heart pounding, certain that our world will fall apart. Then the mind, an ambassador of this plague, jumps in to list the countless horrible realities that could—no will befall us. After a few hours of this mental torture we jump out of bed and get something to eat, trying to shake off this fear flu that has already sickened our thoughts and sapped our courage. We might walk around the house as we try to deny this sticky, clingy poison of fear's absolutism. But there is no negotiating with fear. Like the medieval black scourge that wiped out Europe, the "bacteria" that carries fear—the fear bug—bites us hard, leaving us to wait in trepidation for the inevitable agony of disintegration to befall us.

Where does this fear come from? We work so hard to be positive, brave, optimistic. But still we are infected. This global pestilence is rising to a point of feverish collective terror. Even the strongest of us seem destined to perish in the Swamp of Terror where visions of possibility are contaminated. Coming in for the final kill, the paralysis sets in—the last stage of the fear plague when we simply stop moving forward in our lives. We may tell ourselves we are open, growing and taking risks. But if we look deeper inside, we see ourselves huddled up in a corner of our psyche, hoping that somehow we will be able to survive the inevitable horror on the horizon.

No wonder we can't unleash our creative power, joy and acceptance. When we wonder why we aren't growing, expanding, trusting, we blame others, politics and God. But most of us haven't explored the full range of fear that saturates our cells which forever reminds us that no matter what we do in life, something horrible will happen—failure, disease, violence, betrayal, lovelessness, etc.

This level of subliminal fear is the Dread Zone. Like an iceberg, most of it lies massively present in our unconscious with just the tip showing, presenting itself as the surface fears that we try to dismiss and ignore. Like a Band-Aid, we attempt to smooth over our apprehensions with a rational exploration of the presenting fear, support from our friends and family, by forcing ourselves to breathe more deeply, or by saying a quick prayer to God to give us courage. But few of us scuba dive down into the arena of the collective DREAD, the iceberg fed for thousands of years by our negative expectations of earthly life.

We try to ward off the Dread Zone by taking flight in our imaginations, hoping to explore and embrace our magnitude. But trying to soar with thousand-pound weights attached to our feet pulls us in half. It's impossible to integrate ourselves into an expanded consciousness with our feet cemented in the paralysis zone of Dread. If we can't align our entire being with our highest intentions, we cannot successfully energize and manifest our visions. This feeds the fear bug (ancestrally injected into our roots) that is already streaming through our system, blackening hopes and dreams for the future. Instead we unwittingly energize the Dread Zone with collective karmic, fear-filled expectations that unbalance us, kick the creative platform right out from under us and undermine our best intentions. Yes, we've caught the plague one more time as we second-guess our decisions, actions, understandings, visions, dreams, and pathetically hand our power over to fear. After all, don't we all agree that fear knows better than we do about the "reality" of things? Better to let fear guide our path. Doesn't it protect us from foolishly blundering into disaster as it convinces us that we need to be prepared for devastation—as if one could ever be prepared for catastrophe?

Daily my awareness increases of how the Dread Zone permeates my consciousness. It is the counterpoint to an emerging sense of profound well-being and aliveness. As soon as I touch this fresh joy, the Dread Zone reminds me that we are all on the brink of destruction, and I better not forget it! In response I contract, scurrying back like a scared rabbit to our communal Worry Ward. Fear wins, crushing my delicate attunement to the potential of these times. I slink back into the morass of collective catastrophic visions, adding my own particular brand of nightmare to the mix, which leads to thoughts of giving up on everything that I believe in. I know in that moment that I am colluding in the chronic negative paradigm. But I cannot stop myself as the quicksand of fear blackens my perspective.

When I am in channel the Tibetan shows me this nasty Dread Zone on the inner planes. It looks like the earth is shrink-wrapped in thick, black plastic—compressed tight as a drum, unable to breathe through this synthetic (artificial) barrier. This is not the nature of our organic world! The negative force eclipses our natural brilliance. However, the plastic is wearing thin, torn in places, to reveal the verdant harmonious green of our collective healing which inspires the realization that this veil of darkness is truly an illusion—counterfeit—NOT REAL. When we open to the awareness of our true spiritual identity, old illusions are prevented from holding that plastic in place. It starts to shred, allowing gaps of brilliant light to emanate forth.

When we dare to touch these shafts of light, ancient negative conditioning cautions us not to trust this greater realm. Continue to keep paying homage to the Fear God! We hesitate to bask in the long-awaited awareness that there is NOTHING to fear. I continue struggling to withstand the seduction of the Dread Zone, determined to sustain an outlook free of fearful expectations while touching the innate lightness of my spiritual essence. I challenge myself to not look back at historical events that "prove" our fears to be true. Like Lot's wife, I know that if I look back I will turn to "salt"—a useless pillar of frozen fear. In this moment, as I look to the horizon of my liberation, the plastic dread wall appears stupidly flimsy, and I understand that ultimately nothing can stop our evolution into enlightenment!

The Tibetan smiles in support of my fleeting moment of inner peace and encourages me to breathe this fearlessness deep into my cells. He teaches:

Humankind expects things to go wrong—to be victimized by its very existence. It attaches to fear like a God. Fear shrinks one's world through suffocation. Then the spirit appears to be snuffed out, the light of inspiration exhausted by storms of dread that ravage the emotional and mental body.

There is a blanket of dread, like a dark cloak of ruin, surrounding the earth. This blanket is a distorted force field of astral quicksand, filled with dread vortexes. The more that self fights it, the more the dread vortexes pull self down. The true nature of the cosmos is a positive upward vortex that magnetizes the soul's evolution. The darkened grid surrounding the planet inverts this magnificent magnetic calling of the soul's true glory and drives it down into dread's existential wasteland. The dark force celebrates fear as its ultimate weapon against the light. Humankind is truly blinded by fear. The ball of dread in the solar plexus is the connecting chord to this negative grid.

Unplug the dread! It is NOT humankind's true nature to be fearful. Crippled for centuries by this dark garden of horror embedded in the earth's emotional (astral) body, humankind assumes (without reflection) that fear-based limitation is Source's mandate for earthly existence. Remember that self's light factor carries a greater voltage than the magnetic draw of the Dread Zone.

The Masters encourage students to rise up from their wheelchairs and discover that they will not fall. Take a step out of the Dread Zone, the breeding domain that continually hatch millions of fear bugs thirsty for the blood of humankind's negativity. This negativity leaves humanity open to infection, repeatedly bitten by fears that convince them that joyous health, well-being, happy endings, true fulfillment, success, enlightenment and liberation are foolish yearnings never to be known while human. Students relegate these possibilities to the etheric planes:

"After death I will go to heaven and finally be safe, happy, loved, light and joyful."

Humankind has continuously, unwittingly energized the dread zone and crystallized the dark grid surrounding the earth as they resign themselves to fearful visions like chains that enslave their imaginations, harden their hearts and congest their solar plexus. This contracts all channels of inspiration. *"Fear indulgence"* must cease in order to enter the Aquarian Age. In response to the Masters' urgings to evolve, students argue: *"I can't, I'm too scared,"* as if fear justifies shirking their responsibility to their Higher Self's mandate for full soul expression. Fear is not a reason to hide one's light to opt out of this current collective spiritual emergence. The Dread Zone is the most dangerous place to live. When self caves in to fear, self fuels the dark force, shrinks planetary light and postpones world evolution.

To leave the Dread Zone, all fears must be tracked with the eye of a detective. Search for clues that validate anxiety voices. Track them back into childhood and past lives. All fear images do nothing more than paint a picture of what humankind has experienced for thousands of years. Once explored, students need not attach to these memories as forerunners of the future.

Many students are beginning to sustain a greater awareness of the truth of humankind's destiny even as familiar fears grip their minds. Align the personal will that emanates from the solar plexus with the Higher Will, to refocus the mind away from fear. Be fully open to the present moment. Students have the choice to turn the mind away from fright-filled compulsions. Daily, self's determination to leave the Dread Zone tonifies psychic muscles that prevail over the downward pull of fear and sustain extended attunement to the Free Realm beyond the fear paradigm. As this fearless consciousness expands, just like a well-conditioned athlete's training becomes effortless, students need less strength and resolve to resist the Dread Zone. Eventually they forget that it exists. The student then serves as an example of reclaimed innocence and trust. In time the students will completely fail to remember all chronic apprehensions and teach others not to fear their own pathways to enlightenment. Then they serve as a shining demonstration of life beyond the Dread Zone where exuberant well-being issues forth into a magnetic field of optimum safety, peace and Divine Nurturance.

As heightened vibrations intensify earth's magnetic field, the gooey grasp of the Dread Zone is loosened because it can only adhere to a diminished voltage of light. Then the "black plastic" ruptures, allowing the earth and collective consciousness to finally breathe in the overwhelming nature of Divine Love which instantly washes away the small world of terrifying nightmares that humankind assumes is its inevitable destiny. Relish the ripping open of this plastic obstruction. Realize self's innate birthright to be free of all fear. Open the solar plexus to its full glory of pure alignment with the Divine Will.

Remember that humankind has shared a mandate in this lifetime to reveal a greater world bathed in LOVE so profound that all dread is neutralized. Then the entire dark grid crumbles. There is nothing to prevent humankind from embracing the limitless Aquarian Age. Students no longer need to fear their vulnerability because to expose their jugular to Source is to receive a Kiss of Safety in the soft underbelly of the open soul. The reign of terror can no longer be energized because the old dread paradigm is metamorphisizing into a higher plane of shared wisdom and true KNOWING that all exist within the Domain of Love.

✧ The Illusion of Failure ✧

May 2005

I often sit in my office and listen to tales of failure. Clients lament that they made a mess of their lives, didn't turn out to be the person they hoped to be, should have been so much further along, let too many opportunities pass them by, never developed their gifts, or failed at marriage, parenting, loving, living. I open my heart to their pain and feel my own dread of nonsuccess surface to intermingle with theirs as we sit together in the collective stew of failure—cooked to a crisp in our shame-filled disappointment.

What would our lives be like if we knew there was no such thing as failure? Probably, filled with the gusto of buoyant certainty that fertilizes confidence and self-esteem, we'd jump headlong into our dreams—unstoppable! But demons of failure haunt our souls and convince us not to even try in the areas that matter the most. Conditioned to anticipate failure, we freeze in the face of possibility, fearful of the disgrace of falling short of our potential. We convince ourselves that we don't care as we cycle downward into failure's seductive web. We betray our greatness in resignation to a failed existence. Ironically, the only failure is when we don't try. All efforts are pure victory for the soul because willingness is fail-proof.

Children assume that family problems are their fault—somehow they've failed their parents. This starts the failure ball rolling as it mows down the truth of who we really are. Parents who feel inadequate pass on this failure legacy. Certainly we can't humiliate them by highlighting their failure with our success. So we hide behind conclusions like: "I blew that one," "I don't live up to my potential," "I can't do anything right," "Success is for others, not me." Parents who are blind to our gifts tell us that we don't have what it takes. Perhaps they were successful in areas foreign to our nature, like a father who is a bank president discounting his son's passion to be an artist. If we're designed for success in areas that don't match our parents' values, they withhold acknowledgment. In their eyes we've failed. But the only "failure" is that we aren't clones of them.

I entered this life feeling like a failure. Distant memories of unfulfilled past-life agendas bled through my delicate psyche not yet armored against the knowledge of where I'd been in previous incarnations. This failure imprint, like a condemnation from on high, convinced me that I would be doomed to nonsuccess no matter how hard I tried. Crippling failure disease was in my bones, calcified from lifetimes of wrong conclusions about my performance as a human being. My parents ignited this illusion by viewing me as a flop not worth their investment of encouragement. So I learned not to invest in myself but rather to comply with this failure doom and try to be satisfied with a fraction of who I really was. This narrowed my world and shrank the possibilities of positive mirrors that reflect the illusion of perceived failure.

I wanted permission from Source to succeed but felt unworthy. So I unconsciously sustained the failure illusion by raising the bar higher every time I neared success. Regardless of positive feedback from others, I faithfully adhered to this "failure contract" to reenact my past-life selves' illusion of insufficiency. Now I know better and happily reframe my interpretation of how I've shown up for life. Life is no longer a string of failures, but rather a stream of cosmic feedback.

The feeling of failure is always a setup. We hold expectations (lifetimes old) that undermine the ability to appreciate our current successes. Our distorted self-image mirrors back only endless shortcomings which add to fears of failing. Self-disappointment projects outward and convinces us that others also judge us as failures. But who decides what failure really is? What is the root of this painful illusion?

Failure is fueled by the fear that we're not enough. Because we dread the humiliation of our inadequacies, we'd rather stagnate than try to be all that we can be. Our inner saboteur has a field day with these unconscious karmic seeds of unsuccessfulness. Failure phobias energize our resistance to evolution. It takes courage to view shortcomings as works in progress rather than failures. Then we'd have to face our deficiencies and not simply slink off to eat humble pie as hopeless spiritual students who have flunked earth school yet again.

Society defines success/ failure according to its current value system. But these values shift throughout time. Prerequisites for a successful life change in the fickle eyes of those in charge. When others experience success we wonder, what's wrong with us? But maybe their souls have agreed to manifest society's values through an easy alignment with these qualities while others have the karma of experiencing great success, not from external recognition but through internal self-acceptance. Because society only sees a peephole of the Divine Plan, its perception of failure/ success is distorted. It makes no sense to judge ourselves with condemnations of failure when we can't perceive the big picture that reveals the true rules of the cosmic game. So how can we know who the winners or losers really are?

We're scientists trying to prove the hypothesis that our magnitude really exists. All efforts in this cosmic experiment are well-rewarded with a release from the prison of failure. We can gleefully interpret the results of our experiments and deposit them in our bank account of self-knowledge, regardless of their trial-and-error nature. After all, we don't condemn scientists as failures because they must try over and over again to unveil life's mysteries. We patiently honor their process of exploration, expectant that eventually something beneficial will result from their efforts. So why not treat ourselves the same way and release the illusion that we have failed in our quest? We're truly free to have the audacity to know that we are successful beings who have all won the race!

The Tibetan holds up a flag of flying colors that affirms humankind's arrival in the Land of Success. He teaches:

Source does not give pass/fail grades to Its students! To go to one's deathbed believing self's life was a failure is a tragic statement of spiritual blindness. Yet, often students bring this veil of perceived failure to the spirit realm when transitioning the earth plane—ashamed to face the karmic board.

When life doesn't unfold as expected, or is filled with obstacles/ setbacks, humankind assumes it's their fault. They forget that those setbacks were divinely mandated to strengthen, mature and evolve the soul. Some of these obstacles are not meant to be surpassed in this lifetime, but rather to be integrated as learning modalities that continually agitate the soul into greater awareness. True success comes from interacting positively /lovingly/ creatively with these impediments rather than making them disappear.

Humankind remembers unfinished past life assignments as failures. But sometimes the karmic board gives directives that are purposely designed to be impossible—not to torment the student but rather to break down their egoic will to allow a deeper alignment with the Divine Will. These setbacks are devised to erode long-standing defense structures in the soul and teach surrender to the mystery. Therefore, to interpret reversals/ disappointments as nonsuccesses causes needless suffering and self-hatred as these "failures" ferment undigested in the soul's belly and turn into the vinegar of defeat.

Humankind senses its innate magnitude and projects that forth into a rigid set of expectations that represent success—then sorely judges itself when life turns out differently. Often the soul describes its notion of success based on obstinate karmic values. However, this lifetime the soul needs to be steered toward a new value system. So obstacles are established to prevent the successful embodiment of all obsolete values.

To perceive self as a failure because expectations based on antiquated soul agendas can't possibly be fulfilled in this lifetime would blind the student to information/ guidance that these supposed failures are providing. They teach the student to embrace an alternate pathway based on the Divine Call toward a new set of virtues. To curl up into a ball of discouragement because self appears unsuccessful is to thwart the very purpose of one's lifetime. Humankind must integrate the past into a meaningful acceptance/ understanding of what the soul needs now. Open to the comprehensive developmental picture that tells the story of the soul's transformation. Nowhere in this Cosmic Cinema is there a need for failure. Therefore, it doesn't exist.

Only through the lens of unconditional love can humankind embrace life's challenges as a vote of approval from the karmic board. After all, why would Source set up Its own beloved offspring—humankind—to hopelessly fail? This would imply that Source Itself failed in Its creation of the human condition, which would undermine the evolutionary journey homeward and retard the expediency of the Divine Plan.

It is a statement of success to have the honor of being selected to come to the earthly plane. All incarnations carry a predestined triumph as they build upon themselves to manifest the height of success. As the cloak of the failure illusion dissolves, the Joy of Attainment sings its song of celebration and accelerates this Universe into the Unimaginable!

✧ <u>Part Five</u> ✧

SOUL LESSONS

✧ Karma ✧

May 2001

Karma, the glue that binds the Divine Plan, is based on the law of cause and effect. There are very specific consequences for our actions, thoughts, feelings and the overall energy we emanate. The old adage, "Everything that goes around comes around" perfectly describes the law of karma. If we accept life on this planet as "Earth School," we can appreciate the role of karma as our Soul's Curriculum Advisor. Our life lessons express unresolved issues from previous lifetimes. Rather than gripe about how tough our karma is, we can see it as an opportunity to develop much-needed soul qualities.

Karma is a neutral force. Like an absolutely unbiased judge, it isn't swayed by begging for mercy, plea bargaining, threats, or denial. It is simply a metaphysical dynamic carrying the laws of the universe, dictating ultimate accountability for all that we create.

Karma is not always "bad." It's satisfying to consciously take note of our good karma—hard-earned gifts, resources, talents and grace showered upon us from this lifetime and previous lifetimes of willingness, overcoming obstacles, maturation, discipline, determination, hard work, endurance, self-responsibility, the development of creative abilities, service to others, selflessness, self-love, and faith. Every effort we have previously made to further our evolution is "rewarded." Nothing goes unnoticed.

When I first learned the concept of karma I felt immediately relieved. Thank God I didn't have to get it right in only one lifetime. I couldn't imagine working through all of my illusions, confusions, frustrations and blind spots in the short span of 90 years (figuring I live that long). Karma is a byproduct of reincarnation. Assuming that we get to incarnate over and over again, karma describes the results of efforts to uncover our essential nature while exploring divinity through earthly life.

Even if one doesn't believe in past lives, karma still exists in this lifetime. Life orchestrates precise situations, placing us on the receiving end of our previous actions or thoughts. This may take

50 years or one day, but eventually the results of our actions circle around either as rewards or difficulties.

We can't escape our karma no matter how hard we try. There are certain people, events, and circumstances we just can't walk away from. We're stuck with them. We may complain and moan like the high school student resenting teachers who give too much "unfair" homework, but the work has got to be done!

It is pure illusion to think that self or others can slip-slide through life, somehow "getting away" with cruel, selfish, thoughtless behavior, free of consequences. It is very comforting to know that all actions catch up with us. Being aware of this metaphysical principle eases my instinctual need for revenge when someone has hurt me. Trusting that their karma will provide them with exactly the situation they need to realize the negative impact they had on me, I am released from having to drive the point home myself. I don't have to "sink to their level" to get even. I just have to hand it over to the great Karmic Board.

The Karmic Board is made up of the guides, teachers, Masters, angels and loved ones who are entrusted in the care and development of our souls. They review our lifetimes, establishing areas that need further development, purification and refinement. Appropriately difficult and challenging situations (course requirements) are mandated to fulfill karmic obligations to one's Higher Self and others.

Karma motivates like nothing else. Being acutely aware that whatever we do, think, or feel comes around to meet us again, whether in this lifetime or some future one, makes one slow down a little to consider the repercussions automatically generated from moment to moment.

Once I understood the implications of karma, I became obsessed with every thought, action, impulse, and expression, knowing full well that whatever energy I generated would eventually circle back around, demonstrating to me its full impact on the world as well as myself. My mind, eagerly overactive, microscopically scrutinized all actions and thoughts, wondering what subtle, or not so subtle, karmic impact my behavior was producing.

It's easy to get carried away with this, examining one's life with relentless vigilance fueled by the fear of generating "bad karma." After all, I figured I had probably created enough bad karma in past lives to keep me busy for eons, cleaning up all the messes my former selves had made. God forbid I should trigger more bad karma. I'd be stuck "staying after school" for eternity to catch up on endless soul homework.

The idea of karma has been misused rather mercilessly by "spiritual" students who explain away other's difficulty and suffering with, "Well, that's their karma." Understanding the law of karma does not negate the need for compassion. Karma or no karma, life's lessons can be painful. We all need support and caring for the tremendously demanding process of being human.

At some point in our evolution we are all blind. Because this blind spot leads us to unconsciously do or say hurtful things to each other or the earth does not mean we "deserve" the "bad" karma it generates in subsequent lifetimes. Karma is not a punishment laid down by a judgmental God. It is simply an energetic response to our learning curve. It is very tempting to judge other people's difficulties as indications that they are not very evolved. However, often "old souls" carry highly challenging karma orchestrated to propel them into heightened levels of consciousness.

Karma has incredible staying power, no matter how hard we try to obliterate cosmic obligations to our Higher Self, each other and the earth. When we don't apply ourselves to consciously evolve in our soul's "course work," karmic patterns just keep repeating over and over again until we finally "get it right." It's that simple. The beauty of this indefatigable metaphysical dynamic is that it gives us infinite opportunities to learn our lessons. Staying in first grade for hundreds of lifetimes is an option. But it's a lot more exciting to graduate to higher-level challenges resulting in extended wisdom.

When faced with difficult karmic situations, I'm the first to protest to the Tibetan, "What did I do to deserve this? It's not fair. Aren't I doing a good job down here on the earth plane?" He laughs off my indignation with:

Karma, a gift from the Universe, provides the guidelines for self's evolutionary curve. It is the road map through which self describes the specific journey of the soul in this particular lifetime. Ultimately fair, karma establishes cosmic justice. It dispenses lessons uniquely tailored to the individual student.

Karma is not literally an "eye for an eye, a tooth for a tooth." Rather, it is the end result of energies established long ago or the need for developing new soul qualities. Someone may experience great levels of abandonment by loved ones in this lifetime. Yes, it may mean that they abandoned others in previous lives. Or it may mean that through the pain of abandonment, they can learn the precious quality of connectedness and loyalty. These may be new lessons for the soul, not necessarily corrective lessons for previous mistakes.

Karma illustrates the circular energetic nature of the Universe. Energy doesn't move in a linear format but rather arcs back to itself in ever widening, or narrowing, concentric circles. Every energetic impulse that self projects eventually returns to self precisely the way it was issued.

Narrow concentric circles indicate karma that returns quickly. For example, if a parent harshly scolds a child for taking too long to tie their shoelaces, later that day their boss might reprimand them for missing a deadline. The challenge for the student is to recognize this energetic karmic return rather than see the two events as random and unrelated. Once the connection is made the student's awareness is heightened. A deep learning has taken place.

Other karmic conditions are carried on wide concentric circles. Within this format it may take several lifetimes before the karma "comes around." The delayed reaction allows the soul to evolve while developing other qualities in preparation for this karma.

To the current self, who may be working hard to be the "perfect" student, these karmic mandates may feel unrelated and harsh. After all, why should the gentle, loving student have to struggle with the consequences of a past-life self's murderous rage? Yet deep inside one's being, there is a memory of unresolved behavior, even if it is not conscious. This is an opportunity to resolve that behavior no matter how ancient. The beauty of karma is that its purpose is for learning and <u>release</u>. Once resolution occurs, the karma dissolves, liberating self from the sticky sensation of having to deal with certain people, situations, governmental climates, health conditions, spiritual challenges, blind spots, etc.

The karmic mandate is paradoxically set in stone while also subject to change, depending on self's efforts. Like the teacher who drops the lowest grade to allow for the inevitable slips and slides of human nature, so too can the student dissolve certain karmic criteria when self has earned a level of consciousness no longer requiring the rigors of karmic events previously tailored to shape and maturate the soul. While self cannot jump over karmic requirements, the student can open wholeheartedly to these assignments.

One's attitude toward their soul's homework makes all the difference. A positive embrace of all karma circling into one's life lifts the heaviness of the work, speeding up its completion. So surrender to karma, rejoicing in the great wisdom and understanding that it brings, allowing the soul to circle around and around, exploring the multi dimensions of its divinity through human passions.

There are no time mandates on karma. Self can ride the Wheel of Karma for as long as needed. And finally the glorious day arrives, a day of triumphant celebration in the Universe. Self steps off the Karmic Wheel, liberated at long last, encircled in love and appreciation for the masterpiece that is the soul's fruition.

✧ Judgment and Beyond ✧

April 2001

Don't be in your judgment. It's a basic spiritual principle. To offer unconditional love requires going beyond judgment. Are we foolish human beings really capable of that? It's impossible not to judge. Biased preconceived evaluations spring from an instinctual impulse as automatic as a muscle reflex.

When introduced to someone, before they even have a chance to tell me their name, my mind immediately obliterates their character—smashed by the waves of the Sea of Judgment. The moment I see their face, hair, body and clothes, a judgment is formed, for better or worse. It's instantaneous! Then, as I get to know this poor stranger, the judgments compound upon themselves. If that person has a negative effect on me, the judgments explode, burying the person in my superior notions of good and bad.

Struggling to be spiritual, I keep telling myself, "Don't judge." This is like trying to hold back the tide. I experiment with allowing all judgments free reign to surface, without judging my judgment, hoping these biased assumptions will discharge, dissipate, and leave me free to simply be open to what is. But no, there is no end to it. Judgments feed off perceptions like vultures, twisting simple observation into condemnation, once again, for the good or the bad. My mind is intricately wired to form opinionated conclusions. Always the ego lurks in the background, making sure the judgments buoy my self-esteem through put-downs of people with whom I don't resonate, or by elevating others who hold mirrors of my "greatness."

As I "advance" spiritually this judgment process becomes more subtle but no less powerful. I find ways to couch it within spiritual language: "He is less along on the path." "She needs to do some work on herself." "Don't they realize the karmic implications of their actions?" "One of these days they will wake up and boy is their karma gonna hit them between the eyes." "That person is totally unconscious—he has a long way to go." And so the litany goes, on and on, with endless possibilities for this merciless process of dissection, evaluation and presumption.

To be honest, if I'm going to indulge in the delicious act of judging others, it's much more satisfying through cruder expressions springing from gut-level reactions: "What a jerk that person is. How can anyone be that stupid?" "They don't have a clue." "That person is a real low-life." "That idiot has nothing to offer." My mind loves this activity, sparking off endless nasty pictures of "distasteful" people found guilty before they were even tried.

The geyser-like source feeding this relentless reckoning of others is the hot-bed of *self-judgment* charging the climate in my soul. As if caught in a perpetual blizzard, the voices of self-condemnation blur inner vision, drowning out the internal voice of guidance and endlessly engulfing me in negations of my being. This inner judgmental force cripples my spirit. It is like constantly being followed by someone shouting harsh evaluations of my thoughts, actions, dreams, words, interpersonal dynamics, work—EVERYTHING—with the stony austerity of a terribly biased critic. In this critic's eyes, everything must be judged. Nothing can simply exist in its essence, beyond the unreasonable realm of distorted evaluation.

I know that I am not alone in this inner onslaught of juried reality. We all suffer from the courtroom within, endlessly on the witness stand, trying to represent ourselves to the archetypal judge who has already pounded his gavel, concluding the trial before it has begun.

All judgments are based on lies. These lies constellate around telling ourselves we are BAD—not enough, inferior to others and God. We seek relief from the pain of this inferiority illusion by claiming superiority, making ourselves more than others and even our God. Then acceptable others are enlisted into our "superior camp"—those we judge as the good/ great ones, the in-crowd, the advanced ones, etc. This crystallizes the duality of our earthly condition, forcing us to relegate all remaining refugees into the "inferior camp" of those who just don't cut it, who are unworthy of life's gifts, love and, "most importantly," of our acceptance.

All judgments reflect a need for superiority as we look down from our ivory tower at the actions of others, deciding which are acceptable in the eyes of God and which aren't. We forget that we are part of that seething mass of humanity, with all of its foibles.

The Tibetan persistently encourages me to let go of all judgment, as if there could actually be a reality that exists beyond judgment. My imagination falters in its attempt to conjure up a state of consciousness free from the lacerations of perpetual critique. Struggling to stop the immediate impulse to form evaluative conclusions (usually based on illusion), I remind myself, "Let this person or situation be what it is. Open to the mystery in others and self without conclusion."

Catching my inner judgmental dialogue midstream, I bite off my words, suspending these critical bullets mid-air. My frantically determined mind searches for little bits of evaluative "zaps" to sneak in past my noble efforts. If I can ward off these instinctual torrents of assessment, a place of spaciousness opens within my thinking. Immediately I breathe a sigh of relief. A heavy weight has been lifted off my shoulders.

Even if the judgment was directed at others, I feel as if I have been "pardoned" when permission to levy a verdict is denied. I am free at last to experience self in a state of unconditional acceptance. This feeling washes over me like soothing warm water, healing wounds continually reopened through judgment. Lightened up, my solar plexus relaxes its vigilance against projected condemnation, finally able to breathe freely and easily.

Everyone is fearful of being judged, if not by people then by God. This demonstrates how all judgments directed toward others are nothing but inverted self-judgment. Externally directed judgmental energy boomerangs back at self, ironically re-energizing wounds of self-negation.

Life beyond judgment brings a new level of freedom, a reality where it is so much easier to love. In this new reality no one has to fear being fundamentally invalidated, releasing the collective contraction held as protection against the onslaught of judgment. Accepting each other and ourselves unconditionally is to be free to truly be ourselves at all times.

The Tibetan, smiling at my efforts to go beyond judgment, chimes in:

The heart's capacity for acceptance extinguishes all judgment. In curbing the impulse to judge, the student can experiment with placing all judgment of self and others in the center of the heart. The heart cannot tolerate judgment. Like food-poisoning to the body, the heart immediately rejects this foreign thinking, unable to assimilate anything falling outside the realm of Universal Love.

The natural process of discernment is to describe, without bias, one's process and experience. This requires no examinations, no grades. It is folly to judge one's being, because all beings are ultimately enlightened. Out of time and space, this enlightened self already exists, waiting to emerge. The Sea of Judgment delays this process, offering identifications of a self only referenceable in a punishing paradigm. This adjudicating model cannot reflect self's divinity. All judgment is repulsive to the true Self. The Divine, in its infinite nature, washes away all judgment.

Judgment originates in the illusion that Source approves of only certain qualities of the human experience, only certain chosen ones, harshly denouncing all those who "fall short" of the cosmic mandate. Judgment, a force of great contraction, is based on fear. The fear is that Source presides as a censorious magistrate in the Celestial Supreme Court, parentally belittling and spurning a great portion of the spectrum of human experience judged as unworthy to enter the heavenly kingdoms. From this perspective, humankind keeps itself separate—unworthy, bad, wrong, inferior/ superior, and diminished—certainly not on par with its Creator and its inherent birthright of divinity.

It is impossible for Source to judge Itself or Its creation. Love cannot judge, but only embrace. When all judgment is released, reality opens up like a blank canvas, available to the great creative flow that is liberated from the inhibiting effect of judgment. Self is then free to become a co-creator with Source, joyfully with the abandon of a child, participating in the process of self-creation and transformation.

Self then realizes that the various levels of consciousness, like classrooms in different grades, do not require damaging evaluation. Someone is not better or worse because they are in elementary school rather than graduate school. Everyone goes through the entire shared process of the "earth school" system from beginning to end. Levels of consciousness are not to be disdained as inferior or smugly exhibited as superior, but rather seen as simply streams of perception the soul journeys through in its return home.

From this awareness of all-embracing acceptance, self is free to clearly perceive the essence of others undistorted by the collective judgment that veils the light inherent in all beings, regardless of their "level" of development. Then self is free to explore the compassion of Master Jesus and the Buddha—a compassion that dissolves the judgmental straitjacket arbitrarily worn by humankind in the assumption that it is second-rate to its Creator.

Dare to release all judgments. Challenge their insidious seduction, so tantalizing to the lower mind. Bring forth the originality of spacious perception, unbounded by negating forces. Challenge self to see the divinity in all aspects of earthly life. It is truly possible to go beyond judgment and touch the sweet serenity of deep well being that exists in all phases of the great awakening process upon which Source smiles in sheer delight.

✧ Nobody's Perfect! ✧

May 2004

Why do we all have to be so perfect? Where did we get the idea that flawlessness is what Source wants from us? We project perfection onto the spiritual plane, which renders us imperfect, and then spend most of our lifetimes trying to live up to the Impeccable Divine. Attempts to climb "Mt. Perfection" leave us feeling resentful, discouraged, and inferior. We believe that the gap between perfection and imperfection is our fault. We simply haven't tried hard enough!

To assuage the guilt over our endless shortcomings, we remind ourselves that nobody's perfect. But the bedrock of guilt is resentment. We feel guilty (resentful) when too much is being asked of us without enough given in return. It seems that Source is asking too much of us if we are not allowed to make mistakes when we haven't been given the raw material for the full embodiment of excellence.

The perfection quest riddles us with guilt about our inability to level the playing field between the All-Mighty Divine and us defective earthly peasants who can't even imagine accessing the atmosphere of the Realm of the Perfect Ones. We believe that if we fail in our efforts to be perfect we can never return Home (where only the Ideal Beings exist) because we are unworthy of our Source. So we ride the karmic wheel throughout eternity, trying to figure out how to be good enough in order to be released from this world into greater realities.

We often don't even register the subtle but persistent pressure to "get it right." This relentless demand insists that we do it better next time and/or completely meet other people's needs—as the perfect mate, child, parent, employee, devotee, etc. Every once in awhile we get a momentary reprieve from the perfection tyranny and are actually able to rest quietly in "enoughness." There we bask in the beauty of our imperfections and relish the exquisite design of a Divine Plan that purifies our consciousness through lifetimes of trial and error. But historically somewhere along the line, we decided that life on the earth plane was just trial—no room for error—only punishment for our interminable faults.

How many of us accept our flaws without judgment? I'm the first one to scrutinize myself in the mirror with a Geiger-counter designed to pick up all obvious or hidden blemishes—physical, mental, emotional and/or spiritual. When someone points out one of my defects, I endlessly chew on it trying to extract every last morsel of remorse and self-criticism—as if that brutal process would purify me enough to be "the perfect one."

I embarked upon my perfection quest in early youth. Deep wounds of emotional isolation in childhood fueled my determination to be the "perfect" friend, therapist, partner. If I could tune in to what others wanted from me and supply it, I wouldn't be hurt by abandonment, betrayal, rejection. However, behind my perfection armor I was terrified that others would eventually discover my failings and not be willing to put up with them—the deal would be off—all love would be withdrawn.

To be this perfected responsive person, I focused on others and denied (abandoned) myself. The more I tried to be perfect in my relationships, the more isolated I became from myself. Perfection did not insure me protection against my childhood wounds after all.

How many of us orchestrate our relationships and actions around hiding our foibles? In spite of highly functioning outer lives, ripe with accomplishment, inwardly we fear being discovered as frauds because the perfection we assume others require of us (because we tend to defy other people and the perfection we assume they require) can only be a facade. The fear of falling short in the eyes of others drives us into slavery—shackled to the constant repairs required to uphold our "flawlessness." Western culture thrives on this perfection illusion in its false superiority over other cultures that practice true modesty by purposely weaving flaws into their creations. Real humility is the loving acceptance of our imperfections with a gratitude for the never-ending process of purification that deepens the soul.

It's helpful to observe where we hold ourselves most accountable to be perfect. What is it about these particular areas that represent our greatest fears? It is our wounds that compel our need to be flawless because these injuries drop us to our knees to teach the lesson of vulnerability and acceptance of our modest place in this vast Universe of Excellence.

I am still determined to be a perfect channel for the Tibetan. After all, isn't that what he wants—a fully purified vessel for collaboration? The Tibetan shakes his head "no" and reminds me that my imperfect human self is exactly what augments the interface between the spiritual and earthly planes.

What is the price of perfectionism? Aside from the obvious weariness that springs from trying to be someone we are not, we never really experience the sweet self-acceptance that allows us to relax our grip on life and trust that all good things will come our way regardless of our blemishes. It is only in that precious self-acceptance that we can heal the original wound of human impoverishment that results from perceiving our Source as inherently dissatisfied with our endless failings. Self-disappointment abounds as we scramble to find the magic button that would return us to the perfected state we must have embodied eons ago. So we live in the stress zone of the gap between our idealized self and our lowly, vice-filled ordinary selves. The more we judge our shortcomings, the more stressed we become, like a tight rubber band stretched to the max in our determination to "touch all the bases."

Ultimately, all my efforts at perfection have backfired leaving me exhausted from too much effort. In those rare moments when I can accept that "I'm good enough" I am flooded with relief, the heavens part, the sun shines and I trust that Source really does love all my blotched attempts at creating a sterling existence. The biggest challenge is discovering when enough is enough.

Ironically, our goal of perfection blocks our awareness of who we really are, complete with qualities so rich in their shimmering imperfection as representatives of our soul's evolving essence. We throw the baby out with the bathwater, discarding all that hasn't yet arrived at the high peak of Superbness. Then all we have is our attachment to the fortress of perfection which is a lie to others and ourselves, as we try to convince the world that our virtues are impenetrable. Like marble statues in the park we stride about in idealized form, all the while suffocating our priceless imperfect soul as it struggles to humbly bring itself forward.

The more we try to be perfect, perhaps trying to be everything to everyone, the more we fear our mistakes. They expand in our minds like towering monsters, screaming in our ears that we "blew it," as if this were our only chance.

How often does our need to be perfect prevent us from starting new life adventures? We assume that our imperfection automatically disqualifies us from running the race. We throw up our hands in self-demerit, ironically postponing the very actions integral for our evolution. We assume that others started from perfect rather than worked up to it.

What do we tell ourselves about our defects? We all have our favorite words of criticism that burn like acid into our soul and eat away at our emerging wholeness. These harsh reproaches reveal our individual illusions about perfection because the cruel voice of disapproval always holds a higher model that we will never, ever, live up to. This voice of absolutism holds a collective spiritual ideal designed to compensate for our terribly handicapped human condition. The Land of the Perfect is a place we never reach.

The quest for perfection extinguishes the fire in our passion. It becomes too painful to face our inadequacies over and over again. Attachment to perfection produces only humiliation which results in a hotbed of shame that engulfs our right to be alive. Self-shredding in the name of perfection reaches a peak until our soul protests against this insistence that we are not enough. This protest is the Divine Knowing that our existence is not about our lacks but about learning to love ourselves. When we accept that we are all in the same "imperfection boat," we drop the collective false pride designed to cover our warts. We can then laugh at our inadequacies and honor them as the very vehicles that ferry our souls homeward to the Land of Flawlessness.

Perfect in his ethereal beauty, the Tibetan strides toward me filled with an all-encompassing impeccable love. He teaches:

All of creation is evolving, even Source. For evolution to occur, the unrefined essence in all beings is magnetized forth to make full impact with Source's consummate vibration. To attach to perfection blocks this refinement process through fear of spiritual judgment. Humankind, frozen in its awe of Source's magnificence, has been determined to tolerate no less than their own Sourceness within.

However, humankind exists on the earthly plane to demonstrate the PROCESS of evolution in form. Imperfection, the required starting point in all dynamics of transformation, is key to this substantiation process of evolution. Without imperfection there would be no dynamic tension within the duality of becoming vs. being. To embrace and work with this dynamic tension—highly creative—is central to spiritual artistry and Self's eventual mastery of the physical plane. To avoid unnecessary suffering, students must make peace with this aspect of the Divine Plan that demands the loving acceptance of the soul's raw material offered forth in human expression. This acceptance releases the students from the relentless pressure in the collective consciousness to be in full mastery before they are ready.

Ask for assistance from the Masters and Angelic Force to throw off all attachment to perfection based on humankind's early perception of the Godhead as an "exacting" being who punishes all inferiors. Be willing to release self-judgment, self-criticism and perceived spiritual demands of absolute correctness. Remember that students get as many chances as needed to learn from their mistakes. Only when the students surrender their endless litany of "requirements" and deeply accept all defects will they be ready to begin the process of transformation at the core level. Otherwise self grips the perfection model which allows no room for the Process of Becoming. One cannot be at the finish gate until he/she has run the race.

As students move closer to their enlightenment the pressure to be perfect increases. Yes, more is expected of them—more awareness, responsibility, maturity, creativity, compassion. But more does not mean perfect.

Please know that Divine Love has never been withheld because of self's faults. Rather, Source's great Love increases in its magnetic response to those flaws because they are the central reasons for the soul's incarnation, and consequently, the most responsive to the Magnificent Devotion that arcs all of humankind Home.

What would it be like if all of humankind brought it flaws to each other as precious jewels in the rough, eager to share the process of refinement without shame for their "original sin" of imperfection?

Try to go through one week without defending against, struggling with, denying or covering up self's defects. Prideful in its grandiosity, the ego thrives on the need for perfection as a compensation for the duality with the human psyche.

Experience the ego's critical reactions with compassion and reassurance that these very flaws place self exactly where the soul needs to be. This revelation of flaws, unjudged, describes self's pathway. Imperfections unfurl one's Divine Destiny. Self's inevitable mastery will have its specialty precisely in those initial areas of shortcoming.

Most importantly, attachment to perfection inhibits inner peace. Dare to feel the lightness of being that springs from breaking free of the old Godhead of Judgment. Discover a new Source Who only wants joyous reunion with Its beloveds. Then, like an adored child, self feels held by a "parent" Who chuckles at his/her growth mishaps while appreciating so deeply the journey of becoming, and rejoicing in the exquisite nature of the child— flaws and all. From this place of supreme trust in Source, the student relaxes, breathes deeply—finally free from the cruel perfection wheel—and eagerly works to refine all raw material for the sheer exhilaration of transformation: the fulfillment of turning lead into gold.

As humankind's evolution unfolds, the line between perfection and imperfection blurs because ultimately the only distinction is one of judgment. Then, being and becoming are unified and all that needs correction is already reflected in the fully-realized Self. This is the "perfect" moment—to let all perfection demands go— and relax into the consciousness true Enoughness where Unconditional Love abounds!

✧ Worthiness ✧

February 2004

I wonder how my life would change if I could fully release all levels of unworthiness. Many of us struggle with false beliefs like, "I'm not enough." "I don't deserve more." "I should settle for less." We may compensate for this deep sense of unworthiness through grandiosity and ego-inflation. Delusions of superiority are empty puff bubbles—feeble attempts to buffer a devastating sense of inferiority that relentlessly insists that we are not up to the task of whatever is expected of us from others, our Higher Self and God. Unworthiness, like a silent cancer infiltrating our thoughts, feelings and spirit, ultimately eats away at our birthright of self-acceptance, magnitude, abundance, unlimited joyful expression and success on every level. Consequently, we give ourselves away too easily, assuming that we should grab what we can because we don't deserve the best. We sell our souls for security or a quick fix to stave off the inevitable hunger that arises from depriving ourselves of the genuine recognition of our unalterable core value—the essential gold within us.

If we all truly perceived the limitless value of that gold, we would surge forth to deliver denied gifts, releasing a glut of pent-up energy. Our worth, then in full dominion over our lives, would display our value like gemstones of the soul sparkling in the light of an awakening consciousness. We would truly behold the full caliber of our worth in all of its glory, releasing all hesitation as we confidently step forward into our potential—our magnificence.

When I first consciously connected with the Tibetan in this lifetime, he informed me that my biggest stumbling block was unworthiness. Eighteen years later, I'm still working on this issue. How do we actually establish a sense of profound value—really experience our worthiness? The sticky web of lies proclaiming self to be shabby, wretchedly flawed and mediocre corrupts our ability to attune to the treasure of our being, an excellence that merits all good things to come our way.

Djwhal Khul's invitation to be his channel was a glorious assignment to "live up to" a higher calling from an Ascended Master. Fear of this heightened responsibility as well as chronic long-term unworthiness surfaced in response to the Tibetan's proposal of ambassadorship. So began the arduous process of trying to force myself into believing that, just maybe, I had a shred of value that could be cultivated to produce fertile soil on which to offer this gift of channeling. Mostly, I just wanted to hide in dread of the inevitable humiliation in front of others who would surely know how unworthy I was of this important assignment. Trying not to feel like a fraud, I was afraid to be taken as an impostor ... afraid people would detect my "not enoughness." I had to resist the impulse to recede. Struggling to try to step into shoes that seemed way too big for little ol' me, I was shocked when others applauded my work. Every gesture of appreciation stimulated a healing crisis as, with true humility, I bravely battled to move forward into my greatness. My struggle is something everyone faces because indeed we all have outstanding treasures that we are challenged to accept.

Slowly the web of unworthiness began to shred as I tentatively inched my toes into the Blessed Waters of Deservedness. I still dance with the devil when it comes to *totally* believing in my value. But the voices of denigration, belittlement and condemnation have lost quite a bit of steam. Their seduction fades like a distant movie that used to be a way of life. Uncompromising, the Universe keeps raising the bar higher for me to climb into greater and greater "shoes" of magnitude and to believe that they actually fit! I am forever grateful to the Tibetan for this opportunity to at long last break the unworthiness spell that has imprisoned my soul for lifetimes.

When clinging to unworthiness in order to hide our Light and resist the spiritual responsibility that requires our display of significance (the offering of magnificence that demonstrates the inherent treasure—divinity in form—that is the human condition) we often protest, "I couldn't possibly do that, have that, be that!" The more we *all* dare to expose our worthiness to ourselves and each other, the more everyone recognizes the divine permission to claim their particular specialty of non-rescindable cosmic value.

To leave our "unworthiness comfort zone" is to expose our profuse quality of being to others whose judgment might rear its ugly head. "How dare we!" They unconsciously prey off our unworthiness to support their own heavy investment in the collective agreement that there is only so much we can do with ourselves as damaged goods.

Fearful, we capitulate, give up too easily, and believe in our inferiority. We assume that we'll be more popular if we hide the full extent of our deservedness. Why be a target for jealousy, anger, envy and competitiveness by others easily threatened by our quality? So we sentence ourselves to lowly positions of scarcity, failure, unfulfillment in order to be compliant with everyone else's illusion. What a price to pay to be part of a human tribe terribly handicapped by a profound sense of spiritual inferiority. If we expose our value at all, we fear being hunted down like an animal, destroyed for the nerve of allowing ourselves to embrace the fact that we are truly priceless beings of profound significance to each other and to the Divine Plan.

Many of us are tired of resisting the full expression of our soul-jewel, with all of its rich bounty and spiritual holdings. I, as well as countless others, have spent lifetimes brainwashing myself to believe that I am a trivial, meaningless, inconsequential, measly, paltry being who has only mere crumbs to offer this world—and of course, should expect no more for herself. Perhaps we believe that we deserve less because we must have committed horrible acts in past lives. We often assume that our wounds/ traumas from childhood/ past lives are the definitive statements of our unworthiness. Can we finally discern the lie in the perceived need to live a second-rate existence? Ironically, this hard karmic stuff is simply part of a large learning curve designed to refine our consciousness, just as the jeweler brings out the facets in a diamond. Even in the rough, a diamond is still a diamond!

When we attempt to override/ deny our unworthiness wounds, we run the risk of grandiosity. Unconsciously we project our valuelessness onto others. From this platform of superiority, we disdain people we deem inferior to ourselves, ironically feeding our disowned impoverishment. Eventually we must fall from this empty pedestal to encounter our own wound of inadequacy. The "fall" opens us into the rich process of claiming the precious internal gold that resides within the earthly crevices of our soul. From this place of true enrichment we cannot help but recognize the worthiness in others, which instantly charges them to "go the distance" into their deservedness.

When we "step ourselves down," we are unconsciously directing creative energy into the undermining force of the inner saboteur who relentlessly reminds us that we dare not touch the success that powers and expresses our deservedness. The more we deny our worthiness, the more potently this unconscious energy works at pulling the rug out from under us. The tyranny of the saboteur dictates that we accept a diminished, frustrated, misrepresented life on planet earth as victims and failures. Deeply indoctrinated, we become convinced that we are less than others and God. To claim our magnitude seems like a sacrilege. Unworthiness convinces us to stay in unpleasant, abusive, starvation situations too long because we assume that's all we deserve. We become blind to the subtle manifestations of unworthiness that shrink our lives into smaller and smaller islands of self-diminishment and impossibility. We assume that this is the way life is. Our challenge is to be vigilantly watchful of this automatic programming that takes over and pushes away relationships, employment, material prosperity and/or spiritual, mental, emotional opportunities offered to us from the Divine Platter of Abundance because we're too "second-rate" to claim our spiritual due.

Eventually we comprehend that we are not destined to be Source's whipping post. There is NO spiritual mandate to cheapen and underrate ourselves. How can we possibility respond to the profound spiritual opportunities available to us during this time of accelerated energy if we are too shy to step forward through the many initiations available to us now at this time in human history? Life keeps giving us chance after chance to feel good about ourselves. We must stay awake to the multitude of opportunities available to demonstrate our deservedness to ourselves and others. This is the basis for our next great evolutionary leap into possibility.

Smiling, the Tibetan shows me an image of the common ground that unites us all through horizontal rather than vertical alignment, indicating that ultimately we are all equal, however differentiated, treasures of the Divine. He teaches:

Worthiness is everyone's birthright. To have the opportunity to incarnate on planet earth is a statement of this deservedness. In order for students to collectively pass through the Portal of Interdimensional Shift, they have to feel worthy enough to step into a greater reality which mirrors their glorious majesty— profound merit never known in this or previous lifetimes. They must stretch into an expanded perspective and look into the Great Vault of Breathtaking Value that is their Divine Root.

For centuries humankind has been blind to its innate value. This distortion in perception originated from religious doctrines that, in efforts to induce humility and break down the ego, encouraged humankind to perceive itself as unworthy of its Creator. Today many students, after lifetimes of exposure to these false beliefs, are deeply convinced at a cellular level that they are hopelessly inferior beings, non-deserving of the great spiritual fortune that earthly life, the human condition, offers. Believing that they don't deserve "heaven on earth," students push away what is truly possible and opt for sparseness and deprivation. They rationalize this lack of fulfillment, under-supply, scarcity with the false belief that self-deprivation will bring them closer to God. This connects to the false belief that humankind must stay in its place and not hope to expand beyond.

Does self ever dare to ask the question, "Do I deserve more in my life?" However nobly determined to be positive, underpinnings of guilt surface for even considering the question. How dare self want more! The collective wound of undeservedness causes humankind to hang its head in shame for even dreaming of an earthly life that would reflect a level of lavish joy way beyond what the "lowly" human condition should deserve. Consequently, many students stop far short of their potential. Uncertain that it is "permitted" to open their receptivity valve or to expect the best, they refuse to envision great possibility, fruition, success, love because their imaginal muscle is stunted by lifetimes of supposed spiritually-mandated scarcity, often resulting in the opposite of true humility—humiliation. Every time that students attempt to open to full alignment with their Higher Self and Source, an instinctive unconscious alarm like an electric fence repels them back into themselves in shame and unworthiness. This drops them to their knees. However, in the effort to tame the ego, ward off arrogance and control, humankind has thrown the baby out with the bath water and reduced its sense of value by 98%! Students have been taught to say, "I am not worthy of God" and therefore I do not deserve my own enlightenment and full union with my Higher Self.

From the Masters' vantage point, humankind stands before a colossal banquet table with an overflowing cornucopia of treasures. Students timidly stand there with their hands clasped, fearful of reaching out and partaking of this bounty. They convince themselves that they are not worthy of such rewards and refrain from claiming what is rightfully theirs (regardless of their imperfections). So they wait for the day when they will be given permission to go beyond unworthiness. Some wait for lifetimes. Today is the day to release all self-devaluing thinking and to accept one's Divine Stature of Goodness. Remember that no one is innately flawed. No one need see themselves as inconsequential, shoddy or useless.

When students rightfully claim their full worth, then they are able to thoroughly avail themselves of the spiritual/ earthly bounty that supports their soul's journey into full liberation. This allows them to fully register the value of their gifts and to offer these gifts with complete confidence. Then no one will hesitate at the Gates of Initiation, subjugating themselves to a false sense of inferiority. Rather, all will audaciously stride forward in full assurance and declaration of their deservedness. There will be no holding back. The crimes of instilled unworthiness will cease. All of humankind will then experience the Paradise of Treasures that honors the value, the Cosmic Bank Account of Worth, deeply established in the souls of all beings. Bask in the Heavenly Applause that acclaims salutes and honors the stellar Divine Quality of Excellence that fills all beings within this Universe and greater Universes.

✧ Guilt Free! ✧

July 2005

Many of us are drowning in a sea of guilt. We feel guilty if we have food on the table while our global neighbors are starving. We're guilty if we've left an unhappy marriage and found joy with a new partner while our ex-spouse is struggling with loneliness. We're guilty if we live in a warm, safe house while the homeless struggle on the street. We're guilty if we're not helping the world become a better place because our personal life is more compelling. We're guilty if we survive while others die in tsunami waves or terrorist attacks. We're guilty if we say no to others' needs because we'd rather do something for ourselves. We're guilty if we procrastinate on our goals. We're guilty if we eat too many cookies, don't exercise, speak harshly to a loved one, don't clean our houses, buy a new dress, go out to eat because we're too lazy to cook, don't send our resume in on time, forget that it's Mother's Day, relax in the hammock while others are toiling away—and on and on.

The "guilts" become so far-reaching; they meld into one towering amorphous guilt-trip that pervades our every moment with its endless lists of crimes. Eventually we don't even know why we feel guilty—we just do. We resign ourselves to that nagging feeling that we've screwed up somehow and hope that the higher courts take pity on us.

Guilt trippers sniff out the fertile hotbed of feelings in our gut and have a field day. We fall for it every time, as if they are prosecuting attorneys for the Cosmic Court, ordained to reveal our crimes in Technicolor. To relieve ourselves of the weight of our secret guilt, we eagerly give them our power. Then we're furious with others who seem to sail through life guilt-free. How dare they not lie with us in our collective sticky, suffocating acid-bed of guilt!

Most of our guilt is nothing more than resentment. Guilt springs from our habit of "shoulds" and thrives when we're at odds with our real needs. Inability to accept our needs reflects a bottom-line self-condemnation. When we fall short of people's notions of whom we're supposed to be, we fill up with the guilt that disguises our resentment for having to adhere to a standard that betrays our soul's true path. Deeply buried conflicts about our needs force us to "hire" others to be make impossible demands. This flushes out our unconscious internal struggle. These people hold a nonverbal contract over our heads, insisting we should give more to them than they give in return. When they guilt-trip us with unreasonable expectations we attempt to quell our rising resentment with guilt—to persuade ourselves that their demands are reasonable and that we're bad for not fulfilling them. But our gut indignantly registers this inequity.

If our relationship ideals mandate that we should respond to the needs of others regardless of their lack of generous return, then we're prime candidates for guilt. There are always GOOD reasons why we behave the way we do. The challenge is to identify the deeper reasons for our behavior rather than guilt-trip ourselves for actions that fall below our standards. Most guilt from saying no to others reflects a fear of our own soul's requirements.

Guilt can be a genuine ambassador of our conscience when it makes us uncomfortable about ways in which we have hurt ourselves and/or others. Guilt triggers an alarm to signal that we are out of alignment with our highest intentions and need to pay attention to unconscious impulses that undermine our ethics. Guilt warns to us to make it right. Unfortunately we often attach to the guilt itself rather than follow through on the work mandated by our conscience. We're more inclined to berate ourselves for our crimes rather than take responsibility for them.

Perhaps our lofty expectations of perfection make it unbearable to directly face our wrongdoings. It's too painful to accept the discrepancy between our highest ideals and how we really live our lives. So we attach to the guilt itself and relentlessly fester in shame and self-castigation instead of going the distance to work through the lesson that guilt carries. To learn about our unconscious conflicts/ wounds we must undeviatingly acknowledge the infringement and then take responsibility to correct for that aspect of our shadow. This correction is not punishment but restitution. We have to return the appropriate energy to balance out what we took from ourselves or others in our crime. Penance is not self-debasement, but rather a true adult assessment of how to take responsibility for learning the lessons in our destructive impulses.

The more we attach to guilt, the less we practice self-forgiveness. We can only forgive ourselves if we've resolved our actions, not through endless guilt, but through appropriate restitution. Otherwise our crime continues in our psyche, renewing itself daily, because there is no outlet for its resolution and transformation. We fear that the higher courts are non-forgiving—reviling our crimes for eternity with no possibility for reparation. Resigned to guilt's endless punishment, we suffer from a lack of the imagination required to create a venue for making amends. Terrified to release our crimes, we cling to guilt to prevent us from repeating our wrongdoings because we don't trust that we've really learned the lesson. Guilt harnesses us to the past as we discount the natural process of evolution that resolves our crimes through self-responsibility. To truly understand the nature of our crimes empowers us to redress them. Then we're FREE. Guilt has served its purpose. Do we really dare to be guilt free? Do we trust our learning enough to release guilt's poison prick to the gut that relentlessly reminds us how bad we've been? Can we trust the wisdom harvested from our transgressions?

We may have been born riddled with a nasty hangover of guilt from old past-life crimes that we don't even remember. We just feel bad about who we are. Hundreds of lifetimes of unresolved guilt are cellularly registered in this lifetime through countless opportunities for self-recrimination. Wherever we are eaten up by guilt, the soul is unresolved. We may have clung to our "wrongness" in previous lives. Guilt's unclean, sticky energy is impossible to shake off. We have to work it through, not override it, by tracking the symptoms of chronic guilt.

The Tibetan playfully slams down the court gavel—"Case Closed!" He teaches:

The illusion of original sin implies that humankind should feel guilty about its innate nature. The ironclad notion of original sin is so hard-wired in the collective unconscious that most of humankind, regardless of their religious upbringing, carry some level of guilt, however vague, that seems intrinsically linked to the very texture of their being—a rotten disposition that is unfixable and unavoidable. Therefore, human beings are victims of their original sin because they are powerless to be born without it and thus powerless over their guilt. Humankind forgets that the interplay of shadow and light in human nature was created by Source, not by humankind's defective impulses.

Like being covered in paint, guilt suffocates the soul. The pores of the soul's energy body are clogged with unremitting self-accusation, with no hope for pardon. Humankind employs guilt to restrain the ego and keep it in check. They uphold false courts that believe in punishment rather than education. These courts thrive on guilt—societal guilt, emotional guilt, spiritual guilt—that intimidates the students with rivers of collective remorse and disfavor. These rivers flow along quicksand that sucks the students down into the dungeon of suffering where indemnification is forbidden. There is only a great ocean of shame about what disappointment humankind has been to its Source. The fundamental religious pathways have used guilt as a tool to corral their followers into appropriate behavior. This is a rather uncreative response to the limitless options available for guidance, education and illumination.

Now humankind must release its attachment to guilt. To live a life beyond guilt would indicate that humankind has at long last comprehended its Divine Imperative and approves of the human process. Then students are willing to work with their nature to refine all shadow impulses through good intention and willingness—not guilt.

If there are crimes that haunt the soul, take them to the truest High Court, a dimension of pure Justice, which resides in the heart chakra. Place these crimes on the Court's Altar and allow the Sacred to sanction the resolution of misdeeds that only reflect the blind sleep state of the immature soul.

This High Court is held in the Temple of Love, Compassion and Acceptance where all crimes are immediately forgiven in the Light of Self-responsibility. Here the student can objectively view the offense and decipher the riddle that holds its deepest lesson. Then guilt becomes an obsolete hair shirt. Humankind rejoices in its liberation from guilt's punishing blanket of recrimination and evolves forward into full acquittal for all crimes, imagined or real. It now makes a leap into acceptance, mastery, maturation and self-responsibility—a realm of heightened conscience where the Divine Compass steers the soul forward along the high road to Sublime Standards that form the bedrock of collective transformation.

✧ Forgiveness ✧

October 2000

"Make the big spiritual leap and just forgive them. Turn the other check. If Master Jesus and other great spiritual teachers can do it, so can you. Just let go of your anger and rise above it." *Forgiveness*! What a challenge it is to really forgive and forget.

Forgiveness is one of the central "food groups" for nourishing our connection to the soul. If we can't forgive those who have hurt us, how can we move on with our lives? How can we expect others to forgive us? How can we forgive ourselves when we have hurt others?

When friends suggest I practice forgiveness in a situation where I have been wronged, a rising surge of anger lands like a fireball in the pit of my solar plexus (the energy center/chakra just below the rib cage). Retreating from this impossible spiritual demand, my usual self-righteous mutterings explode out loud as I rant and rave at all the spiritual teachers who I imagine are shaking their heads in disgust at my inability to forgive. Defensively I respond, "I hate this forgiveness thing. Why do I have to do it; no one else does? I can't pretend to forgive someone if I am really furious at them. Why do I have to do the work of trying to forgive them when *they* were hurtful to *me*? They should be doing the work of making it up to me somehow." And so the litany goes, deepening my resentment as hopes of forgiving dissolve into the boiling waters of rage and victim hood.

If that isn't bad enough, this process is eventually topped off with a good dose of self-criticism as I berate myself for these rebellious thoughts. How will I ever reach enlightenment if I can't even forgive someone for harmful actions or words that may or may not have been premeditated? How can I swallow all that rage in order to find enough love in my heart to forgive?

As long as we are stuck in unresolved anger, we cannot release whatever "crime" is committed against us. We remain victims of other people's hurtfulness. As long as we believe we are victims, we have no power. To be disempowered is to be angry. How can we break this cycle to allow forgiveness to surface?

234

We cannot simply jump over negative feelings in order to arrive in the land of forgiveness; a realm we imagine is inhabited by advanced spiritual beings. *Forgiveness is not a transcendent function.* It is impossible to simply rise above the heavy, hot feelings bubbling up from wounds inflicted by those who devalue our being and violate boundaries. The only road to true forgiveness is *through* the intensity of our rage and hurt and out the other side. This is an alchemical process, one that literally transmutes the energy of anger into love.

The key to this transmutation is acceptance. If we can accept that we have been hurt, not judging our angry response to that hurt, then we can allow our emotions to flow freely dislodging the illusions that set us up to be injured in the first place. Releasing these illusions empowers us with greater understanding of how to take care of ourselves. This frees us to let go of the anger, knowing we are better equipped to prevent future betrayals of our trust. The more we feel empowered in self-knowledge and self-love, the more we can accept human nature with its inevitable pitfalls leading to "crimes" of the heart and soul.

The Tibetan teaches:

Forgiveness is the softening action that opens the heart to the soul. It emerges through the heart's wisdom based in a realm beyond preconceived judgments of right or wrong. This allows acceptance of the full range of the human condition, complete with all of its loveless actions.

Forgiveness is a prerequisite for enlightenment. Self cannot fully embrace the soul while clinging to wounds and hurts no longer necessary for growth. Each perceived wound has a function to clarify the soul's needs. When this function is fulfilled, it is necessary to release the negative emotions surrounding the wound. The wound is not simply a hurtful situation but a lesson that springs from illusion. This understanding allows self to forgive those who are hurtful, accepting them as a vital part of the process leading to self knowledge and soul connection.

Painful relationships are often carried over from previous lifetimes, generated by karmic agreements mandating experiences which recreate wounding, hurts, betrayals and neglects. This offers insight into belief systems about self, others and Source (God) leading to forgiveness of others as well as gratitude for the opportunity, however painful, to come to terms with behaviors that are lifetimes old. Attempting to forgive without examining why one attracts the wounding experience to begin with forfeits the opportunity to grow in awareness. Ironically, the anger and sadness in need of resolution is then pushed into the unconscious. This allows the ego/ personality to identify itself with the spiritual "virtue" of forgiveness without having really earned the experience of true forgiveness.

Forgiveness is based in the heart. After digesting the hurt, anger and grief, and resolving to address the issue through self-love, the solar plexus relaxes its contraction which stemmed from feelings of powerlessness. All beings have the power to transmute wounds into wisdom. Only when this is accomplished can the realm of true forgiveness be accessed.

Forgiveness starts with self. To forgive self for being a victim is as necessary as forgiving self for being a victimizer. Forgiveness is not an act, but a vantage point on the human condition. From this vantage point the student can see and accept the imperfect world of humankind. Because humanity has not yet achieved the ability to love unconditionally, it continues to hurt itself through its illusions of separation.

When the student moves deeply into the heart center, he/she can try on the perspective of Master Jesus, the Buddha or the Divine Mother and understand, with compassion, the process of becoming spiritual beings. The acceptance of this process makes it easier to forgive self and others for the illusions that bring hurt and pain. While in this expanded state of consciousness, one sees the foolishness of holding onto former wounds. Forgiveness is the only mechanism for truly letting go of past hurts. In the act of forgiving others, self experiences universal compassion which elevates consciousness, allowing greater access to the Higher Self.

True forgiveness is not a patronizing pat on the head to those that have hurt self, reflecting a superiority that obscures the common ground that unites all beings. Forgiveness is an act of humility. To forgive self for creating experiences of being hurt, neglected and/or threatened allows self to forgive the abusers.

Forgiveness is the only road to freedom. It makes it possible to release the past and rejoice in the liberation that awaits those of heightened compassion. This compassion stems from a deeper knowledge and understanding of the human condition and its process of spiritualization. Vigilance is needed to discern whether all "splinters" of hurt and resentment are resolved into greater self-acceptance and self-knowledge. When all past wounds are licked and healed, true gratitude flushes the psyche with sweet appreciation of the human spirit that embraces acceptance. Then a fount of forgiveness opens up, ushering in the soul with its full capacity for compassion and understanding."

As I listen, the Tibetan helps me to accept the pace of the process of forgiveness. It doesn't happen overnight. As with all healing, time helps to expand the vantage point on the hurts that plague us, so that we may come to terms with our part of the karmic collaboration leading to injury. To bring compassion to self is to accept our co-creation in whatever "messes" develop with others. We don't have to project our anger at self onto others within some arbitrary system of "They are wrong and I am right" or "I would never do such a thing, how could they?" We are free to embrace all wounding experiences with curiosity, a willingness to take responsibility for our participation, and surrender to this strangely wonderful human process that allows us the free will to bombard each other with our illusions/ projections in order to eventually extract our souls' truth. Acceptance, compassion, self-love and wisdom all yield the real forgiveness—a gift from the Divine that allows us to start again and again, until our trust is complete.

✧ Letting Go of Control ✧

August 2003

"Unfasten your seat belt! Prepare to be flung from your seat!" The Tibetan teasingly offers this remedy for my obsession with control. Yes, I'm a control freak and proud of it! It's how I manage this insanely chaotic life on a planet that seems to be spinning out of control. There are many steps down the enlightenment path that I am willing to work at, but letting go of control is just pushing things too far. After all, if I'm not in control, who is? When I'm in charge, I know it will get done right.

I'm in awe of people on roller coasters who throw their arms up in the air when the ride takes a sharp turn or steep descent at breathtaking speed. My gut reaction is to white-knuckle the iron bar supposedly holding me in while frantically looking around to catch the operator's eye so I can get him to stop the ride.

Ironically, the more I attempt to hang onto control, the more it seems to slip through my fingers. My best efforts at precision management of my journey crumble in the face of an increasing wave of chaos pummeling all my ironclad expectations into fragmented dust, revealing the distinct smile of the great cosmic joke. The more I tell myself to ease off and surrender to life's unfoldment, the more tightly I grip the steering wheel, revealing a level of distrust so far-reaching that I can't imagine any force-field strong enough to pry my fingers loose from their clenched command

Is this a stubborn refusal to align my personal will with the Divine Will? Or am I smart enough to know that *somebody* has got to get a grip on this earthly life, and it might as well be me!

As the heightened frequencies impacting our collective consciousness up their voltage, chaos increases. Always ready for a good fight, I struggle with the chaos, determined to be in control of its whimsical attempts to undo my best-laid plans. When the mystery pulls the rug out from under my rigid daily life strategies, I get angry and redouble my efforts to be top-dog in this battle for supremacy.

The more I lament that I should be the conductor in charge of my own symphony, the more the Divine Jester laughs at my obstinacy. My gritty persistence to hang on for dear life lodges itself in my neck and shoulders, tightening those muscles and my upper back into a shield of ego-will determined to have the last stand on the control battlefront. Of course, I always lose. Sooner or later, my body implores me to just let go, relax, and drop my shoulders down several inches, where they belong, instead of having them pretzeled around my neck, poorly armored for ultimate supremacy in my latest showdown with the Divine Plan.

Do we have any control over our lives, or is the concept of free will an illusion? Are we humans innately designed to be impotent control freaks? Is this related to a feeling of being cut off from Source by our very earthly incarnation? Do we grab on so tightly because our fear—of change, chaos, helplessness, overwhelm, disintegration—fuels our efforts to control our environment, relationships, work, vacations…everything?

We attach to a fixed idea in our minds of what is supposed to happen, leaving no room for the mystery. Fiercely clutching these notions, determined to have things work out the way we "know" they should, we unwittingly block the divine surprises waiting in the wings.

Excessive efforts to control our external life often stem from a need to keep ourselves in a box. Vigilantly monitoring the parameters of this self-imposed container, we are afraid of being surprised by whatever destructive, unloving monsters might emerge if we relaxed our surveillance. Assuming that control is the glue that holds us together, we expect to fall apart if we let go. But when we ward off chaos through excessive control, we inadvertently block the Higher Order trying to evolve us to an elevated consciousness.

All control issues spring from expecting the worst. If I let go of control I believe people will be mean to me, I will be abandoned, I will be irresponsible, I won't be able to function, the chaos will overwhelm my mind and emotions, others will block my process, I won't like myself, I might lose my marriage, home, work—all evidence of the glue that appears to hold my world together.

Refusing to accept vulnerability with grace, my need for control escalates as I open psychically and feel the innate fragility of life. My false beliefs state that to lose control is to lose dignity, integrity, strength, resulting in defeat, overwhelm, insignificance, weakness. Ironically, control only fosters rigidity, fear, domination, bullying, arrogance, anxiety, tension, contraction, blockage, and the deep inner sorrow that springs from the isolation of not believing we are part of a larger sphere designed to make sure all our needs are met.

How do we surrender control so that we can make the leap of faith into pure trust, permitting ourselves to experience the real stuff that holds/ orchestrates/ unfolds our lives precisely to fulfill our souls' needs? Like holding our nose, closing our eyes and wildly dashing into a stormy ocean, maybe we need to block out our rational mind (just for a moment) and believe in the best! It is letting go of control that allows the greatest impact on the energetic flow/unfoldment of our lives.

Going beyond control doesn't imply abdicating self-responsibility, however. Those who simply take a back seat, passively witnessing life while they blame God/ Goddess for their difficulties aren't in collaboration with the Divine Will. We all have the opportunity to exert healthy control—defined as focused intention and creative initiative in spearheading our Higher Self's mandate for this lifetime. We just need to know when to release the attachment that obsessively energizes our intentions/ desires/ wishes/ dreams. Like blowing in the wind, our intentions are then carried by the stupendous cosmic genius who ultimately fulfills all wishes within the labyrinthine mystery encoded in the torch of our destiny.

What's the difference between making something happen vs. letting it happen? How can we align our personal will with the Divine Will and actively implement our Calling without attempting to control its expression or outcome? When we grip too tightly we contract the cosmic flow and block the creativity underlying our purpose. This feeds the fear that we won't be able to fully align with our soul's desires. So we redouble our efforts at control, trying to achieve whatever goal we envision. Does this desperate exertion spring from an illusion of unworthiness that insists we're not up to the task?

Releasing control, we could relax, laugh, trust and enjoy the cosmic ride of our shared unfoldment. We would realize the illusion of our fears, gratefully accepting the inevitable chaos that invokes necessary change, fertile creativity and divine improvisation.

Chaos informs us of the edge of mystery that surrounds our little island of the known, with its barbed wire boundary of control. Fully accepting our chaotic interface with the Unknowable, we accept the inevitable buffeting-about that propels our evolution, the cosmic disorganization required to leave outgrown attitudes behind. How else would we wrench ourselves out of the karmic straightjackets suffocating our souls for lifetimes? Releasing control clears us to attune to messages, intuition, guidance, signs, timing—all designed to enlist us in a collaborative relationship with the Divine Plan.

We begin to trust our spiritual instincts like the wolf who sniffs the wind, following nature's vibrations to discover his next meal, mate, cave, or soulful alignment with the moon. Ironically, we humans are the only living beings who block our destiny. When we participate cooperatively, holding the steering wheel lightly through the tumult of life's challenges, we access extensive spiritual opportunity. Then we bathe in the full power of our Beingness as it magnetizes to us just the right events, people, places required for evolution.

To my inner eye, the Tibetan appears in a chariot driven by eight wild, unrestrained stallions. He sits there calmly, no reins to grasp, with a twinkle in his eye daring me to LET GO AND ENJOY THE RIDE!

The heightened energies accelerating humankind's collective learning curve bring amplified chaos. As deeper levels of karmic debris are kicked up for transmutation, students momentarily spin "out of control" while their core is being reorganized at a higher level. This promotes fluidity in self's essence, facilitating full surrender to the next dimension in consciousness. To accept the chaos within the Higher Order allows students to discern the illusion that they alone control their reality. It is impossible to control a reality based in a predestined matrix established eons ago.

Paradoxically, students can exercise a profound effect on their experience through attitude. Self can control his/her attitude, work to release negativity, but cannot guarantee through control the outcome of any shift in attitude or any other inner work. The more responsibility taken for awakening, the more self realizes how little ego control is possible over one's process. Yet, through the willingness to take full self-responsibility, the student experiences the transformative impact of right attitude. This yields a potent creative flow that manifests all the desired outcomes self believed required ego-control in order to fulfill. Yes, letting go of control is mandatory for full mastery of the human condition, true collaboration with the Divine Will and deep understanding of the workings of the Divine Plan.

When students hang on too tightly, determined to control reality, they experience needless suffering. The current mountain of karmic debris dislodged and flowing through students' energy bodies is challenging enough to assimilate and heal without contracting the process by attempting to orchestrate the timing or type of material surfacing, the quantity of debris, or the outcome. As self relaxes into trust, this soul material can resolve fairly smoothly as it deepens wisdom and lightens self's karmic load. However, when students try to control this accelerated soul cleansing, their higher channel contracts. Then the material being released chafes against the ego walls of control, creating a "soul rash" prickly with the heat of fear, dread, worry that elongates the process and makes the student miserable.

The powerful torrent of cosmic forces at this time in human history demands true surrender to the alchemical process of transmuting erupting karmic material. These forces pummel the personal will like a meat tenderizer, making it impossible to hold on to notions of control. This softens the soul body, inducing fluidity, elasticity and expansion.

Ego control equals contraction. Ironically, it is when the students most need to relax, let go and open in order to ease them through this transitionary initiation that they resort to every control mechanism they've ever known—frantically searching for the brakes and steering wheel in a vehicle stripped of such elementary devices.

This last-ditch attempt to outwit one's destiny distracts and exhausts the mind/body, creating lacerations from where the lower mind scrapes up against the genius of the Greater Mind of Source. It's best to appreciate the inevitable softness/ vulnerability/ lubrication that these pummeling energies produce with true humility. Self is then liberated from the claustrophobia of soul armor, no longer able to maintain the tight grip of control. Students can at long last be unshackled from the illusion that the ego/ personality alone is sitting in the soul's driver's seat.

Humankind need only remember that they are ultimately safe in a universe based in love. When releasing control, reference this innate platform of sanctuary in order to quiet the mind/ego and unwind the solar plexus. Like sitting back to watch a technicolor movie, allow self to relax into the unfoldment of the story—not attempting to control the story but completely present in self's multileveled response to it.

From this place of deep acceptance of soul transformation through the human process, students are profoundly impacted by life's journey. Control defenses melt away, allowing the cosmic forces full penetration to one's core. Joy mushrooms forth as the student relinquishes the controls, turning them over to a Higher Knowing. The higher mind is emancipated from the steel chains of iron-handed, cramped ego control to creatively respond to the Divine Plan with jubilant input—deeply at peace with the knowledge that a monumentally merciful, compassionate and benign Force exists to shoulder the summons of evolution. Beyond control lies humankind's birthright and unavoidable destiny—a true JOYRIDE into awakening!

✧ Vulnerability ✧

September 2004

Most of us are terrified of being vulnerable. If others see our vulnerability, they might judge it as weakness. We armor our soft underbelly with rigid steel defense structures to convince ourselves and others that we are impervious to the "tenderizing" process pivotal to our human condition. Ironically, acceptance of vulnerability, the true center of our human power, is an indication of real potency. Our learning curve of duality teaches than we can only embrace our power when we have encompassed its opposite—helplessness. We can pretend to be impregnable, but our fabricated invulnerability is a flimsy front fueled by the dread of exposure. Yet, naked visibility is exactly what we need to fully open. When the duality comes full circle and we discover the strength in our vulnerability, unification is possible.

Fear drops us to our knees, exposes our fragility on all levels and initiates the process of making deep inner contact with self. Unprotected defenselessness facilitates full surrender to Higher Powers. This disarmament advances us to drop the false pride of control and accept our Divine Fate. Vulnerability is our access point to the Divine Flow. Nothing stands in the way—no armor, shields, veils, numbness—NOTHING!

Do we hide our vulnerability because it would put us at a "disadvantage" in our dog-eat-dog society? What are we trying to protect—ego, pride, identity, reputation, competitiveness? We equate vulnerability with humiliation—a deep collective shame over our unclothed essence. Perhaps we don't want others to see our soul. But vulnerability *is* the gateway to our soul. So we strangulate the soul in a rock-hard fortress that suffocates the chakras. Yes, we may feel safe, even invulnerable. But the price of this security is true contact with the Divine Flow. Our razor's edge brings us Home only when we strip away all defenses and yield to our delicate, tender, mushy essence.

Often we react in anger to our vulnerability. If we become enraged maybe others will be afraid of us. Hot tempers drive others away before they can hurt us. Maybe they won't notice how much we're hurting as we dash to find a private place to cry our eyes out. God forbid others should witness this. But uncurtained vulnerability without the smokescreen of anger paves the way toward deep emotional intimacy, compassion, and understanding.

We pride ourselves on rugged durability—"I can take it." Who wants to be the laughing stock of others' judgments of our "weakness?" *But vulnerability is not a weakness, it is permeability.* Life ups the ante with insistent blows to our "toughness" until we can't take it. Finally tenderized, we accept our delicate self and disallow its rejection by others.

I feel most vulnerable when my emotional needs are exposed in close relationships. If I let down my defenses will others simultaneously follow suit? Or will they imperviously lord their disdain over my fragility? Am I a fool for exposing my soft underbelly? It feels counterintuitive to strip down when others are zipped up. But it is the only way in which we can know real trust. I've discovered that expressed vulnerability has strengthened my relationships and deepened emotional credence. (It's hard to trust an "invincible" person.) Vulnerability is the ultimate "crazy glue" that binds relationships and nurtures real soul bonds.

So what are we so afraid of—a blow to our pride, revelation of our inferiority, acknowledgment of fear, dysfunctionality, being controlled or overpowered, spineless, insubstantial, and feeble? But aren't we all in the same boat? If we think that we are less vulnerable than our global neighbors, we might want to reconsider. Collectively, we collude in the illusion that we can live in a realm beyond our vulnerability if we just patrol and screen our sensitivities. But denial relegates them to the unconscious where they subliminally eat away at us driving us to shore up greater buttresses of munitions.

What are your secret areas of vulnerability? Are you afraid of being exposed through your emotional needs, your creative expression, your truth, your spiritual orientation, the way you parent, your aging process, the way your mind works, your loss of physical beauty or strength? Why do you hide them? What self-judgmental false beliefs support your secrecy? Whatever we judge in others, we are terrified of discovering in ourselves.

It would certainly level the playing field if we all removed our armor. Equalized through our collective human fragility, we might tend to be more compassionate, nurturing, sensitive, patient with each other. With a deep caring (not coddling) and attunement to the human predicament we would receive everyone's vulnerability as a sacred domain—the portal to the soul—to be cherished and swaddled in loving attention. Once all defenses are expelled, we finally have a starting point for global healing.

Many clients start session with, "Thank God I'm here. Now I can let down my guard. No one knows how heavy my life is right now." I wonder why we are only allowed to share our vulnerability with our therapists/ healers—as if in confessional, where we shamefacedly reveal our underbelly for examination and forgiveness. Must we be forgiven for our fragility? Isn't it something to be PROUD of—to be honored? Vulnerability is the ultimate place of freedom. We no longer have to pretend to ourselves and others that we can override our delicacy.

Vulnerability is our only path to wisdom. We can't know our spiritual nature until we drop our ego's illusion of omnipotence. Then, as fresh-skinned babies, we can begin to look around at the larger Universe with awe and the soft saturability that allows us to fill with LOVE.

The Tibetan sprinkles rose petals through the air—demonstrating the dance of lightness that unfolds through exquisite delicacy. He teaches:

A newborn's head is soft to amplify continuing contact through the crown chakra (top of the head) with the spiritual plane while the soul is adjusting to its new physical body. Softened chakras keep the psycho/ spiritual self flowing and available to maxim celestial contact. The human experience is designed to break down one's defenses to allow the soul to emerge unencumbered. The students might as well make it easier on themselves by voluntarily accepting/ exposing their vulnerability without needing to be clobbered into submission. Humankind blocks the enormous spiritual wealth, guidance, support, protection with dense, coagulated energy willfully forged into armor, designed to support the notion that it is completely on its own. Humankind is NOT "duking it out" autonomously. It is unremittingly "tied in" to the spiritual plane. No action, thought or feeling is immune to the Compassionate Response that is Source. To obstruct spiritual energy (it literally bounces off hardened defenses) burdens one's journey through earth school and delays the inevitable recognition of Source's powerful SOFT nectar—the essence of the human condition. Identification with ones defenses feeds the ego's pride, willfulness and illusion of control. The sooner one lets go, becomes vulnerable, the sooner one touches the Plane of BLISS. The release of all defenses is the final initiation into enlightenment. The ego craves separation through invincibility. The soul aches for pure openness—final alignment—Cosmic impact.

Practice vulnerability! Ask for the courage to be authentic, exposed, to reveal needs, to release control, to unashamedly share experiences of vulnerability. Ask others about their vulnerability without assuming they "have it all together." Release all judgments of vulnerability. Scan for congealed areas in the heart, throat, solar plexus. Invoke loving gentle Light to soften these "boulders." Assume trust instead of distrust. Risk being the first one to reveal vulnerability. When arguing, remember that the other person is equally as vulnerable as self. Remember that all man-made notions of protection are illusion. Divine Custody is the only truly invulnerable source of immunity.

As more students expose their vulnerability, nations will follow suit. It will no longer be politically popular to put resources into defenses. Rather, disarmament will be the "in" political statement. As long as countries still need to prove their invulnerable sovereignty, war will proliferate. Bullheaded national boundaries can only be softened by exploring the mutuality of collective vulnerability. Students believe that if they have more defenses (political, emotional, and mental) then others, they will win or be safe. May everyone simultaneously drop their fear of vulnerability and play "naked" together in Mother Earth's great playground.

This is the onset of a New Cosmic Day—truly an Aquarian Age when Heaven and Earth merge into a shared embrace of soft receptivity. The fierce softness of Source's Love-Light permeates all bastions of encrusted defenses. Unencumbered by HEAVY armor, students will finally be liberated to create a sweeter world where all can show and tell the gifts that vulnerability brings— wisdom, compassion and receptivity to the Divine Mother. Like delicate meadow flowers, humankind will fully bloom through the joyful expression of its exquisite transparency.

The Divine function of vulnerability is to keep the chakras open, pliable, elastic and accessible to the Higher Self. It teaches humility, surrender, receptivity. Vulnerability reminds humankind to not override its fundamental nature. Life pushes through all defenses, no matter how rigid, to help the students "drop to their knees" in deep acquiescence to vulnerability. *Resist the temptation to protect self. Celebrate times of extreme vulnerability as a magnificent opportunity to enhance connection with the Greater Worlds.*

We remind the students that both the Masters and the Angelic Force cannot interfere with their karma. Only when students ASK for help can we respond. When the students can't accept their vulnerability, they either don't ask for aid at all (and therefore block our access point) or they request only surface assistance which aborts the deeper, soul-sustaining support and nourishment needed by all students during this momentous time in history. Joyfully accept the gift of self's uncovered vulnerability and bathe in the Divine Waters of Solace and Bolstering needed to gladden the heart into full trust of the Divine Plan.

✧ Trust ✧

March 2001

To trust is to be a fool! Everyone knows there is a real good chance that when you allow yourself to fall into the sweet oblivion of innocent trust in someone, something or God, something bad will happen: It always does. Just when you think you are safe in your trust the bottom falls out and trust is shattered—replaced by a heart a little more hardened and by renewed determination not to be hurt again—not to be so stupid next time or so foolish.

I have always been the "queen of suspicion." Just hearing the word "trust" sends instant signals of caution rippling through me as my mind searches for a reason to distrust. I know only too well how dangerous it is to trust. Putting full trust into a lover, friend, parent, or child is like asking for betrayal. After all, human beings inadvertently, or sometimes even purposely, hurt each other as we unconsciously blunder about in our relationships. The "lone wolf" part of me concludes it is simply better not to trust—safer, cleaner, and more reliable to keep that jaded edge in place, small bits of armor, chain-linked together by burning hot memories of betrayal of an earlier trust fueled by foolish innocence. Is the price of maturity and wisdom the loss of a fundamental trust in life?

Many of us have trust issues with the earth herself, having experienced past lives of starvation in drought, being buried alive in an avalanche, sucked up by a tornado, drowned in a flood or burned in a raging forest fire. How can we trust our precious planet to support and nurture us if she is capable of such betrayals?

The trust issue gets really interesting when we consider Source (God). Then every trust issue we have ever experienced in all of our lifetimes surfaces with a vengeance. Trust a God who would let people suffer, allowing such horrendous losses and tragic endings brought on by war, famine, disease, cruelty, persecution, and on and on? The trust issue is vast, extending from the personal immediacy of our current relationships, to our country's relationship with other nations, to our relationship with mother earth, and ultimately to our relationship with our God.

And then there is the final frontier of trust—trust of self. So often people say, "I'd be willing to make a change, but I just can't trust myself to make the right choices in life." We all know what it is like to feel as if we've made bad decisions in relationships, employment, finances, living arrangements, etc. Perhaps we are afraid to trust our intuition, our values, our wisdom, our strength, our loyalty to ourselves. Yet if we can't trust ourselves, who can we trust?

Djwhal Khul, the Tibetan, has persistently whispered "trust" in my ear for many years, reminding me that distrust is one of my greatest stumbling blocks to liberation. If he dares to even mention the word I tighten up, annoyed at his demand that I stretch beyond my fearful, cynical expectations of betrayal and loss.

He insists: *You must become like the newborn baby with its mother—open, trusting. Trust is the mechanism that softens defense structures and allows in a greater Universe, a yielding to the Higher Self. No student can make a leap in consciousness unless the trust factor is established. It is trust that allows self to relax, letting go of all known reality to fall into an embrace with the Divine.*

In spite of my resistance, I know the Tibetan is right. It becomes increasingly painful to sustain distrust, for to withhold trust is to push away all possibilities, including love. Clutching my distrust around me like a cold veil narrows my world, unbearably reducing abundant life bounty to a mere trickle of energy. The irony is that any efforts to stay "safe" in my small jaded world of cynicism create the very reality I'm trying to avoid—one of limited support, lack of loving relationships, a feeling of disconnect from others, mother earth and the universe. I become so fearful of opening in trust to the Cosmic Waterfall, nothing can flow in past the contemptuous gates of suspicion and pessimism. Shrouded in festering justification, I remind myself that I've been "burned" before by loved ones and life, not to mention God. So why should I trust now?!

Djwhal Khul tells me that trust is the bridge to the Higher Self, to enlightenment. He reminds me of past lives, when spiritual teachers encouraged their students to jump off a cliff, reassuring them that they would be caught by the teacher's "spiritual powers." I think in response, "How many students fell to their death, caught in the shock of shattered trust when the teacher didn't fulfill his end of the bargain?"

Perhaps those were exercises in making leaps of faith. Without trust, it is difficult to sustain faith. Without faith we can't let go and take the big swan dive into the mysterious abyss that holds our potential. The Tibetan teaches that for most students trust is the bottom line, the final barrier to self-realization. His favorite challenge is, *Just trust and all else will follow.*

To trust is to remember that love is the true nature of the universe. In a cosmos based in infinite love, there can only be utter safety. Stretching to accept that ultimately we are truly invulnerable beings is a potent process. Reacting immediately, the unconscious conjures up a vast array of horrible memories, personal or collective. It frantically reminds us to stop that feeble-minded wishfulness and get real, because if we dare to let down our guard our trust will be shattered yet one more time.

All of us have trust issues. If we had no trust issues we would be completely open. If we were completely open we would be enlightened. Perhaps it is our final lesson to be learned—how to open to our reality with the trust of a newborn babe, assuming that all of our experiences are in perfect alignment with the Divine Plan. How would life be different if we really trusted our reality, no matter how difficult or unfathomable it may be?

Learning to trust is a process involving one step forward and two steps back. Whenever freshly established levels of trust are shattered, there is the opportunity to review expectations. Shattered trust reveals expectations based on illusion. These illusions are usually rooted in false beliefs from past lives, often re-energized through this lifetime's childhood.

Every time we fall from trust we learn more about life's complexity. Our wide-open expectations are then tempered with a philosophical wisdom that includes the unexplainable level of our experience. Human beings don't live in the realm of absolute ideal. Our human plane of duality holds opposites. Therefore, we must include the worst in our trust! This is the alchemical tension between feeling ultimately safe and realizing we are all just hanging by a thread. We must broaden our trust to include the larger paradigm, the knowledge that our being is eternal and therefore can be trusted.

The Tibetan jumps in to add:

From the human perspective, to open to complete trust is impossible. The "pinhole vision" through which humankind perceives the universe does not fully represent the true picture. Trust is easily shattered because only fragments of the universal story can be seen at one time from this pinhole vision. Yes, it appears as if Source may have been having a good laugh at humankind's expense when It offered this minuscule vantage point. This was a challenge to stretch beyond the narrow framework of duality, tearing away the veils to behold the larger meaning infusing all earthly experiences.

So indeed, the trust has to be blind, like jumping off a cliff at midnight into blackness. This trust is seeded in one's core, permeating the mind and body. It is an innate knowing that everything occurs for a wondrous purpose, one of transformation and love. Trust is essential for making the leap across the dimensions from the old consciousness into the new. Don't look back. Don't try to <u>think</u> self into trust. Simply let go of all the haunting voices of the past cautioning self to be wary about opening. Take a big breath and allow self to believe that all is what it should be and therefore all will be fulfilled.

In the alchemical process, the blackening stage (the first stage of turning lead into gold) is discouraging to the student. When the inevitable breaking down of the outgrown self occurs, through whatever mechanism needed, the trust that the old self would never be "harmed" is shattered. The old self feels betrayed and unsafe. Yet the old self must be released in the transmutation process—the old skin shed. The Core Self, eternal and forever young, then emerges at a new level, more clarified and delighted than ever before.

Yes, self cannot trust a world attached to changelessness. But self can trust the process of change and metamorphosis. Change is a gift from Source, the gift of transformation. No matter how difficult the inner or outer storms of transformation may be, they <u>always</u> result in a glorious outcome, one eventually leading to cosmic consciousness.

There is truly nothing to distrust in this Universe of Everlasting Love. No being has ever been lost in the eyes of Source. It is as difficult to get away from the Divine Canopy of Safety as it is to get away from the sky. This is a colorful process full of "black and blue marks" along the way, all alchemizing into golden light.

To dare to trust this opportunity of transformation is to rejoice in the storms that shape the soul and temper the heart's fire while the student eagerly awaits the culminating flower that is Self's exquisite beauty. There has always been Light. There has always been Love. That is the foundation for trust catapulting self beyond all imagined realities.

So trust each other to be divine soul mates, carrying each other along the ladder of love, escalating the soul in its return arch homeward to Source. Trust your beloved planetary home that has served you for lifetimes in rich form and substance, vivifying and making human life possible. And trust your Source—for from It you carry your breath, your spirit, the eternal flame that lights all worlds.

✧ Divine Discipline ✧

March 2005

"Discipline is the key to freedom," exclaimed my piano teacher 20 years ago. However, freedom and discipline seem as incompatible as oil and water. Discipline's "shoulds" provoke the rebel in me. In anarchistic moments of sheer revolution, discipline appears to be a tedious, heavy, burdensome drag that blocks my freedom to do whatever I want, whenever I want! I temporarily ride the wave of this heady rebellion. But inevitably the stagnate sludge of unstructured laziness, indulgence, free-for-all good time becomes boring and turns me into a "free" but miserably brainless, blobbed-out couch potato. Could it be that my piano teacher was right?

Why do we hate discipline? What are we afraid of—too much hard, painful unimaginative work, deprivation, loss of spontaneity, drudgery, restriction, dullness and most importantly—not enough fun? Discipline's rigors appear to be a prison rather than a liberating tool for self-mastery. It all boils down to attitude, especially after the initial enthusiasm of change fades. We must remember discipline's rewards of gratification in order to feed the optimism that carries us through all stopping points—roadblocks that have sabotaged our enterprises for lifetimes and convinced us that "it's too hard" to do this discipline thing.

When our negativity resists self-government, we forget that we are the architects of our lives. The atmosphere of discipline feels parental in its policing of our childlike spontaneous impulse for pleasure by reprimanding and curbing all playful abandon. This triggers frustrating memories of parental boundaries—too many "nos"—enforced discipline for requirements that seemed stupid and irrelevant to us as kids. Sometimes we forfeit the rewards of self-chosen discipline by "hiring" others to be our parental disciplinarians who force us to tow the line, like slave drivers from previous lifetimes. We eventually hate those taskmasters. When our disciplines are perceived as encroaching tyrants of pressure, we lose sight of our original vision of possibility and are robbed of the incredible quality of life that discipline provides. It helps to remind our inner child that as adults we get to *choose* the meaningful disciplines that carry our passions to their ultimate fulfillment.

Olympic athletes who defy the odds and move into the realm of the extraordinary have certainly made discipline their ally! What sustains their discipline through hours of grueling training? How do they resist the Voices of Undoing that say, "Why bother?" Usually by March we've given up on our New Year's resolutions. Why can't we buttress our willpower?

Perhaps we don't believe that we're strong/ determined enough to uphold discipline's demands. We suffer from the illusion that we're weak or lazy. But discipline is only bearable if we truly believe it will take us where we want to go. Otherwise it becomes a jail of drudgery that kills our joy. Maybe our default to laziness is a protection against fears that discipline won't yield the satisfaction of fulfilled intentions, and will only lead us down a disheartening dead end. Discipline devoid of the vision of its eventual harvest feels like a straightjacket designed to tighten whenever we step out of line. In addition, our intentions may be riddled with unconscious conflicts that undermine our efforts to cement in daily disciplines. Far from lazy, we may simply be at odds with ourselves over our goals. Often we have unconscious secondary gains from the status quo that we are loath to give up. Therefore, we may be unable to fully welcome the changes that discipline brings even though our conscious selves are begging for metamorphosis.

We have to set realistic, self-compassionate goals. If we're too strict, the psyche will revolt and overthrow discipline's tyranny within a month. So, we must gently coax ourselves into deepening involvement with our disciplines as we breathe with the natural resistance that surfaces—and forgive ourselves occasional slips into chaos. These momentary "discipline disintegrations" provide the psyche with refreshing breaks from holding concentrated intentions and need not be interpreted as defeat, which would only justify a descent into juvenile irresponsibility. Step by step, discipline will broaden our horizons and provide rich cornerstones that anchor and structure the soul while we journey through the human condition.

What truly sustains discipline? Is it iron will or devotion to an ideal—perhaps an interplay between the two? Iron will's male yang energy helps us stay one-pointed in our purposefulness, resoluteness and perseverance. But too much iron will makes us rigid, dry, and controlling as we white knuckle our way to our goals. How much can we grit our teeth without imprinting a permanent grimace on our faces? Discipline addicts, fearful that any interruptions in their daily rituals will evaporate all progress, sometimes forget to relax and trust that it's okay to take a break. Devotion to an ideal, feminine yin energy employs yearning and love to sustain the heart's discipline that feeds the passion necessary for the spark of inspiration to continue to fire up our determination.

Ultimately, without discipline we can't manifest anything. We need discipline to accomplish this incarnation's spiritual mandate. Discipline is intention put into action. It glues commitment to our goals and structures the pathway that makes our dreams come true. Discipline deepens resolve and solidifies the matrix of our intentions. This matrix, a vessel for the Universal Flow, must be strong enough to receive, contain and focus the potent Force that evolves us into the Realm of the Extraordinary. Without discipline the structure of our intention's matrix becomes too flimsy, and precious cosmic creative energy is dissipated.

Ironically, discipline is not the work ogre that we dread, but rather a vehicle for self-love. The attitude, "I do this for me because I love myself and trust that I can be so much more," opens the door to discipline's transformative magic and enlivens our willingness to sacrifice obsolete life patterns. Discipline builds character, maturity, focus, responsibility, self-esteem/ confidence and a garden of fulfilled goals. This transforms our attitude to, "I can do it," and excites us to add more impassioned disciplines to our lives as we bask in their gifts of strength and self-satisfaction. Discipline breaks new ground, wears away at the inertia of past lives, and opens new vistas of possibility as we touch our magnitude and taste all that we can be and MORE.

The Tibetan teases about the discipline it takes to manage unruly students like myself! He teaches:

Discipline's ability to manifest intention in form, although perceived as backbreakingly toilsome, makes ensoulment possible. Through discipline, humankind encounters the tension/ friction point between the etheric and physical planes. Discipline links the boundlessness of the etheric plane's sensitive, untroublesome, effortless response to the soul's creative imagination with the earth's weighty, gravitational pull within the Time-Space

Continuum of Limitation. The soul needs this earthly tension to develop the strength, conviction and persistence that deepens its essence. Discipline focuses the otherworldly unfettered self and provides an alchemical container for spiritual energy.

Students frequently complain that earth school is too hard. They assume that discipline chains them, like convicts doing 'hard time,' to the density of earth's gravitational field. Humankind's 'too hard' assumption automatically invokes karmic patterns of arduous laboriousness, defeat, slavishness, resignation and joylessness. To succumb to the false belief that self doesn't have what it takes to go the distance in this lifetime demolishes determination as waves of resignation engulf the soul. Can self really dare to beat the odds in this lifetime?

Only the positive attitude of self-love can overcome the Wall of Stoppage established through lifetimes of inertia. To evolve beyond this wall and dispel the soul's sluggish resistance to its earthly contract, self must instruct the mind to establish new thought patterns/ beliefs that associate discipline with the happy fruition of all soul desires. Stances like, 'I hate discipline,' generate adversarial conflicts with the course requirements that must be accomplished in this lifetime, like it or not! Students don't believe that they can possibly master the human condition. Therefore, they fear that all the discipline in the world won't bring them liberation and will only further enslave them to earth's 'barren wasteland of fruitless effort, toil and difficulty.'

Ironically, humankind's real resistance to discipline is the fear of touching its magnitude and allowing the Extraordinary Self to be visible at long last. When experiencing the fruits of self's disciplines, all attachments to unworthiness/ shabbiness are challenged and must be released. Is humankind allowed to feel this good? Yes—cosmic permission granted! In this delicate juncture between the etheric flight of the imagination and earthly mastery, discipline is the self-proving that anchors the soul onto the earth while being the chariot that transports humankind to the stars.

At this momentous juncture in humankind's evolution, the Divine Imperative of Maturation is at hand. Humankind must leave its childish irresponsibility. To 'grow up' is to embrace discipline as a key modality for honing the soul's readiness to enter the Gateway of Heightened Consciousness that spearheads the New Age. There is no time to waste. Therefore, release all physical, emotional, mental and spiritual levels of lethargy. Grab the cosmic bull by the horns and gratefully accept the required disciplines for self liberation. Be cheerleaders for each other to develop the spiritual muscle and virtue that links humankind to the Realm of Exceptional Discipline required to literally reshape the human condition into its ultimate truth—beings of such momentousness and distinction that all of the intergalactic family cheers for this Olympic event that truly defies all the odds!

✧ Gratitude vs. Entitlement ✧

June 2004

How can we learn to be grateful for what we have rather than "entitled" to what we don't have? I fluctuate between being overwhelmed with thankfulness for all the gifts in my life and being consumed with discontent about all my unrealized desires. Then, guilty and ashamed of being greedy, grabby and selfish, I scurry back to thankfulness to resist the entitlement trap that I find so distasteful in others.

My expectations of entitlement only bring frustration and a wounding sense of failure, hurt and rejection from the Divine. (Have "they" forgotten about me when they handed out all the goodies?) Entitlement blinds me to the real treasures in my life. Instead, I only perceive what others have that I don't—more money, more leisure time, more fun, more friends, more freedom, more inner peace—more, more, more! I rage at Source for not "delivering the goods" that I expect to come my way, especially in the face of everyone else's plenty.

Envy carries deep levels of entitlement. We assume that we are supposed to have what others have. This belief homogenizes our pathways by wicking out the uniqueness of our needs. Caught up in a sense of entitlement, we miss the very specific requirements of our particular soul's journey in this incarnation. What is our fair due? How do we measure our soul's necessities? We must trust that we are given exactly what we need to complete our life assignments. Why would we envy someone else's path when it would only lead us astray from our most exciting learning curve? Their bounty, if inappropriately given, would only rot in our laps by blocking our soul's needs and crimping our evolution. Others' riches, irrelevant to our soul, are ultimately meaningless to the core Self.

Entitlement may also reflect past-life memories when we had more—material, emotional and/or mental excesses that require moderation and non-attachment in this lifetime. These cellular memories fuel demands for more. We can be continually frustrated by these unmet expectations or learn how having less grows us in new ways—extended wisdom, humility and balance. But it sure is challenging to overcome the gnawing hunger pains of not-enoughness springing from vague unconscious memories of having had more. Willing exploration of the deeper benefits we have gained from the areas of "scarcity" in our lives fertilizes an all-pervasive gratitude that transports us through illusions of deprivation.

When my giving to others is not appreciated, I feel devalued, invisible and disconnected, which contracts my generosity of spirit. (I can only imagine how the Universe feels when we are stingy with our thankfulness.) This demonstrates the power within the Force Field of Gratitude. To broadcast genuine thankfulness substantiates worth, which then augments the positive effects of gifts received. Expressed gratitude toward Source for all aspects of life magnetizes the Great Flow that showers our needs with Plenty. Potency of appreciation expands our reception channel. Gratitude withheld because we selfishly assume we are entitled to what we receive, with no requirement to "return" the energy, contracts our channel. The Universal Generosity that is Source—our Holy Ground—becomes untouchable. The moment we fill with gratitude, our lives change. The humbling effect of appreciation allows us to happily yield to what we have rather than stew over being "ripped off." To surrender to gratitude softens the ego and enhances our higher alignment. Perhaps enlightenment is to be in a constant state of thankfulness.

Fear, unworthiness and anger are the usual log jams that sabotage my efforts to *sustain* gratitude. Unrealized desires stimulate self-criticism. Rather than revise my expectations, I wonder how I have sabotaged opportunities for fulfillment. Yes, unworthiness wounds may block my ability to receive, but some areas of perceived lack are really appropriate conditions for my current evolution. Bottom-line thankfulness for all lessons and the exquisite Divine Plan that orchestrates these opportunities is the true path to joy. Attitude is everything. Gratitude expresses the willingness to collaborate with my Higher Self.

Entitlement represents the attitude that I'll wait for eternity, with arms squarely, defiantly folded in front, until I get my fair share. This isolates me from true communion with the Divine. Entitlement is my way of scrambling for whatever crumbs I can steal when I've decided that Source has forgotten about me.

It's deflating to joyfully give a gift to someone who arrogantly (grandiosity) expects it. The delight of giving freezes in our heart and is replaced by resentment. We make a mental note not to be too generous with that person again. Perhaps the Universe responds to our entitlement that way as well. People who don't practice gratitude must feel spiritually bankrupt.

Entitlement is our way of taking things for granted, which we often regret after losing what we had. The true loss was an appreciation of the moment which would have highlighted our experience a million-fold. Instead we are left with empty memories based on the hollow pleasure that "satisfied entitlement" may have temporarily produced. It's far easier to release life experiences that we have deeply appreciated rather than the ones we took for granted. I must be vigilant about any numbed-out aspects of self that thanklessly devour life. Gratitude is an incredibly effective form of RETURNING energy. If energy is miserly withheld, the Loop of Cosmic Exchange is interrupted.

Sometimes I feel unbearably overwhelmed by gratitude because it reminds me how precious *everything* is. Then I feel painfully vulnerable to loss. It helps to remember that gratitude doesn't magnetize loss, but rather increases sensitivity to the rich essence within the moment. Gratitude allows us to honor each other and to realize our deepest value. It melts our defense structure of insular self-sufficiency (based on the illusion that we alone create all the goodies in our life—no need to be grateful to others or a higher power). This insular focus severs us from the Pipelines of Fullness. *Every* moment requires gratitude. Recognition of all help received expands our narrow paradigm. When thankful, I relax, smile and know that all is well with the world. When feeling entitled, I am tense, untrusting, resentful of others and frustrated with my lot in life. To challenge myself to be grateful for everything inspires the creative process of searching for the gift within my darkest moments.

How can we be open to abundance without puffing up with entitlement? Through profound thankfulness based on true humility in the acceptance of our specialness/ value, we remember that we are extensions of a Higher Self that places us in the unpretentious position of teamwork. We can want more, not from expectations and demands, but rather from referencing the infinite nature of our being—the never-ending possibility for expansion. The "more" we desire is not only for ourselves but for all beings and the earth. Ultimately, the more we truly want is the More that comes from knowing LOVE.

The Tibetan bows in deep appreciation of the moment and teaches:

What would the world be like if humankind was truly grateful for EVERYTHING? When humankind initially incarnated, it assumed that to be relegated to the earthly plane was punishment—an exile from Source's hearth. Consequently, humankind feels devalued and diminished by its very nature and earthly existence. This illusion, encoded in the students' root chakra at the base of the spine, has fostered all levels of entitlement.

Humankind subliminally remembers its true spiritual essence (and value) and struggles to bridge the apparent discrepancy between the "lowly" human condition and its Divine core that beams like a diamond through the soul. Plagued by feelings of abandonment by Source, humankind took it upon itself to establish "its proper due" based on this vague memory of being more than just an inferior human being. The attempts to commandeer its proper due were based on the illusion that humanity was not given the "keys to the Kingdom" because of Source's apparent rejection. This makes humankind "grabby," like a child throwing a temper tantrum who seizes what he/she wants because of fears of non-deservedness. When grasping from a place of entitlement, humankind automatically blinds itself to the bigger picture of Divine Bounty. Consequently, entitlement results in impoverishment.

To receive requires gratitude. Gratitude is the electrical matrix that triggers Source's outpouring of Abundance. Metaphysical law insists that only true emptiness stimulates receptivity. Therefore, emptiness begets fullness through the magnetism of opposites. If the student is too full of self (ego demands/entitlement), then there is no space through which to magnetize the responsive flow of Wealth. This blocked energy fuels the primordial rage that humankind harbors against Source for its supposed loss of value through earthly incarnation. Consequently, the ego is determined to snatch what it needs regardless of others on the earth. Entitlement then reaches full dominion in the collective consciousness. Ultimately entitlement springs from a deep sense of unworthiness—humankind still caught in the sticky web of perceived rejection from Source. The only avenue for full recovery of one's worth is gratitude, which represent the humility required for enhanced awareness of one's true spiritual nature.

Can self be thankful for ALL experiences—good or bad? Full gratitude for difficult life challenges provides a boost to the energy body, fortifying it with the best attitude to access all the resources available for self's "assignments." All karma has its ultimate antidote. Gratitude lubricates access to this soul remedy. Gratitude implies ego surrender in the acknowledgment that ultimately whatever self receives is beyond the ego's control. If self entrenches in entitlement, seething with resentment about others' abundance, then difficulties increase in order to break down the ego. Ultimately through complete thankfulness humankind realizes that it can only truly function in conjunction with the Higher Forces. Gratitude is prayer—conscious contact with LOVE. Shower each other with appreciation. Take nothing for granted. All life experiences are gifts to the soul. All gifts thankfully received return to Source doubled in value!

✧ <u>Part Six</u> ✧

THE TRANSITION PROCESS

✧ The Process of Transformation ✧

December 2005

Can you turn lead into gold? Impossible? But ancient alchemists were undaunted in their determination to practice transformation. We assume that transformation only happens in fairy tales that magically transpose adversity into happy endings. Grown-ups must be realistic about their limitations and disregard these childish fantasies. Yes, we make important modifications in our lives. But, let's face it, we can't fundamentally change—or can we? Is a RADICAL metamorphosis of our being possible, or are we stuck with the status quo?

Currently we're being challenged to open our minds and imaginations to very real opportunities for total transmutation at the cellular level. Are we willing to believe that this is possible?

Transformation isn't something that suddenly happens, magically, to lucky people. Rather, it's a relentless moment-to-moment PROCESS that activates everyone. The heightened evolutionary frequencies impacting our planet have brought us full circle, back to the ancient alchemists' goal. Divine mandate insists that we change the lead in our souls to gold.

Transformation is a three-step process that consists of an initial blackening (nigredo) stage, a whitening (albedo) stage and the culminating gold (rubedo) stage. The blackening stage comes on like gangbusters and floods us with dark, upsetting feelings, sensations, and thoughts. We're driven down into our deepest self to unearth all blockages in need of conversion. It takes a mighty force to pummel/ bombard the defense structures that guard these soul deadlocks. We feel like we've been hit by a Mack truck and wonder why God is punishing us. This alchemical phase of "rotting" catalyzes self-repulsion and harsh self-judgment.

As the armor disintegrates, our worst nightmares surface to represent the hidden material stockpiled in our unconscious. (Needless to say, I would much rather skip this phase!) Old crystallized chunks of self begin to decay. Death feels pervasive. Terrifying inner monsters erupt from their caves as the shadow-self floods our awareness. A blazing alchemical fire cooks the parts of us divinely charged to transmute. We don't bargain on how far down the alchemical tunnel we must travel to transform our wounds at their roots. The extent of the decent seems unsparingly formidable.

Because the far-reaching alchemical impact of "spoiling" leaves no stone unturned, we can't rush the process. Our dependable vision/ orientation is being eaten by alchemical fire, creating a temporary blindness that sucks us into depression, hopelessness, frustration, exhaustion, despair. We can only surrender to this undoing just as the caterpillar accepts its dissolvement into a mush-filled cocoon. All expectations, victories, assuredness and confidence crumble to make way for the transforming self.

To cling to the "dead body" part of ourselves undergoing transformation would drive us into a crazed, frenzied stagnation as we resist full immersion into the murky waters that decompose the old psychic structure. The blackening phase is a corrosive process. We feel devoured by forces that push us to our "boiling point" with the imperative heat that disjoins and dispels the integrity of the obsolete self to make room for the new. All unresolved conflicts, traumas, illusions from previous lives are revealed. The ghostly presence of the death stage reduces the old self to a crumbling empty shell. Our egos are overwhelmed, baffled, frightened and demoralized as the rug is yanked from under us, dismantling the platform of our outmoded being.

Can we resist the impulse to judge ourselves as bad, inferior, unworthy during this "ugly" stage? Self-condemnation exacerbates the blackening process by fixating on the soul's dark impasses and missing the glimmers of gold beginning to surface. We must remember that transformation is a *process*. The descent is not the endpoint.

The blackening stage informs us that the fire is hot. But our feet aren't held to the coals without respite. Periodically we surface from the deep cauldron and begin to touch our emerging potential. Such glimpses are short-lived as we're dragged back down again to undergo more divine decay, which yields the fertile compost essential to grow the soul's newly-sprung garden. This roller coaster ride of ascent-descent allows for alchemically produced change by heightening awareness. We lose our bearings, release levels of expectations and "knowing," and tumble into the void.

Now we're well on our way. The past has crumbled—the old forms are wrecked. The discarded matrix is unrecognizable. Reality as we've known it has fermented into a powerful "bitter"—the potent alchemical element that cuts through the "sweet" of fruition. Like the over-ripened apple, fruit of the soul, that is too sweet, we "turn" and submit to our unmitigated decomposition.

During the whitening stage, like the pure mush of the caterpillar, we sit in the emptiness, like sawdust figures, as undifferentiated blobs of consciousness. We're NOTHING. We must surrender to the formlessness and wait on the Tao— emptiness that often really aggravates my impatience. With the pain of the descent over, we're challenged to sit in the void without filling it with galling interpretations as to why we find ourselves in this Godforsaken vacuousness. There's no point in personalizing this obscurity. No one is exempt from periods of pure undefined shapelessness. We must trust the Master Alchemist within our soul whose genius guides this razor's edge journey of transfiguration.

The whitening stage demands flexibility and fluidity. The turbulent oceanic Storm of Blackening is hushed. The soul waters are placid. We're like a blank canvass—white...formless. Our bud-like emerging ego structure is barely perceptible. We've been thrust far from our familiar shoreline. Who are we? Our breath reminds us that our essence still flourishes as we simmer in the White Cocoon that stills, purifies and regenerates the soul. Our trust is buoyed by the victory of having weathered the storm. Curiosity about our next step starts to percolate while we're held in the deep Not-Knowing. There's no turning back. Can we cultivate an attitude of receptivity, humility, reverence and quiet faith during this time of purgation and sanctification?

Then, suddenly we've arrived! The sun is shining! We take flight! We're GOLD! Our boundlessness focalizes into new forms—new consciousness, new identity, new purpose. Wisdom gushes forth from the transformational wellspring as understanding, lucidity, empowerment, joy and creativity usher in an invigorated boldness, redoubled energy and a new appreciation of our prolific, enduring essence. The butterfly takes flight, exuberant in its glorious rainbow colors, and touches heights unimaginable to its old caterpillar self. How does it feel to take to the skies and receive the big picture after crawling on the ground for centuries? It is the reward for our courageous efforts, which were not unnoticed by the spiritual plane.

The Tibetan, dressed in shimmering gold, teaches:

Embrace transformation! This process of shifting forms reveals the soul's honeyed nectar and advances the divine union between the Higher Self and its human extension. Today's heightened frequencies are accelerating everyone's transformational process in order to ready humankind for its next evolutionary leap. The alchemical fires within the soul burn hotter than ever when riding this transmutational express train.

Accept the blackening stage with gratitude for the opportunity to finally unshackle from ancient blockages. Marvel at the wonder of Cosmic Nature as it decomposes and reorganizes at superior levels. What an honor to ride this roller coaster of dismantlement and regeneration. Enjoy the surprise of seeing self newly reflected in the mirror each morning. Observe the transformational stages with curiosity and neutrality, like a scientist who marvels at the wonder of transfiguration. In spite of earth's density, its predilection to transubstantiation reveals its core etheric essence. The transformational impulse in the cosmic agenda pervades the entire earthly plane.

Transformation is relentless, exciting, unnerving and bone-penetrating. Taste the deep excitement within comprehensive CHANGE. Trust that self is inevitably metamorphosing into a light body of heightened refinement. Transmutation guarantees that self's greatest dreams will inevitably manifest. As you embody your soul's essential gold, you can be all that you ever hoped to be and so much more. Transformation reveals its counterpart in the changeless, eternal, ever-present heart of the soul. Enjoy this process of watching self disappear and reappear in dazzling splendor.

Most people easily recognize that they're not the same person they were 10 years ago. While their transformational journey may have been rigorous, in hindsight they're thankful to have been "shoved" into the alchemical oven. Embrace the heat of transformation as a loving fire that precisely pinpoints the fossilized bottlenecks in the soul awaiting the gift of softening. No one is ever burned by these alchemical fires. Their temperature is carefully set to consume the dross without scorching the tender pink of the soul's innocent underbelly. Trust that the Divine Torch of Transmutation flames with LOVE to accelerate the soul's evolution and liberate it from the confines of obsolete parameters.

Teach others the stages of this process so they can joyously submit to the Divine Alchemy which yields the glorious glow of golden streams of Light that emanate from refreshed chakras, heightened alignment with the Higher Self, a purified energy body and a refinement of being that exquisitely represents the soul's elegance and true majesty. Soon all of humankind will be fully "cooked." A new World Order of Incandescent Gold will unfold as the earthly plane ennobles the Universe with its dazzling demonstration of the transfiguration of lead into GOLD.

✧ Embracing Change ✧

September 2003

Earth's vibrational field is quickening, relentlessly forcing us to evolve swiftly, like pulling an all-nighter before a final exam with no respite. This vibrational headway is a mandate for growth. Growth means change. We all clamor to grow. But how much are we really willing to fundamentally change deep down inside?

My clients say they want to change, but they don't know how—or they are afraid to. They feel stuck, stagnant, impossibly mired in chronic conditions. Without change, we cannot transform our consciousness. Yet feeling trapped in our patterns, we don't really believe that profound change is possible. We fear that if we do somehow manage to change, it can't be sustained. Like losing weight, we may be disciplined enough to take off the pounds, but keeping them off is another matter. Anchoring REAL change seems as illusive as climbing Mount Everest.

Whether it's initiating or sustaining change, CHANGE WE MUST if we are ever to open to the Age of Aquarius—an unprecedented world order based on a vastly different paradigm. Because this age brings in such NEW information, understanding, wisdom, we must set aside traditional perspectives and open to the original. Are we willing to truly let go of habits, fixed mind-sets/beliefs and frozen emotional patterns in order to transform the roots of our being? We're starving for transformation while trying to incorporate the new paradigm into our familiar third dimensional consciousness, only to find that it doesn't translate. So we must open to a pioneering, cellular change…one so far-reaching, we may not know ourselves afterward.

Our resistance tells us that we can't transform. After all, no one ever *really* changes. We are who we are! We pray to somehow liberate ourselves from chronic patterns of thinking, feeling, acting, and interacting. But our bottom-line shared belief that humanity will never truly evolve into full collective awakening reinforces the illusion that basically we are powerless to full-blown change. As long as this negative belief is woven into the bedrock of our conditioning—a doctrine that freezes us into sameness—all our best efforts to change seem to falter.

Change is terrifying. We buoy up our reality by struggling to hold onto the tried-and-true that supposedly sustains our sanity, in spite of the shifting sands of evolution undermining our foothold. Desperate to cling to the known, we tighten our muscles to adapt to that amorphous footing, causing intense tension as the acceleration amps up, alchemically designed to disintegrate crystallized blockages within the soul body.

FULL root-level change requires us to face the breakdown of the old, let go and surrender to the inevitable ego disorientation. If our society embraced change, there would be provision for passages of madness and bewilderment, when we celebrated each other's metamorphosis instead of feared it.

Change is especially threatening when everything seems to be going well. Why would we want to change? Better to sit tight than try to improve on an already acceptable life. However, the nature of evolution is CHANGE. Only by embracing change can we touch the eternal nature of our being.

We don't trust change because we can't see the larger picture of what is emerging. But now we must blindly welcome change because the cosmic winds are blowing apart our knowns, casting them off like shattered splinters of wood—fragments of an old world metamorphosing into a greater arena of divinity. To resist change is to suffer. How can we convince ourselves to surrender to the change and disappear into a new being—unidentifiable yet deeply recognizable at the essential level?

I love change—that is, unless it threatens to introduce chaos, dismantle precious attachments, deposit me where I don't want to be, invoke an unacceptable part of myself, steal my stability, shatter my perspective. Then I fight tooth and nail for security, determined to anchor in some semblance of predictability. But with the energies so intensified, I'm actually safer untethered—resilient, elastic, open to change. I try to believe that change heralds liberation, healing, transformation. Yet my gut insists that change means loss. I forget that changelessness equals stagnation, which suffocates the soul.

Change allows us to inhale the pulse of the universe and flow within waxing/ waning intergalactic currents. Changelessness feels like the stultifying, oppressive humid heat that makes us beg for a violent thunderstorm to clear the air. Still, we cling to changelessness, assuming that we can remain the same forever and still evolve. If our bodies change 95% of their cells yearly, how can we hope to batten down the hatches and avoid our metamorphosis?

Paradoxically, I desperately *want* to change negative patterns, but feel impotent to do so. After all, I don't believe I'm strong enough to sustain innovations. I'm certain that my best intentions will be undermined by the Inertia Vortex—that deep groove in my soul that has always made me view, and therefore experience, earthly life in a certain way. Fearful that if I look back I will be further cemented in my soul's chronicity, I try to turn away from entrenched patterns—imagining myself born anew each moment…fresh as a daisy, ready to embark on life in a completely new way.

This illusion quickly shatters as the incarcerating tug to the familiar weighs down my adventure into possibility, reminding me that: this is my life's fate; we're all "doing time" here without parole, caged by deeply incised negative karmic patterns forever limiting, asphyxiating, squashing the emerging garden in my soul. Like struggling to bail out a rowboat on the ocean during a nor'easter, the persistent currents of "the way it's always been" nullify feeble efforts to build a new self.

From this perspective, I'm blind to the far-reaching transformation that has already occurred in my life. Reflecting on ten years ago, I barely recognize myself. How did that metamorphosis occur if I'm still feeling like I can't change core patterns? Does life change us in spite of ourselves? Does our attachment to the known block recognition of what has already changed? If we really allowed ourselves to recognize the cellular transformation in our physical, emotional and mental templates, would we celebrate or go mad?

So we struggle with the razor's edge of change—fearing it when it bears down upon us, expecting the worst and begging for it as a release from the Pit of Constancy at the center of our inner prisons We're challenged to greet change with curiosity, a joyous heart, the trust of a babe, and the wonderment of the miracle of rebirth. We're challenged to register the avalanche of change that has already imbued our lives with expansion, depth, healing. We are challenged to accept what appears changeless in our lives— realizing that the water is heating up even if hasn't yet come to full boil.

The moment we issue an intention to change, universal energy is invoked, setting that change into motion, whether it circles around as a recognizable form/ experience immediately or fifty years from now. Somewhere deep in our souls, all ancient skins of illusion are falling away—reorganizing our very core.

The Tibetan's shape-changing energy flows toward me on the inner planes, joyfully teaching:

The emerging new paradigm for the collective consciousness is COMPLETELY different from all that humankind has ever known. The forefront of the consciousness revolution necessitates a wide-open receptivity to absolute metamorphosis. Humankind resists change because it is afraid to see itself fully revealed in its divinity. Ego attachment to the small self blocks awareness of the potentiated Self.

Students beg for change when they feel imprisoned by a karmic process requiring them to dwell within a particular situation for a prescribed duration—the time it takes to "cook" the soul. During this term, self feels impotent to break free of chronic conditioning. Nonetheless, although imperceptible, change is occurring. All karmic stints impact/ transform the soul. Like water over rock, it may take time for the crystallized karmic debris to thaw, creating the illusion that these patterns are rigid beyond softening. However, like water, the spirit softens all density in the soul to allow greater light/ love to enter.

Eventually students realize they have changed when they can no longer energize outworn attitudes. Incredulous, they may scurry around to reinvest in the old behavior, but its essence has metamorphosed and cannot be accessed. The change is complete. The lower mind has to catch up and reorient to the change, establishing a higher level of self-identification.

Prescribed karmic agendas demand a holding pattern to be sustained long enough to simmer the soul wounds and burn away the dross of illusion. Students may feel condemned to this karmic "prison." Remember that even the most severe chronicity eventually breaks down. Self is painstakingly inching along on a protracted inner pilgrimage that eventually harvests great wisdom.

No one is ever required to be eternally imprisoned in a changeless hell. True transformation cannot be rushed or skimmed over. It is a process that must be endured through the illusion of time. Trust that the timing for change is precisely orchestrated. If a cake takes an hour to bake, don't undercook it—but don't let it burn, either! Look within to appreciate where self is in the cooking process. Acceptance allows joyful witnessing of the unfolding changes. When students realize they are completely cooked, they are challenged to fully release all attachment to their karmic chronicity. These patterns have outlived their purpose.

Transmitting the message to the Universe that self wants to change is like putting the foot on the gas pedal and leaving it there. Most students issue this Change Invocation conditionally based on what their ego assumes needs changing. But the universe responds to the soul's revisionary Turnabout Call and provides exactly what is needed for alchemy. Allow self to be surprised at the changes that the universe offers, trusting that these transfigurations ultimately heal the ego as well as the soul, yielding a garden of joy beyond all belief.

Everyone is right on schedule. Daily, upon awakening, state: Today I am changing from moment to moment as I allow the full spirit within my divinity to fill my being. This change ushers in my magnitude, stripping away the veils that obscure true vision. This change reveals my enlightenment.

With the accelerated energies expediting the awakening process, predestined karmic timing is shortened. Many students feel unprepared for the changes they are experiencing, panting to keep up with their process. All incarnate beings have agreed during this time in history to endure the rigors of acceleration, necessitating greater leaps of faith as self releases old constructs of being perhaps a tad sooner than usual. While the cake may not look totally solidified, it has baked enough.

Trust that in spite of the bombardment of change, self is prepared for the onslaught of movement on the inner planes. Everyone is required to respond to this galloping evolutionary cooking formula. Change must occur at the roots. The ego is smugly satisfied with superficial change, knowing that its domain is unthreatened at that level. But the higher self requires cellular change—reorganizing the karmic matrix that is the DNA structure of the soul. Changes are taking place at great depth, issuing a broad-brushed wallop to all aspects of life.

Students suffer when they believe they are unable to sustain their changes, falsely concluding that they haven't really changed at all. After sustaining a metamorphosis for a while, deeper layers of the karmic conditioning surface, creating the illusion that self has regressed. This is not the time to give up. These subliminal layers surfacing indicate how profoundly self really IS changing. Self has not failed. Persist in the spiraling process of meeting inner chronicity with an open spirit, filled with the knowledge that of course self is sustaining and deepening the change. When transformation occurs cellularly, at the soul level, it is so complete that, ironically, students can't return to the old patterns if they try.

Humankind sits at the edge of the precipice looking toward the Horizon of Metamorphosis. There is no choice but to change. Stagnation is no longer an option. The luxury of "being stuck" is over.

The intergalactic family awaits the earthly plane—celebrating its great metamorphosis. This transformation elevates the entire Universal Body to a more exalted level.

Trust change. Embrace the opportunity to be born anew. The ego need not strive to control or repress change. The soul beholds its destiny and gladly reorganizes itself moment to moment, allowing the great loving Wave of Alchemy to birth the great Changeover that thins the veils between the worlds, offering portholes into the new Dimension in Consciousness. The world as humankind has known it has already metamorphosed. Open the eyes to see what is emerging. Fill with gratitude for the inevitability of transformation. Through Source's magnificent liquefied Love, all beings are transported through the Initiation of Change into the realization that All is possible as illusions dissolve into Truth.

✧ Disorientation ✧

November 2005

Lately, many of us don't know which end is up. The energetic blizzard of heightened frequencies that is bombarding our planet makes it impossible to clearly decipher our unfolding pathway. We've lost our sense of direction. We reach for trusty life maps to get an exact read on our location so we can choose the best possible route forward. But they are obsolete. We are being propelled into uncharted territory with graphs that we're not yet able to decode. Our familiar grid work of electrical possibilities has been short-circuited by these accelerated vibrations. Unable to orient ourselves with our normal infallible life compass, we are flung far and wide, randomly adrift on a sea of CHANGE. How confusing!

Many of my clients report: "I'm not sure where I'm going." "I've lost my sense of purpose." "Sometimes I don't even know what day it is." "Why am I here anyway?"

We witnessed our brothers and sisters become displaced by hurricane Katrina's wrath. Their world was turned upside down. And so were we, as we empathically placed ourselves in their shoes and felt the cosmic shakedown—the roller-coaster ride of disorientation that comes when we can't even trust the ground under our feet. Big disasters remind us that we're not in charge. The impact of disbelief, shock and loss stimulates the awareness that deep down inside, we are shifting at a fundamental level so profound that we can't begin to grasp the magnitude of this process that is dislocating our usual consciousness. It is being displaced through the Divine Plan's insistence that we leave the familiar to evolve into the emerging paradigm. Like the refugees from the storm, we are wandering around shell-shocked, deeply confused and wondering what to do next, how to find our true home and how to hold together as a global family.

Aside from the external crises, internal hurricanes are slamming away at our Cornerstones of Certainty. We can't believe this level of destruction (inner breakdown) could possibly happen to us. We aren't prepared for its total undoing of our old way of being. We've attempted to prime ourselves for this profound time in human history—the entry into the New Age—when we are all being spiritually mandated to inaugurate a new era of enlightenment and unification. But we didn't bargain for the full-blown devastation of the old order as it gives way to the new archetype of human consciousness. Shaken to the core by inner and outer upheaval, we wonder how we got here. How are we going to hang on?

Our ego/ personality disassociates from this frenzied delirium, unable to integrate these cosmic blasts into any kind of traditional context. This sends us reeling into the Vortex of Disorientation where we succumb to vertigo, dizziness, spaceyness. We forget to breathe. All proven orientation points are vanishing. Our only option is to open up to the mystery that so lovingly awaits us.

Even if we manage to keep our outer lives quiet, ordered, calm, simplified, we're still subject to bouts of severe inner disorientation because we feel/ sense energies moving that are new to our consciousness. They are mobilizing with a velocity that puts Katrina to shame. The kundalini (primal life force dormant at the root chakra until it awakens and travels up the spine to activate enlightenment) is being dynamized in everyone, regardless of how much or how little they meditate. As these waves of energy sweep upward to the top of our heads, it feels like our "roofs" have blown off. Destabilized, disoriented, our slant on life is turned on its head like the Hangman card in the Tarot. We feel suspended upside down with no bearings in sight. How do we manage this?

We all agree that time-space is an illusion—a well-loved mirage that delineates our expectations of earthly life. The heightened vibrations provide the opportunity to experience ourselves holographically—as a point of consciousness beyond the time-space continuum. As our presumptions about space lose their validity, we feel as if reality is folding in on itself. This produces a strange uneasiness in our connection with the gravitational field. EVERYTHING seems to be shifting—or is it simply our view shed that is shifting?

As these energies open our portals of perception, we begin to comprehend our soul's earthly history. All previous lifetimes make their presence felt at a cellular level. This is profoundly disorienting to the ego, which designates itself as the conductor of our life, not simply another "face" in a long lineup of personnas that have served our soul. As our ego flails in its loss of centrality, we lose direction.

I experienced severe vertigo when I visited Athens in 1990 and had to sit down on the steps of the Acropolis as hundreds of tourists walked around me. Extreme disorientation flooded my cells as I recognized my Grecian lifetimes. The past-life dimension collided with my current life and sent me reeling. Internally we're all remembering our journey through incarnations. We don't have to travel to a specific physical location. Our souls are harmonizing all previous lives to align/ cleanse themselves for this monumental consciousness shift.

It boggles the mind to fathom that all lifetimes take place simultaneously—holographically. Our official, indisputable orientation tools of space and time are beginning to take their leave. As they lose their validity, our traditional conceptual framework of direction crumbles. This is incredibly exciting, as long as we ward off the impulse to go crazy from disorientation. We must trust that Greater Forces are unveiling the Universal road map as they set the magnets of the Cosmic Compass to a veracious dimension.

Being an organized, list-making, clock-watching person, I'm determined to ward off disorientation. I ground myself through daily practices of hiking, chi gung, and piano. But all the practices in the world can't prevent waves of nausea, disorientation, nebulousness because we're in an unavoidable inner process of change—regardless of our external clamps. As the level of our consciousness transmutes, our balance point shifts. We have a vague feeling that we're in transition. But without a discernible destination point, we fall into a wobbly, uneasy existential churning as our stomach turns in on itself. We are changing— FAST. The sensation is like that of being out to sea and then stepping on land; we feel as if we are still moving, even though the ground is stationary. This describes the interface between the soul's movement and our ego's need to stabilize reality.

How do we accept the wrenching away of our usual parameters/ boundaries and yield to the Bridge of Disorientation that conducts us to the new paradigm? All we can do is surrender to the Cosmic Compass and allow ourselves to be "drawn" in the right "direction" as we follow the clues in our innate response to the new magnetics. When I release resistance to the enveloping waves of disorientation, I actually enjoy the sensation of interdimensionality, where the past, present and future collide in a rapturous shattering of illusion. My usual moorings are uprooted.

I'm swept off my feet into a new vantage point on my soul's vaulted voyage. As our consciousness elevates, we find ourselves at previously unexperienced altitudes—High Ground—that invariably launch us into a swirling vertigo vortex of disorientation, which breaks apart stuck patterns by shattering the margins of reality. Let us be grateful for these disorienting episodes of unearthed bewilderment. They express profound cellular movement, the purification and release of all habitual cornerstones, and the flexibility to flow with the massive birth contractions of our emergence. They bring the promise of a new and truer direction.

The Tibetan holds a Cosmic Compass filled with Universal symbols and graphs. He teaches:

Humankind is adjusting to a new relationship with the gravitational field. This vibrational acclimation lubricates the interface between the old world order, and the passage through the void and out the other side into the New Cosmic Day. The ego resists the mandate to release its attachment to linear spatial reality in order to embrace the true holographic nature of one's divinity. This is the only pathway into one-pointed consciousness.

The earthly plane and human nature will be unrecognizable as the process of transmutation completes the birth of the New World Order. The change need not be associated with loss or gain. It is simply different. Let go and embrace the metamorphosis. The heightened frequencies are increasing daily. This is just the beginning of a transition that causes the usual mirrors of self-reflection to fall away and reveal the New Self.

Although transformation is disorienting to the ego, it is deeply orienting to the essential Self because the soul has been disoriented by the illusions of third-dimensional earthly life throughout all of its incarnations. Bask in this new but ancient feeling of the soul's original alignment and allow it to soothe the temporary process of energetic disorientation. This process initiates the onset of the new collective direction—the new human truth. It is so profoundly orienting to the soul that all energetic systems fire up at once in ecstatic response to this deepest reunion with the Universal Directive that unveils the ultimate highway HOME!

✧ Coping With Chaos ✧

August 2004

Don't you just hate it when everything falls apart—when "the best-laid plans of mice and men" go awry? Precisely when you think you have it all together, life unravels.

Fragmentation is the necessary anarchy that liberates us from outgrown reality blueprints. But the process heralds the onset of a much-dreaded chaos that seems to destroy everything we've built up and relied upon.

The nature of transformation is extremely chaotic, yet in our most chaotic moments, a larger order is laying seeds and beginning to root itself. How do we simultaneously attune to that higher order while being thrashed about by the chaos? Perhaps it is a question of faith. Chaos allows the Divine Order to "sneak in" and establish itself when we aren't looking.

I've always been intimidated and unnerved by chaos. God forbid my world should collapse. The pressure to bring new growth into my life wicks the adhesive out of the glue that holds my reality intact, compelling me to confront my fears of physical, mental, emotional and/or spiritual disintegration. So I try to hold on to order—my routine—while, at the same time, invoking change.

Impossible? No! We all face radical chaos as we shift into the new consciousness of the emerging paradigm. To embrace full metamorphosis, we have to accept internal and external chaos. How can we cope with it? By finding, or creating, some new sense of order through which we can orient ourselves to the current process of collective spiritual awakening: a reference point, a buoy, that tethers the old world order to the new, helping us surrender to the chaotic primal energy of transformation.

What false beliefs do we project onto chaos? For me, it's the fear that it will lead to helplessness, impotence, loss, dysfunction and frustration. Many of us dread having the "rug pulled out from under us." Hungry for permanence, we despair when chaos rears its ugly head. If only we could keep life stuffed into neat boxes to reinforce our existential grip. We create reality clamps designed to buffer us from the ever-looming chaos monster. I could spend hours making lists and double-checking them, putting my possessions in their "proper" places, planning ahead to the minutest detail—making my feeble efforts to forestall chaos. We often believe that we can't be creative unless our house in order...or, perhaps, we simply fear the inherent chaos of the creative process and want to batten down the hatches before that part of ourselves is unleashed.

It's futile to fight chaos. It will not be squelched or repressed. The body, mind and soul stiffen when we rigidly clutch our pre-described order. If we are to transform, we must accept chaos. Chaos initiates birth. In addition it is the precursor to the blackening stage in alchemy, when the old leaden form begins to decompose and transition into full metamorphosis—gold. The more invested we are in our personal game plan; the more life sends us curve balls that sideswipe our projected reality programs. We can't control the times when "everything goes wrong." But we can work on our reactions.

How are we to weather the chaotic bombardment of the massive paradigm shift that's on the horizon? The Tibetan encourages us to celebrate the chaos, but it's hard not to get cranky when our "schedules" slip through our fingers. And, although challenged by external chaos, it's my inner chaos that has the power to annihilate my mind, clarity, certainty and self-identity.

This motivates me to work double-time to order my outer world, repeatedly checking my appointment book, so to speak, to ameliorate the inner derangement. When I walk around the house, placing things neatly in precisely designated spots, the tumultuous disarray of my inner world mocks my efforts. Do I really need all my socks lined up in rows to be able to function? How much order does anyone need?

The chaos monster, perched on the edge of our reality, just waits for the right moment: When we're really feeling on top of our game—BANG—anarchy erupts and nothing is predictable, manageable, reasonable or moldable. It's the frustration of spending hours on an important project, only to have the computer crash and devour our work before we even had time to print it out. Was that moment of chaos really necessary?

Sometimes we "hire" people to be chaos ambassadors They keep us waiting on the street far beyond our agreed upon time; they lose the keys to our car when we are running late to catch a plane; they forget to give us important phone messages; they stash our unpaid bills under a pile of paper…We're drawn to them, although there's often something about the relationship that sets us on edge or flashes a warning. We may ignore the signals, but these connections can decimate our life formulas within moments.

Are we willing to relinquish the grasp on our carefully fabricated order to be able to absorb the fertile promise within the chaos? The lessons of duality dictate that if we cling too tightly to our orderliness, we will inevitably be clobbered by chaos to balance that rigidity. Wouldn't it be great if we could dose ourselves with just enough mayhem to keep the gods happy without needing to be fully dismantled by tidal waves of chaos because our life has been too tightly wrapped!

Fearful of venturing forth into the mystery, we assume that the untrodden path would plunge us into such pandemonium that we would be completely lost. The determination to outwit the forces of chaos feeds our compulsively neurotic agendas. Our response to destructive chaos is, "This is not the way life is supposed to be." But preconceived human agendas are pathetically flimsy matched against the genius of Chaos. Ironically, chaos is the road to a higher order—the ultimate liberation from our fear-based systems. Eventually we surrender to chaos and accept that we don't know "the ways it's supposed to be." Then we don't have to lament the loss of certainty and watch our faith eroded by judgments of chaos.

Even though we think we are flexible/ adaptable, most of us have a place inside that is our designated Cornerstone of Order, and so we often take chaos personally, assuming that the Universe is punishing us for God knows what. But chaos is the dynamic wave that shatters any stringent, obstinate prison of meticulousness that suffocates the soul's need to ride the Wave of Disorder as it jumbles our reality, unhinges the mind and provides just enough brouhaha to open fissures into greater possibilities. When that ultimate attachment to order is overturned, we have a choice: to go stark-raving mad, or acquiesce to the quiet faith that Source's genius orchestrates all chaos…that, indeed, chaos is Love.

Through my mental clutter I sense the stable presence of the Tibetan—serenely durable and unswayed by the cycles of disintegration and integration in the conflicting cross-currents of my thoughts. He teaches:

Embrace chaos! When feeling unstable, it's best to destabilize! To trust chaos is to trust the Divine Plan. Chaos is the ambassador to a Higher Order. Evolution requires that chaos disorient and untether self's consciousness from the status quo to create room for movement. Surprise is a key element in chaos because it truly ushers in the NEW!

Chaos is the interface between dimensions. In daily life, students are experiencing increasing levels of chaos that foster feelings of ineffectiveness, exasperation, helplessness. Such feelings stem from a bedrock of disorientation. The chaotic shattering inherent in these times of collective awakening is like the Hoover Dam suddenly breaking apart and releasing an onslaught of "soul waters"—karmic discharge from unresolved past lives. The discharge floods the psyche with converging karmic issues that often make no sense to the contemporary ego's well-defined boundaries/identity. When students protest that they feel incapable of handling life, they must learn to place self's consciousness in the middle of the maelstrom of chaos—like the hub of a merry-go-round as it spins off all soul attachments to previous templates.

The issuance of the magnetic vortex that generates humankind's collective movement into the Aquarian Age carries a potent electrical vibration that expands exponentially in concentric circles, as when a pebble is dropped in a still pond. The energy feels like an electrical shock, however subliminal, and is registered by the psyche as jolts of chaos. The jolts are literally pummeling and extinguishing the old paradigm, level by level, to allow amplified spiritual energies from the higher planes to merge with earth's denser vibrational field.

Expect chaos! Help each other embrace disorientation with positive anticipation of a New World Order far superior to the obsolete systems that have governed human nature. Please don't interpret chaos' "mess" as a setback, but rather as a sign of advancement. Allow deep grief for the loss of the old paradigm and all that it has meant to the soul. Although the ego resists when its "house of cards" is blown away, the soul rejoices in the enhanced contact that the disruption provides. Ironically, vitalizing moments of sheer chaos that liberate students from the "dead body" of outmoded prototypes produces a heady intoxication.

DO NOT BE AFRAID OF CHANGE! Chaos teaches that control is nothing but illusion, and awareness of this brings great relief to the soul. There is no earthly precedent for the emerging paradigm—no recognizable historical overlay. Timeworn navigational tools for unfolding consciousness no longer apply. The New World Order initiates new avenues and provides new compasses for the soul's earthly journey. So do not succumb to the madness, depression, and fear that intensified chaos provokes. Rather, focus on self's spiritual destiny.

Chaos is an overflowing, fast-moving spring river that carries dead debris from the winter cycle—a scouring of the soul to make it fresh for the dawning paradigm. The debris— ancient defense structures—may tempt the students to re-affix their reality to imprisoning notions of order. Do not give power or truth to these defenses as they rush up through chaotic intervention. Simply observe the ego's attempts to reclaim them, and reassure self that Source's Higher Order is truly a cosmic infrastructure that supports Universal Balance-Coherence.

Then life "clicks" into place and humankind watches the River of Chaos flow into a clarified sparkling Ocean of Totality, where all loose ends knit together to smile back in gratitude for the audaciously turbulent journey of chaos that makes this exalted trail-blazing metamorphosis possible.

✧ Spiritual Growing Pains ✧

November 2002

Many people believe pursuing spirituality requires giving up family, lovers, work, and play. They fear that the cost of practicing the spiritual principle of non-attachment is alienation and loneliness. When inundated by people trying to convert us to their spiritual-religious beliefs we often think, "I hope I never do that to anyone. See what happens when you get into spirituality—you become a fanatic." Others struggle with thoughts like, "How will I function if I open to a spiritual life? I won't be able to think straight, be a good business person or handle my responsibilities."

We seek spirituality because our soul is pushing up inside of us, begging for attention—insistent that the time has come to look to Source (God/ Goddess). From that moment on, it may feel as if our lives aren't our own but rather belong to something larger. The impulse to focus on our spiritual growth is usually connected to a deep desire for transformation—liberation. But we fear who we might become through this transformation. Do we have to let go of everyone who might not fit into our pathway of liberation? How can we stay on the same page with the people who share our lives while going through a spiritual process that inherently breaks down all structures and false beliefs that block our awakening? To practice non-attachment feels like an impossible assignment in the face of our human needs for relatedness, support and contact.

We can't force our loved ones to take the step with us. That would only backfire. Yet spiritual practices open our awareness, kick up karmic issues, stimulate our wisdom and broaden our perspective—all of which CHANGE the way we have always been. The moment we decide to commit to spiritual growth, evolutionary pressure is invariably placed on all those we are connected with to grow alongside us. If they don't, we either have to bridge the ever-widening gap through compassion, acceptance and patience, or let go.

Adding to the heat, often our friends and family are resistant to our evolution, fearful of losing us to our spiritual path. Perhaps unconsciously trying to reel us back into our "normal" way of being, they pour out subtle, or not so subtle, judgmental critical comments about our new spirituality. Spiritual growth magnetizes ancient karmic wounds, bringing them up to the surface for healing. When this material surfaces, it appears that we are doing worse than we were before we started "getting spiritual." It is a choice moment for skeptical loved ones to encourage us to stop this foolish nonsense—it's only causing us pain anyway; how good could it possibly be—which feeds our internal doubts about "doing this spiritual thing."

Common ground with loved ones begins to slip out from under us as we forge our way into the adventure of developing spiritually. Like a ship setting sail out onto the open sea, we look back at what we have left on the dock and wonder where this journey will take us. If all our loved ones are standing on the dock beckoning us to turn back, it takes considerable courage, willpower and determination to move forward, especially when we are traveling into a sea of uncertainty...mystery. In that moment, we may question our sanity. False beliefs try to seduce us into aborting the entire process: "There is too much at stake." "It's not worth it." "Your loved ones really care, why would they lead you astray?" "Let go of this spirituality stuff and appreciate what you already have." Will our burgeoning spirituality cost us our most cherished relationships?

Getting spiritual often involves energetic refinement through practices like prayer, meditation, yoga, chi-gung service to others. As our energy purifies, our personality changes. Loved ones protest that they no longer recognize us and can't relate to who we are becoming. Our heightened vibratory rate changes the previous harmonious resonance binding our relationships into one that temporarily feels discordant. Is there enough glue to hold relationships together within these shifting frequencies?

Our perceptions start to expand, dissolving old judgments, invoking wisdom. If we can't join our loved ones in the usual negative banter about life, it may seem as if we are elevating ourselves right out of our support system and emotional security. While many people attend church or temple weekly, few truly live a daily spiritual life. Spiritual growth is an ongoing process, inextricable from our employment, family, lovers, and friends. When we begin to model spirituality to our tribe, will they exile us or embrace our efforts? Bucking the system is something few of us wish to take on, especially if we have spent much of our lives trying to be secure within the tribe.

Once we spiritually catch on fire, there is a burning desire to share and celebrate our new discoveries, which often leads to rejection. People may not be interested, or they simply don't want to hear it. Perhaps we have gone a little overboard with our spiritual gusto and inadvertently driven them away. Or maybe they simply aren't ready to entertain this greater dimension of being. When rejected, our personal stamina for spiritual questing can be undermined. Is it a crossroads between choosing God, leading to loneliness, or choosing human relationships while silently starving for the spiritual dimension?

How can we share our new discoveries so that others can hear? The Tibetan teaches that our awakening process is going to occur in groups. Relatedness and shared communion propel us forward into heightened consciousness. This group format counters the old false beliefs that the spiritual mystic is fated to be a loner, unable to integrate into the community.

Teaching or preaching may create the opposite of its desired effect—a throwback to old ideas. Modeling is a neutral approach. We can practice non-attachment and accept our loved ones' lack of acceptance or disinterest while we embody the glorious changes and enhancements that spiritual life provides. The trick of walking the razor's edge is to not let others' negativity snuff out our fire by remembering earlier times when we believed spiritual life to be stuffy, puritanical, demanding, austere, and inconvenient. If we woke up to the hunger for more, so will everyone. Spiritual rewards of enhanced clarity enable us to sense when others are hungry to hear our message. They absorb our energy with joy and excitement. When force-feeding our discoveries to those still deeply asleep and needing to stay that way for a while, our words bounce off the walls of their resistance and return to us with a thud.

Growing pains also include the ego's reaction to this process. As our consciousness opens, initial spiritual intoxication makes our ego drunk on grandiosity. It may latch on for final control by deciding that this heightened awareness is *its* domain—resulting in superiority, inflation, judgments of others not on the path—which fuels alienation. We may try to hide these changes, "staying in the closet," so others won't be threatened. Ultimately we are found out. Our light factor can't be dimmed or contained by any closet. Yes, it seems to be a perilous journey as we undertake spiritual growth, but it's well worth the commitment, knowing that others farther down the evolutionary road have paved the way for us as we pioneer the spiritual trail for those ripe to flow into our slipstream of awakening.

The Tibetan strides forward to meet me, teasingly stepping over the rubble of these illusions—false beliefs that indicate it is perilous to embark on a spiritual pathway. He says:

Everyone is on the path. All of life is spiritual. Assume that the path is filled with grace and ease. Open-hearted spirituality magnetizes others, infusing them with trust in the process. Embody the joy, insights, wisdom, love and acceptance that spirituality bestows. Others will notice with curiosity, anticipation and excitement as their cells quicken in response to the mirror of their own destiny.

Self has agreed to catalyze the awakening of specified others karmically designated before this incarnation. Don't assume that they are only the ones self is close to. Be open to the serendipity that brings just the right people in contact for self to fulfill this agreement. Practice patience with those closest to self, trusting that they will inevitably prioritize their spiritual life when they are ready.

The tender process of spiritual emergence, aligning the relationship between the Higher Self and ego, requires sensitivity. The ego, sensing a higher frequency infusing self's being, reacts with an increased need for control. The student lovingly accepts the ego's reaction while continuing on the pathway.

Students may initially need to hold silence regarding their process to protect this delicate new commitment to the Higher Self. The ego needs little opposition from others to trigger its constricting impulse, which retards the initial opening. Connect with other spiritual students. Dispel the myth that spiritually has to be suffered in isolation. Support from like-minded groups nourishes the new student's trust and commitment. When firmly anchored on the pathway, the student, stable enough to share openly with all eager to hear about this wondrous adventure of awakening, cannot be knocked out of balance by those whose eyes and ears remain tightly shut.

To proselytize about self's spiritual pathway reflects the illusion that others need to be knocked on the head or captured in order to commit to their divinity, and that self is the one who knows what is best for them. The enhanced awareness resulting from spiritual growth enables the new student to begin to perceive blockages in others. This doesn't mean self is designated to break through these obstructions. The mystery within the Divine Plan is full of surprises. People open up in unusual ways through unexpected circumstances. Contain the hubris of the ego's reaction to the initial spiritual gifts flowing in. Don't assume that self knows the truth for others. Be alert to the ego's impulse to judge others who do not seem to be "on the path." All are on the path, whether they know it or not.

Others will ask self for spiritual guidance, inspiration and support as self grows beyond the ego's initial reaction. When others are awakened by a voracious hunger for Source, self becomes a reservoir of divine nourishment. The accelerated energies are quickening this process for the collective. Self will not be alone in the quest for communal spiritual relatedness. Soon, spiritual support systems will be proliferating.

Stay connected in the heart with those loved ones who have yet to consciously initiate their spiritual advancement. Hold them with compassion, internally reminding them that spiritual life is ultimately all there is and ever has been. Like blowing on a cocoon to prematurely witness the emergence of the butterfly, to push them would abort the delicate unfoldment of their destiny, so sensitively timed within the Divine Plan. Remind self that all are already enlightened, thereby releasing fear that self will evolve beyond loved ones and be forced to abandon them due to their lack of consciousness.

Bring the expanded self home to family, friends, community as a radiant example of what is probable for all. Self's spiritual growth inevitably opens the heart chakra, strengthening the adhesive that unites self with loved ones. Karmically, self agreed to go first, pioneering spiritual life in a way that is digestible to loved ones' energetic fields not acclimated to this "foreign" food. Allow them to take little bites as inquisitiveness gets the better of them, trusting their "digestive tracts" to purify and expand its capacity for MORE. Enjoy the exquisite timing of this ordinary miracle of awakening. Trust that the more self lets go of the need to "get through" to others, the more others will circle around self in deep appreciation of self's growing metaphysical being.

All are unfolding to become teachers within this mystery of collective awakening. Bring the unconditional love and patience of the great sage that is Self with arms stretched out wide to embrace the young in evolution as self is transported by the magnetic gifts of those already initiated into the wonders of spiritual life. Rejoice in this moment of amplified possibility with deep gratitude toward all who have patiently held self's awakening in the golden chrysalis of Self's enlightened being. From this place of true humility, spiritual growing pains dissolve, liberating self to view the big picture of collective fellowship, where Source's fire sparks the Light of Love, and sweeps all into the Ocean of Cosmic Consciousness.

✧ Are You Overwhelmed? ✧

August 2005

Do you feel buried alive by life? Is it all too much? Many of us feel like we're coming apart at the seams as today's heightened vibrations are bombarding the planet and kicking up deeper and deeper levels of karmic debris to be cleared. We're in a blizzard of new frequencies impacting us internally and externally—blasting us from all directions at once. This is all too much to handle. There's not a moment to surface for air. We're deluged with energies from within the soul demanding the healing of wounds/delusions from all previous lifetimes. We're swamped with external changes as we attempt to accommodate the emerging paradigm that forces us to reconsider life direction, relationships, health issues, creative venues, our soul's service—everything. We're dumbfounded as to where to even begin with all of this. Negativity abounds on the planet as we struggle not to be paralyzed in a state of demoralization. Political, environmental, medical, educational arenas all demand transmutation. There's so much to fix in ourselves and with each other.

As soon as we revolutionize, integrate and advance one aspect of our lives, ten more pop up for attention. These energies compound upon themselves exponentially until we're ready to implode and/or explode. Engulfed in today's endless requirements for personal and collective transformation, this flood of energy propels us downstream into the Vortex of Overwhelm. There we're sucked into reactions of impossibility and disorientation as the crosscurrents of enormous change wallop our ability to respond and render us down to a misfiring ball of static electricity. There are no medications for overwhelm. Most of us, in the attempt to function as "normal," are walking around in a daze—shell-shocked by life on planet earth in 2005.

Children protest when teachers give too much homework. As a human race we are swamped with soul work- everywhere. With no earthly "principal's office" where we can lodge a complaint, we keep trying to accommodate these increasing demands. Life is raining down upon us as we run from one "assignment" to another, desperately trying to keep up with the multidimensional impact of this paradigm shift. Heightened communication through the Internet bombards us with global information while we struggle to synthesize millions of different points of view and become One Human Heart. As our increasing sensitivity to the needs of others floods our awareness, we feel pulled in new directions. The thundering Call of our Soul becomes ear-piercing. With our perception of time speeding up, there is no down time to synthesize or come to terms with our lives. There is simply too much of everything. The nonnegotiable immediacy of our soul's requirements and destiny is pressing in. Intuitively we sense that there's more to come. This is just the beginning of a massive cosmic *tsunami* wave gaining momentum. Our feeble little egos can't run fast enough to stay in charge of these energies. There is so much NEW emerging in the collective consciousness while simultaneously old, frozen wounds are melting and surfacing to be healed. How much can we handle as a human race?

Life in this cosmic pressure cooker, intensely compressed, drives our stress levels over the top. There's no control. We're losing our sense of priorities as they rearrange to accommodate a new set of emerging spiritual values. Shock and pain overwhelm our emotional body as unresolved soul traumas, carried for thousands of years, surface for integration. False beliefs are being smashed, leaving us uncertain as to what to believe. We're so stimulated by the volume and depth of inner material surfacing in conjunction with the heightened "insanity" on the planet that we're fried. The ego, mind, emotional body, even physical body short-circuits when the voltage of change overwhelms our "normal" range of assimilation/integration. Must we raise our white flag in surrender to the Universe and plead for mercy and the cessation of this cosmic burst? Surely we can't be expected to manage this Niagara of soul homework.

My initial response to overwhelm is very *yang*. I run through life putting out brush fires like a madwoman desperate to keep up with this accelerated process. (Too much *yang* takes quite a toll on our adrenal glands as stress levels skyrocket.) Then I collapse into a pile of exhaustion and cry over the impossibility of coping. I hide under the covers and pretend that life isn't happening. Slack-spined, forceless and unfit, I hope that if I ignore my life's assignments, they will simply go away. All sense of possibility evaporates. Overwhelm has dropped me to my knees.

We become victims of overwhelm by giving our power to this energy blizzard and allowing it to incapacitate us after we've fruitlessly struggled to integrate this onslaught. Like a lone doctor on a battlefield of thousands, we struggle with knowing when to give up. When we finally cave in we conclude: "I can't do anything." "I'm helpless." "I'm going to lose my mind." "I'm not capable of handling life." "I can't deal with all these intense emotions and mental confusions." "The world is too much." "I'm going crazy." "I'm ineffective." "I can't cope." This "defeat" drives us into frozen passivity—too much *yin*—as we search for justification to give up, hoping that the karmic board will waive this lifetime's assignment of full cooperation and involvement with this personal and collective metamorphosis.

How can we maintain balance and presence during these concentrated times? Attitude is everything. When we accept that overwhelm is a natural reaction to enormous CHANGE, perhaps we can see the gift in this gushing overflow of life. Gigantic evolutionary forces are at play on our planet, and in our collective soul. We can use overwhelm to help us shed familiar priorities, understandings, controls and defenses. Then we're carried through the Gateway of Disorientation which appropriately scrambles our consciousness right out of the old paradigm into the New World Order. Overwhelm cues us to regroup in our psyches with the positive expectation of a long-awaited evolutionary leap.

It helps to ground ourselves in simple, basic ways. A good long walk, listening to beautiful music on a rocking chair, looking out the window and watching the sky, meditating, practicing chi gong, smiling at ourselves in the mirror, singing a song and luxuriating in a long shower all create Rituals of Essence that touch our changeless Selves. This provides respite from this overpowering process, calms and anchors us- quieting the waters of this tumultuous flood.

Overwhelm challenges us to review all self-expectations. If we can't keep up with life, it doesn't help to criticize or judge ourselves. We don't have to collapse into helplessness. We aren't hopeless failures. We're just shooting the rapids, at breakneck speed, of a mighty, invincible, relentless cosmic current—without paddles or life jackets! If we can remember this, we might even enjoy this hair-raising ride!

The Tibetan teasingly reminds me that the Masters and the Angelic Force are in the boat with us, navigating these tremendous tides. He teaches:

Humankind is opening to a consciousness of its holographic nature and beginning to experience itself as multidimensional, multifaceted beings emanating from a one-pointed unification. The collective consciousness, newly awakening to its holographic essence, experiences this unfamiliar awareness as points of energy emanating likes planes of perception extending in all directions at once. This consciousness shift opens humankind to the emerging new paradigm that lies beyond the time/space continuum. When this new awareness interfaces with the traditional third dimensional linear reality, humankind's innate understanding of life on planet earth is challenged at a fundamental level.

To make the consciousness shift from linear to holographic reality feels like being bombarded by an exotic blizzard of experience, internal and external, that cannot be assimilated in the usual manner. This is overwhelming, not only to the personality/ego, but also to the soul's historic orientation to earthly life. All third dimensional circuitry, currently under transmutational pressure, must be restructured to embody the true Divine Matrix at the heart of human potential. Therefore, predictable thought patterns are being scrambled to short-circuit established pathways of perception. This opens the door to the following: a torrent of new information, immediate access to the eternal self (including the history of the soul prior to its earthly incarnations), the experience of the urgent need to be awake to this momentous collective shift, the challenge to undo ALL previous understandings of humankind's place in the greater Universe and be happily shocked by the NEW.

Accept overwhelm as a blessed sign that self is letting go of the known. Rigid, predictable internal/ external structures of earthly life soften under overwhelm's gush of chaos. Without overwhelm humankind would still be convinced that it knows what's going on based on its historic existential context. The old paradigm, swiftly disintegrating moment to moment, is no longer a compass for the soul's earthly journey. Overwhelm delivers humankind to the Gateway of the Fresh and Unfamiliar. <u>Overwhelm is the inversion of awe.</u> *Overwhelm startles, unnerves and astounds humankind into the Realm of Reverence—where awe opens the crown chakra and the bliss of Source's gift of transformation fills the soul with the cosmic champagne of astonishing wonderment!*

✧ Leap of Faith ✧

March 2004

The Masters declare: "Now is the time to make the big plunge into the New Age." This raises the question of our ability and willingness to make a leap of faith. Our evolution has always required the need to make a significant leap of faith, at least once in our short lives, from an old existence to a new not-yet-proven reality. This might mean leaving a stagnant job, a dead marriage, an unfulfilling home life, outmoded ways of thinking and feeling. To open our hearts to someone new, to believe that our dreams could come true and/or to make a spiritual shift in consciousness as we discard false beliefs all require leaps of faith. While we talk a lot about leaping, we often freeze at the edge of the abyss, momentarily blocking the trust required to fuel our jump, convincing ourselves that we don't really need to leap—at least not now, anyway.

Collectively perched on the edge of the old world, we are all getting the divine kick in the butt to leap—NOW. Yet few of us joyfully approach this Abyss of Not-Knowing that must be crossed before arriving in the new world. Terror seeps into our bones— 3:00 a.m. anxiety attacks—reminding us that indeed we are on the EDGE and not ready or equipped to make such a foolish jump. Quivering, we wonder how long we can postpone the leap.

What does it mean to leap from one paradigm to another? How much trust do we have to place in the mystery?

The physical body carries the unconscious. If the only way the Masters can reach us is through our unconscious, because we're too dense to hear their subtle messages, then our bodies receive the messages to leap. If we freeze, our bodies pay the price because thwarted energy designated for leaping turns in on itself. This feeds our fear, which makes us dig our heels in a little deeper.

What are the ramifications of never making a leap of faith in our lifetime? Yes, it is daunting to leap into the unproven, but it is far more dangerous NOT to make required leaps.

Lately I feel pressured to make *ongoing* leaps of faith. Typically rebellious, I go kicking and screaming across the abyss. When my soul demands that I stretch out into the new, my resistance prefers to sit tight and wait this one out. Stomach clenched, mind racing through rationalizations, I'd rather cry about how hard life is. However, there is no negotiating the karmic necessity to jump when my soul says jump.

Our souls are being pushed to leap when we receive relentless internal pressure to "go forward." This higher command propels us into the "dread zone." False beliefs threaten that all required leaps of faith will fail as we fall, crushed to death by the mystery and its infidelity to our well-being—once again, victims of the great cosmic joke! I tell myself that I need to grow or heal more before I can jump. However, leaps of faith are designed, by their very nature, to feel premature.

We all have aspects of self that have reached fruition. The point of harvest catalyzes the Call to move on. To attempt to extract something more from these saturated arenas is like planting food in depleted soil. Therefore, leaping is our most exciting—and ONLY—possibility. Even if we can't fathom what it means to leap from an old to a new paradigm, we can certainly pinpoint stagnant areas in our lives to which we cling. As fear shrinks one's life into a narrow, insulated cage, the idea of a leap of faith becomes inconceivable. The imagination needed to describe enhanced life possibilities atrophies, unable to lubricate the flow of creative energy that builds a dependable etheric bridge across the Chasm of the Unknown. The accelerated energies impacting the planet refuse us the luxury of waiting to jump. The Divine Plan mandates that, like cattle, we be herded by the masters and angels to the edge of the cliff and OVER…into God knows what!

It helps to practice making smaller leaps of faith, to get used to letting go. Ferret out the one area in life that feels the most stagnant. Then imagine releasing it, trusting that something more sublime awaits. Don't reference statistics here because they always indicate that the odds are against us—we should just sit tight. The faith that fuels the truest leap on the soul's behalf has to be blind.

It helps to envision a landing point on the other side of the chasm. Trust the third eye (intuition) that displays an inner picture or sense of the destination. Then issue the intention to land there. Employ a one-pointed focus. If the targeted landing site is vague, undifferentiated, we run the risk of losing the magnetization required to literally draw us to the other side. If our focus is ambiguous, fuzzy, we won't have the chi (life force) to rocket us across the mystery, invulnerable to the chasm's gravitational pull. Successful leaps of faith must be based on forward movement and growth, not running from karma. Of course, in spite of our best efforts to project a landing point, clearly honed vision must be coupled with an absolute surrender to the Mystery.

To creatively imagine the highest and best version of our destination aligns our soul to enhance success in this opportunity to evolve. We must trust our inner vision and the intuition that describes our soul's next step in order to put our ALL into the leap—like Olympic athletes who direct 100% of their energy to transport themselves beyond the normal limitations of consensus reality. The possibilities in the new paradigm are unknown and need not be limited by ordinary expectations. We can anticipate MORE; expect to be surprised and to surprise ourselves! This is the inherent joy and wonderment that rewards us for having the courage to take giant leaps. Nothing feeds self-respect more than pulling off a well-timed jump, ignited by deep faith, into a superior reality that mirrors our magnitude.

To keep pace with this cosmic push, we can help each other take evolutionary leaps. Like a game of leap-frog, as one of us jumps, others are compelled to follow suit. This tethers us together like a necklace of pearls. Our leap-frogging generates a line of energy that keeps magnetizing itself forward through the joy of letting go into a shared attunement to the Divine Plan.

There isn't anyone who perches at the edge, attempting to leap, who doesn't experience profound resistance. Resistance kicks up hidden pockets of doubt, issues of distrust, past-life memories of leaping and falling, collective false beliefs that insist we play it safe, be practical and never, ever take action based on faith. The content within the resistance tells the soul's story through time.

Before leaping, release all ambivalence that flushes up the Voice of Undoing. Ambivalence makes us grip the familiar while simultaneously trying to leap. Then, torn and split in half, our full being isn't behind our intention. If half of us remain attached to the other side, the leap is sabotaged. Sadly, this fuels the belief that leaps of faith aren't safe. Entrenched, we burrow deeper into our stagnancy. The yearning that compels us to jump must be soul-based, not ego based.

Leaps of faith can last a long time as our soul transforms consciousness. We may leave the familiar world only to realize that the chasm we assumed would be speedily transversed seems to stretch on forever. Probably Columbus felt that way. Midway in our leap is too far from the old shore and nowhere near the new land. This is truly a place of the VOID—neither here nor there. The Void is the Gatekeeper...the Matrix of Initiation...the Middle Point, where there is no duality. While rich in its potential, this realm is not always the most comfortable place to hang out. The shock of having left the old, with no new ground to count on, floods us with fear and disorientation. There are no hand-holds in the Void except the soul's determination to plant itself in the soils of a greater reality. Nausea and vertigo reflect this disorientation. Every pocket of mistrust festering in our soul bubbles up—unleashing the "hungry ghosts" who would devour our conviction, laughing as we drop to our demise.

I motivate myself to "jump" by flashing ahead to my deathbed in this lifetime and looking back at how I'd feel if I hadn't made the necessary leaps of faith. A pawn of fear and stagnation, I would have lived a flattened, wasted life suffering from failure of imagination—a profound disappointment to my soul. It helps to take stock of the leaps I have already taken as demonstrations that, although not without challenge, these leaps have carried me the "full distance."

We all become saturated with the known. To augment our aliveness, we must plunge into the Mystery. Faith is nourished through the conviction that all that lies ahead is a gift for our soul—Cosmic Kindness from our Creator. On the Edge, our greatest adventure awaits us. The price of admission: take a deep soul-filled breath and JUMP!

On the inner plane the Tibetan teasingly demonstrates mile-long leaps that indicate our future "course work." He teaches:

All students' pathways unfold through ever-increasing leaps of faith. Faith is a deep KNOWING in every fiber of one's being, registered at the cellular level, that there is a momentous Destiny that awaits all of humankind. This Divine Destination calls self forth when all of one's energy bodies—physical, emotional, mental, spiritual—are aligned and ready to take the next step. There is no turning back. Indeed, students leap INTO faith when they release the old before the new is fully recognizable. This courage is greatly rewarded. Faith is the KNOWING that self will land safely in the loving arms of the Cosmos.

If humankind never applied this Dynamic Law of Faith, leaping into new soul territory, then our shared universe would diminish in its magnitude. The borders of the old would constrict and crystallize the Collective Dream that amplifies the earth plane's potential. Vision and imagination would collapse. The third dimension would become two-dimensional. Suffocating, humankind's "ceiling" would lower. Access to the Guiding Heavenly Resources would be severed.

Students cannot grow if they don't learn to leap. Advancement requires the completion of the earthly course work assigned to the soul. Courses culminate through final exams that ascertain how deeply one believes in the learning gleaned from the course. If the student simply experiences the course material but doesn't demonstrate full confidence in its effect on their being, then they revert to who they were before the course started. Course work negated, they have to start all over again. To solidify and apply the newly acquired wisdom gained from the course requires the initiatory process of making a leap of faith into full alignment with their new wisdom.

Leaps of faith are a prelude to flying! When self learns to let go and ride the currents of the Winds of Fate, then there is an opportunity for one's trust and vision to be proven true. This "proving" profoundly strengthens one's experience of connection, safety, and purpose.

Leaps of faith are possible through a deep commitment to the meaning that one gives to their process. This meaning carries the Code of Direction—the Map of Destiny that connects the dots— that relentlessly draws self to the edge and beyond into the soul's frontier. Faith links the lower mind to the higher mind through an essential energy of certainty in the face of the unknown. Through repeated leaps of faith, students create elasticity—a bounce and a delight in the opportunity to jump into the new. Then they realize that the old worlds they have released are eternally tethered into the new. Usually, this is only understood in hindsight. The exercise is to leap as if the past would disappear forever. This increases the energetic charge that amps up the electrical body just before the leap.

There is a final moment when all of the old world must be released. Self is momentarily suspended beyond time, where the confluences of all past-life pathways culminate in the up-rushing recognition of the emerging dimension. To leap from one paradigm to another is to be fully open to all those moments when the Inexplicable makes its Presence felt through the urge for expansion and the Divine Desire to experience a truly different world.

Leap! Don't look down. Don't look back. Keep your channel open—chakras aligned and joyous. Place full trust in the mystery, self and Source. Be willing to unconditionally accept whatever awaits self. Do not strive to get to the other side. Rather, open to the recognition that the Leap has already occurred outside of time and space. The heart reacts to this awareness with an outpouring of Love that magnetizes the soul body into the fifth dimension. Then allow self to free-fall into a vast dimension in consciousness—creativity unleashed to greet the Unimaginable— and Rejoice!

✧ Got Purpose? ✧

April 2006

We all need purpose. My clients, feeling lost, seek the gifts of purpose: direction, guidance, focus, vision, possibility, destiny, karma and responsibility. Purpose is the rudder that steers the soul on its authentic path. It stimulates enthusiasm, faith, clarity, potential, and causes our values to evolve. It gives us a reason to get out of bed in the morning, orchestrates our day and bathes us in the sweet satisfaction that we exist for a very significant reason as we drift off to sleep at night.

This link to the soul's desire declares the basis for one's incarnation. Purpose is a vividly stimulating frequency that electrifies the heart and gut, as it reverberates throughout all the cells—quivering in anticipation of fulfillment. It is also mysterious—emerging from out of the blue and often disappearing as quickly.

Is purpose simply a composite of our fantasies, desires, dreams—a random lightning bolt that startles our imagination with a gush of goals? Or is it a separate wavelength uniquely encoded with the archetype of our soul's becoming that fills us with a deep yearning and determination?

We're now required to transform our sense of purpose to match the consciousness revolution currently unfolding. We're burning through illusions at breakneck speed, which pulls the rug out from under our usual citadels of purpose. As old frameworks of meaningful action and intention crumble, our reasons for living fall into an aimless heap devoid of the spark that ignites motivation and inspiration.

The new paradigm, still hovering indecipherably on the horizon, is not anchored in our waking consciousness. Because our lower minds and egos cannot yet connect with the original imagery that out-pictures of the New Cosmic Day, we're unable to respond fully to the magnetic pull inherent in our collective purpose. Many of us are floundering around in a haze, sensitive to this developing shift in consciousness but unable to integrate its intent into our life structure. We've left the outworn purpose that propelled humanity to its current consciousness, but we are bewildered as to how to cognitively hook into the command that's lurching us forward to complete this Shift of the Ages.

How do you react when your once-steady sense of purpose starts fluctuating, sputtering, and then evaporates? We count on visions of the larger picture to ignite our purpose and fuel initiative. But when the Divine Plan seems to be a distant mirage of false promises, indistinct mandates and mysterious curveballs, it seems that Source has retracted the cosmic injunctions required to propel us forward with conviction. This stimulates karmic wounds of abandonment/ betrayal.

Purposelessness fosters a type of insanity as coherence gives way to fragmentation and disconnection. It generates a sticky malaise that veils the Divine Directives—the sparkling diamonds issued to claim our attention and undying commitment—and squelches our fire. Purposelessness is the portal to the void. The void holds a greater purpose, disguised as a riddle, to taunt us forward in pursuit of direction—our soul's unavoidable karmic agenda.

Without purpose's high beams on the path, we assume that we're lost. But that haze of purposelessness is actually part of the transition from the old into the new. Often, our sense of purpose carries false beliefs from past lives—beliefs that limit our vision and convince us we are much less than we really are, obscuring our perception of the magnitude of our soul's intent. We constrict our purpose with narrow self-expectations. In addition, our purpose may be confined by the values instilled by family and society, which must be purged to clearly discern our absolute destiny.

Purpose feeds my fire and I love it! When falling into the vortex of purposelessness, a great existential vacuum sucks me up into despair and deposits me in a wasteland of self-doubt. I don't respond well to free-floating, and often feel like an idiot when I encounter the pulsating purposelessness of the void, oblivious to the awareness that I'm immersed in my own unformed potential. Yet, paradoxically, a deep hunger is always present—a craving that persists until this lifetime's precise intendment is revealed and fulfilled.

The Tibetan teases me that just *being* is sufficient purpose to guarantee my existence. Is that really enough? I always assume that purpose involves action, goals, serving and creating, which contribute to Source's Divine Purpose—evolution. The Tibetan reminds me that evolution cycles back to itself because everything becoming already is, and that dispels my judgment of inactive phases as "non-purposeful."

True purpose never abates its internal insistent nudging. Although it may be eclipsed by negativity and fear, at any moment we can ask our soul to portray this incarnation's intention. If we can suspend our ego's need to manipulate that description, a fresh energetic response, however abstract, immediately reveals this lifetime's ultimate animus—which may not match what we think we're supposed to be or do. Yet we must embrace it as our evolutionary razor's edge. The content of our purpose may change as life assignments evolve, but its essence just deepens into richer hues of the same calling we've always sensed. The clearest display of purpose is only perceptible on a completely blank canvas, free of all "shoulds."

If we try to create a sense of direction that is discordant with our true purpose, we can't sustain the fire that fuels it—like forcing ourselves to marry someone we don't love. It might seem to be the correct thing to do, but it lacks the pizzazz that keeps us interested.

We often follow an empty purpose because we resist the full demands of our soul. We seek safety in comfortable, familiar, controllable directives where there isn't too much at stake, and that fosters a sinking feeling in the belly as the soul responds, "You're missing the point...not keeping your promise." This creates a "near-life" experience in which we aren't fully hooked up to the locomotive that joyrides the soul into fulfillment. To go through the motions of clinging to a life purpose devoid of the sizzling pitch that keeps us on the edge of our seat prevents us from being genuine ambassadors of the soul. We must reach for the stars and dare to embody the Divine Purpose that thrusts us forward at light speed into our ultimate Destiny.

The Tibetan purposefully enters my consciousness and teaches:

Humankind's usual perception of purpose is shifting during the current transition into the new paradigm. As each person enters the void that previews the remarkable unmet potential of these times, ironclad conviction of one's direction disintegrates. As the soul interacts with the accelerated vibratory rate impacting the earthly plane, a new agenda emerges to influence one's personal sense of purpose.

Normally, purpose describes the individual soul's karmic conditions. Now, under the Divine mandate for humanity to awaken together, one's purpose is geared to the need for everyone to contribute to the collective awakening. One's personal docket is losing its charge in the light of this overall evolutionary thrust. The student is challenged to hold a sense of purpose that reflects their vision of the unfoldment of the Divine Plan for ALL of humanity. The question is no longer "What is my purpose?" but rather, "What is our purpose?" This orientation then floods self with awareness about the particular intention—gift—that the soul has chosen to offer during this great time of Birth.

Please eliminate all false beliefs that describe self's life as purposeless. It's impossible to exist without the Divine Directive. The cocoon stage of transformation includes an incubation period of formlessness, yet the evolutionary purpose of the caterpillar doesn't crumble when it is in the cocoon just because its previous structure has disintegrated. Purpose is the essence of the soul, sustaining itself through all levels of metamorphosis. It serves the students to focus attention on their eternal texture when trying to decipher the clues that illuminate purpose. Within that essence is encoded the soul's ultimate contribution to the intergalactic family.

Indeed, the supreme purpose of all beings is to learn LOVE. There are many secondary scenarios of purpose that tantalize the student to move forward, sometimes against all odds, like carrots held before a donkey. These enticements thematically accumulate over time to display self's unique cosmic thread in the great Rainbow Tapestry of Creation. Once the soul's Divine Specialty is fully manifest, the initial purpose of all incarnations is concluded and the soul's full glory is revealed. Self is then free to unleash into the potent, joy-filled purpose of heightened collaboration with the Divine Plan in the creative improvisation that ushers in the New World Order designed to flourish for millennia to come.

Do not question self's right to have an IMPORTANT PURPOSE. Do not allow illusions of unworthiness, failure, confusion and distrust to block self from carrying the torch of the soul's splendor. Ask to see self's purpose revealed from moment to moment. Embrace dormancy periods with the anticipation of the arrival of an even higher purpose. As all students realize the distinction of their individual purpose, they will stand up straight and tall, grateful for this Divine assignment to impact all of Creation at this very potent juncture. Allow this Magnitudinal

Purpose to be the basis for all decisions, actions and non-actions as self lives a life of fierce intendment that anchors a mighty vibration of Love into the rich fields of wonder known as the earth plane.

✧ Beyond Training Wheels:
Self Responsibility ✧

October 2004

Do you remember how it felt to face that great rite of passage when your parents removed the training wheels on your bicycle? Did you find just the right balance point and cruise off into the sunset on your own (despite hovering parental anxiety), or did you fall flat on your face as the pavement sucked up that moment of glory into a black hole of humiliation, insecurity, failure?

We are all facing this same threshold in our shared evolution. The latest word in New Age circles is that our spiritual protection is being removed. Needless to say, this current cosmic gossip kicks up no small amount of anxiety. Isn't it challenging enough to live in a world drenched in fear of terrorism, global warming, mosquito-carrying diseases, rampant cancers, war and prophecies of the "end times?" That we're losing higher protection is the last thing we want to hear. It's like driving a car with no brakes or steering wheel, and knowing its insurance has just been terminated. Are we plummeting toward a predestined date with disaster? Or do we need to consider this issue of "spiritual protection" in a new light?

I'm certainly not immune to the massive collective anxiety about the state of our world. I attempt to take refuge in prayer, deep inner reflection and nature's sweet voice to bolster up my trust in the Divine Plan. Especially if I've been exposed to countless horrors on the nightly news, my anxious soul hungrily searches for a soothing balm—some cosmic reassurance that, yes, everything is truly going to be okay (whatever that means). There is only so much our sad and frightened little egos can assimilate on this cosmic stage of dramatic change.

Anxiety about the possible loss of spiritual protection immediately drove me into meditation to exact an explanation from the Tibetan. He displayed a picture of a child's first attempt to ride a bike without training wheels to illustrate that this is truly a time of collective maturation. We must embody complete self-responsibility. We can no longer make a mess of things and expect our "divine parents" to clean up/ repair our damaged earthly "playpen." So we've been put on "cosmic notice" that from now on, what we do is up to us.

That means we have to find just the right balance to ride our existential bike in a rush of achievement, honor, autonomy. Otherwise we'll fall flat on our faces—poor little victims of spiritual negligence overwhelmed by the demands of self-responsibility.

With our world floundering in negativity, it's frightening to think that we might continue to forestall our full maturity in the expectation that the Higher Forces will intervene on our behalf. We have to at least meet them halfway and attempt to bring full awareness to all that we think, say and do. In our current state of numbness/ indifference, we assume that we can't watch for obstacles in the road, too. If the bike crashes or topples over, we hope that scraped knees will be our only consequence—but we doubt it.

Yet the process of removing training wheels brings us the potential for increased free will and collaboration with the Masters, Angelic Forces, and all the other spiritual guides/ teachers/ friends who have so generously lubricated our collective "childhood" in its experimentation with earthly life. In spite of feeling wobbly without the reassurance of training wheels, the rush of our own personal mastery seduces us forward—compelling us to ride on our own steam/ knowing/ instincts. Now we can proudly ride *alongside* our spiritual "parents" like the grown-ups we hope to be as we accept our creative responsibility in the unfoldment of our world. All reflections of immaturity—narcissistic agendas, ego-based concerns, victim mentality, cutthroat competition, unconsciousness and escapism—must be released as we enter this monumental process of unprecedented world evolution in consciousness.

As we are released from our customary cocooning spiritual protection, we open to the true security that springs from expanded awareness. This heightened consciousness deepens the alignment with our Higher Selves—the ultimate pipeline to all spiritual resources. Old enough to finally "leave home," we view the vast horizons of possibilities before us. Gifts of freedom, initiative, self-respect, exploration and self-knowledge beckon us into our emerging adulthood and a profoundly stimulating collaboration with the spiritual plane. No longer allowed to hide in false beliefs that say, "There is nothing we can do—we are hapless victims of our own shadows," we feel the fresh air of new possibility and powerful interaction with superior Forces. Our creative input will be taken seriously as we finally step on the Cosmic Panel alongside all the spiritual greats of our Universe. The spiritual plane will no longer spoon feed us, implore us to take notice of lessons, or slap our hand with a Zen stick when we are lazy about our advancement. We will only have to transmute the inevitable consequences of our childish indulgences.

As the training wheels are being removed, we may momentarily flood with internal voices of doom as we reference failed past efforts to "ride on our own." That old conditioning will try to convince us that we're not strong, savvy, aware, creative and wise enough to sustain the ultimate balance that keeps us from falling. We all need to look at our inclination to lean on the spiritual plane to alleviate our responsibility for the messes in our lives.

Divine intervention never meant that all we had to do was wait for some Higher Force to post bail on our crimes—especially the "sin" of carelessness which mocks Source's great Care of all of Its creation. The inertia of the immature attitude that justifies the acceptance of ourselves as helpless fools who can't function independently on the earthly plane has us in a stagnant mire—a holding pattern that condones mindless destruction, insensitivity, victim hood and obliviousness.

I remember how people in the '60s thoughtlessly littered the roads they traveled, assuming someone else would clean it up. Forty years later, it's a rare person who tosses garbage out their car window. Somehow we learned to take responsibility for that simple act. Now, if we can only extend that attitude throughout every facet of our lives, indeed the spiritual plane would be released from the drudgery of monitoring our every move. Then our world would be filled with self-responsible adults who take pride in their creation of heaven on earth.

The Tibetan rides a shimmering diamond-studded bicycle toward me with a big grin—happy to demonstrate the joy of freedom from training wheels. He teaches:

Now is the time to break free of the torment of waiting for Divine intervention. Presuming abandonment, many students angrily accuse the Masters, Angels and even Source of ignoring their pleas for help. Unified through cosmic adhesives of Love, it is impossible for us to forsake humankind. Rather, the spiritual plane is now giving students the opportunity to explore on their own—to discover what they are truly made of. This allows humankind to experience a self-proving so profound as to shatter all preconceived notions of failure, ineffectuality, inferiority, insignificance. It is only in this moment of self-proving that humankind can witness and therefore trust itself enough to make the giant shift in consciousness required to step into the Aquarian Age.

If humankind cannot believe in itself, then it cannot sustain faith in dimensions/ worlds beyond itself. Humankind stunts itself through under-extension due to self-doubt that undermines its range of influence in this galaxy. Consequently, this time requires students to meet the challenge of facing all fears in order to realize their innate resources of wisdom, brilliance, lovability, and creativity. Once these gifts/ resources are realized, they can be used to claim and apply one's spiritual heritage to earthly life. When students meet life with self-responsibility, the Universe <u>*matches*</u> *this energy with equal support. Self-responsibility frees up more Universal energy to propel humanity to evolve quickly and spectacularly toward greater horizons, rather than being used to maintain the simple safety net of the "playpen."*

Once children ride autonomously on their bicycles, the whole neighborhood is at their disposal. They can choose directions, destinations, and routes on their own without the limitations of parental control. So, too, is humanity liberated to explore its earthly mastery, expanded consciousness, deepening wisdom, connection with the Higher Self, as well as the greater intergalactic neighborhood. This leads earth to interdependence with all extraterrestrial and inter-dimensional beings.

Humankind will finally truly have a "say" in the metaphysical policy-making central to the Divine Plan rather than feeling like earthly life is "happening to them" (like children who are told what to do). The newly liberated potential for potent collaboration will stimulate a tremendous creative outpouring from humankind.

The process of self-discovery through self-proving requires the acceptance of one's karmic assignments in this lifetime rather than attempting to negotiate/ escape its demands or "turn it over" to the spiritual plane. It is like a fifth grader trying to get permission to watch TV while his parents do his schoolwork. Full conscious involvement, willingness, focus, discipline, initiative, maturity and self-responsibility are the "price of admission" to this exciting new paradigm.

The removal of stagnant forms of spiritual protection is the necessary next step for world evolution. It is a wake-up call to humanity to stand on its own two feet and touch the sky. It is a call to release all blame and become an individuated ADULT who demonstrates autonomy, self-trust and exquisite sensitivity to all beings.

Trust that this process is precisely timed. Humankind is ready. Accept this liberating mandate with glee, curiosity and an eager willingness to join the great Forces of Mutuality that compel all beings to evolve side-by-side into the Heart of their great Source.

✧ <u>Part Seven</u> ✧

THE NEW CONSCIOUSNESS

✧ Answering the Higher Call ✧

April 2003

Lately I've been feeling a distinctly potent Call from the higher planes. This Call carries a sense of urgency—ethereal, vague, and undecipherable. I wonder what I'm really tuning in to. Is this just a figment of my imagination? Or is something trying to get through to me, to us? The Tibetan urged me to write about the Call this month, interrupting our usual conversation with "Call waiting" from the Masters, trying to get our fully conscious attention.

How many of us feel a Call from the higher planes? Do we know how to respond to it? Is it discounted as simply mindless imagination? Are we embarrassed to admit that we may be electronically connected to higher frequencies that spark the synapses in our brain, hooked to some primal code established eons ago, to fire up just when the planet/ universe needs our attention? When we live according to a sense of calling, we can be more sensitive to the Great Call when it is issued. When we live with blinders on, mechanistically moving through our days, it is harder to hear/ receive larger messages from the universe. If we ever needed to pay attention, now is the time. With humanity seemingly out of control, everyone teetering on the edge, we need to be as tuned in as possible.

Many of my clients are feeling the pressure of these auspicious times. They intuit that something much larger is being asked of them. Eager to be of help, to ward off/ neutralize this awful feeling of collective impotence, we strain to decipher the Call that most of us can only vaguely register in the pit of the stomach, through a strange buzzing in the head or from a feeling of restless imminence.

Trying to decode this amorphous Call, I recognize the message: We must become very clear on our unique soul's purpose NOW. Opening to our sense of elevated purpose magnetizes the greater Self within to come out into this world, representing our soul's highest energetic capacity. The Call exclaims, "There is a great birth occurring." We must gather around, supporting each other, joining forces to act as anchors/

acupuncture needles/ magnets for the Higher Forces to assist this stupendous transition. If we can embody our magnitude, our soul's magnificence, the alchemical balance in this world will dramatically shift to the good.

Terrorists are often trained and then put on hold for years until the day they are given the orders to destroy. We, too, have been trained and put on hold for years—to heal, strengthen, gather wisdom, enjoy earthly life—until we are given the Call. Now is the time—not for destruction, but for CREATION. The Call impresses on me that we must leave the old paradigm, obsolete patterns filled with stagnant energy that left us dry, blank, dead. We must evolve beyond the dulling resignation of defeatedly accepting whatever life presents us. Collectively, we are being asked to set aside our smaller concerns, not repressing them but rather expanding, daring to include and embody our potentiated Self. We must challenge ourselves to open our minds to the Horizon of the Original—where all new inventions, breakthroughs and whirling dervishes of revolution, reside—to carry us into the new paradigm where our minds are joined as one.

Putting myself in the Tibetan's shoes, I would "call" people to claim their souls to stay awake, take the risks and do what they are really passionate about, to open their hearts to each other, to resist going numb, to challenge themselves to see their unique contribution to this current collective spiritual emergence, to be ready at all times to serve, to stop looking back at how things used to be, to speak their truth at all times, to teach others new levels of awareness, to face their shadow. But this is my sense of the Call. What is yours?

What does it mean to receive our "induction papers" from the Universe? If we receive these papers, do we consider going AWOL from the cosmic army? Do we wish to postpone our stint in "the service" and continue going numb, burrowing into complacency to wait out this horror show. I hate being told what to do. Being a rebellious Aquarius, I don't like take orders from anyone, including the Masters! But not even my obstinate spirit can withstand the roar of cosmic marching orders as they are delivered to me through this great CALL.

Where are these induction papers sending us? What are we being called to do? What *can* we do? In the war between the Light and dark forces, is the real front simply within as we battle ourselves, always at odds with who we truly are?

Many of us feel hopeless in the face of world events. We don't know whether to be politically active, to pray/meditate or simply to hope for the best. Overwhelmed by the current wave of chaotic destruction, my own powerlessness sets in when I view our world. I want to fall to my knees in despair and curse the karmic board for sending me to incarnate at a time in human history when so much seems to be going wrong.

The Tibetan urges us to recognize that we must mature, step out of the playpen, and take responsibility for every thought, feeling, and deed. Lazily we put it off—maybe next week, year or lifetime—when we are ready. There is no way to feel ready for this unprecedented collective process. Ready or not, the time has come. Selfish egos aside, we can no longer indulge insular narcissistic agendas. The Tibetan emphasizes that now is the time to "get spiritual." Aren't we already spiritual? I assume we must shift our focus and values to more urgent Universal demands. We must open our eyes, ears, and hearts to the CALL.

What does it mean to step up to the plate when we have no point of reference for this time in history? When we have so much power to self-destruct and yet, paradoxically, are more united in consciousness as a global village than ever before. For me, stepping up to the plate means that I can no longer hide my Light, dwell in fear, postpone karmic homework, be too tired, too lazy, or too numb, claim "I didn't know," or indulge in feeling lost/ unloved/ abandoned/ betrayed.

Struggling to respond to this persistent, internal, nudging Call, I wonder how to direct the pressure. Fearful of despair undermining my idealism, I hold back my passion and belief that collectively we can transform the world, and shamefully settle into mediocrity, collapsed by the inevitable "limitations" of the physical plane. It's so easy to get distracted from the Call. I'm too busy, exhausted, confused, downright frightened, and would much rather withdraw and wait it out. My ego cautions me about sounding delusional: "There is no Great Call, whatever you think you hear, keep it to yourself. Don't share these higher impressions/ knowings with anyone or they'll write you off as a flaky New-Ager, some Pollyanna with her feet in the clouds."

But at age 54, I'm old enough to know better. I have never felt more purposeful, driven and determined not to waste a minute, tenaciously holding my own feet to the coals—laboring to stay conscious and open my ears to the Call—the directives from on high instructing us how to successfully birth this "New Cosmic Day." If we can't freely share common impressions on what is REALLY going on here, how can we unite our force fields to transmute the dark grid of negativity devouring our world? The Call insists: Stop living at the level of ego. Stay awake and tuned in. Trust that humanity is not simply in a nightmare with a horrendous ending. Most importantly, we are being called to discover our unique gifts to this world/each other and to recognize how these gift are an integral part the emerging new consciousness being born as we walk this dangerous razor's edge together into unified consciousness.

The Tibetan strides forward, hard-wired to my questions as they magnetize his consciousness into mine. He summons:

CALLING all light workers, teachers, channels of love, students who dare to express their truth. The Masters ask humankind to sign a cosmic petition to end the old paradigm—to join as One. To view many names on a petition demonstrates that self is not alone. This communal awareness allows students to open their collective force field and recognize their birthright, authority, and contract to assist in ushering in the New Cosmic Day. This requires rigorous clearing, self-examination, braving the corridors of the shadow where stored on-going karmic afflictions are waiting to be touched, healed and integrated.

Dare to embody the Light at the most potent level imagined. Then multiply this Light times 10,000. At least do that much. There is no time to be off-duty. Know that self can transform much faster than ever imagined. Whatever breakthroughs self experiences need to be communicated, shared, expressed. With full consciousness of the darkened energies surfacing for final resolution, dare to be positive. Remember that all make it to the threshold of awakening, and that the earth herself is held within a Universe of Love. Then create a plan of action. Commit to it. Start eliminating all aspects of life that are meaningless, at odds with self's sense of purpose.

Don't underestimate the impact of just one student's full ensoulment, radiant in light, on the collective consciousness. Receive the joy of being propelled by an inner force that knows exactly what self signed up to do before this incarnation. Self's mission need not be unduly dramatic, sacrificial, overwhelming. It may be fulfilled through humble, subtle levels of contribution that are no less impactful. Ironically, it is the subtle energy that carries the Call. This subtle energy is streaming in to conduct the rarefied vibrations of the New Cosmic Day.

Students are Called to refine their ears, eyes, hearts to attune to the subtle nuances of higher, refined, etheric energies. When trying to decipher a newspaper written in a foreign language, self has the opportunity to feel the energy from the words, subtly picking up the message carried within the form. Trust self's intuition. Don't question it to death but rather embrace this knowing with the innocence of a child trusting that the play will emerge. This trust opens portholes of perception. Soon self recognizes the meaning of the newspaper's foreign words.

Release pride. Ask each other for help with this experiment. Don't allow the ego to convince you to hold on to outmoded models of learning. Humbly sit in the Mystery as it impresses the Call on your heart, igniting a soul agreement made well before this incarnation. Know that self has a uniquely important contribution to make and it must be made now! Don't worry about self's imperfections. Continue to improve character, thought, deed as self goes forth—the imperfect warrior of light daring to mix with all of the frailties, vulnerabilities and illusions of the human condition

Humankind's greatest illusions are the following: Self can't make a difference. Self isn't enough. Self isn't worthy. These are all constructs that feed darkened energies, closing in their deadly grip on the earthly plane. Don't underestimate self's impact. It is time to consider self's mastery. Pretend to be a Master. Go forth as if self's spiritual life were the most important event in the Universe. Yes, continue to have the feet on the ground, deeply rooted into mother earth, while daring to IMAGINE a new world. Then do whatever self feels CALLED to do.

Follow the pathway of least resistance, holding the channels of grace well-developed in previous lives that are now storehouses of the soul's gifts, so that those gifts can be offered at this time for a very precise reason. Practice generosity. Share self's gifts eagerly, unconditionally, knowing that they carry just the right ingredients for the collective soup that is cooking humankind into its full awakening. Commit to listening within, every morning, mid-day, evening. This weaves one's externalized consciousness into the sacred fabric of the soul, calling it forth.

As the Masters issue the Call, so too, do the students issue the Call urging their own souls to emerge—urging each other to transform—and urging the world to make its leap. Holding hands at the edge of the cliff, millions of souls take the leap together, demonstrating the trust, wonder, excitement of responding to the Call that moves all of humankind to a greater world in consciousness. This is a time of Renaissance of Spirit - where all illusions of negativity, destruction and suffering melt into the waters of Cosmic Love and are overtaken by this burning mandate for liberation. Hear the Call. Respond to the Call. Be the Call. All will KNOW. And all will be served.

✧ Triggers to Awakening ✧

December 2002

Sitting comfortably in our ego's "house," fully furnished under our control, and perhaps with a smug knowing, we imagine ourselves safe, impervious to life's pitfalls. We have it all figured out. We are on the top of our game. Pleased and self-satisfied, there is no need to pursue the larger picture. Then—WHAM—we lose a loved one, sudden unemployment leads to financial disaster, disease robs our health, our lover betrays us. Suddenly we are on our knees, groveling in the dark, desperate to find the light switch. Why is this happening to us? What did we do to deserve this? The ego tries to regain control but there is no going back. Our fortress of security has fallen and can never be rebuilt. At that moment we set foot on a higher pathway fueled by the anguish and angst of life's unanswerable questions.

When reality throws us a curve ball that cuts to the quick, we are triggered to open to greater possibilities never before imagined. To crash and burn is not our only option. Hitting bottom opens the possibility of touching the "top" of our awareness. We are forced to put our world view into a larger perspective because our ego can't handle the pain of integrating crisis or trauma within its narrow perspective. Harsh blows dealt by an austere reality are calls from the Higher Self to explore the spiritual meaning/knowledge that will fuel us through these crises as our ego falters within its limited paradigm of control and victimhood.

Overwhelming collective tragedies like 9/11 are obvious signals to refocus us into embracing our spirituality. However, on an individual level, most of us meander through our days, adjusting, perhaps numbing ourselves to the slings and arrows of life and missing the "wake-up call" nature of these difficulties. We assume that we have to tough it out, "this is the way life is," without realizing that "bad things" have a specific Divine purpose orchestrated with just the right timing to initiate (or deepen) our spiritual quest. To the extent that we miss these cues is the extent to which the "calls" get more potent—demanding recognition, usually through pain.

I have always rebelled against the notion that we need to experience pain in order to grow. Can't we just hear the celestial call to open up, like flower buds to the song of the warming spring sun without having to suffer? Is our ego's defense structure so dense that it requires the jackhammer of misery; affliction and mishap to break it open to the higher light? The Tibetan reassures me that eventually we will be able to grow spiritually through joy, when our egos have found their proper place within our cosmological view shed. In the meantime, we apparently need to be clobbered over the head to get the message that there is more to reality than meets the ego's eye!

Often it's a traumatic event that triggers our awakening. Sometimes, rather than an event, an amorphous existential ache surfaces, apparently from nowhere wicking the color right out of our reality, dumping us into a joyless wasteland. If we can learn to open to this pain, sitting in its mystery, we can accelerate our spiritual growth by leaps and bounds. Our society is chock full of pain suppressors—pharmaceuticals, anti-depressants, T.V.— geared to pushing our agony as far from our consciousness as possible. While this may offer temporary comfort, it obliterates the "call" our soul so desperately needs us to respond to. So we heap on the numbing agents of our resistance, increasing the dosage, to ward off the impact of the bad stuff that happens. We don't realize that this bad stuff is reorganizing our energetic field to open us to higher knowledge NOW. Ironically, we push off the rewards of heightened consciousness by denying or attempting to destroy our torment. If we absolutely knew for sure that difficult experiences (both external and internal) were signals to step onto a higher path, we might be inclined to embrace these challenges with gratitude and the eye of a detective looking for clues on this scavenger hunt to expanded consciousness.

These painful triggers to awakening are timed when we are ready to embrace a spiritual life. We may have fully developed a personal, ego-based existence. Having completed this assignment, the next one awaits—to align with our Higher Self. The pain required to catch our attention is not only for wake-up call purposes. It is also the tip of the iceberg that suddenly surfaces when we think the sailing is clear.

The "presenting" pain (the current expression of accumulated past-life pain) is just the beginning of a major clearing process of karmic wounds lying dormant until we are ready to "go the distance" into full soul-alignment. It isn't necessary to laboriously plow through layer after layer of karmic pain. Today's trauma/ difficulty carries the matrix, the core essence, of the soul's wounds. If we can embrace this pain, allowing it to have an alchemical impact on our approach to life, we have the opportunity to simultaneously clear hundreds of past-life clusters of trauma. When these bad things happen they seem larger than life because they are!

The ego assumes it's the sole occupant of Self. Unable to fathom that it is a mere piece of the larger puzzle, the ego is overwhelmed when trauma catalyzes an ancient soul-based pain with which it cannot identify. The ego is then faced with a choice—to either believe that self is a victim in a random universe or to surrender its dominion to an amplified life of spiritual growth that includes the full range of the soul experienced through countless lifetimes.

Hitting bottom shatters the ego structure, providing just the right breakdown required to liberate us from the blinders of the small self. Then we have the opportunity to behold and follow our pathway of spiritual growth. Ego-death symptoms of loss of control, disorientation and failure ultimately lead to the surrender required to start getting spiritual. This is a challenging junction because the ego, so inclined to resist the mystery, views these bad things as dead ends rather than as the process of initiation that they really are. If the ego clamps down on its domain, the breakdown process (the blackening stage of alchemy) is unnecessarily prolonged.

We may be able to resist and postpone our spiritual life, but ultimately we all pass through the gateway of spiritual initiation. The "breakdown tunnel" is only as long as is needed to alchemize the ego and defense structures—pummeling them down to a pulp to allow the Higher Self to finally breathe through at long last. Bad events blow open the door to a new direction with pain as the ambassador to a dimension way beyond our familiar personal reality. Our Higher Self knows exactly when it is time to issue these wake-up calls. Larger forces take over our lives, granting us a great opportunity to flower spiritually. This alchemical process softens, humbles, and elasticizes the ego to allow it to flow with greater attunement to impermanence, mystery, wisdom.

In spite of understanding these concepts, I, too, put up a valiant fight to resist the call of spiritual growth. Although I know this is ultimately what my soul wants, my ego tenaciously clings to its version of reality no matter what. It tries to control all the bad things that happen, as if it had ultimate dominion. It declares: "I don't need to grow more. I already know all that I need to know. I'm spiritual enough!"

Triggers to spiritual growth occur at all points along the pathway, not just to initiate our process but to deepen it. As soon as we get too cozy with our certainty, even our spiritual certainty, our ego clamps down in a statement of final authority. Then we have to be catapulted into the "no man's land" of despair, anguish, upheaval, chaos—whatever it takes to grow our spiritual essence through our human experience. I'm not thrilled with this growth format! However, I'm slowly learning to cultivate an attitude of ongoing surrender to minimize the shocks of boot-camp-like wake-up calls, attempting to convince my Higher Self that indeed I am finally willing to cooperate and extend my spiritual ground. My ego still quivers at this process, wondering what horrible things have to happen for me to grow me spiritually, knowing that ultimately it will experience itself as undifferentiated oneness, whatever that is!

The Tibetan chuckles at my trepidation, reassuring me that these triggers don't have to be so melodramatic. He teaches:

The soul rejoices when the time has come to step on the spiritual path. It signals the imminence of ultimate reunion with Source—the greatest adventure Self has ever known. Ironically, there is more chronic subliminal pain/ discomfort in the complacency and stagnation of residing in the small self too long, resisting spiritual growth, than there is in the bad events that propel self beyond the ego. The passionless state of ego control dulls the spirit, extracting the magic out of life. Bad events reflect the soul's energy pushing up to the surface to shake things up, challenge old belief structures to provide a crack in the cement through which to allow magnified light to enter. It is the ego's nature to secure itself to a one-pointed reality that it believes it manages. The ego's mechanism doesn't yet register the spiritual call without pain. This is not a reflection of a cruel Divine Plan but rather of an immature humanity.

Respond to these bad events with curiosity, willingness, open-mindedness and trust. They are NOT punishments. These disturbing upheavals that catalyze self to an enhanced land beyond the ego's island are interpreted as signs of failure, inadequacy, and stupidity. This reflects the ego's impotence within this expanded reality of the soul. Most of the pain from these bad events is the result of the ego's attachment to the status quo. When fully surrendered to these challenging events, self opens to their full impact. Relaxation within acquiescence eases some of the pain/ difficulty into a greater flow through which self can harvest a deeper attunement to the brilliant guidance inherent within these triggers. Self is then in full cooperation with his/her predestined soul's curriculum.

Once established on their spiritual pathway, most students look back upon these triggers of initiation with great appreciation. Without this momentary disruption of the psyche, self would be permanently imprisoned in the small, windowless room of the ego. The long range gifts of spiritual growth far outweigh the temporary discomfort of these passing triggers. Just like ignoring the alarm clock when self wishes to stay submerged beneath the covers, the ego is innately resistant to the self's divine impulse to rise up out of its cocooned state to greet a superior reality. To stay under the covers, suffocated within the grasp of the ego, is to miss the magnificent Universe that awaits self through spiritual growth. Traumatic triggers to awakening advise the student to break down, to ask what is life all about, to look inside, to reexamine one's values, to explore the terrain of one's deepest self, to experience the heart's trust, to be notified that the Higher Self is ready and waiting, to remember that Source is within self's breath, to yield to the mystery, to let go.

Devastatingly painful experiences need not forever be the central mechanism that propels students beyond their ego. As humankind embraces its spiritual reality, the collective ego will assume its rightful place within the psyche. This maturation of humankind will allow the soul to grow through other forms of heightened vibrational influence besides pain, such as powerful currents of joy, ecstasy and love. There will no longer be a need to shock the student into looking toward higher ground. All will already be awakened and in Love. The paradigm of mandated nightmarish disturbances will recede. Humankind will respond to the great Call, ushered forth through Source's magnificent organizing magnetism of Self-discovery, Self-creation, Self-initiation, with the gleeful joy of a child running with arms outstretched to embrace a Land of Wonder.

✧ Beyond the Realm of Duality ✧

December 2001

The Tibetan alerts us that it is time to go beyond the realm of duality. What does that mean? We have only experienced our human condition through a dual focus—good/ bad, high/ low, dark/ light, happy/ sad, yes/ no, strong/ weak, etc. There has always been a counterpoint to our experience, there to balance our reality through an opposite adventure, perception, feeling, impulse.

The Tibetan's instructions carry an urgent quality to them, almost commanding us to make this paradigm shift NOW—in a moment—from lifetimes of dual focus to an immediate emergence into Oneness. With current events stepped up to an unbearable pitch, and everyone perched on the edge of their seat waiting to find out whether the "good guys" or the "bad guys" prevail, there's a natural collective inclination to pick sides, righteously describing the evil ways of the enemy vs. the saintliness of the heroes.

Collectively, as a global family, we run the risk of moving into extremes with no middle ground, taking the duality to the "nth degree," convinced we are right, they are wrong. We rigidly hold on to philosophies and belief structures that describe whatever is ours as the "right" way, eclipsing any inherent value or truth in other people's vantage point of the human journey. This reduces us to a level of fundamentalism—a bottom-line arena in which there is no longer any discussion, no meeting point within the divergence of paradigms.

Extreme polarization can lead to a frightening level of absolutism. This kind of indisputable, godlike hold on "the truth" is fertile ground for fanaticism in any culture. When we totally block out the reality of "others," we back ourselves into a corner where we have to fight to the finish to justify our take on reality, leaving no room for reconciliation…for mystery…for common ground. Tremendous passion fuels the rigidity, baking it in a stew of judgments projected "out there" while disowning any personal contribution to the collective darkness we say we're determined to scourge from our planet.

Yet, if we look at the duality inherent within all aspects of our human condition, we have to own that within all "good" causes is a negative underbelly, and conversely within all "bad" causes there is a thread of light-filled truth. If we embrace this duality, where does that put us? Right smack in the mystery, the uncertainty that emerges when we dare have the courage to release our tight-fisted grip on polarized reality.

Our egos don't want to face uncertainty, warding it off with inflated crystallized decrees of knowing, impervious to questioning, scrutiny, confusion, befuddlement, and wonder. Yet this perplexity is the expression of authentic movement beyond the duality into a new paradigm in consciousness. This emerging consciousness includes *everything* within it, holding all contradictions equally, simultaneously.

Forever on a quest for the ultimate truth, I have often fallen prey to the seduction of knowing that "of course I'm right." I assumed that there was ONE ultimate truth that prevailed over all other realities. I have played this out not only in philosophical discussions and metaphysical explorations of the Divine, but also in personal relationships where I *"knew"* I was right. I expected the other person (friend, lover, teacher, employer, whoever) to eventually see "the light" and come around, not to my way of thinking but to the truth about which I was so "certain."

This belief system constantly backfired on me when inevitably I had to acknowledge the undeniable version of truth in the other person's reality; it typically came full circle as I placed myself in their shoes for a moment. I finally got it through my stubborn mind-set that there are many facets to human existence, each valid while seeming contradictory. To let them all in at once was to blow the circuits in my taut-wired mental program about truth. The short-circuiting of old programming catalyzed my immersion into a sea of creative, chaotic confusion, which opened profound doors of perception and insight.

The road to the Oneness lies in the process of abandoning our "ultimate" grip on reality, freeing ourselves to be flooded with a bewilderment that is the gateway to a wisdom that springs from a mutual neutralization leading to transformation. I have to confess that both my spiritual and psychological egos still love to battle for their stand on the truth, determined to prove others wrong for the sheer satisfaction of winning the corner on truth. How empty I feel when others inevitably retreat in alienation, unheard and judged.

At that moment I have forfeited the opportunity for the rich alchemization that occurs when paradoxical realities collide within my brain and heart, blackening my walls of self-righteousness and metamorphisizing my rigidity into a smooth flowing river of golden insight.

We all have to grapple with the duality knowing that the moment we assume we have our version of reality pinned down its counterpart will present itself, eager for the same passionate embrace we gave our opposite truth. Buffeted back and forth between conflicting realities softens our defense structure allowing us the opportunity to take the next step which is to embrace multiple realities at once. The Tibetan calls this "embodying the paradox". At this point we break the attachment to either pole and expand into a realm that exists beyond the duality—the Oneness within the Multiplicity. From this vantage point our tenacious judgments dissolve freeing up our ability to love ALL beings. Liberated, our global family then unites in mutual understanding and acceptance.

Nodding in agreement, the Tibetan adds:

The Duality has been the primary learning vehicle for humankind. This vehicle has provided a full spectrum of experience that enriches the soul through multiplicity and contradiction. At this point in history, with the accelerated energies impacting the earth plane, the poles are moving to an extreme. It is the "Armageddon" spoken of in prophecies.

Armageddon is <u>not to be feared</u> in its catastrophic sense, but rather to be celebrated. Yes, the prophecies were correct in their description of a global clashing of wills. However, the Divine Plan does not indicate that this critical apex in diametric realities will result in devastation, horror, and the downfall of the human race. Yet, like all birth processes, an air of danger fills the earthly chamber as humankind witnesses the energetic conclusion of a way of life long established since the beginning of time and space. There is no need to charge this climate with fear, apprehension, and negativity. That only fuels the illusion of divergence. Allow self to cultivate a world-view of unification and inherent harmony, which indeed is its true nature.

The energetic patterns of oppositional forces, perceived by humankind as good and evil, are increasing in intensity as they accelerate to their optimum potential in expression. This is reflected in the agitated political arena. Humankind has always felt the need to assert its existence through opposition to itself, still confused by notions that the Divine infuses only segments of its population and not its entirety. Do not contribute to this hollow battle by aligning one's mind/ heart/ soul with one side or the other, for this only empowers the unilluminated terrain within self. Also, do not hide one's head under the covers, hoping that the crisis will go away by itself. All of humankind must align their will with the Divine Will and step forward to assist in this collective shift in consciousness. No one is exempt from the responsibility to detach from the dramatic influences of disunity, no matter how compelling the unfoldment of events may be.

The climax of the poles ushers in a new paradigm in consciousness wherein the human mind no longer orients itself through opposites. Through this unification process, humankind has the ability to contact a higher vibration of Light that exists beyond the light factor referenced through its polar opposite, dark (the absence of light). This heightened Light factor can be imagined as a million times brighter than the sun.

While no reference to it exists in humankind's historic experience, this Light factor is available nonetheless for integration into the collective consciousness. The light that humankind has known can be compared to the illumination of a 40-watt bulb lighting a huge gymnasium. While humanity assumes that this is the "light" of the Divine, it merely casts a faint glow compared to the magnificence of the heightened Light factor that is truly the Source of all illumination.

Humankind must act as conscious physical channels to anchor the heightened Light factor onto the planet during this delicate process of polar climax. To access the magnitudinal Light, humankind needs to hold the larger picture in mind and not be seduced by the magnetic collective illusions that reflect the divisive nature of duality. The expanded perspective describes a collective transformation currently peaking momentum. It is a transformation that compels ALL beings to awaken from the collective sleep cocooned within a paradigm of separation, unrelatedness and conflict.

In meditation and prayer, imagine this magnificent Light filling self's emotional, mental and physical body. Conduct this Light into the earth through the feet. Know that this Light is not subject to the laws of duality and need not attract an equal and opposite darkened vibration. To be incarnate at this time on the planet carries a karmic contract signed before birth, when self agreed to serve as a bridge/ conduit for the Light factor during this predestined pinnacle juncture. Now is the time to step forward to fulfill this agreement and apply self's willingness, imagination and openness to the process of being a vessel for a new frequency of Divine Fire that burns away the dross within the collective attachment to the duality.

Unleash self's imagination to picture a world beyond duality, where humankind no longer needs to experience its divinity in a bifurcated format. Know that the emerging unification blends the spiritual plane into the physical plane, anchoring a phenomenal Light force never before experienced in the collective consciousness of humankind. Remember that the Masters and Angelic Force are actively encircling the earth as she moves through the labor pains birthing a New Cosmic Day. We hold all of humanity with the exquisite care of boundless love, devotional 24 hours a day to this miraculous process of regeneration and transformation. When humanity finally releases the duality, a window opens, offering a view and understanding of the extraordinary interconnectedness within all beings—not only on earth, but in the intergalactic family as well. Then humankind will assume its rightful place in a Universe anchored by cornerstones of LOVE, LIGHT, HARMONY, and JOY.

✧ The Possibility of Enlightenment ✧

April 2002

How many of us really believe we are going to reach enlightenment in this lifetime? Enlightenment is often viewed as an unreachable horizon to be considered and explored in future lifetimes, after we have made more progress. Certainly we don't dare to believe that it is an attainable state of consciousness in *this* lifetime. How could that be possible? We associate enlightenment with mountaintop meditators from India or western spiritual teachers who have somehow mysteriously made the miraculous leap from mere human into the realm of the awakened ones. Most of us are more comfortable with spiritual goals we consider "reachable," such as: "I just want to be a good person…find a little inner peace from the incessant turmoil…have a comfortable life…stop judging others," or "I want to learn how to love…manage my anger…" To be able to shift our consciousness into a state of enlightenment filled with bliss, extrasensory gifts, fearlessness, present-centered awareness and unconditional love for all beings seems too much to ask.

Lately, more people are exploring the concept of enlightenment. This reflects a shift in the collective consciousness, an opening to consider the full range of possibilities for humanity. The Tibetan continually talks about enlightenment, encouraging us to accept that not only is it possible in this lifetime, but probable. Opening to that possibility is a stretch for most of us blind, crazed mortals struggling to simply hang on to our sanity.

The state of enlightenment is hard to language. Without a solid conceptual base to reference, our imaginations flounder around trying to latch onto an image or vision, seeking a lifeline to orient our passage into awakening. If we can't imagine ourselves enlightened, it is harder to open to enlightenment. The imagination is the rainbow bridge aligning our creative body with archetypal patterns waiting to be tapped. Usually our refusal to consider ourselves worthy or ready for enlightenment collapses the imagination, blocking an intuitive connection that opens our paradigm to catch glimpses of how our individual enlightenment might be experienced.

My understanding of becoming enlightened is that it is a long process (spanning lifetimes) of self-exploration, purification and healing that leads to a moment of "sudden" awakening. The Tibetan teaches that one of the biggest blocks to enlightenment is our inability to imagine it possible in this lifetime—in this moment. He reinforces the usual teachings that we can't strive for it, attach to it, or force it.

How do we open to enlightenment without investment? What an assignment! Most of us throw up our hands in frustration and impossibility, saying: "This is too hard, too far out of reach. Maybe in future lifetimes my turn will come to be honored with the miracle of awakening."

When I was 30 years old, I sat with a dear friend on a hilltop in the gorge-filled upstate New York town of Ithaca. As we mused about life's possibilities stretched out before us, I asked her, "Do you think we will reach enlightenment in this lifetime?" She answered, "Of course." We both laughed, delighting in the audacity to believe that we could make that much progress in one life. From that hilltop, with its mystical view of Ithaca's whale-back hills, anything and everything seemed possible.

A bit more than 20 years later, I often feel I am farther from enlightenment than ever! What happened? Did I regress? Has all the work I've done on myself been for nothing? Was I just a foolish young woman fantasizing about the impossible? Perhaps she needed more humility, patience, purification. Am I running out of time? Maybe I don't know how to "measure" the growth I've made.

When I am embroiled in frustration, anger, resentment, envy, jealousy, or simply flattened by exhaustion, depression, worry and fear, I wonder how I could possibly ever become enlightened. The Tibetan lightens my discouragement by telling me that usually when we feel farthest from awakening, ironically we are closest, and are reacting to the impact of our egos dissolving into a sea of humility, sweeping us into a greater reality.

My skepticism kicks in. Maybe I can be forgiven for the emotional turmoil, but when scanning my daily life, I critique all the "bad" things I do: self-involved, controlling, craving addictive foods, zoning out with foolish videos sedating my consciousness, ignoring world issues to protect myself from the collective pain, and basically wanting to "get by" without the discipline required to do the mountain of purification and alignment work required to go beyond the ego. Surely these spiritual crimes have retarded my awakening process by at least a few hundred years!

The Tibetan smiles at my resistance, taking it in stride, joking that I can't use those "crimes" as excuses for not allowing myself to *imagine* my own awakening. His charming persuasion melts my defiance. Armor dissolved, I begin to reflect on those fleeting times when a deep feeling of joy permeates the moment; or I catch glimpses of an exquisite light filling the room; or an overflowing love suddenly expands my heart, dissolving all judgments; or a sweet sensation of inner peace seeps into the pores of my psyche, easing the sharp edges of my soul; or I am propelled by a great desire to help others—to serve the world. I find myself smiling in acceptance of the mystery as it fill me with delight and awe at the unanswerable nature of life…as clairvoyance opens my inner eyes as I gaze spellbound at the bright rays of colors emanating off the wildflowers dotting the hill behind my house…or as I am overtaken by an irresistible urge to sing—a shout out to the heavens in the sheer exuberance of being. Could these flashes be a sneak preview of my enlightened self?

My negativity discounts these precious tastes of possibility. They are unsustainable, therefore not valid signposts of spiritual progress. I am struck by our natural inclination to discredit these bleed-throughs from the awakened self. It is so much more familiar and comforting to nestle in with our favorite blockages, feeling safe from the challenges of opening to a new dimension in consciousness, and the shock of 360-degree vision.

The Tibetan picks up my thoughts and runs with them:

One's enlightenment has already happened outside the illusion of time and space. The students are simply evolving into it! The accelerated energy currently impacting the earth plane heightens the momentum of intense cosmic forces engineered to sweep self into recognition of what already is. Because it has already happened, enlightenment is inevitable for ALL of humankind. The awakening process is an organic dynamic encoded in the soul's matrix. The only effort required is to get self out of Self's way.

Students just need to gently focus their attention on their own unique enlightenment, assuming it to be immediately available at any moment. Release notions that one must be a perfect human being in order to be ready for this momentous breakthrough. Yes, much purification and refinement work is required to heighten the student's ability to take the imaginative leap into the awakened self. However, paradoxically, no matter what level of evolution the student is at, the opportunity to touch the enlightened state is always available.

In addition to disciplined industriousness, the mysterious serendipity of the confluence of energies and unexpected openings can shift the consciousness, like suddenly discovering just the right combination that opens a vault. Does the student simply happen upon it? Yes and no! The energetic field of enlightenment is the potentiated Self in all of its magnitude, existing side by side with the unawakened self. A shift in perspective, a moment of sheer letting go, a willingness to trust and surrender to what already is, all provide the exquisite opportunity to open.

Release all notions of what the enlightened state is supposed to be like. Students often feel that once enlightened, they will be in perfect physical health, emotional body always calm, mind completely pure. Yet each student, each soul, is a unique expression of Source's prismatic Being. Therefore, everyone's enlightened self exhibits different combinations of qualities interfacing the human condition with the universal Oneness. Enlightenment is a state of consciousness regardless of the state of the physical body, emotional currents or conceptual energies of the mental body. What changes is the student's relationship to these aspects of self. When awakened, self dwells in a state of unconditional love and acceptance for all expressions of self at the earthly as well as spiritual level. In this supreme acceptance, the student is liberated from all attachments.

The enlightenment process is no longer a solitary journey, or contingent on following a teacher/guru for energetic transmissions. Neither way is efficient at this time. The birth of the New Cosmic Day on planet earth involves a collective awakening experience, meaning that awakening occurs at a group level. As the students share with each other the very real probability of their individual enlightenment, they spark one another's recognition of the immediacy of potential. Then more and more students catch the spark of awareness that ignites their awakened self, and the collective awakening gathers great momentum. This compounds upon itself, heightening the speed with which humanity wakes up. Remind each other to imagine enlightenment, to accept its probability in this lifetime, acknowledging the inevitable expression of the Divine Plan as it ushers in a new paradigm in consciousness.

Many students are temporarily blinded by the intensified clearing of momentous levels of karmic debris. Amid the storm of unresolved past-life issues, it is difficult to imagine the enlightened state, much less assess self's progress. Please assume that self is heading in the right direction.

Become sensitive to the moments of enlightenment peppering daily life. Record the occasions, however fleeting, when self experiences a transcendent state of consciousness. Allow self's intuition to recognize these moments, usually highlighted by an amplified sense of light, love, connectedness, compassion, peace, and joy-filled willingness. This discipline expands the students' awareness of the presence and immediacy of the enlightened self.

Humankind is more likely to notice what is not *happening, especially if one loses clarity momentarily in a cloud of karmic debris, and remembers the disconnect rather than the moments of supreme connection. Most students experience several flashes of enlightenment each day. However, these spectacular events are immediately suppressed by the inertia of the conditioning that instantly snaps the consciousness back to its familiar narrow paradigm fueled by expectations, developed over lifetimes, of limitation in consciousness.*

To attempt to record or share these moments, however ephemeral, anchors their "reality" in one's consciousness. This has a cumulative effect of rearranging habitual thought patterns, catalyzing the release of the false beliefs indicating that self isn't worthy or ready for awakening. Collect these gifts of awakening like treasures foretelling the truth of self's being and the predestined inevitability of soul harvest. As this bundle of favors accumulates, the cells in the body start to fire in recognition of the vast realm beyond illusion. Like a match to gasoline, suddenly the entire energetic body is filled with light— enlightened...awakened...reborn to Truth as the veils of distortion fall away to reveal Self's magnitude at long last.

✧ Sustaining Enlightenment ✧

January 2003

How many of us assume that once we reach enlightenment we're all set—no more work to do, clear sailing all the way. We expect enlightenment to be a self-sustaining state of consciousness, like popping into another dimension with its own innate trajectory. Yes, leaving our gravitational field can be quite the struggle, but once we're launched, don't we naturally orbit at a higher level, never to fall from grace or contract in awareness, effortlessly and truly within a dimension of ease? Do awakened people still struggle with their egos after enlightenment? Does it require constant vigilance to ward off the pull of the old consciousness? These theoretical questions may seem irrelevant to our present struggle to even imagine ourselves enlightened. Just getting to the finish line is challenging enough, much less contemplating what lies beyond.

The Tibetan teaches that we have countless moments of enlightenment during the course of one day. We simply don't recognize, or are unable to sustain them. The ego rushes in to obliterate these moments of pure truth. These repressed flashes fall into the unconscious, stored as fragments of the awakened self, disconnected and unintegrated. If we can't extend awareness of these moments, how will we ever maintain the awakened state once it arrives? To nourish motivation for the enlightenment quest, we need to know that it is indeed possible to uphold the awakened state while still being human. Our challenge is to bring credibility to these breakthroughs, however fleeting, and to connect the dots that interface these moments into a unified experience of enduring enlightenment.

The Tibetan's directive is to record and remember daily moments of enlightenment in order to anchor their "reality." When attempting to sustain my experience of these transient awakenings I catalyze their opposite, falling back into the gravitational field of duality. How can we substantiate our moments of breakthrough if the second we recognize them, our ego attaches? Attachment instantly shatters gateway encounters.

When mining for crystals in Arkansas in the early 1980s, I discovered that the best way to spot those iron-cloaked gems was from a sideways glance. To look head-on somehow obscured my recognition of them. Similarly, generating a state of non-attachment requires a sideways glance at my consciousness—not too focused as to induce attachment, but focused none the less to authenticate the reality of these breakthrough flashes. The Tibetan says that as we are able to retain the awareness of these moments without attachment, a momentum builds, blending these instants into a fully revealed awakened state. This momentum breaks down old conditioning that suggests we are not ready/ worthy/ able to reach, much less sustain, enlightenment.

The ego is captivated by its desire to identify with and control the enlightenment experience. It claims these gateway glimpses as its own doing, immediately lowering their vibration. This task seems impossible. Attempting to track twinklings of enlightenment without attachment is like trying to restrain excitement when we finally meet our long-awaited soul mate. The grabby nature of the ego is instinctual. How can we override this automatic response pattern when we behold our greater Self?

We are taught to resist the ego's desires. However, the soul also has desires—for divine union. How do we discern the difference between the ego's lust and the soul's profound hunger for its liberation? How do we ride the current of "higher desire" without dropping to lower levels of attachment?

My consciousness continues to expand regardless of incessant ego pulls to duality. This subtle but definite climatic shift in my soul endures in spite of personal trials and tribulations, suggesting that once accessed the awakened state overrides duality. It prevails regardless of my ego's melodramas. As the presence of this light-filled soul environment increases, the domain of my ego shrinks to the size of a small island in a universal ocean of joyous cosmic waves. But when I feel stranded on that island, my link to this Sea of Love breaks down, reinforcing the belief that I'll never be able to get off the island, no matter how hard I try. However, when I shift my perspective, I realize that this Source Ocean is closing in on my awareness from all sides, not taking NO for an answer. Yes, it seems to sustain itself, regardless of my resistance to the Sublime.

Clients of mine have experienced states of sudden breakthrough, some after receiving energetic transmissions from gurus and others seemingly from nowhere, out of the blue. They describe suddenly being filled with overwhelming love, insight, compassion, energy (needing no more than a few hours of sleep each night). These heightened states lasted for a few weeks and then mysteriously evaporated, like a broken spell, sending them reeling back into their small selves, disoriented, disappointed, confused, out of balance. Did they fall from the "Garden of Eden" because they needed to integrate their enlightened self within the field of duality? Did they lift off prematurely, with unfinished ego work left behind demanding their return? Why didn't this amplified consciousness sustain itself? Did past life conditioning undermine these precious few weeks of liberation?

I assume that in simply touching the enlightened state, we are reorganized by its biochemical/ electrical change. From this higher order of being, we cannot return to, or even recognize, our old self. It has disappeared into the matrix of our soul, rearranged into a truer essence. This suggests that enlightenment is self-sustaining because there is no other reference for self other that what is in the moment. So, why do people "fall" from this state? Does the energetic grid of the old self hover in the background, like a ghost determined to haunt the awakened self out of its domain?

Energy is neutral. Whatever energy fuels our life sets the tone for our consciousness. If our temporary experience of super-flow is short-circuited by the inertia of historic energies, patterned through duality for lifetimes, we can be easily pulled out of the Enlightenment Zone. Ironically, the breakthrough into higher consciousness catalyzes past life debris to surface for clearing. The tenacity of this karmic material challenges the fragility of our emerging relationship with this newly discovered sphere of liberation. Must we vigilantly fight back the demons of duality rooted in our historic selves in order to anchor enduring roots in the "E-zone"?

The Tibetan gladly responds to my barrage of questions, deeply appreciating the stretch which is involved in comprehending this leap in consciousness. He teaches:

Enlightenment is a natural state of being, humankind's birthright. Once uncovered, enlightenment automatically sustains itself. However, self must practice commitment to this expanded consciousness through watchful efforts to anchor one's ultimate truth onto a planet of duality. As the awakening mind gathers momentum, it perpetuates itself. The winds and storms of life test one's root system at this high level, deepening humankind's commitment to establish heaven on earth.

When completely non-attached to the quest for enlightenment, self is free, unencumbered by striving, to flow within this magnificent orbit. Enlightenment is an expanded state of consciousness within which the human drama continues to unfold without identification with a past or future personality. Within this present moment, Self expands into the infinite that naturally sustains itself because it can be none other than itself. The historic self is not obliterated. Rather, it is integrated within the awakened consciousness.

Since all are already enlightened out of time and space, Self need only anchor awareness beyond past and future. With eyes steadily turned to Source, an arch is generated that is fueled by the already awakened collective consciousness. The only tug back to duality is the mighty pull of collective false beliefs describing enlightenment as an unreachable state while in the human condition.

The gift of sudden breakthrough (from guru transmissions or kundalini awakenings) is an opportunity to touch the already awakened self, to taste the realm of expansion, to know Love. This expanded consciousness must be integrated into the soul body, requiring all past life selves to dissolve into the enlightened Self. To sustain contact with the spiritual dimension of the enlightened Self demands resolution of all unfinished business from past lives as well as one's current incarnation. Kundalini transmissions charge the energy body with an enlightenment frequency for the express purpose of providing a crisis in consciousness—a break with the stagnancy of three-dimensional reality. This serves to catapult the student out of the prison of ancient false beliefs, to blow open their grid. However, students are still responsible for mastering their enlightenment. Mastery necessitates the profound integration of heightened soul consciousness through its interface with all earthly experience.

There are many levels of enlightenment, instead of one shared generic, undifferentiated pinnacle of awareness, rather, there are striations of perception, insight, knowing. Source keeps evolving and so does all of Its creation. Therefore, Self's evolution never stops. States of enlightenment forever refine and deepen themselves. The student does not simply sit back after enlightenment, all set up for eternity. There are challenges all along the way. Yet, having arrived in the new land offers a great boon. There is no turning back because Self finally understands that the unawakened self is only an illusion. It takes tremendous resistance to drown this new awareness in forgetfulness—an act very few students would ever consider.

The commitment to work one's process continues, like chopping wood and carrying water, within the context of the enlightened realm. Students continue creating their unique versions of enlightenment. Mastery of enlightenment requires full embodiment of one's precisely individuated being—full expression of Self's distinctive sound and truth eternally metamorphosizing through the expanded dimensions of the many planes of enlightenment. Students explore the multifaceted nature of Self-experience within the enlightened state which generates superior ripples of light throughout the cosmos.

The earthly plane is inherently an enlightened plane, with the veils of illusion concealing its true brilliance. Therefore, it does not go against the grain to sustain the enlightened state while still being subject to the human condition. Historically it has been formidable for the lone student to maintain the awakened state within humankind's collective field of enlightenment denial. However, as more and more groups awaken in concert with each other, the barrier of illusion melts away, making it infinitely easier for the enlightened ones to establish themselves permanently in this threshold of awareness. Remove false beliefs that indicate it is impossible to sustain enlightenment while human.

As students connect the dots between moments of awakening, they realize that the emergence of this new dimension is real and cannot be denied. Once this is deeply comprehended, the student can enhance his/her enlightened state through creativity, curiosity, joy, and the Magnetic Pull of Emergence through which all creation issues forth. Yes, even enlightened ones continue to practice the art of daily surrender, embracing the mystery within. This necessary vigilance matches that of a great musician who could not fall to the level of beginner yet must practice/play music continually to express and charge their state of mastery. This training need not be seen as heavy work because the rewards of the enlightened Self bring profound delight and freedom, inherently motivational for the continuance of the self-generating (already established) mysterious arch of expanded consciousness.

Responsibilities for Self-creation never end. "Making up" one's enlightenment generates the imaginal bridge to greater consciousness. Having crossed the bridge, the journey is just beginning as students continue to reinform themselves, through action, thought, love, devotion, and surrender of their ultimate destiny of liberation. This is a never-ending process regardless of whether self inhabits a physical body or not. Yes, the Masters are still joyfully reinventing their enlightenment as the wheels of the cosmos turn into infinitude, exposing unseen vistas to even the most all-knowing beings. This is a dance that recharges itself through ecstasy and possibility. So connect the moments of dimensional leap. Know that once awakened, Self is free to truly begin to explore the dimension of enlightenment, to master the realm of the Unknowable within a pathway of devotion to the great well-spring of LOVE that would offer enlightenment as the razor's edge—the only pathway Home into the exalted limitlessness of Source's never ending unfoldment.

✧ *You* Make a Difference! ✧

October 2005

We don't realize how powerful we are. Individually, we have the capability to heal ourselves, transform evil, refurbish mother earth, establish peace—all through the simple act of intention.

Most of us, myself included, feel impotent in the face of the gigantic political, economic, social, environmental problems flooding today's world. We consider all the groups we should join to help turn the tides of destruction, but then throw up our hands in futility as we return to our personal worlds, already filled with too many responsibilities. We pray that someone else will take care of this huge mess—this undoing of all that we value…our pipeline to the sacred—because we simply can't. We barely manage our own lives, rife with transformational challenges. There's no time, energy, or inspiration remaining to attempt to make the world right.

But the Tibetan insists that we CAN make a difference. Individually, we ARE the difference.

How can we augment our birthright of divine impact as transformational vessels? We're all inherent healers, teachers and light workers just by the very breath that we share. But we must REMEMBER this divine legacy in order to inaugurate the moment-to-moment potency of our effect on the collective consciousness. We've brainwashed ourselves into believing that we are helpless, ineffective children who make a mess and hope that some adult will clean up after us.

Yes, we face colossal dilemmas as we watch our world fall apart. These challenges appear insurmountable from our traditional third-dimensional perspective. We must comprehend ourselves as holographic beings. Then we can truly experience the mighty effect that comes from simply the flicker of a new thought pattern, a momentary sweetness that emerges when our heart softens, or a willingness to suspend our egos' tyranny for just a second in order to glimpse our greater self.

We make a difference when we practice the "spiritual arts" of kindness, reverence for the earth and all living beings, compassion for ourselves and our endless failings—maintaining awareness that we are part of a bigger picture, acknowledging that our planet is made up of mostly good people, and taking a moment to reflect on the presence of the spiritual realm in our lives. Let us dare not succumb to the planetary bad news that increases exponentially. Assumed spineless inadequacy only sustains the brainwashing fostered by the Forces of Undoing.

We can choose the planetary arenas that call to us for help, knowing that our endeavors are not circumscribed by our small domain of influence. Rather, all efforts augment our basic intention to anchor Light on the planet. Our vehicles of service/ assistance become beacons in the dark—vibrant crystalline refractors of Light, Love and Healing. At this point, we are more than enough.

What would it be like if, deep in our bones, we really grasped the impact on our collective psycho-spiritual environment every time we felt hatred or Love? We have a divine responsibility to use intention to focus our essential truth and spiritual nature into daily life. Only then can we turn the tides of our destruction. It's not just that our own singular Light counterbalances the darkness of one other being. Rather, our individual Light, dynamically efficacious, can nullify the deleterious effects generated by *hundreds* of people who vibrate at the lower frequencies of negativity, fear and lovelessness.

In homeopathy, the minuscule dose of a remedy has the electrical capacity to resolve an entire systemic pattern of ill health. These remedies stimulate the immune system in the energy body to restore balance. They make the precise vibrational connection needed to undo illness. So, too, we use the power of intention and willingness to focus our thoughts and attitudes to connect with a preeminent GOOD, available to all, to align the entire "body" of the collective consciousness with higher principles. This allows a greater spiritual flow to invalidate dense harmful vibrations by kicking in our spiritual immune system. Individually, we are simply a "small dose." But our focused positive intention, innately far-reaching, can change the vibratory rate of our entire unilluminated collective unconsciousness.

To practice the Art of Transformation, we must develop spiritual muscles through the use of intention. We must decide— INTEND—to fasten our thoughts and feelings in a prescribed direction rather than allow ourselves to be cast about by our common negativity. When we travel, we concentrate intention on getting to our destination as efficiently as possible. We don't hope that someone else will intervene to accomplish this. We place ourselves in charge. We don't scatter our mind and forget the road while driving. We would never get anywhere. We have to stay focused. To truly be the Ambassadors of Transformation, the Cosmic Alchemists who turn the "lead" of this world into GOLD, we must use determination to direct the high intentions that develop the spiritual arts with the full knowledge that this IMMEDIATELY MAKES A DIFFERENCE in the ennobling of our darkened vibrations.

I'm the first to fill with guilt and despair when I read the newspapers' reports of our planetary hell. Self recriminations abound: "I'm not doing enough...I'm too lazy...too involved in the mess of my own transformation (and melodrama)...too overwhelmed by the responsibilities I'm already carrying without taking on such gigantic collective offenses." I regretfully fail to uphold the archetype of Mother Theresa—an earth angel 100% devoted to assisting this world out of its suffering. I minimally slog through my days, hoping that I'm not annihilated by my own ever-surfacing karmic debris. The winds of futility howl, trying to convince me to give up. There will be no happy ending to this awful earthly story. But the Tibetan whispers the truth sweetly into my ear, that this is just a momentary storm for humankind that will resolve into a bright new dawn—but only if we ALL use intention to harness the powerful energetics of our being that make us the true transformers.

The Tibetan points a wand of shimmering Light at the planet to demonstrate that one individual gesture can change the world. He teaches:

To raise one's light factor has the effect of putting an infinitesimal drop of Divine Love into the great sea of the collective consciousness. It instantly ripples out and merges into humankind's entire oceanic body, leaving no speck untouched, because one's concentrated Divine Light Essence holds in its core the "Changer Molecule." The chemical nature within this heightened vibration of Light infiltrates and transforms everything. One moment of focused, loving thought (positive intention) can infiltrate the dense, lower vibrational environment of the collective unconscious and raise the efficacy of that generic vibration to unheard-of levels. This is made possible when self is WILLING to embody love, practice compassion, be awake and TRUST in positive outcomes. This stockpiles Divine Light, which enables humankind to resist the quicksand of the denser collective frequencies that pull the human psyche down into the abyss of annihilation and despair.

Humankind alone cannot maintain contact with higher consciousness. It's still too weakened by its illusion of separation/ fear. But with the right use of intention, the alignment of the personal will with the Divine Will, humankind could right itself in an instant. This is not wishful thinking, but simply the application of metaphysical law, as demonstrated by Master Jesus, the Buddha and all the resplendent avatars who have graced the planet with their sacred presence. Their "Changer Molecule" magnifies Divine Light through the Intention of the Divine Plan, which sustains humankind on its journey through darkness into Light.

Spiritual adepts aren't the only ones who can make a difference on earth. Indeed, each individual is the true star whose light shines into the Cosmos as brightly as all illustrious teachers and makes an even greater difference, because humankind's process of enlightenment carries a potency that startles and shocks the collective consciousness. People simply don't expect their own awakening.

To make one small insight into self's blockages/ illusions creates a consciousness shift that catalyzes an influential force field, highly electrical, that stimulates the circuitry woven throughout the collective consciousness. One small light center turns on in the brain, one moment of 'ah ha,' and like a string of Christmas lights, the same light bulb turns on in EVERYONE'S consciousness. All dine at the Table of Illumination simultaneously. Even if self quickly forgets that "ah ha" and tumbles back down to the familiar negativity, the impact of that moment is indelibly etched in the collective brain patterns. This pioneers original grooves of awareness never before blazed. This is how the world really changes—from the inside out.

The potential opened by one moment of reflection, prayer, openheartedness, forgiveness, surrender and love is boundless. PLEASE TRUST IT. Old conditioning blinds humankind to this truth. Fearful of disappointment, people hesitate to put faith in their innate power of intention. They don't dare believe that heaven on earth is possible—no, inevitable. Instead, humankind passively waits for Divine Intervention. But humankind is Divine Intervention, holding the keys to transformation. It is the gatekeeper that it waits so longingly for.

✧ The Power of Unity ✧

February 2006

We're all together in a great alchemical stew that cooks our human condition. So why do we create arbitrary distinctions to set ourselves apart from one another? Are we afraid that our individual distinctiveness will be homogenized by the Ocean of Oneness? But separateness does not foster uniqueness.

If we are to collectively ignite our mutual awakening, we must unite. But how can we join forces if we are afraid of becoming each other?

We're all cut from the same cosmic cloth. We all travel the same path to liberation, filled with hurts, fears, hopes, dreams that are, energetically, identical. We all experience similar life stages. We share the same planet. We're all students with mandated soul assignments that shape our lives. We're all equally responsible for humanity's evolution. No one is exempt from the depths of the human soul or the heights of the human spirit. No one is spared the "dark night of the soul," or robbed of the possibility of transformation. So, why do we feel so alienated?

If we could just team up, it would be so much easier to fulfill our earthly course work. We could "study" together and grow in leaps and bounds. Yes, our egos would have to rescind their insistence on separate dominion. But we ought to be able to make that leap by now. How much longer must we indulge our need to be better/ less/ different from everyone else? Such a victory is hollow, only generating the pain of isolation and loss in the face of the amazing power that emanates from our unified being. Yes, each one of us *is* unique—special, individuated—but only within the greater context of our shared essence.

All of Source's Creation demonstrates unity. When we resist oneness, we buck our divinity and oppose the Divine Plan. The animal kingdom survives and thrives through group consciousness; there are *schools* of fish, *packs* of wolves, *gaggles* of geese, *herds* of deer, *prides* of lions, *colonies* of ants, *flocks* of birds, *pods* of whales, *mobs* of prairie dogs, etc. Cosmic Affinity empowers these creatures to flourish in deep communion with each other and Mother Earth. Typically, an animal who strays from its group will perish because it's cut off from its congregation's endurance power.

We must follow suit if we are to handle the heightened vibrations that compel us forward into the emerging paradigm.

The New Age requires humankind's collective consciousness to emanate from a deep bond of mutuality. We're the only ones who can conjointly awaken each other. The recognition of our essential common ground fills us with amazing dynamism as we draw on the concentrated energy of the whole rather than dissipate resources through estrangement and opposition.

Humanity stands at a crossroads. If we don't band together to meet the accelerated planetary frequencies, we will surely miscarry this gargantuan opportunity to evolve en masse to a level never before experienced. Instead, we'll fall into a chaotic disintegration, where our essential Oneness is obliterated by a sea of separate egos willfully highlighting their stance of apartness as a basis for survival. It is a position of utter weakness that causes our souls to wither and mourn for the communion that makes earthly existence feasible.

We must experience the human family as one body, one heart, one mind. When our neighbors half-way across the planet are starving, struggling with disease or devastated by natural disasters, we have no choice but to feel their pain. It's so tempting to try to insulate ourselves with the illusion of separateness and become numb to the vicissitudes of others…to carefully screen those with whom we're willing to blend and only accept people who are like us. We can't imagine uniting with anyone we consider creepy, ugly, derelict, criminal, lost, uneducated, poor or ill.

But our essential unity summons us to be all people at once in order to perceive the soul in everyone, no matter their walk in life. To dissolve our judgmental estrangement, we must dare to perceive life through their eyes. It won't kill us to feel their pain. Rather, it cultivates a potent empathy and warm-heartedness that softens our armor. Compassion unites us.

We're evolving toward true interdependence. Our advancement obliges us to become One. We can't possibly make this last leg of the journey unlinked. So how do we put our differences aside and reference our mutual essence—the place of real empowerment?

We must suspend all territoriality and sense of unrelatedness, and release the secret fear that we're no different from everyone else. The more people we can imagine as extensions of ourselves, and vice versa, the more we are likely to treat them accordingly. The heart chakra then becomes crowded, like a packed subway, with millions of people drinking from the same cosmic loving cup. Once we accept the genius within our unity and allow it to be our guiding force, total transformation is possible.

I certainly struggle with this unity thing. Why should I blend with others whom I find distasteful? After all, I've worked hard to get where I am; why do I have to "sink" to their level in order to evolve through the Unity Gate? Can't I sidestep this communion process, hang onto my particular uniqueness, and still move into advanced consciousness? But alas, my ego will have to humble itself so that I can take responsibility for my shadow's narrow-minded assumptions.

Our egos, replete with the need to be "most special," are baffled by the notion of expressing the soul's uniqueness while simultaneously erasing all distinctions between self and the tribe. We're challenged to embody the paradox of differentiation in the Oneness. We must reassure the ego by highlighting our significance as we coax it to release its insistence that it is separate from all other egos. Then we're ready to make the colossal shift and fully accept our birthright of wondrous unified consciousness—our ticket to fly.

Once we begin to live this unity consciousness, our heart chakras will bubble over in gushes of love. Unity repairs all broken spirits and demonstrates that we're never alone or abandoned. As we experience the amplitude of this unity, we realize there really is strength in numbers. We become a wave of awakening humanity that initiates, sparks and unfurls its own liberation. Suddenly, we have access to the Primordial Heartbeat that pulses us together in the Ocean of Light and Love. How inspiring and joyful it will be to genuinely share the ride.

The Tibetan, holding all beings in his boundless heart, teaches:

Historically, there has been a tremendous emphasis on the vertical axis that reflects humankind's evolution up the scale of refined consciousness. Everyone pulls those on the rung below them up onto the next step of this cosmic ladder. Movement along the vertical axis allows students to view spiritual heights, and plummet into the depths of the soul. However, this emphasis on verticality has reinforced the notion of hierarchy. Students, daunted, perceive the advancement of these "higher-ups" as a reflection of their own inadequacy. Vertical spiritual status becomes a hotbed of comparison, pressure, and competition.

Like children who transfer decision-making and self-responsibility to parents and/or teachers, students often turn their power over to the hierarchy. This supports the illusion that self is not ready to collaborate with the Divine Plan because he/she is too far down the evolutionary ladder to make a difference, and therefore not worthy of this level of participation. But the new paradigm requires humankind to be in full co-creation with the Divine Plan. Therefore, the reference point must shift from vertical to horizontal.

All beings, however latent or undeveloped, are equal in their divine potency. Everyone faces the same opportunities and challenges. No one is overshadowed by the "advanced." As humankind references itself and the spiritual plane from a horizontal perspective, it can more readily experience its ONENESS with all life in the Macrocosm. WE ARE ALL THE SAME! All beings on the spiritual plane, earthly plane and extraterrestrial dimensions are inextricably bound together by the identical force field that created this Universe and those beyond.

To make the great shift into Unity consciousness authorizes humankind to take its rightful place BESIDE the Masters, Angels and other "elevated ones," who gladly relinquish their vertical status to blend into the profound wave of Oneness that unites all of Source's Creation in the NOW. The ultimate lesson for humankind is to move through the Enlightenment Gateway as one being. Only then can it establish the new paradigm in which spiritual principles and values are fully embodied and applied in earthly life.

None can really extract themselves from the One Pulse that harmonizes all beings. When humankind comprehends this, the Force of Unification will penetrate and knit the collective consciousness into a togetherness so profound, it will melt all insurmountable evolutionary obstacles. At long last, the body of humanity will embrace its destiny as the supreme Herculean channel for Light and Love.

✧ The Extraordinary Self ✧

April 2005

Do you ever dare to think big—I mean really big? Maybe in quiet moments your imagination momentarily escapes the prison/tyranny of the negative ego just long enough to play with the truth of who you really are—an extraordinary being trying to recollect the rich potential within its wondrous divine destiny. To embrace our extraordinary nature would have an amazing impact on self-esteem, life choices and self-expression. To grant permission to believe that we can be so much MORE, we must push the envelope of the status quo and release attachment to our "ordinary" self. Once envisioned, we ultimately embody our superb beingness.

What are all the "good" reasons why we should stay small? An unconscious collective contract chains us to mediocrity with childhood pressures to "not get carried away with self" and societal mandates to "not outshine others." It would be sacrilege to dare to open the mind/imagination to an exceptional version of self. Even those who accomplish extraordinary lives struggle with insignificance, self-diminishment, and failure. But in order to graduate earth school, we're required to manifest our utmost potential. We must leave the "security" of the prosaic self in the dust if we are to run the race to the finish—no half-stepping.

In our comfort zone of homogenized unnoteworthy ordinariness, we blend in with the rest of the sheep called humanity. But the emerging new paradigm involves groups of highly individuated unique beings whose distinction blazes past the generic humdrum dead end of the stifled human spirit. We must be bold enough to discover and declare our special brand of brilliance destined to illuminate this world.

However, we love commiserating about our wounds as we reinforce attachment to the protection/ defenses that buffer those hurts from deep contact. If our lives revolve around wounds, we never even contemplate the prodigious core that dwarfs the terrain of our afflictions. We're so accustomed to mirroring negativity inwardly and outwardly that we're blind to our extraordinary essence. We've forgotten that it even exists. After all, isn't it egotistical folly to consider ourselves extraordinary? We're taught that it's virtuous to be small, humble, unassuming. But that particular "virtue" cages us into self-effacing invisibility with low impact on ourselves and others. At the risk of swelling our egos, we must dare to claim our extraordinariness so we can confidently, expansively, readily meet the heightened vibrations impacting our planet. Just because we're oblivious to our gifts doesn't mean they're out of reach. Through leaps of faith we can dig into ourselves to uncover and share our soul's gems.

In what areas of our lives do we dare NOT think big? What secondary gains do we receive from staying insignificant? Perhaps we've "signed" unconscious agreements with family members, mates, and employers to stay ordinary so they don't feel outshined or threatened. Fearful of abandonment, we've got to make sure they continue to love us. It's just not safe to evolve past them. Or perhaps we fear that society will punish us with attack, exile, imprisonment for exposing our magnitude. We subliminally remember past lives of being ousted from the human family for daring to exhibit greatness. To belong to the tribe, we hide our light and pretend that the extraordinary self is a distant mirage. Then we don't have to take responsibility for our super-excellence. We can wallow in a small lifetime and simply wait for it to be over, content in our cocoons of ordinariness.

We all agree that only a handful of people are allowed to be phenomenal, as if there was a scarcity of extraordinariness in the Universe. But *all* the wonders of nature are exceptional. Even a simple leaf displays splendor and noteworthiness. So why would we relegate the realm of the extraordinary to only a chosen few? Nobody is exempt from the challenge to uncover his/ her remarkable essence. On our collective stage of human drama there's plenty of room to shine—to be amazing... to blow people away with who we really are—and the world is only enhanced as a result. We don't need to compete to enter the realm of the extraordinary. This platform of splendor holds everyone.

We often disown our extraordinary self because we believe we are damaged goods, as if the unfailing grandness of our divinity could ever be tarnished. But "damaged" parents pass down this legacy of blemishes as we continue to bespatter our souls with distortions of "not enoughness" that lock us into a commonplace flatness. We believe that we don't deserve the big MORE because we haven't worked/ tried hard enough, suffered enough, figured out the mystery, sacrificed enough, given enough, evolved enough. Totally out of touch with our inherent value, the veil of unworthiness cloaks our light and shrinks our largeness into a manageable package. We're afraid to reach out for our extraordinary self and discover that nothing is there, or if we do recognize it, it might be taken from us. What unbearable disappointment to be cast out from the altitude of our greatness and re-imprisoned in the stockade of the unremarkable. Perhaps it's easier just to stay in the cramped box of the inconsequential. Isn't that better than falling off the mountaintop into a black hole of shame?

I've always felt more comfortable being small and unnoticed. I assumed that any expressions of extraordinariness would invite criticism/ pain, and feared the isolation of being exiled for going beyond the commonplace. It was safer to downplay my accomplishments as I mumbled my qualifications/ achievements, hoping no one would notice! My highly competitive, spiritually stingy parents were threatened by expressions of prominence. They enacted my karmic beliefs that it was far too dangerous to exhibit the extraordinary on a planet of rivaling, jealous, frightened people. Although I've had to open to the realm of the extraordinary in order to channel the Tibetan, I still quiver at the prospect of being seen for who I am (as we all do). Even though I know better, my gut still presides with its visceral insistence of danger when my extraordinary self tries to peek out from under my denial. Determined to reach for the star that wants to shine through me, I wrestle with the seduction of self-diminishment. How foolish to hide the very gifts that our soul asked us to bring to earth.

Deep in the privacy of our internal terrain, there are moments when we KNOW we are more. We only settled for less because we thought we were supposed to. If we're brave, maybe we permit a part of ourselves to shine. But self-diminishment drains the energy of this small island of the remarkable and prevents it from gathering the steam to ignite the conflagration of magnificence just waiting to animate our exalted being. Why not give ourselves permission to be exceptional in *all* ways as we DARE to leave no stone unturned in our reunion with the extraordinary self.

Emerging in a blaze of smiling cosmic glory, the Tibetan delights in the full expression of his tremendousness. He teaches:

Part Seven: The New Consciousness

The increasing vibratory rate impacting the planet is designated to redesign human nature. Students must open their imagination, to invoke a new version of self where all potential is manifest. The New World Order materializes through the creativity of extraordinary human beings who usher in a previously unimaginable level of consciousness. The Divine Plan REQUIRES humankind to embody its magnitude in order to carry the spiritual load of re-creating a race of uncommon beings who fearlessly walk tall in their significance. Enter the Extraordinary—a realm of true safety and unification! Today's mandated maturation cycle necessitates the release of all childish cries of subordination that block humanity's spiritual heritage of magnificence. It's an illusion that the extraordinary self can be spurned through a fall from grace. To "fall" from one's cardinal nature is impossible.

History convinces humanity that it cannot access, much less maintain, its extraordinary core. But new vibrational frequencies fire up ancient memories of humankind's original exalted consciousness lying dormant in the collective unconscious until humanity was ready to pick up its Torch of Greatness. Now is the time!

Envision a superior human race! Open to the mystery. Dare to assume that the emerging self is BIG and readily available for full engagement.

To be fully anchored in one's extraordinary identity feels like the entire Universe is bolstering self through celestial applause. Sensations of prominence, genius, compassion and creativity fill the heart with recognition of its marvelous constitution. All actions are propelled by newly awakened memories of the soul's earthly agenda, only perceptible through Portals of the Extraordinary. The physical, emotional, mental and spiritual bodies align within the Joy Stream of Illustriousness. Self starts experiencing a life far beyond his/her wildest dreams. Unearthed levels of extraordinariness compound upon themselves to create a positive vortex that magnetizes the unexpected potential of humankind into full flower. As humankind pioneers its towering destiny, the Universe expands. It's never too late to watch the miraculous unfold in self's life as the Call to the Extraordinary sounds forth for humanity to claim its birthright of inter-galactic prominence and esteem—as giants of love, brilliance and creative joy—offered to this Universe as leaders extraordinaire who will pave the way for Source's next sublime issuance of LOVE.

GLOSSARY

Akashic Records: Records stored in a non-physical library on the causal plane which is an etheric dimension. These records hold the soul's entire karmic history including all lifetimes on planet earth.

Alchemy: A process used in medieval times to turn lead into gold. This term is used symbolically to describe the transformation process in the soul.

Astral Plane: The next dimension beyond the earth plane, the energetic field surrounding the earth plane. It is the initial place our spirit goes after death, the place where ghosts reside.

Chakras: Seven energy centers in the body, described as vortexes that receive and emit cosmic energy.

Channeling: Attuning and opening to receive wisdom, guidance and teaching from the Higher Self, and/or spirit-plane teachers and guides.

Chats: Monthly groups sponsored by the School of the Golden Discs when the Tibetan is channeled by Moriah Marston for teaching metaphysics.

Etheric Plane: A non-physical higher dimension where refined and evolved beings from the spiritual plane reside.

False beliefs: False conclusions made during times of trauma and difficulty, usually based on experiences in previous lifetimes that hold negative patterns that limit our openness to our present life potential.

Fifth Dimension: The dimension of enlightened consciousness, the new paradigm, that humankind is collectively evolving into.

Higher Self: The essential, eternal level of self that exists beyond the earthly realm. The Higher Self extends itself to earth as a human being with an ego and personality.

Kundalini: The central life force that runs through all beings. It lies curled up like a snake at the base of the spine while dormant. When activated, it rises up the spine and sparks the electrical system of the body that catalyzes awakening.

New Cosmic Day: The next chapter of humankind's evolution that heralds a New World Order and a new paradigm for the human condition.

Shadow: The unclaimed, unintegrated, unconscious aspects of self.

Self: A shortened term for Higher Self.

Soul-alignment: The process of self-realization. The integration of the Higher Self and one's karmic history into full conscious awareness in this present lifetime.

Source: God, Goddess, "All that is," the Ultimate Supreme Being, the Creator.

Moriah Marston and the School of the Golden Discs

In 1990, Moriah journeyed with a group of people to the sacred sites of Greece in a reenactment of the Eleusinian Mysteries. It was in Delphi that Moriah had a vivid dream of the Golden Discs. This dream inspired her first vision of this school. The Golden Discs are objects found in ancient Greek art. They are covered with symbols the meaning of which has never been discovered. It is in the domain of the Greater Mysteries in which the human spirit dwells that this school is founded.

The primary binding influence of this school is Ascended Master Djwhal Khul, the Tibetan. Djwhal Khul guides from the spirit plane the overall program with wisdom, compassion, humor and inspiration.

The acceleration we are feeling at the onset of the third millennium brings us increased chaos, crisis and opportunity. We have a choice to creatively work with these heightened energies rather than be overwhelmed by chaos. We live in a period of history where there is a major paradigm shift occurring on the planet as we move from a model of individualism to a different form of consciousness—a group consciousness. The paradigm shift is occurring through a collective awakening experience. The school provides a vehicle for opening to the great potential of these times.

OFFERINGS

COURSEWORK

The School of the Golden Discs offers the following processing and channeled group exploration sessions facilitated by Moriah, including channeled discourses by Ascended Master Djwhal Khul. These events are held in Shelburne Falls,

Massachusetts and are offered to interested groups throughout the nation. Contact Zayne @413-625-6754 for information about hosting an event.

"Chats with the Tibetan" are held monthly on Sunday afternoons. These sessions inspire the group with the Tibetan's wisdom, compassion and humor as he explores themes pertinent to the new millennium and the collective transformation that is occurring on the planet. Join us in this special communion as the Tibetan explores the spiritual process of integrating and applying the higher perspective into daily life.

"Seminar Intensives with Moriah Marston and the Tibetan" These half-day and weekend long workshops address the psychological and metaphysical process of transforming core issues we all experience in order to evolve our consciousness. As facilitator of the group, Moriah applies her psychological background to assist the participants in exploring and working through current issues and past experiences related to the seminar's theme. Then Moriah channels the Tibetan who provides the spiritual perspective on the work. This helps the participants to release false beliefs and to expand their awareness of the topic, leading to greater self-acceptance and insight. Bask in the Tibetan's transformative energy as he heats up this alchemical process with his original insight, compassion and humor.

The Transformational Times with Show Moriah Marston & the Tibetan: An Internet based interactive Talk Radio show with Moriah Marston which addresses a range of topics covered in *Earth School*. Visit www.transformationtimes.com to check the schedule, link to the weekly, hour long show and to access the show's archives.

"Inward Unbound" Correspondence Course: Keep the heat turned up on your transformational process in the privacy of your own home! This is an opportunity to work with tapes/CDs and journaling questions related to the topics in *Earth School*. Rolling enrollment allows you to begin the program at any time. The program will offer you the following:

*An inexpensive and convenient way to accelerate your spiritual transformation on the path to full soul alignment and awakening.

*Heightened awareness of your soul's journey, false belief systems, childhood wounds, past life material, unconscious patterns and blocks.

*Tools for working through the karmic material that surfaces as a result of accelerating your process through this program.

AUDIO CASSETTES AND CDs

90 minute audio tapes/CDs of the Tibetan's general discourses from the School's monthly "Chats with the Tibetan" as well as 60 minute seminar tapes that cover most of the topics in this book.

CDs of Moriah's narration of *Earth School*.

PUBLICATIONS

Soul Searching with Djwhal Khul, the Tibetan, A dramatic, multidimensional, autobiographical story of Moriah's soul-alignment process, which includes past life memories, the impact of suicide, verbal abuse and how childhood trauma can be instrumental in opening psychic doors. The story centers on Moriah's relationship with Djwhal Khul, the Tibetan, including her process of opening to channel. Moriah's personal story is crosshatched with psychological insights coupled and enhanced with the Tibetan's metaphysical teachings. The book explores the process of releasing blockages and negative beliefs while embracing the interface between the human condition and the spiritual plane.

"I enjoyed reading *Soul Searching* tremendously! It is so powerful and loving told. The author's honesty and vulnerability—the richness that is there spiritually and otherwise—is breathtaking. The story, words and Higher understanding speaks volumes and connects me in deeper ways to wholeness, trust and faith."

--Terri C, New York City

Soul Searching with Djwhal Khul, the Tibetan

By Moriah Marston

Transformational Times, the School of the Golden Discs' quarterly publication, is dedicated to building group consciousness through the exploration of digestible metaphysics which expands our awareness beyond ordinary day-to-day reality. This allows us to recognize and embrace our true potential as spiritual beings. As a continuation of ***EARTH SCHOOL***, each quarterly issue includes three new articles by Moriah Marston and the Tibetan.

PRIVATE COUNSELING SESSIONS WITH MORIAH

INDIVIDUAL

Moriah offers individual ongoing soul mentoring sessions either by phone or in person at her office in Shelburne Falls, MA. She works with your astrological chart to help flush out your "life lessons." Moriah includes dream analysis in her session because dreams offer an uncensored glimpse into your unconscious which will assist the process of soul "uncovery."

In her sessions Moriah intuitively links with the Tibetan, who offers the larger perspective on your soul's process. The sessions are deep, rapid and penetrating as we explore false belief systems from past lives, early childhood wounds/patterns, life purpose, relationships and any other areas that are calling for your immediate attention. You will be sent a tape of the session to assimilate the information.

COUPLES

One of Moriah's specialties is couples counseling. She works with the astrological charts of the couple to examine the underlying issues that might create power struggles, blocks to communication and projections on one's partner stemming from childhood wounds and karmic patterns. Once again, the work is very deep and penetrating. Moriah provides tools and assignments for the couple to apply outside of the session. The session can be done either by phone or in person.

To find out more information about her soul-mentorship, healing work and/or couples sessions or to set up an appointment call 413-625-6754 or contact School of the Golden Discs, 26 Monroe Ave., Shelburne Falls, MA. 01370

Contact Zayne 413-625-6754 for Chats and Seminar Intensive schedules, and list of topics on CDs and audio cassettes or visit our website: www.transformationaltimes.com.

CREDITS

Book Cover:
Concept: Zayne Marston,
Design: Zayne Marston and Jeanne Marie Sutherland
Earth Picture: NSSDC is the supplier of this data (NASA)
Cover Art: Nona Hatay

Nona Hatay Visual Artist
Cover photo art from the
Natural Illusion Visual Meditation series 2006

Throughout her 35 year career, Nona has photographed musicians and performers in New York City, fashion & events in San Francisco and landscapes in New England. She has had three books published, two of her experimental photoart of Jimi Hendrix, "Jimi Hendrix the Spirit Lives On …and "Jimi Hendrix Reflections & Visions" and a children's book of photographs of her son called "Charlie's ABC ".

Her work is in Hard Rock Cafes world wide and many museum and Gallery collections. Always interested in color, form and energy, she is now expanding into DVD film programs that she calls Visual Meditations. She designs the short film programs with colors and images from Nature to help relax and inspire. The pictures are accompanied by soothing music. More information on the website www.nonahatay.com or (413) 210-7907

Nona has studied the teachings of the Tibetan and Moriah Marston since 1992. She is happy to see this compilation of some of the most important topics and feels many will benefit by these valuable and practical teachings.